Equivalences

Any expression may validly be inferred from any other that is equivalent to it, according to the following principles:

"*p*" and "*p* ∨ *p*" and "*p* & *p*" all are equivalent.

"*p* ⊃ *q*" and "−*p* ∨ *q*" and "−(*p* & −*q*)" all are equivalent.

"*p* ≡ *q*" and "(*q* ⊃ *p*) & (*p* ⊃ *q*)" are equivalent.

"−(*p* ⊃ *q*)" and "*p* & −*q*" are equivalent.

Double negation:	"*p*" and "−(−*p*)" are equivalent.
Contraposition:	"*p* ⊃ *q*" and "−*q* ⊃ −*p*" are equivalent.
Commutation:	"*p* ∨ *q*" and "*q* ∨ *p*" are equivalent.
	"*p* & *q*" and "*q* & *p*" are equivalent.
Association:	"*p* ∨ (*q* ∨ *r*)" and "(*p* ∨ *q*) ∨ *r*" are equivalent.
	"*p* & (*q* & *r*)" and "(*p* & *q*) & *r*" are equivalent.
Distribution:	"*p* & (*q* ∨ *r*)" and "(*p* & *q*) ∨ (*p* & *r*)" are equivalent.
	"*p* ∨ (*q* & *r*)" and "(*p* ∨ *q*) & (*p* ∨ *r*)" are equivalent.
De Morgan's laws:	"−(*p* ∨ *q*)" and "−*p* & −*q*" are equivalent.
	"−(*p* & *q*)" and "−*p* ∨ −*q*" are equivalent.
Exportation:	"(*p* & *q*) ⊃ *r*" and "*p* ⊃ (*q* ⊃ *r*)" are equivalent.

Tautologies

The following list includes a number of forms of tautologies. Our rule will be that any sentence having one of these forms may be written down as a new line in a formal deduction.

p ∨ −*p*	−(*p* & −*p*)
p ⊃ *p*	*p* ≡ *p*
p ⊃ (*p* ∨ *q*)	(*p* & *q*) ⊃ *p*
(*p* & −*p*) ⊃ *q*	*p* ⊃ (*q* ∨ −*q*)

THE ELEMENTS
OF LOGIC

As an additional learning tool, McGraw-Hill also publishes a study guide to supplement your understanding of this textbook. Here is the information your bookstore manager will need to order it for you: 003732-9 STUDY GUIDE TO ACCOMPANY THE ELEMENTS OF LOGIC, Fifth Edition

THE ELEMENTS OF LOGIC

FIFTH EDITION

Stephen F. Barker

Department of Philosophy
Johns Hopkins University

McGraw-Hill, Inc.

New York St. Louis San Francisco Auckland Bogotá
Caracas Lisbon London Madrid Mexico City Milan
Montreal New Delhi San Juan Singapore
Sydney Tokyo Toronto

This book was set in Melior by the College Composition Unit
in cooperation with The Clarinda Company.
The editors were Judith R. Cornwell and Bernadette Boylan;
the production supervisor was Denise L. Puryear.
The cover was designed by Betty Binns Graphics.
Arcata Graphics/Martinsburg was printer and binder.

THE ELEMENTS OF LOGIC

11 AGM AGM 998

Library of Congress Cataloging-in-Publication Data

Barker, Stephen Francis.
    The elements of logic / Stephen F. Barker.
    —5th ed.
    p. cm.
    Bibliography: p.
    Includes index.
    ISBN 0-07-003730-2
    1. Logic. I. Title.
BC108.B25 1985   88–20930
160—dc19

This book is printed on acid-free paper.

ABOUT
THE AUTHOR

STEPHEN F. BARKER teaches philosophy at Johns Hopkins University. He has been awarded several fellowships, including the John Simon Guggenheim Fellowship. He is a member of the American Philosophical Association, the Hume Society, North American Kant Society, Washington Philosophy Club, and the Board of Editorial Consultants of *Philosophy Research Archives*. His other books include: *Induction and Hypothesis*, *Philosophy of Mathematics*, and (as coeditor) *Thomas Reid: Critical Interpretations*.

CONTENTS

PREFACE

This book offers a general introduction to logic, emphasizing the practical criticizing of reasoning. It deals with traditional logic, with modern symbolic logic, and with induction, and also it considers philosophical issues related to logic.

It has been my hope to make the exposition concise, accurate, and clear, and to provide accompanying exercises that really illustrate the points they are supposed to illustrate. To achieve such goals in full is difficult, but in this fifth edition I believe that some further progress is made toward them. In this edition the basic character of the book remains unchanged, but there have been many revisions in the wording and in details of exposition. Some revisions are for the sake of greater clarity and correctness; others are to make the prose more readable. A majority of the exercises are new for this edition, and their total number has been increased.

Some able teachers of logic disagree with the range of topics which this book covers. They consider that an introductory course which includes comparatively traditional topics such as the theory of the syllogism, fallacies, and induction, must become a mere "grab bag of topics," lacking formal rigor. They prefer a more highly unified approach that omits these topics and presents instead an abstract exposition of deduction, mathematical in style, with emphasis on the nature of formalized systems. By teaching introductory logic in this way, these instructors have the satisfaction of being able to deploy the knowledge of mathematical logic which they themselves have acquired during their own advanced studies, and they can regard themselves as imparting rigorous and up-to-date material.

A first course in logic along these lines can be a good course, I admit. However, it will appeal to only a minority of students—the ones who have a definitely mathematical turn of mind. As I see it, a course covering a more varied range of topics and treating these in a less formal style will be better suited to the intellectual needs of most students. This more varied and less formal type of course has greater chance, I believe, of enhancing understanding of the actual reasoning that students find themselves and others engaging in. It has a greater chance of offering constructive guidance toward better reasoning, and better thinking generally. Moreover, it need not be an excessively easy or frivolous course, since many nonformal aspects of logic involve hidden difficulties and intellectual challenges which it is by no means child's play to master.

In recent years a new movement in the teaching of logic has been gaining momentum under the banner of "informal logic" or "critical thinking." This approach gives little or no attention to symbolic logic and instead seeks to train students to recognize arguments in ordinary language, to identify unstated premises, to avoid fallacies of ambiguity and irrelevance, and to deal with kindred informal matters.

This increased emphasis by teachers on nonformal aspects of logic is to be welcomed. These aspects indeed ought to be taught, for they are important to the evaluation of actual reasoning. However, I believe that any wholly nonformal presentation of logic will be somewhat unsatisfactory. The student who has been taught nothing but nonformal logic is unlikely to have gained a strong grasp of the distinction between valid and invalid reasoning. To learn to appreciate this distinction, some study of formal principles seems to me to be needed. Therefore, I continue to believe that the type of logic course which will be best for most students should combine both formal and nonformal elements. The formal and nonformal aspects should be presented in ways which connect them and show their relevance to actual reasoning.

This book contains more material than can conveniently be covered in an average one-term course. A teacher willing to omit one or more of the chapters can do so without appreciable loss of continuity, since the chapters are largely independent of one another. Chapter 5 can be omitted by instructors who do not want to go this far into the logic of quantification. Chapter 2 can be omitted by those who prefer to move directly into symbolic logic without studying traditional logic. Chapters 7 and 9 can be omitted by those who do not wish to deal with induction or philosophical questions about logic. The chapter on fallacies (Chapter 6) comes in the middle of the book following the chapters on deductive logic. I realize that some teachers of logic are accustomed to discussing fallacies near the very beginning of a course. Those who wish to do so can assign Chapter 6 before starting with deductive logic.

However, I would counsel against doing that. As I see it, the study of fallacies is not something easy, bland, and straightforward that belongs at the beginning. On the contrary, I consider this part of logic to be fraught with pitfalls. It is the part of logic from which students are most likely to carry away some terminology which they will try to apply to real-life reasoning which they encounter. And it is all too easy for them to carry away crudely oversimplified notions about fallacies. This will encourage them to censure the remarks of others by crying out more or less at random the names of various fallacies—a procedure which can have the strong rhetorical effect of intimidating others who are unacquainted with the jargon of logic. Responsible instructors, however, will want to guard against encouraging sophistical habits. To learn to distinguish between arguments that are genuinely fallacious and ones that are not requires the development of mature judgment and sensitivity to varied forms of reasoning. The student who has mastered deductive principles will have acquired a notion of what logical validity is, and this will make it more likely that study of the treacherous topic of fallacies will be beneficial rather than harmful.

Chapter 8 may appear to be unimportant, but I believe it has a significant place in the presentation. It deals with the application of logic to actual reasoning and has some basic points to make about the application of formal rules. It also contains the discussion of enthymemes, which would traditionally have accompanied treatment of the syllogism, but is placed here because it is an informal matter that pertains to all reasoning, not to the syllogism alone.

Those who use the book should be aware that a study guide and other supplementary materials are available from the publisher. The study guide, by Christopher Dreisbach and Robert Cavalier, contains supplementary explanations and exercises for students to use. Also, it now contains answers to a sizable selection from among the exercises in this textbook.

My warm thanks are due to many people who have provided me with helpful suggestions. I am especially indebted to the publisher's several anonymous reviewers, who made many valuable comments. To Carolyn Loring I am grateful for her excellent assistance, especially regarding some exercises in this edition. Also, I am indebted to many others who have communicated with me about the book over the years, offering criticism and comments. I regret that these persons are too numerous for me to be able to list, but I extend to each of them my thanks and appreciation. Even though I have not adopted all their suggestions, I have benefitted from them. I shall be glad to hear from others who use the book and who care to offer criticisms or suggestions.

Stephen F. Barker

NOTE

From place to place in the following chapters arabic numbers appear as superscripts. The superscript numbers refer to notes that are found at the end of the book, after the Glossary of Symbols. The notes discuss controversial points and give supplementary information. Readers who prefer to concentrate only on the basic ideas will not need to consult the notes.

In the exercises, an indication of level is given. Groups of easier or more basic examples are marked with an asterisk (*). Groups of examples that are considerably more difficult or less essential are marked with a dagger (†). Examples of intermediate level are given neither sign.

THE ELEMENTS
OF LOGIC

CHAPTER 1

INTRODUCTION

1 LOGIC AND ARGUMENTS

Most courses in the curriculum of a college or university today are relatively new ones, which were not taught a few decades ago. Logic is an exception. Logic probably was taught regularly in the schools of ancient Greece, and certainly in Western Europe courses in logic have been offered to students ever since the first universities came into being some 800 or 900 years ago. What is there about logic that for so many centuries has made people regard it as deserving to be a part of higher education? The answer has two sides. Logic—the critical study of reasoning—is a subject having both theoretical interest and practical value.

On the one hand, the study of logic can be intellectually rewarding as knowledge for its own sake. This is because of the clear and systematic character of many of its principles and its close relations with basic philosophical questions and (in recent times) with the foundations of mathematics.

On the other hand, the study of logic is also of practical use. A mastery of its principles can help us to recognize and avoid mistakes in reasoning— both in the reasoning we do ourselves and in the reasoning that others use in trying to convince us of things. A person who can recognize and avoid logical mistakes in reasoning should be able to think more clearly and correctly, more soundly and surely, about any subject. To be sure, we probably should not expect the study of logic all by itself to make people who reason badly into good reasoners. Good reasoning is a very complex skill which requires sound judgment and broad knowledge concerning the subject matter about which one is going to reason. A single course in logic can hardly sup-

1

ply these. But it is to be expected that people who already have some skill at reasoning can improve and refine that skill through studying logic.

This book will deal with both theoretical and practical aspects of logic because both are important and both have educational value. Although it is not always easy to connect both these aspects closely together, ideally the theoretical principles of logic should be studied in living relationship with their application to actual reasoning.

Logic and Philosophy

Logic is a subject with a long history. Like so much of our intellectual heritage, it goes back to the ancient Greeks. Among the Greeks the formal study of logic began with Aristotle in the fourth century B.C. Aristotle's most important contribution to logic was his theory of the syllogism. (The nature of the syllogism will be discussed in Chapter 2.) Later, Stoic philosophers worked out some of the principles of truth-functional logic. (Truth functions will be explained in Chapter 3.)

Thinkers during the Middle Ages admired Aristotle's writings on logic far more than anyone else's, and so the medieval tradition came to regard the theory of the syllogism as the central and most important part of logic. This view persisted into the modern period. As late as the eighteenth century, the great German philosopher Kant reflected the prevailing opinion of that time when he declared that logic was a "completed science"—that is, a subject whose elements were fully understood, so that no new principles remained to be discovered in it.

Kant proved to be mistaken in this opinion, however. In the nineteenth century the Irish logician Boole showed that the field of truth functions was far richer than had previously been realized, and he devised powerful new methods for treating problems in that branch of logic as well as for generalizing the theory of the syllogism. Also, the German mathematician Frege originated the theory of quantification. (Quantification will be discussed in Chapter 4.) Then Whitehead and Russell systematized the new developments in logic in their famous work *Principia Mathematica*, written early in the twentieth century. In that work they presented the new logic in a comprehensive way, and they also tried to establish the controversial philosophical idea that the laws of pure mathematics can be derived from those of logic alone.

This modern logic does not in any way contradict the traditional aristotelian logic, when both are properly understood. However, modern logic differs from traditional aristotelian logic in two important ways. It is much more general, dealing with a far wider variety of forms of reasoning; and it uses more symbolism, its style and method being more akin to mathematics. In what follows, we shall be concerned both with the main ideas of traditional aristotelian logic and with some of the ideas of modern symbolic logic. In studying these ideas, we shall be trying always to keep in view their application to ordinary reasoning.

The more advanced logical studies nowadays have taken on a character resembling that of pure mathematics, while elementary parts of logic have their special interest because of their practical value in helping to detect mistakes in reasoning. Thus it perhaps seems that logic does not have much relation to philosophy. Yet logic has always been regarded as a branch of philosophy, and there are good reasons for this. Let us briefly consider what some of the various branches of philosophy are, and what they have in common.

Moral philosophy, or *ethics*, is the branch of philosophy that investigates the notions of good and evil, right and wrong, duty and obligation, and the like. It tries to clarify the nature of these notions in order to answer general questions about their meaning. Are there objective standards of value and rightness? How can we determine what things are good or right? What general kinds of things are good or right? In dealing with such questions, moral philosophy seeks to analyze the critical standards used in making moral judgments.

Metaphysics is the branch of philosophy that tries to understand the nature of the real universe, considered in its most general aspect. It deals with questions about what kinds of things really exist. Is everything physical, or are there real nonphysical things? What is the nature of space and time? Does everything that happens have a cause? Metaphysics seeks to handle these questions by emphasizing the standards employed in judgments about reality.

The *theory of knowledge*, or *epistemology*, is the branch of philosophy that investigates the nature and scope of knowledge. It asks what it is genuinely to know something. Can we have knowledge of things outside our own minds? Does all knowledge depend upon sense experience? The theory of knowledge seeks to analyze the standards employed in judging the genuineness of claims to the possession of knowledge.

Aesthetics is the branch of philosophy that deals with the notions of beauty and ugliness and with the value of works of art. It asks what the nature of beauty is. Are there objective standards of beauty? Can experiencing beautiful things give us insight into the nature of reality? Aesthetics tries to deal with such questions by examining the critical standards used in making judgments about what is beautiful or ugly.

Four of the main branches of philosophy have been mentioned, and they are akin to one another in important ways. They deal with questions which are extremely general. Moreover, these are not questions that can be dealt with by the methods of the special sciences: we cannot settle these questions by scientific observations or laboratory experiments. These philosophical questions are ones with which we can make headway only by reflecting upon our own standards of various kinds (our moral standards, our standards of what counts as reality, our standards of what counts as knowledge, and so on). By obtaining a clearer view of these standards, we may be able to make progress toward unraveling philosophical questions—toward answering them in some cases, and in other cases toward clarifying the misconceptions that have given rise to the questions.

Although the study of logic differs in some ways from the pursuit of other branches of philosophy, it is no accident that in the past logic has always been classified as a branch of philosophy. Logic has a basic kinship with these other branches. Like them, it deals with some very general questions: questions about what good reasoning is and about the difference between correct and incorrect steps in thinking. Moreover, like other branches of philosophy, logic is a reflective study; experiments are not necessary, and no laboratory work is appropriate for verifying its principles. Like other branches of philosophy, logic involves the critical analysis of standards. In logic, standards of correctness in reasoning are central.

Someone might object that there is no need for a reflective, philosophical approach to reasoning, because reasoning is a phenomenon which can be studied empirically by the science of psychology. This objection rests on a misunderstanding. Of course, observations could be made and experiments conducted to find out how people reason and to discover some of the causes that make them reason as they do. But there is a difference between studying how people reason (a matter of psychology) and studying the nature of correct reasoning (a matter of logic). Logic does not undertake to describe or explain how people think; it has the different and more fundamental aim of analyzing what correct reasoning is, irrespective of whether people do, in fact, reason correctly.

Arguments

In studying logic we shall be studying the difference between good reasoning and bad. But what is reasoning? How shall we identify cases of reasoning? For the present, let us not worry about the difference between good and bad reasoning, but simply consider what reasoning is.

To start with, we can say that reasoning is a process of marshaling reasons. When one is reasoning, one is trying to put forward some things as good reasons for believing something else. Reasoning can take place when one is thinking privately to oneself, but also it can take place when one is trying to prove something to someone else. Let us look at an example of each kind.

Jane is thinking privately to herself. She remembers that last year her employer was in financial difficulty and had to cut her pay by 20 percent. Now business is better, and she is to receive a pay increase of 20 percent. This sounds good to her, but does it mean that her wages will be as large as before? She puts the facts together in her mind and realizes that the increase will be 20 percent of her present pay, and so her new wages will still be only 96 percent of her original pay. "I'll have lower pay than before the cut," she concludes.

In thinking this out, Jane is *reasoning;* she is making an *inference.* She starts from some things which she believes to be true. Then she comes to accept a consequence because she regards it as something that *follows from* these beliefs—that is, as something these beliefs provide *good reason* for accepting. Jane makes a transition from these beliefs (or *premises,* as we shall call them) to the consequence (or *conclusion,* as we shall call it). She comes to believe the conclusion because she regards the premises as showing that it is true.

The situation is a little different when the person who is to come to believe the conclusion is a different individual from the person who presents the reasoning. Suppose that Bill has always rejected astrology, while Jim has been inclined to believe in it. Bill now tries to show Jim that astrology is unreliable. Bill argues that if a person's fate were determined by the positions of the stars and planets at the time and place of the person's birth, then any two people born at the same time and place would have the same destiny. But Bill says that twins born at the same time and place sometimes grow up to have very different destinies. He says that therefore it follows that astrology is unsound.

Here, Bill wants to start from premises which Jim will accept. Then he wants to get Jim to agree that from these premises the conclusion that astrology is unreliable does follow. Bill hopes in this way to get Jim to believe this conclusion. Bill's own belief is not going to change; he presents his reasoning merely in order to change Jim's belief. If Bill is candid and sincere, he will use only premises that he himself believes; if he is not, he may use premises that he thinks will help convince Jim, even though he, Bill, does not believe them.

To generalize, we may say that *reasoning* is a process of thinking which tries to show that a conclusion should be accepted (either by the reasoner or by those being addressed) because there are good reasons indicating it to be true.

When the reasoning is put into words, we call it an argument. An argument may have just one premise, or there may be two or more. But we shall say that each step of an argument has just one conclusion. Where several conclusions are drawn, either there are several separate arguments, or there is one longer chain of argument consisting of several shorter arguments as its steps.

In the examples considered so far, the person doing the reasoning actually comes to accept the conclusion, or actually tries to get a listener to do so. The person does not just suggest a possible conclusion which someone might want to reach—if that were all that was being done, there would be a *potential* argument, but not an *actual* argument.

To illustrate this, suppose that Clara thinks to herself, "If I get a 10 percent raise for next year, and if the consumer price index rises by only 5 percent, then next year I'll be better off financially." Here Clara is trying to understand the logical connection between one possibility and another; to this extent, her thinking is like reasoning. However, she has not put forward any actual argument, for she has not asserted any premise or drawn any conclusion. She has merely made an "if-then" statement, which is not by itself an actual argument.

To be sure, her line of thought does correspond to a possible argument; that is, if she were to learn that she is getting a 10 percent raise and that consumer prices are going up by 5 percent, then she would be able to draw the conclusion that she will be better off financially. However, this mere possibility of an argument is to be distinguished from the advancing of an actual argument.[1]

What we shall mean by an *argument* (or reasoning, or inference, or proof) involves two essential features. In the first place, the person who presents the argument must be claiming that if certain things (the premises) are true, then something else (the conclusion) should be true also. That is, the person is claiming that the premises would support the conclusion, would indicate that it is true. In the second place, the person must be claiming that the premises are indeed true (perhaps the person does not *explicitly* make this claim about each of the premises, for some of them may be assumed but left unstated; but at any rate the person is *committed* to the claim that each premise is true). By making both these claims together, the person aims to give reason for accepting the conclusion as true. We shall say that there is an actual argument (or reasoning, or inference, or proof) when and only when both these claims are present.[2]

In everyday language, arguments can be expressed in many ways. Sometimes the premises are stated first; sometimes the conclusion is stated first. For example, the following are arguments:

National income for the year increased more than population did. Therefore, per capita income must have risen.

The barometer has been falling rapidly, and so there's bound to be a change of weather.

This liquid is acid, since it turns blue litmus paper red.

Octane has a higher boiling point than butane, and butane has a higher boiling point than methane; it follows that octane has a higher boiling point than methane.

There must not be any life on Venus. The atmosphere there is unsuitable, and the temperature is too extreme.

Words like "therefore," "since," and "it follows" are often signs that an argument is being presented. "Therefore" and "it follows" are used to introduce the conclusion of an argument, while "since" and "because" are used to introduce premises. Words like "must," "should," and "ought" in a sentence often serve to show that the sentence is a conclusion being derived from premises. However, none of these words is an infallible sign of an argument. In order to tell whether something that has been said embodies an argument, we need to reflect about its intended meaning. Skill and care in understanding our language are needed here; no merely mechanical rules are likely to be reliable.

Sometimes it cannot be settled whether a remark expresses an argument until we take account of the circumstances in which the remark is being made.

Suppose someone says, "The radiator of the car cracked because it froze last night and there was no antifreeze." To tell how to interpret this remark, we have to consider the circumstances under which it is made. If the listeners are not sure whether the radiator has cracked, the speaker may be making this remark in order to convince them that this has happened; in that context, the remark would express an argument with the conclusion that the radiator cracked. However, if everyone is already aware that the radiator has cracked, then a speaker who makes this remark is more likely to be trying to *explain why* the radiator cracked. If that is what is being done, the speaker's remark is a statement about the *cause* of the event, and is not an argument aiming to show that the event occurred—indeed, it is not an actual argument at all.

Often we come across remarks which are attempts to persuade us of things, yet which do not clearly state conclusions or clearly support them. Consider, for example:

Drink Extra-Light beer! It's the beer of champions.

The Dolores Speedster goes from 0 to 60 in eight seconds. You should be in the driver's seat!

Congressman Brown loves baseball, motherhood, and apple pie. He's the man for us.

Should we classify remarks like these as arguments? In the first place, to regard them as arguments in the logical sense we would need to be able to pick out their conclusions. But what conclusion is the first speaker trying to establish? That Extra-Light is the best tasting beer, the most wholesome beer, the beer with most prestige, or what? In this example no one conclusion can be pinned down, and it is the same with the other examples. In the second place, even if we were able to formulate some hazy 'conclusion' for each example, it is far from clear that the speaker is even trying to say anything to support the supposed 'conclusion.' Thus in these examples the 'conclusions' are very unclear, and the 'premises' amount to very little. If we were to classify these examples as arguments, we would have to regard them as very weak, unsatisfactory arguments. Yet surely it would be unfair to these speakers to criticize them for offering bad arguments, when they do not seem to be trying to offer good arguments. It is better to regard examples like these merely as efforts at *verbal persuasion*, and not as actual arguments.

Longer arguments often consist of chains of steps, with the conclusion of one step serving as a premise for another step. To understand such an argument, we need to recognize how its parts are connected together. As an example, let us consider the following argument.

> When a lawyer suspects a client of being guilty, is it ethical for the lawyer to conduct a vigorous defense? Yes, it is ethical. Look here: Being ethical as a lawyer involves playing by the rules of our adversary system. According to our system, every defendant has the right to a fair trial. It follows that even a defendant everyone thinks is guilty has that right. Now, you can't have a fair trial without a vigorous defense. So even if everyone thinks a defendant is guilty, under our system the defendant still has to be given a vigorous defense. This couldn't be done if no ethical lawyer would take the case and defend it vigorously. So you see it can be ethically all right for lawyers to defend vigorously clients whom they suspect of being guilty.

A number of different points are present in this argument.

1 Even when a lawyer suspects a client of being guilty, it is ethical for the lawyer to conduct a vigorous defense.
2 Ethical lawyers play by the rules of our adversary system.
3 According to our system, every defendant has the right to a fair trial.
4 A defendant everyone thinks is guilty has that right.
5 You can't have a fair trial without a vigorous defense.
6 Even if everyone thinks a defendant is guilty, under our system the defendant has to be given a vigorous defense.
7 The defendant couldn't be given a vigorous defense if no ethical lawyer would take the case and act vigorously.

For present purposes we are not trying to decide just how good an argument this is; here we merely want to unravel its structure. What is the conclusion, and what are the premises? Point 1 is the conclusion which the speaker is trying to establish. Points 2, 3, 5, and 7 are the basic premises. Points 4 and 6 are intermediate conclusions; 4 is obtained from 3, while 6 is obtained from 4 and 5 together. Using an arrow to indicate the direction of inference, we can diagram the structure of the argument in this way:

$$3 \rightarrow \left. \begin{matrix} 4 \\ 5 \end{matrix} \right\} \rightarrow \left. \begin{matrix} 6 \\ 7 \\ 2 \end{matrix} \right\} \rightarrow 1$$

Here the three arrows indicate three steps in the reasoning. From 3, 4 is derived. From 4 and 5 together, 6 is derived. From 6, 7, and 2 together the conclusion, 1, is derived. The diagram depicts this structure of the reasoning.

If we look for arguments in the books we read and in the conversations we hear, we shall find that most writers and speakers are presenting actual arguments only a small fraction of the time. The larger portion of most discourse consists merely of separate statements made one after another, without any of them being put forward as reasons on the basis of which others are arrived at. This is perfectly appropriate much of the time. But where the statements made are dubious or controversial, arguments are needed. Without even considering the arguments pro and con, thoughtless people make up their minds whether to accept dubious or controversial assertions. But reasonable people will want to think over the arguments before accepting or rejecting such assertions, and for the most part they will want to make it their practice to believe in accordance with the best arguments.

EXERCISE 1

*A Interpreting each example in the way it is most likely to be intended, say whether it contains an actual argument. If so, what is the conclusion and what are the premises?

1 Dogs always like bones, so her dog surely will like these bones I've brought.

2 The kiwi isn't a mammal. It's native to New Zealand, and no mammals are.

3 Your honor, the traffic light wasn't red when I went through. I swear it. Believe me, I'm telling the absolute truth.

4 The weather is going to change, because the barometer has fallen sharply.

5 The car stopped running because the gas line was clogged.

6 Anywhere corn grows, soybeans can grow. Corn grows in Iowa, so soybeans can grow there too.

7 They're a healthy, happy family. They eat Shredded Oats. Do you?

8 Everyone at the lecture is bored. No one who's bored is listening. Therefore, no one at the lecture is listening.

9 Matt mounted his horse sadly. Dusk was beginning to fall. He rode off into the twilight.

10 You'd do well to put aluminum siding on that old house of yours. It's not too expensive and never needs repainting.

11 That woman was always complaining, so I packed up and left her.

12 Since inflation is accelerating, the price of gold will increase.

13 Since he had that auto accident, he's been walking with a cane.

14 My former doctor kept telling me to go on a diet, so I changed doctors.

15 Lead is dense and comparatively inexpensive, so it is practical to use as shielding against radiation.

16 Nome is north of Anchorage, and Anchorage is north of Juneau. Hence, Nome is north of Juneau.

17 If all that oil is spilled into the river, serious pollution will occur.

18 There aren't any of my books that I won't gladly lend.

19 If you want to make an omelet, you have to break eggs.

20 No matter how severe the challenges we encounter, we shall continue to fight the good fight. We must emerge victorious in the end.

B Diagram the structure of each of the following arguments.

1 It's no use going to the bank today. This is a legal holiday. The bank will be closed. Banks always close on legal holidays.

2 There's no way we can get to Leadville on time, if we stop at Silverton. When we stop at Silverton we always end up having to stay overnight with your cousins. If we don't get to Leadville on time, we'll miss the auction. So either we stop at Silverton or we miss the auction.

3 The car is worth the price you're asking only if it's in mint condition. But its condition isn't that good. It looks as though the frame has been twisted in a collision. So the car isn't worth your price.

4 Janice is well qualified to work for you as a section head. The job requires understanding of management strategies and experience in handling people. She holds an M.B.A., so you can count on her to understand management strategies; and certainly she is experienced in dealing with people, because she served successfully for two years as personnel director in our Dallas office.

5 Theism is the viewpoint that involves belief in a supernatural God. Now, a supernatural God couldn't be a physical being. That is why you cannot be both a theist and a materialist, for materialists hold that there aren't any beings other than physical ones.

C Construct a clear step-by-step argument establishing what the answer is to each of the following problems.

1 Abe, Bill, Cindy, Don, and Ella each lives in a different city. Abe lives in the third of these cities to the west of Cindy. Bill or Don or Ella lives to the east of Cindy just in case Abe does so as well. Ella lives east of Bill and of Don. Don lives west of Bill if Cindy lives east of Ella. The cities are Albany, Boston, Chicago, Detroit, and El Paso. Who lives where?

2 Each speaker says the following and nothing more: Ali says that Bo speaks falsely; Bo says that Charlie speaks falsely; Charlie says that both Ali and Bo speak falsely. Who speaks truly?

3 There's to be a surprise fire drill one weekday next week. The following statements have been made about it: "It'll be Monday"; "It'll be Tuesday"; "It'll be Wednesday"; "It won't be Monday, Tuesday, or Wednesday"; "It won't be Thursday." One and only one of these statements is true. When will the fire drill be?

4 Theo wants to marry a girl who is blonde, beautiful, and rich. He knows only four girls: Angie, Betsy, Chris, and Deb. Of them, three are blonde, two are rich, and one is beautiful, though each has at least one of these traits. Angie and Betsy are alike in net worth; Betsy and Chris have the same hair color; Chris and Deb differ in hair color. Whom should Theo marry?

†D For each of the following examples, say whether the author presents an actual argument. If so, point out the conclusion and the premises. Identify any intermediate steps of reasoning.

1 You admit then that I believe in divinities. Now, if these divinities are a species of gods, then there is my proof that...I do believe in gods. If, on the other hand, these divinities are sons of gods, their natural sons, as it were, by nymphs or some other mortal mothers, as rumor makes them, why, then, let me ask you, is there anyone in the world who could suppose that there are sons of gods and at the same time that there are no gods?   PLATO, *Apology*

2 I had a farm in Africa, at the foot of the Ngong Hills. The Equator runs across these highlands, a hundred miles to the North, and the farm lay at an altitude of over six thousand feet. ISAK DINESEN, *Out of Africa*

3 Spriggs,...having fallen into a fire when drunk, had had one eye burnt out, one cheek burnt through, and one arm nearly burnt off, and, therefore, in regard to personal appearance, was not the most prepossessing of men. ANTHONY TROLLOPE, *The Warden*

4 Therefore it is clear that, as the soul needs only the Word of God for its life and righteousness, so it is justified by faith alone and not any works; for if it could be justified by anything else, it would not need the Word, and consequently it would not need faith. MARTIN LUTHER, *The Freedom of a Christian*

5 In peace and prosperity states and individuals have better sentiments, because they do not find themselves suddenly confronted with imperious necessities; but war takes away the easy supply of daily wants, and so proves a rough master, that brings most men's character to a level with their fortunes. THUCYDIDES, *The Peloponnesian War*

6 I do not think that one should have children. I observe in the acquisition of children many risks and many griefs, whereas a harvest is rare, and even where it exists, it is thin and poor. DEMOCRITUS, *Fragments on Ethics*

7 To be opinionated is most shameful, for two reasons: Not only can a person not learn what he is convinced he already knows, but also the very rashness itself is a mark of a mind that is not properly disposed. AUGUSTINE, *On the Teacher*

8 *Nora:* And I—how am I fitted to bring up the children?...I am not fit for the task. There is another task I must undertake first. I must try to educate myself—you are not the man to help me in that...And that is why I am going to leave you now. HENRIK IBSEN, *A Doll's House*

9 Every man has a right to risk his own life in order to preserve it. Has it ever been said that a man who throws himself out of the window to escape from a fire is guilty of suicide? Has such a crime ever been laid to the charge of him who perished in a storm because, when he went on board, he knew of the danger? JEAN-JACQUES ROUSSEAU, *The Social Contract*

10 Although animals do nothing which can convince us that they think, nevertheless, because their bodily organs are not very different from ours, we might conjecture that there was some faculty of thought joined to these organs, as we experience in ourselves, although theirs be much less perfect, to which I have nothing to reply, except that, if they could think as we do, they would have an immortal soul as well as we, which is not likely, because there is no reason for believing it of some animals without believing it of all, and there are many of them too imperfect to make it possible to believe it of them, such as oysters, sponges, etc. RENE DESCARTES, *Letter to Marquis of Newcastle*

2 DEDUCTION AND VALIDITY

In order to understand arguments better, we shall divide them into various types which can be considered separately. Let us begin by distinguishing between what are called deductive and what are called inductive arguments. There are good and bad arguments belonging to each type.

Deductive and Inductive Arguments

The basic distinction between deductive and inductive arguments has to do with the type of logical link that is supposed to hold between the premises and the conclusion. Sometimes a person who argues is claiming that the truth of the premises is absolutely sufficient to establish the truth of the conclusion. In other cases the claim is not that the link is this strong, but merely that the link is strong enough so that the premises do support or confirm the conclusion, making it reasonable to believe.

Here is an argument of the first sort:

Whenever it's winter in New York, it's summer in Rio. It's winter now in New York, and so it's summer now in Rio.

Here we have an argument that is *demonstrative*. That is, it has premises such that if they are true, they absolutely ensure the truth of the conclusion. Knowing that the premises are true would give us completely sufficient reason for believing the conclusion. Indeed, it would be inconsistent for anyone who accepts the premises as true to regard the conclusion as false. This is a *deductive* argument.

An argument that succeeds in being demonstrative has the strongest kind of logical connection between its premises and its conclusion, and so in that respect it is a good argument. But we also want to allow for the possibility that a deductive argument can be a bad argument, lacking a sufficiently strong logical connection between its premises and its conclusion. We shall therefore say that if the speaker puts forward the premises with the claim that the conclusion strictly follows from them, then also the argument is deductive, even when this claim is mistaken. For example, suppose someone argues:

Whenever it's raining, the streets are slippery; and the streets are slippery now, and so it's got to be raining now.

Here the wording suggests that the speaker is claiming that the premises are strictly sufficient to establish the conclusion (of course we may have to investigate the circumstances in which the remark is voiced, in order to tell for sure what the speaker's intentions are). If this is the correct interpretation of what the speaker is claiming, then we shall classify the argument as deductive. Of course it is a bad deductive argument, for the truth of the premises in this case does not absolutely guarantee the truth of the conclusion.

In general, then, we shall say that an argument is deductive when and only when either its premises if true would be absolutely sufficient to guarantee the truth of the conclusion or at any rate the speaker claims that they are sufficient in this way.

Now let us look at some contrasting examples:

Jim belongs to the National Rifle Association. Most members of the NRA oppose gun control. So probably Jim opposes gun control.

When I bought shoes of this brand and style before, they lasted a long time. If I buy another pair, most likely they will last a long time too.

We shall regard the sentences "Jim opposes gun control" and "If I buy another pair, they will last a long time" as the conclusions of the arguments. We interpret the words "probably" and "most likely" not as parts of the conclusions but as indicators of the degree of connection claimed to hold between premises and conclusions.

Under the likeliest interpretation of them, these last two arguments are not deductive. That is, their conclusions do not strictly follow from their premises, nor is the speaker claiming this. Moreover, in each case the conclusion makes some prediction or expresses some conjecture that we can find out about by further observations (we can wait until there is an election in which gun control is an issue and then observe how Jim votes; we can test the shoes over a period of time to discover how long they wear). Arguments like this we shall call *inductive* arguments. That is, inductive arguments are arguments whose conclusions do not strictly follow from the premises and are not claimed to do so, but whose conclusions can in principle be tested by further observations.[3]

The conclusion of an inductive argument does not strictly follow from the premises, and this means that there would be no contradiction involved in accepting the premises but denying the conclusion. The premises may render the conclusion probable—but always it remains logically possible that the premises are true and the conclusion nevertheless false.

Deductive and inductive arguments are the only types of argument that are much studied by logicians; indeed, they have studied deduction much more extensively than induction, because deductive reasoning can be described more readily in terms of definite general rules. Whether there is any genuine reasoning that is neither deductive nor inductive is a question to which we shall briefly return later (in Chapter 8).

In practice, when we encounter arguments, we cannot always manage to classify them definitely as deductive or as inductive. This is because sometimes the person who presents an argument does not make clear how tight a link is being claimed to exist between premises and conclusion (the speaker may even be unclear in his or her own mind about this question). In such cases we can at least consider which way of classifying the argument would fit in better with what the speaker would be justified in claiming.

Notice that the conclusion of a comparatively good deductive argument is not necessarily established with any greater certainty than it would have if it were the conclusion of a comparatively good inductive argument. How firmly the conclusion is established depends both on how tight the link is between premises and conclusion and on how certain the premises are to start with. Often, if we want a deductive proof of a conclusion, we have to be satisfied to start with premises that are less certain than other premises we could employ if we were constructing an inductive argument for that same conclusion. For example, suppose that we are trying to establish the conclusion "No marsupials are carnivorous." One way would be to employ a deductive argument; perhaps "All marsupials are herbivorous; nothing herbivorous is carnivorous; so no marsupials are carnivorous." Another way would be to employ an inductive argument, such as "I've observed several kinds of marsupials and never found any to be carnivorous, and so probably no marsupials are carnivorous." The deductive argument has a much tighter link between premises and conclusion than the inductive argument has, but it has to employ premises which are much more doubtful than those the inductive argument uses. So let us avoid the idea that deductive conclusions are always, or even usually, more certain than inductive conclusions.

Truth and Validity

Truth is a feature relating to the premises and conclusions of arguments. Validity is a feature of whole arguments themselves, having to do with how tightly the premises are connected with the conclusion. These two notions are interrelated in important ways, but they are not the same.

What sort of items can be the premises and conclusions of arguments? We shall call them sentences. A *sentence* may be defined roughly as a series of words that form a complete utterance in accordance with the conventions of language. The kinds of sentences with which we are concerned, the ones that can serve as premises and conclusions in arguments, are used to say what is *true or false*. Ordinarily they are what grammarians call declarative sentences. Other kinds of sentences, such as questions or exclamations, usually would not be appropriate as premises or conclusions of arguments, for typically they are not used to say anything true or false. In some cases, however, a question or exclamation can be used to do this ("What a rainy day!" and "Isn't this a rainy day?" each can be used to convey the information that this is a rainy day).[4]

Naturally, a sentence that is a premise in one argument may be a conclusion in some other argument. Suppose I am trying to prove a conclusion, and in doing so I advance an argument that uses another sentence as its premise. My opponent, even if he grants that my conclusion follows from my premise, may question whether my premise is true; he may say that he will not accept my conclusion until I prove my premise. If he challenges my premise in this way, I may be able to meet his challenge by constructing a new argument to establish that premise; that is, a new argument which will have as its conclusion the premise of the first argument. I would hope to be able to choose as the premise of my new argument something my opponent will not challenge; but if he challenges the premise of the new argument also, then perhaps I can prove it too.

We noted earlier that an argument has two essential features: (1) The speaker who presents the argument is claiming that the premises are true, and (2) is also claiming that if these premises are true, the conclusion should be true too (the strength of the logical link can vary, as we noticed). Every argument, whether good or bad, must have both these features if it is to be an actual argument. Now we can see that there are two chief ways in which a person can go wrong and advance an unsatisfactory argument. On the one hand, the person presenting the argument may be going wrong in claiming that the premises are true (perhaps the premises are not all true, or perhaps it is not really known whether they are true). Or the person may go wrong by claiming that there is a stronger connection between premises and conclusion than is really there. Logic is more concerned with mistakes of this second kind than it is with mistakes of the first kind. It is not the business of logic to tell us what premises we should start with in our thinking (except that our premises should be logically consistent with one another); but it is the business of logic to help us see how conclusions ought to be connected with their premises.

The first kind of mistake is the mistake of using false sentences (or sentences not known to be true) as premises. Now, sentences can be said to be true or false, but whole arguments should not be spoken of as true or false. When the premises of an argument are linked to the conclusion in the right sort of logical way, the argument is called *valid*.[5] That is, in a valid argument the premises really do support the conclusion; if the premises are true, then the conclusion should be true too. An argument is *invalid* if its premises are not related to its conclusion in this way. Thus the second kind of mistake is the mistake of employing an argument that is invalid.

To see clearly that there is a difference between truth and validity, let us think about deductive arguments. (For inductive arguments, truth and validity are related in a somewhat more complicated way, which will be discussed in Chapter 7.) A deductive argument is valid provided that if its premises are true, its conclusion must necessarily be true also. Notice, however, that even when a deductive argument is valid, its conclusion can still be false. For example, the argument "All whales are fish; no fish are mammals; therefore, no whales are mammals" is an argument that is deductively valid; that is, if the premises were all true, the conclusion would have to be true also. But the conclusion is false, and that is possible because the premises are not all true.

Also we should notice that a conclusion invalidly reached may happen to be true. For example, the argument "All whales are animals; all mammals are animals; therefore all whales are mammals" is an argument whose conclusion happens to be true even though the argument is invalid. (If someone does not see that this example is invalid, a good way to respond is to make use of an *analogy*. We say to the person, "If you think that this is valid, then you might as well say that 'All pigs have legs and all birds have legs, and so all pigs are birds' is a valid argument." In this way we are likely to be able to show the person that in this style of reasoning the premises do not support the conclusion with the strictness that valid deduction requires.)

The one thing that cannot happen with deductive arguments is for a false conclusion to be validly deduced from premises all of which are true. This cannot happen because it would violate our definition of what we mean when we call a deductive argument valid.

One further bit of terminology: in ordinary language the word "imply" means to hint or to suggest; but in logic this word is used in a different and stronger sense. When we say that the premises of an argument *imply* the conclusion, we mean that the argument is a valid deductive argument. More generally, to say that one sentence or group of sentences implies another sentence means that if the former are true, the latter must necessarily be true also.[6] (We do not say that the premises *infer* the conclusion in a valid deductive argument, because people, not premises, make inferences. Implication is a logical relation that can hold between sentences; inference is an act that people perform when they derive one sentence from another.)

EXERCISE 2

*A For each example, decide whether it contains an argument. If it does, decide whether it makes better sense to interpret the argument as deductive or as inductive; also identify the conclusion and the premises.

1 Our customers always are satisfied. You've bought our product. Therefore, you'll be satisfied too.

2 Our past customers always have been satisfied. You've bought our product. Therefore, you'll be satisfied too.

3 It doesn't snow in Jamaica, because that's in the Caribbean, and it never snows anywhere in the Caribbean.

4 Snow never has been observed in Aruba. So, if you go there this winter, you won't encounter snow.

5 For the party, we need one chair per guest. 38 were invited, and 12 of them are not coming. We have two dozen chairs. So we need 2 more chairs.

6 Only those who've registered may vote in the election. Will hasn't registered, so he isn't permitted to vote.

7 Most large flightless birds are very fast runners. So probably the Moa, which was large and flightless, was a fast runner.

8 The cakes she's baked according to her grandmother's recipe came out well. So probably today's cake will come out well, as she's making it according to that same recipe.

9 Whenever the public fears deflation, demand for gold declines. When demand declines, the price falls. So the price of gold falls whenever the public fears deflation.

10 It's probably going to rain, for the cows are lying down, and almost always when the cows are lying down it rains.

11 If it's a Taurus, it's a Ford. And it is a Taurus. So it must certainly be a Ford.

12 If it's a Taurus, it's a Ford. And it is a Ford. Therefore, it must certainly be a Taurus.

13 No Unitarians are Trinitarians; all Catholics are Trinitarians; so no Catholics are Unitarians.

14 All Sunnis are Moslems, and all Shiites are Moslems; so all Shiites are Sunnis.

15 Small tremors have been getting more frequent, and usually that's a sign of an impending earthquake. So probably there'll be a quake before long.

B Each of the following is to be regarded as a deductive argument. In each case, is the argument valid? Are its premises all true? Is its conclusion true? Notice how each example differs from every other.

1 All Italians are Europeans, and all Venetians are Italians. Therefore, all Venetians are Europeans.

2 All Italians are Europeans, and all Venetians are Europeans. Therefore, all Venetians are Italians.

3 All Italians are Asians, and all Venetians are Italians. Therefore, all Venetians are Asians.

4 All Italians are Asians, and all Venetians are Asians. Therefore, all Italians are Venetians.

5 All Italians are Asians, and all Venetians are Asians. Therefore, all Venetians are Italians.

6 All Italians are Asians, and all Japanese are Italians. Therefore, all Japanese are Asians.

7 All Italians are Europeans, and all Venetians are Europeans. Therefore, all Italians are Venetians.

†C For each example, what is the structure of the reasoning, and does it make better sense to interpret it as deductive or as inductive?

1 A jagged stone was lying among the moss..."This may interest you, Lestrade," he said..."The murder was done with it...The grass was growing under it. It had only lain there a few days. There was no sign of a place whence it had been taken. It corresponds with the injuries. There is no sign of any other weapon."
A. CONAN DOYLE, "The Boscombe Valley Mystery"

2 A dog, used to eating eggs, saw an oyster, and, opening his mouth to its widest extent, swallowed it it down with the utmost relish, supposing it to be an egg. Soon afterwards suffering great pain in his stomach, he said: "I deserve all this torment, for my folly in thinking that everything round must be an egg."
AESOP, *Fables*

3 A struggle for existence inevitably follows from the high rate at which all organic beings tend to increase...As more individuals are produced than can possibly survive, there must in every case be a struggle for existence, either one individual with another of the same species, or with individuals of distinct species, or with the physical conditions of life.
DARWIN, *The Origin of Species*

4 ...You are wise,
Or else you love not; for to be wise and love

Exceeds man's might; that dwells with gods above.

SHAKESPEARE, *Troilus and Cressida*

5　It is necessary that the land and the surrounding waters have the figure which the shadow of the earth casts, for at the time of an eclipse it projects on the moon the circumference of a perfect circle. Therefore, the earth is not a plane, as Empedocles and Anaximenes opined...or again a cylinder, as Anaximander,...but it is perfectly round.

COPERNICUS, *On the Revolutions of the Celestial Spheres*

6　The nature of the mind and soul is bodily; for when it is seen to push the limbs, rouse the body from sleep, and alter the countenance and guide and turn about the whole man, and when we see that none of these effects can take place without touch nor touch without body, must we not admit that the mind and the soul are of a bodily nature?

LUCRETIUS, *On the Nature of Things*

7　"Sperrit? Well, maybe," he said. "But there's one thing not clear to me. There was an echo. Now, no man ever seen a sperrit with a shadow; well, then, what's he doing with an echo to him, I should like to know? That ain't in nature surely?"　　　R. L. STEVENSON, *Treasure Island*

8　[Flaubert in his] letters to Louise Colet...boasts of amorous exploits, which must be true, since he is addressing the only person who can be both witness and judge of them.

JEAN-PAUL SARTRE, *Search for a Method*

3　EMPIRICAL AND NECESSARY SENTENCES

The sentences that serve as premises of an argument are supposed to be true, and their truth is supposed to give us reason for accepting as true the sentence which is the conclusion. However, sentences are not all alike. Let us notice two important types of sentences which differ with respect to how we can know whether they are true.

Most of the sentences we ordinarily deal with are *empirical* (this means "based on experience"). Consider a few examples:

Lead is cheaper than copper.
Some pigs can fly.
Caesar conquered Gaul.
Ted's age plus Jim's age equals thirty-two.

Each of these sample sentences is somehow based on experience; but in what sense? Not merely in the rather uninteresting sense that to know whether the sentence is true one must have had the experience involved in learning the meanings of the words—for us, all sentences are "based on experience" to this minimal extent. No, these sentences are connected with experience in a stronger sense: to know that one of these sentences is true or that it is false, we must possess *evidence drawn from experience*—sensory evidence concerning what has been seen or heard or felt or smelled or tasted. This evidence might consist of direct observations one has made for oneself, or it might be more indirect, consisting, say, of what one has heard concerning what others have seen. Now, to be sure, a person lacking such evidence drawn from experience could still *believe* it to be true that lead is cheaper than copper, or *believe* it to be false that some pigs can fly; but such a person would not *know* these things, because it would be merely accidental whether the person's beliefs were correct. For us, beliefs about such matters cannot be knowledge unless we have properly based them on direct or indirect evidence obtained by use of our senses.

Thus merely understanding the meaning of an empirical sentence is not sufficient to enable us to know whether it is true. In addition to understanding the sentence, we must have sensory experience which we can use to determine whether what the sentence says is true. Empirical sentences are said to be known *a posteriori* ("afterward"), because we can know whether they are true only after obtaining appropriate experience. Also, empirical sentences are said to be *contingent*, in that their truth or falsity depends on more than their meaning; an empirical sentence is a sentence which, if true, might conceivably have been false, or which, if false, might conceivably have been true.

However, there is another type of sentence which can be known to be true or to be false without reliance upon sensory evidence. Such sentences are said to be knowable *a priori* ("beforehand"), because we can know whether they are true before we observe the phenomena of which they speak. Among sentences of this type, we shall concentrate on *necessary* sentences: sentences that are necessarily true because to deny them would involve an inconsistency, or that are necessarily false because to affirm them would involve an inconsistency.[7] Some examples:

> Snow is white, or it is not.
> All dogs are animals.
> Fifteen plus seventeen equals thirty two.
> Caesar conquered Gaul, but Caesar didn't conquer Gaul.

When these sentences are understood straightforwardly in their likeliest senses, the first, second, and third are necessarily true. To deny them would involve inconsistency—something illogical or inconceivable such as snow that is both white and not white or dogs that are not animals. The fourth sentence is necessarily false. To affirm it would involve an inconsistency (Caesar's both doing and not doing the same thing). And all four sentences are a priori, since there is no need to have evidence from sense experience in order to know whether they are true. One can come to know whether they are true just by understanding the meanings of the words employed and by reflecting upon what the sentences say. For example, by understanding the meanings of the words involved, we realize that it would not be literally true to call something a dog unless it were an animal. This enables us to know a priori that all dogs are necessarily animals. No sense experience, beyond what was involved in learning the meanings of the words, is required in order to enable us to know this.

In logic we are interested in learning to tell the difference between arguments that are valid and arguments that are invalid. But to understand that the argument "No birds are cold-blooded; all reptiles are cold-blooded; therefore no reptiles are birds" is a valid deductive argument amounts to the same thing as to understand that the sentence "If no birds are cold-blooded and all reptiles are cold-blooded, then no reptiles are birds" is a necessarily true sentence. The argument differs from the sentence in that it consists of a series of sentences (premises that are asserted and a conclusion that is derived). But to recognize the deductive validity of the argument is to recognize that if the premises are true, then the conclusion must be true too; and this amounts to the same thing as recognizing that the "if-then" sentence is necessarily true.

Thus in logic we are very much concerned with necessary sentences. We are especially concerned with sentences that are necessarily true in virtue of their *logical forms,* that is, because of the ways in which certain logical words such as "all," "some," and "not" are arranged in them. The logical form "If no...are *** and all --- are ***, then no --- are..." is such that, with whatever words or phrases we consistently fill in the gaps (provided we make sense), we always get an overall "if-then" sentence that is true. Regardless of its subject matter, any sentence of this form has to be true. Thus we say that the "if-then" sentence we were considering in the previous paragraph is true in virtue of its logical form, and the corresponding argument is valid in virtue of its logical form. We shall learn more about logical form in later chapters.

Returning to our distinction between empirical and necessary sentences, we must recognize that this is not an absolutely precise distinction. There are plenty of borderline cases of sentences that do not clearly belong in one category rather than in the other. For example, consider the sentence "All spiders have eight legs." When straightforwardly understood, is this a necessary a priori truth, or is it an empirical truth? Is there or is there not an inconsistency involved in supposing that there might be a species of spiders that did not have eight legs? (Suppose explorers found a species of creatures that looked like spiders, behaved like spiders, and were directly descended from spiders—but which had evolved ten legs instead of eight. Would it be incorrect to call such creatures spiders?) There are no definite answers to these questions, because the word "spider" is somewhat indefinite in its meaning. Because of this indefiniteness, there is no answer to the question whether the sentence as ordinarily understood is necessary or empirical. Of course we could decide to change or sharpen the meaning we attach to the word "spider"; then the sentence could become either definitely empirical or definitely necessary—but it is not definitely either one as matters stand.

Thus some sentences cannot be definitely classified as necessary or empirical. However, the distinction between necessary and empirical sentences still has value, in spite of such borderline cases, for many sentences with which we are ordinarily concerned are not borderline cases and do fit definitely into one but not the other of these categories. And even with sentences that do not fit definitely into either category, it can often be enlightening to ask: *To what extent* are they necessary? To what extent are they empirical? How could they be understood so as to be necessary? How could they be understood so as to be empirical? By thinking about sentences in this way we often come to comprehend them better.

Moreover, the distinction between necessary and empirical sentences is of interest in two further ways, one theoretical and the other practical.

First, the distinction draws to our attention a philosophical difference between two types of knowledge: the a priori knowledge involved in logic and mathematics, on the one hand, and the empirical knowledge involved in the experimental sciences, on the other hand. Sentences which express the laws of physics, chemistry, and other experimental sciences typically are empirical sentences. They tell us about what actually is so, although it might have been otherwise. Scientists must make observations and conduct experiments in order to know whether the sentences are true.

In pure mathematics, however, and in logic, we do not have to employ observations or experiments. The sentences in which the principles of mathematics and logic are expressed are a priori necessary sentences (for example, "$x + y = y + x$" and "If no F's are G's then no G's are F's"). The principles of mathematics and logic give us no specific information about this particular world that happens to exist, but apply equally to all conceivable worlds. Such of these principles as we attain knowledge of, we can know by means of reflection without appeal to sense experience.

Second, a practical reason why the distinction between necessary and empirical sentences is worth noticing is that it can help us to evaluate sentences met in ordinary discourse. Sometimes a person wishes to assert an informative, empirical thought, but without realizing the difference the speaker asserts something necessarily true but trivial instead. For example, perhaps the speaker comes out in ringing tones with the declaration "The future lies before us"; the speaker imagines that this is an important insight. But when you stop to think about it, you can see that there is nowhere the future could lie except before us—the remark is a necessary truth, and it does not convey any interesting information. Listeners may give the wrong weight to what was said and may ask for the wrong kinds of reasons in its support, if they do not notice that the sentence is necessarily true rather than empirical. Also, speakers sometimes utter necessarily false sentences without realizing that they are doing so. "Phyllis is younger than Joanna, Joanna is younger than Sybil, and Sybil is younger than Phyllis," someone may say, thinking that this is just a description of the facts. But of course it is an impossible description; this is necessarily false. Here too listeners will give the wrong weight to what is said and may try in the wrong way to evaluate it, if they do not notice the necessary falsehood of the remark.

Of course, trying to distinguish between empirical and necessary sentences brings us face to face with problems about the language we speak. One problem is that many words in our language are *vague*: it is unsettled just where correct use of a word begins and where it leaves off, as things vary in degree. For instance, the word "bald" is vague, for baldness is a matter of degree, and we cannot say just how many hairs must be missing before it is correct to describe a person as bald; there is a 'gray area' between being bald and not being bald. Vagueness on the part of the words a sentence contains can sometimes make for vagueness about whether that sentence is empirical or necessary—for example, the sentence "Bald men have little hair on their heads" is impossible to classify definitely as empirical or as necessary because it contains two quite vague words, "bald" and "little." If by "bald men" were meant "totally bald men," then the sentence would be necessarily true; but if by "bald men" were meant "men at least slightly bald," then the sentence would be empirical and false. So vagueness can cause trouble here.

Another problem is that many words in our language are *ambiguous*: they have two or more different meanings. For instance, the word "heavy" in the sentence "This is a heavy book" is ambiguous, for it may have either of two quite different meanings: "hard to read" or "hard to lift." Ambiguity can make it difficult to tell whether a sentence is empirical or necessary. Thus, "Heavy books are massive" would be a necessary truth if "heavy" means "hard to lift," but would be empirical if "heavy" means "hard to read." In cases like this it is necessary to determine which meaning is intended for the ambiguous word before the sentence can be classified.

Some people who study logic form the mistaken impression that vagueness and ambiguity are always bad features for language to have, and they imagine that ideally we ought to use words that have no vagueness or ambiguity. This is a wrong idea. It would be impossible to eliminate all vagueness and ambiguity from our language. In any case, it would be undesirable to do so; often we want to speak vaguely or ambiguously, and we need language that permits this. What we should do is to become aware of the vagueness and ambiguity in our language, so that in particular cases where these features might cause trouble we can be armed against it. (There will be further discussion of ambiguity in Chapter 5.)

EXERCISE 3

*A When each sentence is straightforwardly understood, does it say something necessarily true, necessarily false, or empirical? If more than one answer is possible, explain the alternative interpretations.

   1 Some roses are red.
   2 All roses are flowers.
   3 There are no living organisms on the Moon.
   4 Whatever will be, will be.
   5 Penguins are not the only birds to be found in Antarctica.
   6 Either Sheila is my friend, or she is not my friend.
   7 Either Sheila is my friend, or she's my enemy.
   8 If no Hindus are Buddhists, then no Buddhists are Hindus.
   9 Every cube has twelve edges.
  10 Some cubes have fewer than twelve edges.
  11 No bishops are generals.
  12 Some whole numbers are not divisible by one.

B Same instructions as for part A.
   1 The centerfielder leaped in vain for McGurk's towering drive; luckily it was foul by inches.
   2 Every electron has a negative charge.
   3 We were incorrect in stating that Halifax is farther north than Edmonton. In fact, Edmonton is south of Halifax.
   4 If you eat an adequate, well–balanced diet, you will get all the vitamins your body normally needs.
   5 All the matter in the universe is made up of chemical elements.
   6 Turn on the pressure and the good guys always come through.
   7 Crocker Corporation increased its earnings during each quarter of the year just ended. However, the gains were not sufficient to bring the corporation's earnings for the full year up to the level of the preceding year.
   8 Radioactive cesium produces dangerous radiation. Although it takes thirty years for half of it to decay harmlessly, the material is gradually excreted from the body so that most of it is gone after a year.
   9 It is not wholesome for a person to spend too much time thinking unduly morbid thoughts.
  10 No thinker can get outside his own world of thought.
  11 The tiny island nations of Lichtenburg and Luxenstein have a long history of border skirmishes.
  12 No statement is wholly true.

C In each case, if your answer is yes, give an example to establish your answer. If your answer is no, explain why there can be no example.
   1 Can there be a valid deductive argument consisting entirely of empirical sentences?
   2 Can there be a valid deductive argument consisting entirely of necessary sentences?
   3 Consider a valid deductive argument all of whose premises are necessarily true. Can its conclusion be an empirical sentence?
   4 Consider a valid deductive argument all of whose premises are true empirical sentences. Can its conclusion be a necessary sentence?
   5 Consider a valid deductive argument all of whose premises are false empirical sentences. Can its conclusion be a necessary sentence?

D In logic it is important to distinguish between what necessarily follows from a remark and what is merely suggested by it. In each case, suppose someone says (a). Then is (b) something that follows as a valid deductive conclusion?

1 (a) Only friends of mine are invited to my party.
  (b) Every friend of mine is invited to my party.

2 (a) All of them who like dancing like music.
  (b) All of them who don't like music don't like dancing.

3 (a) Madrid is farther north than Washington.
  (b) Washington is farther south than Madrid.

4 (a) Boy Scouts are as clean as they are reverent.
  (b) Boy Scouts are clean and reverent.

5 (a) If you buy now, you'll get a low price.
  (b) If you don't buy now, you won't get a low price.

6 (a) The club is open to anyone who is a member or a guest.
  (b) The club is open to anyone who is both a member and a guest.

7 (a) Only buses are permitted in the right lane.
  (b) Buses are permitted only in the right lane.

8 (a) Carelessly, he anchored in the target area.
  (b) He anchored carelessly in the target area.

9 (a) Some of her dogs are well trained.
  (b) Some of her dogs are not well trained.

10 (a) Each human action aims at a goal.
  (b) There is a goal at which all human actions aim.

CHAPTER 2

THE LOGIC OF CATEGORICAL SENTENCES

In this chapter we shall study a traditional part of logic which was first worked out by Aristotle, and which logicians in medieval and early modern times regarded as the most important part of logic, or even as the whole of it. Nowadays we see that such a view is far too narrow; many important forms of argument are not included within this traditional part of logic. Nevertheless, this part of logic is well worth studying. The arguments that it does deal with occur frequently in ordinary thinking, they can be analyzed without much use of symbols, and they form a systematic body of traditional doctrine.

4 CATEGORICAL SENTENCES

Our approach will be to study certain standard forms of sentences, getting clear about the logical relations among them. After that, we shall see that the logical relations among many other sentences can also be clarified, because these other sentences can be translated into our standard forms.

The Four Categorical Forms

Let us focus our attention upon four specific forms of sentence, forms important enough so that they were long ago given the special names "**A**," "**E**," "**I**," and "**O**." These four forms of sentence are:

   A: All so-and-so's are such-and-such's.

E: No so-and-so's are such-and-such's.
I: Some so-and-so's are such-and-such's.
O: Some so-and-so's are not such-and-such's.

Sentences of these four forms, and only these, we shall call *categorical* sentences.[8] Thus, for example, the sentence "All unicorns are animals" is a categorical sentence of the **A** form; the sentence "No natural satellites of the earth are self-luminous bodies" is a categorical sentence of the **E** form; the sentence "Some philosophers are theists" is a sentence of the **I** form; and the sentence "Some birds are not dodoes" is a categorical sentence of the **O** form.

To be in categorical form, a sentence must start with a *quantifier* (the word "all," "no," or "some"), followed by the word or phrase called the *subject* of the sentence, then the *copula* ("are" or "are not"), and finally the word or phrase called the *predicate* (Figure 1). The words or phrases that serve as subjects and predicates in categorical sentences are called *terms*.

Our consideration of categorical sentences will be smoother and clearer if we adhere to this strict and narrow point of view concerning the forms they have. (This will facilitate our discussion of immediate inference, later on, when we shall talk about letting the subject and predicate trade places.) Accordingly, let us insist that in a sentence strictly in categorical form the copula must be plural and the terms must be plural substantive general terms.[9] Thus, the sentence "All gold is valuable" is not strictly in categorical form, because its copula is "is" rather than "are" and because its predicate is an adjective rather than a substantive (a nounlike expression). However, if we reword it as "All pieces of gold are valuable things," then we have a sentence that is strictly categorical.

The **A** and **E** sentences are said to be *universal*, because sentences of these forms sweepingly speak of the whole of the class of things to which the subject term applies. The **I** and **O** forms are said to be *particular*, because sentences of these forms give definite information only about part of the class of things to which the subject term applies. This is called *quantity*. **A** and **E** are said to be universal in quantity, while **I** and **O** are said to be particular in quantity.

The **A** and **I** forms say something *affirmative*, while **E** and **O** say something *negative*. This is called *quality*. **A** and **I** are said to be affirmative in quality, while **I** and **O** are said to be negative in quality. (The four letters used as names

Figure 1

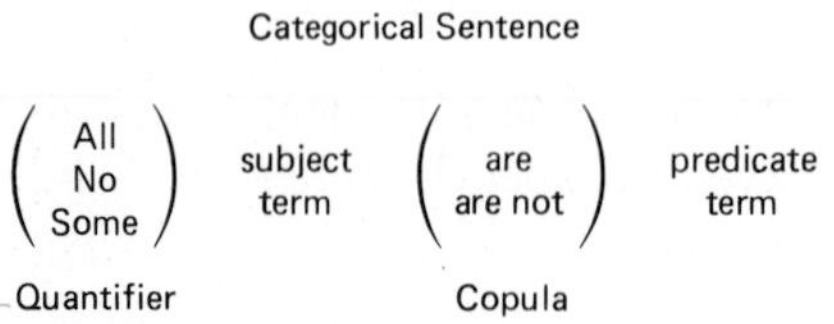

Categorical Sentence

$$\left(\begin{array}{c} \text{All} \\ \text{No} \\ \text{Some} \end{array}\right) \quad \begin{array}{c} \text{subject} \\ \text{term} \end{array} \quad \left(\begin{array}{c} \text{are} \\ \text{are not} \end{array}\right) \quad \begin{array}{c} \text{predicate} \\ \text{term} \end{array}$$

Quantifier   Copula

of these forms come from the vowels in the Latin words "**affirmo**"—"I affirm"—and "**nego**"—"I deny." In medieval and early modern times, logic, like all university subjects, was studied in Latin.) We can use a little diagram to sum up these facts about quantity and quality (Figure 2).

Before we can discuss categorical sentences further, we need to face two sorts of ambiguity that affect our use of the word "some." First, the word "some" is vague as it is ordinarily used. By "some" we mean "a few"; but how many are a few? If a person says that some chairs are in the next room, is the person claiming that there is at least one chair in the next room, that there are at least two, or what? Such questions have no answer, for the word "some" is vague as ordinarily used. Vagueness of this sort is inconvenient for our present purposes. It will be best for us to assign a definite meaning to the word "some." The most convenient way to do this is to assign it the minimum meaning: We shall stipulate that "Some so-and-so's are such-and-such's" is to mean that there is *at least one* so-and-so that is a such-and-such.

A second difficulty is that the word "some" can give rise to ambiguity as it is ordinarily used. Consider a person who states that some men are boring. Is the speaker thereby claiming that some men are *not* boring? In ordinary discourse this occasionally may be part of what such a remark means, although more often it is not. For example, a student who says in an acid tone "Some teachers are worth listening to" is strongly suggesting that some are not, and perhaps we should regard his remark as asserting that some are and some are not worth listening to. But usually to say that some so-and-so's are such-and-such's is to leave it an open question whether some are not.

For the purposes of logic, it is best to choose the minimum meaning of "some." We shall interpret sentences of the form "Some so-and-so's are such-and-such's" as meaning merely that there is at least one so-and-so that is a such-and-such, and leaving it entirely open whether there is any so-and-so that is not a such-and-such. Similarly, we shall interpret the **O** sentence

Figure 2

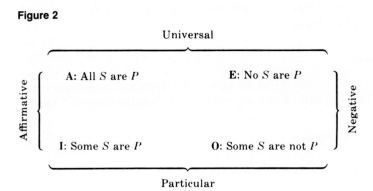

as meaning merely that at least one so-and-so is not a such-and-such, leaving it an open question whether any is.

Venn Diagrams

We can understand the meanings of the four forms of categorical sentences especially clearly if we picture them by means of a kind of diagram devised by the nineteenth-century English logician John Venn.

Let us draw two overlapping circles (Figure 3) and consider two classes of individuals, Swedes and Protestants. We shall now imagine that all the Swedes there are are herded inside the left-hand circle; no one else and nothing else may enter. Into the right-hand circle all Protestants are herded; no one else and nothing else is allowed in that circle. In region 1 of the diagram we now shall find Swedes who are not Protestants, if there are any. In region 2 we would find Swedes who are Protestants. In region 3 of the diagram we would find Protestants who are not Swedes. And in region 4 will be all persons and things that are neither Swedes nor Protestants.

Now consider the **I** sentence "Some Swedes are Protestants." At present we are not concerned with whether this sentence is true or false, but only with what it means. Let us try to draw a diagram indicating exactly what the sentence says, no more and no less. To do this, we put an asterisk in region 2 to indicate that this region is not empty (Figure 4). This diagram indicates that region 2 is occupied by at least one thing, and so it exhibits exactly the information conveyed by the **I** sentence. All other regions remain blank, indicating that the **I** sentence tells us nothing about whether they are vacant or occupied.

Using the same method, we can illustrate what the **O** sentence says (Figure 5). Here the asterisk in region 1 means that there is at least one thing that is an S but not a P.

Diagrams also can be drawn for the universal sentences. Here we shade a region to indicate that it is empty. The **A** sentence says in effect that there are no S's that fail to be P's, and so we shade region 1 (Figure 6). The **E** sentence says that there are no S's that are P's, and so we shade region 2 (Figure 7). Notice that as we are interpreting them neither of these universal sentences implies the existence of anything.

Distribution of Terms

In medieval logic, some of the terms occurring in categorical sentences were said to be "distributed," and others were said to be "undistributed." Tradi-

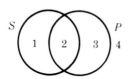

Figure 3

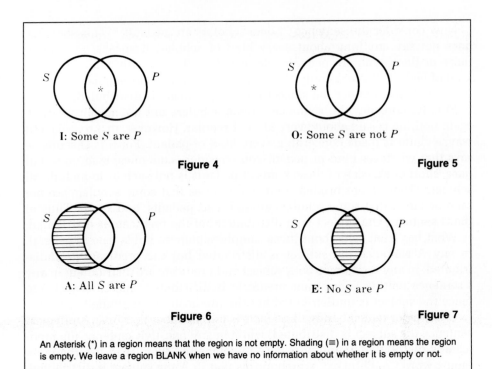

I: Some S are P

Figure 4

O: Some S are not P

Figure 5

A: All S are P

Figure 6

E: No S are P

Figure 7

An Asterisk (*) in a region means that the region is not empty. Shading (≡) in a region means the region is empty. We leave a region BLANK when we have no information about whether it is empty or not.

tional definitions of this notion of distribution were rather unsatisfactory, but the notion is a useful one, as we shall see later on. Let us redefine it as follows: A term S occurring as the subject of a categorical sentence is said to be *distributed* in that sentence just in case the sentence, in virtue of its form, says something about *every kind of* S. Similarly, a term P occurring as the predicate of a categorical sentence is said to be distributed in that sentence just in case the sentence, in virtue of its form, says something about *every kind of* P.

Consider the sentence "All scholars are pedants." Again, we are not concerned with whether this is true, but only with what it means. The sentence says something about every kind of scholar: young ones, old ones, rich ones, poor ones. It says that all kinds of scholars are pedants. However, the sentence does not say something about every kind of pedant; it concerns only ones who are scholars and tells us nothing about pedants who may not be scholars. Thus, in this **A** sentence the subject term is distributed, while the predicate term is undistributed.

Consider next the sentence "No scholars are pedants." Here again our sentence says something about every kind of scholar; it says, of large ones, small ones, fat ones, slim ones, that none of them is a pedant. And, though more indirectly, it says something about all kinds of pedants: whether happy or sad, wise or foolish, it tells us that none of them is a scholar. Thus both the subject and predicate of this **E** sentence are distributed.

Now consider the sentence "Some scholars are pedants." This sentence does not say anything about every kind of scholar; it speaks only about those of them who are pedants. Neither does it say anything about every kind of pedant; it speaks only about those of them who are scholars. Thus in this **I** sentence, neither the subject nor the predicate is distributed.

Finally, consider the sentence "Some scholars are not pedants." Here again nothing is said about every kind of scholar. However, in a roundabout way, a claim is made concerning every kind of pedant. For this **O** sentence says that whatever kind of pedant you consider, sane ones, mad ones, tall ones, short ones, each of these kinds of pedants is not such as to include all scholars. That is, our original sentence implies that some scholars are not sane pedants, that some scholars are not mad pedants, and so on. Thus in the **O** sentence the subject is undistributed but the predicate is distributed.

What has been said about these sample sentences holds true in general. In any **A** sentence the subject is distributed but the predicate is undistributed; in any **E** sentence both subject and predicate are distributed; in any **I** sentence neither subject nor predicate is distributed; and in any **O** sentence the subject is undistributed but the predicate is distributed.

One way of remembering these facts is to remember that in any universal sentence the subject is distributed, while in any negative sentence the predicate is distributed. Another way of remembering them is to use the mnemonic word "**AsEbInOp**," which means that in **A** the subject is distributed, in **E** both subject and predicate, in **I** neither, and in **O** the predicate.[10]

EXERCISE 4

*A Which sentences are in categorical form just as they stand? For those that are, name the form, say what the quantity and quality are, draw the Venn diagram, and say which terms are distributed.

1 No Shawnees are Iroquois.
2 Some ancient Romans were Christians.
3 All igneous rocks are volcanic.
4 Some snakes are not vipers.
5 No leukocytes are phagocytes.
6 All Australia is a continent.
7 Some contestants will be big winners.
8 All sonnets are poems.
9 All toads are not frogs.
10 Some trespassers will be welcome guests.
11 An elephant is a pachyderm.
12 Some real numbers are not rational numbers.
13 All scientific theories are contributions to knowledge.
14 Few people are permanent residents of Greenland.
15 No alleged cases of precognition are phenomena that have actually occurred.
16 Some accountants are highly trained professionals.
17 All things she likes are things he likes.
18 Every blue whale eats tons of tiny animals each day.

19 Some steamships are driven by turbines.
20 Whoever likes Tchaikovsky likes Brahms.
21 No murderers are guiltless.
22 No guerrillas are regular soldiers.
23 All crimes shall be reported to the authorities.
24 Some vegetables are not nutritious foods.
25 There are some carnivorous reptiles.

B Draw a Venn diagram for each of the following sentences. First do so using circles labeled "non-Ontarians" and "non-Canadians". Then do so using circles labeled "Ontarians" and "Canadians".

1 All non-Canadians are non-Ontarians.
2 No non-Canadians are non-Ontarians.
3 Some non-Canadians are non-Ontarians.
4 Some non-Canadians are not non-Ontarians.
5 All non-Ontarians are non-Canadians.
6 No non-Ontarians are non-Canadians.
7 Some non-Ontarians are non-Canadians.
8 Some non-Ontarians are not non-Canadians.

5 THE SQUARE OF OPPOSITION

Suppose that we have categorical sentences of different forms but with the same subject and the same predicate: "All S are P," "No S are P," and "Some S are P," "Some S are not P." What logical relations will hold among them? Before we can answer this question in any particular case, we first must decide from what viewpoint the relations among these **A**, **E**, **I**, and **O** sentences are to be discussed. As we discuss these relations, are we keeping open the possibility that there are no S's, or are we excluding that possibility by presupposing that there is at least one S? It makes a difference.

If we consider the logical relations among these categorical sentences from a viewpoint which presupposes that there exist things of some specified kind, then we are adopting what we shall call an *existential viewpoint.* If we consider the relation among these categorical sentences without taking for granted that any things exist, then we are adopting what we shall call the *hypothetical viewpoint.* Of course there could be intermediate existential viewpoints where we take for granted the existence of some of the kinds of things under discussion but not others. However, for our present purposes, the question is whether to presuppose that there exists at least one thing to which the subject term, S, applies.

First let us consider how the four categorical forms are related to one another if we do not presuppose the existence of S's (or of anything else). Let us consider the logical relations among the sentences "All succubi are poltergeists," "No succubi are poltergeists," "Some succubi are poltergeists," and "Some succubi are not poltergeists." Here we shall keep open the possibility that succubi may not exist. The relationships can be exhibited in a diagram that is called the square of opposition (Figure 8).

As the Venn diagrams show, **A** (which says that all succubi are polter-

Square of Opposition

Hypothetical viewpoint: We do
not presuppose that any S exists.

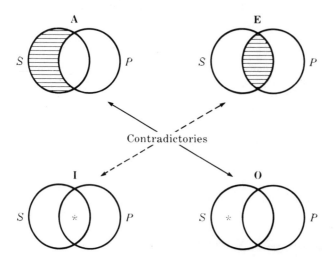

Figure 8

geists) and **O** (which says that some succubi are not poltergeists) are opposite as regards their truth or falsity. **A** says exactly what **O** denies, no less
and no more. **A** and **O** are called *contradictories* of each other. **E** and **I** are
also contradictories, for what **E** says ("No succubi are poltergeists") is exactly what **I** denies ("Some succubi are poltergeists"), no less and no more.

Is **A** related to **I**? You might have thought that **A** ("All succubi are poltergeists") would imply **I** ("Some succubi are poltergeists"). But this is not
so. The truth of **A** does not guarantee the truth of **I**, for it is possible that **A**
might be true and **I** false—this will happen if there are no succubi. Then **I** is
false (when there are no succubi, it is false that some of them are poltergeists), while **A** is true (when there are no succubi, it will be true that none
of them fail to be poltergeists—which is what **A** means). There is no logical
connection between **A** and **I**; knowledge of the truth or falsity of one of
these sentences does not enable us to tell whether the other is true or
whether it is false.

Similarly, **E** ("No succubi are poltergeists") does not imply **O** ("Some
succubi are not poltergeists"), for **E** could be true if **O** is false. This will happen if S's do not exist. In that case it will be true that no S are P but false
that some S are not P. There is no logical connection between **E** and **O**.

Is **A** ("All succubi are poltergeists") related to **E** ("No succubi are poltergeists")? You might have thought that it would be impossible for them both to be

true, but this is not so. These sentences will both be true if there are no succubi (S's) at all. When nothing is an S, certainly nothing is an S that fails to be P, and also there are no S that are P. So the **A** and **E** sentences will both be true. Thus there is no logical connection between **A** and **E**; knowing the truth or falsity of one of them does not enable us to tell the truth or falsity of the other.

How about **I** ("Some succubi are poltergeists") and **O** ("Some succubi are not poltergeists")? You might have thought that they cannot both be false, but it is not so either. **I** says that there is at least one S that is P, while **O** says that there is at least one S that is not P; both these sentences will be false if there are no S's at all. Thus there is no logical connection between **I** and **O**.

Now let us consider the matter again, but this time from an existential viewpoint rather than from the hypothetical viewpoint. Let us consider the four sentences "All Samoans are pantheists," "No Samoans are pantheists," "Some Samoans are pantheists," and "Some Samoans are not pantheists." We want to know how these sentences are related, under the presupposition that there are Samoans. Our results will be brought together in Figure 9.

If it is true that all Samoans are pantheists, then (since we take for

Figure 9

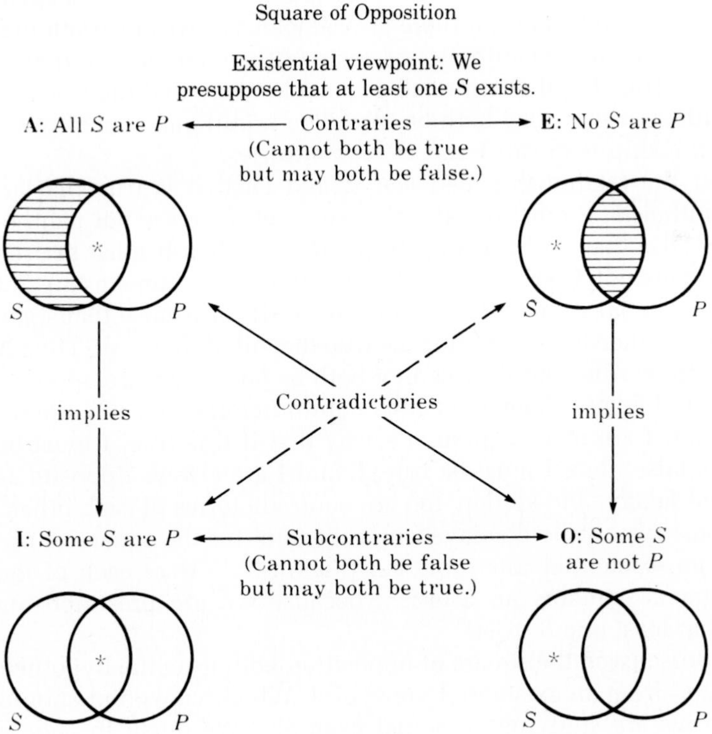

Square of Opposition

Existential viewpoint: We
presuppose that at least one S exists.

A: All S are P ◄———— Contraries ————► E: No S are P
(Cannot both be true
but may both be false.)

implies   Contradictories   implies

I: Some S are P ◄——— Subcontraries ———► O: Some S
(Cannot both be false   are not P
but may both be true.)

granted that there are Samoans) it must be true that some Samoans are pantheists. Thus the truth of the **A** sentence will guarantee the truth of the **I**, and in this sense **A** implies **I**. On the other hand, that some Samoans are pantheists does not guarantee that all of them are (since some might be and some not). Thus we can fully describe the relation between **A** and **I** by saying that **A** implies **I** but **I** does not imply **A**.

Similarly, if it is true that no Samoans are pantheists, then (since we take for granted that there are Samoans) it must follow that some Samoans are not pantheists. Thus the **E** sentence implies the **O**. However, that some Samoans are not pantheists does not guarantee that no Samoans are (for perhaps some of them are and some are not). Thus we can describe the relation between **E** and **O** by saying that **E** implies **O** but **O** does not imply **E**.

As for **A** and **E**, neither implies the other. But if we take for granted that there are Samoans, it cannot be true both that all Samoans are pantheists and that no Samoans are pantheists; that is, **A** and **E** cannot both be true. Might **A** and **E** both be false? Yes, for if some Samoans are pantheists and some are not, then neither **A** nor **E** is true. Thus the relation between **A** and **E** is that they cannot both be true but they may both be false. The traditional way of referring to this relationship is to call **A** and **E** *contrary* sentences.

The relationship between **I** and **O** is somewhat similar. Neither implies the other. Both may be true. But if we take for granted that Samoans exist, then **I** and **O** cannot both be false; if there are Samoans, as we are assuming, then either some of them are pantheists or some of them are not pantheists (or perhaps both). Thus **I** and **O** are related in such a way that they cannot both be false, although they may both be true. The traditional way of referring to this relationship is to call **I** and **O** *subcontraries*.

Now consider the relationship between **A** and **O**. If it is true that all Samoans are pantheists, it must be false that some of them are not pantheists. And if it is false that all Samoans are pantheists, then it must be true that some of them are not. Conversely, if it is true that some Samoans are not pantheists, it must be false that all Samoans are; and if it is false that some Samoans are not pantheists, then it must be true that all of them are. Thus **A** and **O** cannot both be true, and they cannot both be false; they are opposite as regards truth and falsity. They are called *contradictories* of each other.

Similarly, **E** and **I** are related in such a way that if **E** is true, **I** must be false, and if **E** is false, then **I** must be true. **E** and **I** are always opposite as regards truth and falsity, and so they too are contradictories of each other.

These relationships can be displayed in a diagram for the square of opposition under an existential interpretation (Figure 9).[11] Here each of the four Venn diagrams contains an asterisk, because we are presupposing throughout that at least one S exists.

We have now discussed the square of opposition both from the hypothetical viewpoint and from an existential viewpoint. Which viewpoint should we adopt when we are studying an actual example? We ought to choose whichever viewpoint makes the best sense of the remarks we are studying.

Here we need to consider the circumstances under which the remarks are made. Sometimes the hypothetical viewpoint is definitely called for, but often an existential viewpoint is more appropriate. Let us consider an example of each situation.

Suppose that a landowner has said "All trespassers are people who will be prosecuted." We wonder about the logical relation of this remark to the sentence "Some trespassers are people who will be prosecuted." Does believing the former sentence commit the landowner to believing the latter sentence also? Here our answer must depend on whether the possibility is left open that perhaps no one trespasses. In this example it is better to regard that possibility as indeed left open, and therefore our answer should be that it does not follow. There are two reasons for preferring the hypothetical interpretation here. First, the landowner, in speaking that way, may have hoped that the remark would serve as an effective warning, preventing all trespassing. Second, the possibility that there may be no trespassers is a reasonable sort of possibility; so far as we know, not all lands get trespassed upon.

On the other hand, suppose a woman says "All my jewels are diamonds." Is she committed to the consequence "Some of my jewels are diamonds"? Here it would be inappropriate to say that perhaps she has no jewels and so it does not follow. Such a response would not make good sense in this case. By speaking as she did, the woman indicated that she believes she owns jewels, and she should know what she owns. The sensible thing for us to do is to adopt an existential viewpoint and carry on our discussion presupposing that she does have jewels. So the best answer would be that the **I** sentence does follow from the **A** in this example.

Traditional aristotelian logic considered sentences only from an existential viewpoint. Modern symbolic logic usually treats them only from the hypothetical viewpoint. But the best approach is to understand both viewpoints and to be able to use whichever one is more appropriate to a particular case. Of course it can sometimes happen that one encounters a case where the two viewpoints give different answers, and yet neither viewpoint is clearly preferable to the other or more fair to what the speakers are trying to say. Then there is no definitely right answer, and the best we can do is to recognize what the situation is and why it is ambiguous.

EXERCISE 5

*A In each case: (a) Suppose the first sentence is true; what can you tell about the second? (b) Suppose the first sentence is false; what can you tell about the second? (c) Suppose the second sentence is true, what can you tell about the first? (d) Suppose the second sentence is false, what can you tell about the first? Answer first from an existential viewpoint, and then answer from the hypothetical viewpoint.

   1 All frigates are warships. Some frigates are not warships.
   2 Some pantheists are Marxists. No pantheists are Marxists.

3 All Rumanians are Slavs. No Rumanians are Slavs.

4 No pharmacists are realtors. Some pharmacists are not realtors.

5 Some novels are romances. Some novels are not romances.

6 All pines are softwoods. Some pines are softwoods.

7 Some mammals are not land creatures. All mammals are land creatures.

8 No centaurs are nymphs. Some centaurs are nymphs.

9 Some sailors are not puritans. No sailors are puritans.

10 No merchants are saints. All merchants are saints.

11 Some oranges are not seedless fruits. Some oranges are seedless fruits.

12 Some commodities are poor investments. All commodities are poor investments.

B For each example, discuss whether an existential interpretation or the hypothetical interpretation is more appropriate.

1 The preacher declares that no true Christians in the congregation are persons who envy others. Should this be understood as logically implying that some true Christians in the congregation are not persons who envy others?

2 The Watusi chieftain boasts that all sons of his are persons more than 7 feet tall. Does this logically imply that some sons of his are persons more than 7 feet tall?

3 The physics book states that all ideal gases are such that PV equals RT. If this is so, must it be false that no ideal gases are such that PV equals RT?

4 A biologist says it is false that some Loch Ness monsters are reptiles. Does this imply that some Loch Ness monsters are not reptiles?

5 A teacher says it is false that some of her fellow teachers are not pushers of dope. Does this imply the falsity of the statement that no fellow teachers of hers are pushers of dope?

6 A union leader says it is false that some corporations are payers of fair wages. Does this imply the falsity of the statement that all corporations are payers of fair wages?

7 An engineer asserts that no bridges he has designed are unstable structures. Does this imply the falsity of the statement that all bridges he has designed are unstable structures?

8 A politician says it is false that some times when he has been offered bribes are times when he has accepted them. Does this imply that some times when he has been offered bribes are not times when he has accepted them?

6 OPERATIONS ON CATEGORICAL SENTENCES

Next we shall consider several basic operations that we can perform on categorical sentences. These are ways of changing around categorical sentences so as to produce new ones. For each type of case, we shall want to notice how the new sentence and the original are logically related. In certain cases we shall find that one can validly be inferred from the other. Traditionally, these relationships were studied under the title of "immediate inferences"—inferences where only one premise directly yields the conclusion. In discussing these relationships we do not need to worry about any contrast between hypothetical and existential viewpoints except when we come to conversion by limitation; only there will it make any difference.

Conversion

A simple way to alter a categorical sentence is to make the subject and predicate trade places. This is *conversion*, and the new sentence obtained by this operation is called the *converse* of the original sentence. (It is sometimes called the *simple* converse, to contrast it with the converse by limitation, which will be discussed presently.) Let us consider how the meanings of the various forms of categorical sentence are affected by conversion.

Suppose we start with the **E** sentence "No Spaniards are Portuguese." When subject and predicate trade places, we get the converse "No Portuguese are Spaniards." A pair of Venn diagrams drawn from the hypothetical viewpoint (Figure 10) can help us to see how the original and its converse are related. Two sentences are said to be *equivalent* if they are necessarily alike as regards truth and falsity. Here the diagrams are just the same, showing that the **E** sentence and its converse are equivalent. Thus it is valid to infer either one from the other. Notice that a pair of Venn diagrams drawn from an existential viewpoint (putting an asterisk in the S region of each diagram) would give us the same result: both sentences are alike in their diagrams, from either viewpoint.

The **I** sentence "Some Sudanese are pagans" has as its converse the sentence "Some pagans are Sudanese." Here again it is clear that conversion has left the meaning of the sentence basically unchanged; the **I** and its con-

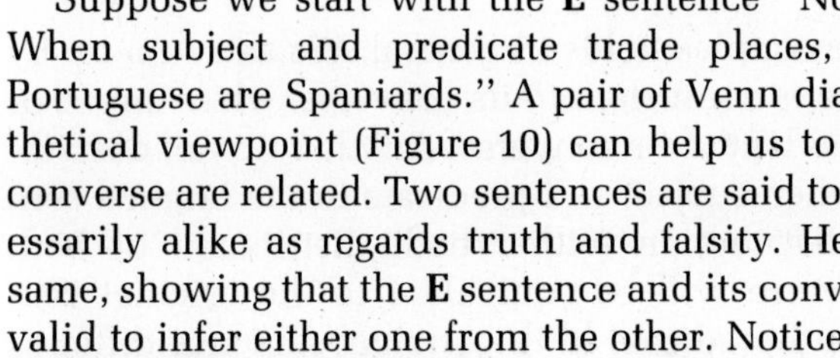

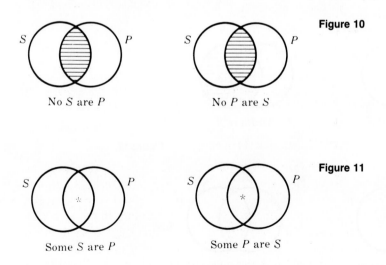

Figure 10

No S are P

No P are S

Figure 11

Some S are P

Some P are S

verse are equivalent, as the diagrams show (Figure 11). Either may be inferred from the other.

Next consider the **A** sentence "All sunflowers are plants." When subject and predicate trade places, we obtain the converse "All plants are sunflowers." How is the new sentence related to the original one? From the diagram (Figure 12) it is clear that the new sentence says something completely different from what our original sentence said. They are logically independent. So of course they are not equivalent, and neither can be inferred from the other.

Finally, if we convert the **O** sentence "Some soldiers are not patriots," we obtain "Some patriots are not soldiers." Here too it is clear from the diagram (Figure 13) that the original sentence and its converse are logically independent of one another.

What holds good in these examples holds in general. We can sum up by saying that any **E** or **I** sentence is equivalent to its converse, while any **A** or **O** sentence is logically independent of its converse. Another way of describing the matter is to say that when subject and predicate in the original sentence are alike as regards distribution (either both distributed or both undistributed), then the converse will be equivalent to the original sentence; but when the subject and predicate in the original sentence differ as regards distribution, then the converse will not be equivalent to the original sentence.

Conversion by Limitation

Although an **A** sentence is not equivalent to its simple converse, we can validly derive from the **A** sentence another sentence in which subject and

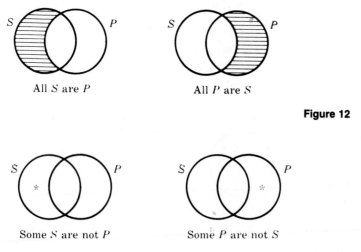

All S are P All P are S

Figure 12

Some S are not P Some P are not S

Figure 13

predicate have changed places. This is a sort of substitute for a simple converse, and it is called the *converse by limitation* (or the *converse per accidens*). This new sentence will be an **I**. From "All sows are pigs" we may validly infer "Some pigs are sows." This inference is legitimate only from an existential viewpoint; it is the existence of sows that must be presupposed here. Moreover, the converse by limitation is merely implied by the original sentence; it is of course not equivalent to it (Figure 14).

Obversion

The operation of conversion has the disadvantage that only sometimes is the converse equivalent to the original sentence. Obversion is an operation free from this disadvantage. However, it involves a slightly more complicated alteration. To form the obverse of a categorical sentence we do two things: we change the quality of the sentence, and we negate the predicate term as a whole.

Suppose we start with the **A** sentence "All saints are puritans." This is a universal affirmative, and so to change its quality we must turn it into a negative sentence. We leave the quantity unaltered. Thus we shall obtain a universal negative sentence, that is, a sentence of the **E** form. Also, we are to negate the predicate, replacing the term "puritans" by "nonpuritans." We leave the subject unaltered. As a result of these two steps we obtain the new sentence "No saints are nonpuritans," which is the obverse of our original sentence. Here we can see (Figure 15) that the **A** sentence and its obverse are equivalent.

If we start with the **E** sentence "No Syrians are Persians," we form its obverse by changing the quality from negative to affirmative and by negating

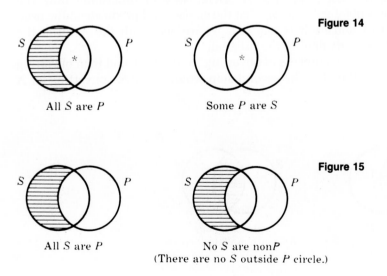

Figure 14

All S are P

Some P are S

Figure 15

All S are P

No S are non$P$
(There are no S outside P circle.)

the predicate. Thus we obtain the obverse "All Syrians are non-Persians." Here again we can see from the diagrams (Figure 16) that the original sentence and its obverse are equivalent.

If we start with the **I** sentence "Some shells are projectiles," we form its obverse by changing it from particular affirmative to particular negative and by negating the predicate. We obtain "Some shells are not nonprojectiles." It is clear (Figure 17) that this is equivalent to our original sentence.

Finally, if we begin with the **O** sentence "Some Senegalese are not pygmies," we change from particular negative to particular affirmative and negate the predicate, thus obtaining the obverse "Some Senegalese are nonpygmies." In this case the obverse is so very similar to the original sentence that it almost looks as though no change had taken place. But a change has occurred, for we consider the obverse to be in **I** form and to have the negation as part of its predicate, while the original is in **O** form and has the negation as part of its copula. When we write such sentences, it will help to avoid confusion if so far as possible we use "non" to express negation that belongs to the term and reserve "not" to express negation that is part of the copula.

Contraposition

Suppose we start with an **A** sentence "All S are P" and obvert it into "No S are nonP," then convert that into "No nonP are S," and finally obvert that to "All nonP are nonS." These steps are performed in such a way that each new sentence is equivalent to the previous one. The final result is equivalent to the original, and it is related to the original in a way interesting enough to have a special name. "All nonP are nonS" is called the *contrapositive* of "All S are P." A briefer way of describing how the contrapositive is obtained is to say that the subject and predicate of the original trade places and each is negated. As we see, with the **A** form, the contrapositive is equivalent to the original.

With the **E** form, this process of obverting, converting, and then obverting again runs into difficulty. The second step would involve converting an **A**

Figure 16

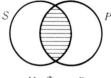

No S are P

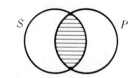

All S are nonP
(All S are outside P circle.)

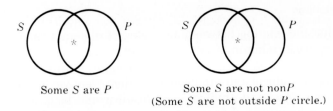

Some *S* are *P*   Some *S* are not non*P*
                        (Some *S* are not outside *P* circle.)

Figure 17

sentence, and an **A** is not equivalent to its converse. If the original **E** sentence were "No S are P," its contrapositive would be "No nonP are nonS"; however, this is not equivalent to the original.

If we start with an **I** sentence, obvert it, and then convert it and obvert it again, we would likewise encounter difficulty. In this case the second step would involve converting an **O** sentence, and the **O** is not equivalent to its converse. Thus the **I** sentence "Some S are P" is not equivalent to its contrapositive "Some nonP are nonS."

However, if we start with an **O** sentence, we can obvert, convert, and obvert again without difficulty. The **O** sentence "Some S are not P" is equivalent to its contrapositive "Some nonP are not nonS."

Summary

Thus we see that while conversion is always permissible with **E** and **I** but not with **A** and **O**, contraposition is always permissible with **A** and **O** but not with **E** and **I**. We may sum up as follows the relationships that have just been discussed.

Conversion (No existential presupposition needed)
"No S are P" is equivalent to "No P are S."
"Some S are P" is equivalent to "Some P are S."

Conversion by limitation (Must presuppose that there are S 's)
"All S are P" implies "Some P are S."

Obversion (No existential presupposition needed)
"All S are P" is equivalent to "No S are nonP."
"No S are P" is equivalent to "All S are nonP."
"Some S are P" is equivalent to "Some S are not nonP."
"Some S are not P" is equivalent to "Some S are nonP."

Contraposition (No existential presupposition needed)
"All S are P" is equivalent to "All nonP are nonS."
"Some S are not P" is equivalent to "Some nonP are not nonS."

Symmetry of These Relations

It is worth noticing that the relation between any categorical sentence and its converse is a symmetrical relation. That is, if the sentence r is the converse of the sentence q, then q is the converse of r. In other words, if we obtain r by transposing the subject and predicate of q, then were we to start with r and transpose its subject and predicate, the result would be q.

Similarly, the relation between any categorical sentence and its obverse is in effect a symmetrical relation. If r is the obverse of q, then q must be equivalent to the obverse of r. For example, if q is "All S are P," its obverse r is "No S are nonP." What is the obverse of r? If we change the quality and negate the predicate of r, we get "All S are non-nonP," and letting the double negative in the predicate cancel out, we have "All S are P," which is q. Notice that this sort of double negation may be canceled out, because any categorical sentence containing a doubly negated term always is equivalent to an otherwise similar sentence with the negations canceled out. But we must beware of supposing that two negatives of different types always cancel each other. For example, "No nonS are P" is definitely not equivalent to "All S are P" (think of "All chows are dogs" and "No nonchows are dogs"—one is true and the other is false, and so it is clear that they are not equivalent).

Also, the relation between a sentence and its contrapositive is in effect symmetrical. If r is the contrapositive of q, then q is equivalent to the contrapositive of r. For instance, if q is "All S are P," then r, its contrapositive, is "All nonP are nonS." But what is the contrapositive of r? If we transpose the subject and predicate of r and negate each of them, we obtain "All non-nonS are non-nonP"; letting the double negations within the terms cancel out, we have "All S are P," which is exactly q.

The relation between an **A** sentence and its converse by limitation is not a symmetrical relation, however. Instead, it is asymmetrical. If r is the converse by limitation of q, then q never is the converse by limitation of r.

EXERCISE 6

*A In each case state how the conclusion is related to the premise (converse, obverse, etc.); and say whether the argument is valid, indicating whether any existential presupposition makes a difference.

1 All Kenyans are Africans. Hence, no Kenyans are non-Africans.
2 No sibyls are prophets. Therefore, no prophets are sibyls.
3 Some submarines are warships. So some submarines are not nonwarships.
4 All tomatoes are vegetables. So all vegetables are tomatoes.
5 Some sailing ships are merchant ships. So some merchant ships are sailing ships.
6 All oranges are fruits. So all nonfruits are nonoranges.
7 Some plays are not comedies. So some plays are noncomedies.

8 Some stars are not luminous bodies. So some luminous bodies are not stars.

9 Some judges are septuagenarians. So some nonseptuagenarians are nonjudges.

10 No passenger vessels are submarines. So all passenger vessels are nonsubmarines.

11 Some logicians are not mathematicians. So some nonmathematicians are not nonlogicians.

12 All scarabs are beetles. So some beetles are scarabs.

13 No spiders are insects. So no noninsects are nonspiders.

14 Some Yugoslavs are non-Christians. So some Yugoslavs are not Christians.

15 All Senegalese are non-Asians. So no Senegalese are Asians.

16 All chairs are not nonthrones. So some chairs are thrones.

17 No supermarkets are nonstores. So all supermarkets are stores.

18 All secretaries are executives. So all executives are secretaries.

19 No nonsandwiches are nonpizzas. So no pizzas are sandwiches.

20 All nonmammals are nonwalruses. So all walruses are mammals.

B By what sequence of steps can the second sentence be validly inferred from the first? Operations of immediate inference and relationships from the square of opposition may be used. Make clear any existential presuppositions.

1 No Africans are Buddhists. Some Africans are non-Buddhists.

2 Some metals are liquids. Some liquids are not nonmetals.

3 No Greek epics are poems about courtly love. Some poems about courtly love are not Greek epics.

4 No Senators are adolescents. All adolescents are non-Senators.

5 All Burmese are Asians. Some Asians are not non-Burmese.

6 All insects are nonquadrupeds. All quadrupeds are noninsects.

7 No sharks are cetaceans. Some nonsharks are cetaceans.

8 All spies are criminals. Some nonspies are noncriminals.

9 Some songs are not anthems. Some nonanthems are songs.

10 All astrologers are nonscientists. Some nonscientists are not nonastrologers.

C Explain why each argument is not valid.

1 No Mongolians are vegetarians. So no Mongolians are nonvegetarians.

2 All rabbis are religious leaders. So all religious leaders are rabbis.

3 All bureaucrats are officials. So all officials are bureaucrats.

4 Some luxury cars are not sportscars. So some sportscars are not luxury cars.

5 No nonresidents are members of the council. So all residents are members of the council.

6 Some sons of his are not fat giants. So some sons of his are nonfat giants.

7 Some volcanic eruptions are catastrophes. So some noncatastrophes are not volcanic eruptions.

8 All French generals are dignified patriots. So all undignified patriots are non-French generals.

9 Some numbers are not rational. So some numbers are not nonrational.

10 No members of the faculty are unrecognized geniuses. So all members of the faculty are recognized geniuses.

7 THE SYLLOGISM

An argument is a *categorical syllogism* (or *syllogism*, for short) just in case it consists of three categorical sentences containing three terms in all, each term appearing in two different sentences. The argument "All Pakistanis are Moslems; no Sinhalese are Moslems; therefore no Sinhalese are Pakistanis" is an example of a syllogism. It consists of three categorical sentences that contain three different terms, each term appearing in two different sentences.

The term appearing as the predicate of the conclusion (in this case "Pakistanis") is called the *major term* of the syllogism. The term appearing as the subject of the conclusion (in this case "Sinhalese") is called the *minor term* of the syllogism. And the term appearing in the premises but not in the conclusion is called the *middle term*. The premise containing the major term is called the *major premise*, and the premise containing the minor term is called the *minor premise*. For the sake of having a standard procedure, let us follow the traditional convention and always put the major premise first, then the minor premise, and last the conclusion.

The example just given is a syllogism whose logical form is:

All P are M
No S are M
$\therefore$ no S are P

To give the *mood* of a syllogism is to state the categorical forms of its sentences. We mention these in the standard order: major premise, minor premise, conclusion. In our example of a syllogism, its major premise is an **A** sentence, its minor premise is an **E** and its conclusion is an **E**. Therefore, this particular syllogism is in the mood **AEE**.

But there is more to say about its form, for other different syllogisms can share with it this mood **AEE**. For instance, a syllogism also is in the mood **AEE** if it has the structure:

All M are P
No S are M
$\therefore$ no S are P

This sort of syllogism differs from the previous kind because of the different arrangement of its terms; and the difference is important, for one syllogism is valid, the other invalid. Saying how its terms are arranged within the sentences in which they occur is called giving the *figure* of the syllogism.

There are four different figures that syllogisms have, that is, four different

ways in which the terms can be arranged. We can represent these four figures as follows:

	1			**2**			**3**			**4**
M	P		P	M		M	P		P	M
S	M		S	M		M	S		M	S
S	P		S	P		S	P		S	P

Here "S" is the minor term, "P" is the major term, and "M" is the middle
term. It is easy to remember which figure is which if we think of the positions of the middle term as outlining the front of a shirt collar (Figure 18).
The first form of syllogism we considered was **AEE** in the second figure; the
second form was **AEE** in the first figure.

Any two syllogisms having the same mood and figure always are alike as
regards whether their form is valid. If one is valid in form, the other will be
too—because mood and figure are the only features that count. Then how
many different forms of syllogisms are possible? There are four possibilities
regarding the form of the major premise (**A, E, I, O**), four possibilities regarding the form of the minor premise, four possibilities regarding the form
of the conclusion, and four possibilities regarding the figure of the syllogism. This means that there are 4 × 4 × 4 × 4, or 256, possible forms in all.
A large majority of these forms are invalid, however.

How can we tell whether a given form of syllogism is valid? Venn diagrams provide the most straightforward method. The method is this: We
draw a diagram showing exactly what the two premises of the syllogism say;
then, by looking at it, we can see whether or not the conclusion necessarily
follows from those premises. It can follow only if it is already contained in
the premises.

The syllogism "All Pakistanis are Moslems; no Sinhalese are Moslems;
therefore no Sinhalese are Pakistanis" is in the mood **AEE** and in the second
figure, as we saw. Let us adopt the hypothetical viewpoint as we investigate
the validity of this syllogism (actually, it makes no real difference in this
case; later we shall consider how to bring in an existential viewpoint). To
test the validity of this syllogism, we form a diagram showing exactly what
the premises say. Since the premises contain three terms, the diagram must

Figure 18

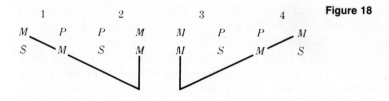

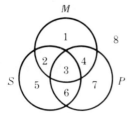

Figure 19

show relations among three classes of beings: Pakistanis, Sinhalese, and Moslems (Figure 19).

We now imagine that all Moslems are herded inside the M circle, they alone being allowed in it. All Pakistanis are put inside the P circle, nothing but Pakistanis being allowed there. And all Sinhalese are confined to the S circle, which non-Sinhalese may not enter. We must be sure to begin the diagram by drawing three circles that overlap in such a way as to allow for all possible subclasses formed by these three given classes. The circles must overlap so as to yield eight distinct regions on the diagram, for there are eight distinct subclasses which we must be able to consider.

Region 1 of the diagram is the location of Moslems who are not Sinhalese and not Pakistanis. Region 2 would contain Moslems who are Sinhalese but who are not Pakistanis. In region 3 would be found Moslems who are Sinhalese and also Pakistanis. Region 4 would contain Moslems who are Pakistanis but not Sinhalese. Region 5 is the location of Sinhalese who are neither Moslems nor Pakistanis. Region 6 is for Sinhalese who are Pakistanis but not Moslems. Region 7 is the place for Pakistanis who are neither Sinhalese nor Moslems. And region 8 is occupied by those who are neither Moslems nor Sinhalese nor Pakistanis.

The major premise of our syllogism declares that all Pakistanis are Moslems. This means that all who are inside the P circle are inside the M circle; that is, that the part of the P circle outside the M circle is unoccupied. We indicate this on the diagram by crossing out regions 6 and 7 (Figure 20). The minor premise of the syllogism declares that no Sinhalese are Moslems. This means that all who are inside the S circle are outside the M circle; that is, that part of the S circle which is inside the M circle is unoccupied. We indicate this by crossing out regions 2 and 3 (Figure 21). We now have a diagram that shows exactly what the premises say, no more and no less.

We now inspect the diagram to see whether or not the argument is valid. According to the diagram, all that part of the S circle which overlaps the P circle is unoccupied. That is, there are no Sinhalese who are Pakistanis. This means that the conclusion validly follows from the premises; if the premises are true, the conclusion must necessarily be true also.

If you have difficulty telling whether the diagram shows the argument to

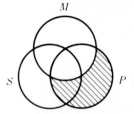

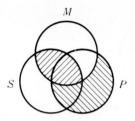

Figure 20

Figure 21

be valid, try this: See whether it is logically possible to add the *contradic-tory* of the conclusion to the diagram for the premises. If this is possible, the argument is invalid. If it is impossible, the argument is valid. In the syllo-gism which we have just been considering, the contradictory of the conclu-sion would be "Some Sinhalese are Pakistanis"; to add this to the diagram of Figure 21 would be impossible, for it would mean putting an asterisk into an area that is entirely crossed out. This helps us to see how the diagram shows the argument to be valid.

Next let us consider the syllogism "All Mormons are pious persons; no Samoans are Mormons; therefore no Samoans are pious persons." This syl-logism is in the mood **AEE** and in the first figure. To test its validity, we again draw a diagram that will show exactly what the premises say. The ma-jor premise tells us that whatever is inside the M circle is inside the P circle; that is, that the part of the M circle outside the P circle is unoccupied. Ac-cordingly we cross out regions 1 and 2 (Figure 22). The minor premise tells us that nothing inside the S circle is inside the M circle; that is, that the part of the S circle overlapping the M circle is unoccupied. So we add to our diagram by crossing out regions 2 and 3 (Figure 23). Here the completed di-agram shows that the syllogism is invalid. For according to the diagram it may or may not be that Samoans are pious persons.

In dealing with the syllogism "All warriors are heroes; some Greeks are not warriors; therefore some Greeks are not heroes," special care must be taken in drawing the diagram. To indicate the major premise is easy (Figure

Figure 22

Figure 23

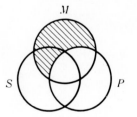

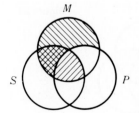

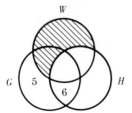

Figure 24

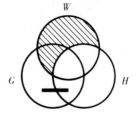

Figure 25

24). But the minor premise gives trouble, for we wish to indicate on the diagram exactly the information expressed, no less and no more. The minor premise is a particular sentence, and it declares that a certain space on the diagram is occupied. But what space? To put an asterisk in region 5 would be to claim that the premise tells us there are Greeks who are neither warriors nor heroes; this is more than what the premise says. To put an asterisk in region 6 would be to claim that the premise tells us there are Greeks who are heroes but not warriors; this too is more than the premise says. All the premise says is that there is at least one individual either in region 5 or in region 6 (although there may be individuals in both places).

The best way to draw the diagram is to use a bar instead of an asterisk. We draw a bar touching region 5 and region 6 but no other regions (Figure 25); we interpret this to mean that there is something somewhere in the space the bar touches. Thus, according to the diagram, there may or may not be Greeks who are not heroes; when the premises are true, the conclusion of the syllogism may or may not be true. We see by the diagram that this **AOO** first-figure syllogism is invalid.

Using the same method, we can deal with the syllogism "No astronauts are Buddhists; some vegetarians are Buddhists; therefore some vegetarians are not astronauts." This syllogism is in the mood **EIO** and in the second figure. When we draw our diagram (Figure 26), we find that the diagram shows the syllogism to be valid. In handling a syllogism like this with one universal and one particular premise, it is good strategy first to enter on the

Figure 26

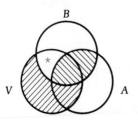

diagram what the universal premise says. Then it may be easier to enter what the particular premise says. If we had entered the particular premise on the diagram first, we would have had to use a bar; then, in entering the universal premise, we would have crossed out half the bar—in effect turning it into an asterisk.

Various generalizations can be made concerning how the diagrams for valid syllogisms must look. For instance, any syllogism whose Venn diagram contains exactly three shaded regions is invalid. And any syllogism is invalid whose Venn diagram contains a bar that touches more than one region (that is, if the syllogism is to be valid, the bar must have been shaded out of all but one region). However, it is better to understand how to use Venn diagrams than to memorize mechanical rules like these.

Now we must consider how an existential viewpoint can make a difference to the validity of a syllogism. With many syllogisms, such as those we have just been considering, presuppositions about existence make no difference to whether the syllogisms are valid. However, there are a few cases where this does make a difference. All these are syllogisms having two universal premises and a particular conclusion. For instance, consider the syllogism "No minors medically fit for military service are paraplegics; all students who can run a mile in four minutes are minors medically fit for military service; therefore, some students who can run a mile in four minutes are not paraplegics."

Figure 27 shows how we can diagram what the premises say. In drawing the left-hand diagram, we adopt the hypothetical viewpoint and leave it an open question as to whether individuals of any of these types exist; from this viewpoint, the syllogism is invalid. However, if we may assume the existence of students who can run a mile in four minutes, then we may add an asterisk to the diagram, and now the conclusion will follow (see the right-hand diagram). Thus this form of syllogism is invalid from the hypothetical viewpoint, but is valid from a certain existential viewpoint (notice that for this particular form of syllogism it happens to be an assumption about S's, not about M's or P's, that is required).

In this case there does not seem to be any obvious reason for regarding

Figure 27

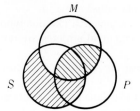
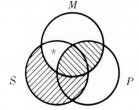

one viewpoint as more appropriate than the other. Perhaps in the context of an actual discussion it would be clear which viewpoint should be adopted; but when we are discussing the syllogism abstractly, the best we can do is to explain the situation, pointing out the ambiguity, and leave matters at that.

EXERCISE 7

*A For each syllogism, determine its mood and figure, and test its validity by means of a Venn diagram.

   1 All ruminants are mammals. All cattle are ruminants. Therefore, all cattle are mammals.

   2 No pharmacists are lawyers. Some realtors are lawyers. So some realtors are not pharmacists.

   3 All existentialists are metaphysicians. Some pragmatists are not existentialists. So some pragmatists are not metaphysicians.

   4 No predators are ruminants. All sheep are ruminants. So no sheep are predators.

   5 No figs are coconuts. No dates are coconuts. So no dates are figs.

   6 No galleys are caravels. Some merchant ships are galleys. So some merchant ships are not caravels.

   7 No Basques are Normans. Some Flemings are not Normans. So some Flemings are not Basques.

   8 All anarchists are radicals. No conservatives are radicals. So no conservatives are anarchists.

   9 Some nations are monarchies. Some language communities are not nations. So some language communities are not monarchies.

  10 Some marsupials are carnivores. All carnivores are predators. So some predators are marsupials.

  11 All Bavarians are Germans. No Bavarians are Rhinelanders. So no Rhinelanders are Germans.

  12 All shot-putters are athletes. Some shot-putters are overweight persons. So some overweight persons are athletes.

  13 All Hegelians are idealists. Some idealists are not theists. So some theists are not Hegelians.

  14 All geometers are mathematicians. Some logicians are not mathematicians. So some logicians are not geometers.

  15 No motorcycles are limousines. All motorcycles are fast vehicles. So no fast vehicles are limousines.

B Determine the mood and figure of each of the following syllogisms, test it by a Venn diagram, and discuss whether it should be classified as valid.

   1 No persons who can run a 3-minute mile are Americans. All persons who can run a 3-minute mile are great athletes. So some great athletes are not Americans.

   2 All natives of Tokyo are Japanese. No Japanese are blondes. So some blondes are not natives of Tokyo.

   3 All contest winners are residents of this city. No Martians are residents of this city. So some Martians are not contest winners.

4 No inexpensive articles are good buys. Some mink-lined sneakers are not inexpensive articles. So some mink-lined sneakers are good buys.

5 All vagrants are homeless persons. All homeless persons are needy persons. So some needy persons are vagrants.

6 All friends of mine are people on the team. Some friends of mine are people 7 feet tall. So some people 7 feet tall are people on the team.

7 All persons whom we want on the team are students who play well. No students who play well are persons 9 feet tall. So some persons 9 feet tall are not persons whom we want on the team.

8 All even numbers are whole numbers. No transcendental numbers are whole numbers. So some transcendental numbers are not even numbers.

8 RULES OF THE SYLLOGISM

Venn diagrams provide an efficient and general method for determining the validity of any syllogism. If we were to construct a Venn diagram for each of the 64 possible kinds of premises that the 256 possible forms of syllogism can have (32 diagrams would do; a tedious but instructive exercise), we would find that the following 15 forms are the only ones valid from the hypothetical viewpoint:

Figure 1	Figure 2	Figure 3	Figure 4
AAA	EAE	IAI	AEE
EAE	AEE	AII	IAI
AII	EIO	OAO	EIO
EIO	AOO	EIO	

Nine additional forms are valid, provided that appropriate existential presuppositions are made[12]:

Figure 1	Figure 2	Figure 3	Figure 4	Presupposition required
AAI	AEO		AEO	S exist
EAO	EAO			
		AAI	EAO	M exist
		EAO		
			AAI	P exist

It is not necessary to memorize this list of valid forms. It is far better to remember how to test syllogisms for validity. Venn diagrams provide one method for testing them. But on the basis of this list, we can develop another method which does not require paper and pencil. If we study this list of valid forms of syllogisms, we can verify certain rules that valid syllogisms obey. One set of rules is the following:

1 In any valid syllogism the middle term is distributed at least once.

2 In any valid syllogism every term distributed in the conclusion is distributed in a premise (but note that this rule allows a term to be distributed in a premise without being distributed in the conclusion).

3 No valid syllogism has two negative premises.

4 Any valid syllogism has at least one negative premise if and only if it has a negative conclusion.

5 No syllogism valid from the hypothetical viewpoint has two universal premises and a particular conclusion.

If we studied the list of valid forms (which we can justify by appeal to Venn diagrams), we could prove that each of these rules is correct.

What do we mean by calling one thing a necessary condition, or a sufficient condition, for another? By saying that *B* is a *necessary* condition for *C*, we mean that nothing is a case of *C* without being a case of *B*. For example, being at least thirty years old is a necessary condition for being a United States senator. By saying that *B* is a *sufficient* condition for *C*, we mean that anything which is a case of *B* is a case of *C*. For example, eating a pint of arsenic is a sufficient condition for promptly dying.

Given that we know by Venn diagrams which forms of syllogisms are valid and which are invalid, we can establish some noteworthy facts about the above set of rules. Each of the first four rules states a necessary condition for the validity of a syllogism regarded from an existential viewpoint. Furthermore, taken together, the requirements stated in these first four rules constitute a sufficient condition for the validity of a syllogism regarded from an existential viewpoint. Also, each of the five rules states a necessary condition for the validity of a syllogism regarded from the hypothetical viewpoint. And taken together, all five rules constitute a sufficient condition for the validity of such a syllogism.

Once we have established these rules, we may use them instead of Venn diagrams for checking the validity of syllogisms. To use the rules in testing the validity of a particular syllogism, we simply observe whether the syllogism breaks any one of the rules; if it breaks a rule, it is invalid, and if it breaks no rule, it is valid.

A syllogism that breaks the first rule is said to commit the fallacy of *undistributed middle*. A syllogism that breaks the second rule is said to commit a fallacy of *illicit process*; it is *illicit process of the major* if the major term is distributed in the conclusion but not in the major premise, and it is *illicit process of the minor* if the minor term is distributed in the conclusion but not in the minor premise. No special names are given to violations of the other rules.

Old-fashioned logic books usually also give the rule "A syllogism must have only three terms." Violation of this rule was called the *fallacy of four terms*. But it is unnecessary for us to include this rule in our list since by definition a syllogism must have just three terms. The fallacy of four terms is a special kind of equivocation (which will be discussed in Chapter 6).

The set of rules stated above has been chosen so as to constitute a brief and easily remembered criterion for the validity of any syllogism. It is also of interest to see how additional rules can be deduced from this initial set of rules. For example, if we wish to prove that no valid syllogism has two particular premises (i.e., that every valid syllogism has at least one universal premise), we can reason as follows:

Suppose that there was a valid syllogism having two particular premises. Its premises would be either (1) two **I** sentences, or (2) two **O** sentences, or (3) and **I** and an **O**. Case 1 is excluded by rule 1, since in two **I** premises the middle term would nowhere be distributed. Case 2 is excluded by rule 3. Case 3 would require the conclusion to be negative, according to rule 4; and in a negative sentence the predicate is distributed, so that by rule 2 the major term would have to be distributed in the major premise. But by rule 1 the middle term would also have to be distributed somewhere in a premise. However, it is impossible for both the major and the middle term to be distributed, since an **I** and an **O** premise contain only one distributed term altogether. Therefore case 3 is excluded, for it would commit either the fallacy of undistributed middle or the fallacy of illicit process of the major. Hence, the rules imply that there can be no valid syllogism having two particular premises.

EXERCISE 8

*A Go back to part A of Exercise 7, and test each of those syllogisms by means of the rules of the syllogism.
 B Identify the mood and figure of each of the following syllogisms. Test its validity by means of the rules. Then check your answer with a Venn diagram, and name any fallacy that has a name.

  1 No Methodists are Lutherans. Some Danes are Lutherans. So some Danes are not Methodists.
  2 Some epic poems are not sagas. No epic poems are comedies. So some comedies are sagas.
  3 No koalas are bears. All grizzlies are bears. So some grizzlies are not koalas.
  4 No philologists are semanticists. Some classicists are philologists. So some classicists are semanticists.
  5 No primates are marsupials. All lemurs are primates. So no lemurs are marsupials.
  6 All hexagons are rectilinear figures. All pentagons are rectilinear figures. So all pentagons are hexagons.
  7 All battleships are warships. No warships are sailing ships. So some sailing ships are not battleships.
  8 All tracts are essays. Some poems are essays. So some poems are tracts.
  9 All detectives are sleuths. Some policemen are detectives. So some policemen are sleuths.
  10 All atheists are positivists, since all positivists are materialists, and all materialists are atheists.

11 All poachers are intruders. Hence, all poachers are trespassers, for some intruders are trespassers.

12 Some seats of government are not metropolises, because some metropolises are not capitals, and all seats of government are capitals.

C Appealing only to the first four rules of the syllogism, prove that the following generalizations hold for all syllogisms valid from an existential viewpoint.

1 If one premise is particular, the conclusion is particular.

2 In the first figure the minor premise is affirmative.

3 In the first figure the major premise is universal.

4 In the second figure the conclusion is negative.

5 In the second figure the major premise is universal.

6 In the third figure the conclusion is particular.

7 In the third figure the minor premise is affirmative.

8 If the major term is the predicate of the major premise, then the minor premise is affirmative.

9 In the fourth figure, if the conclusion is negative, the major premise is universal.

10 In the fourth figure, if the minor premise is affirmative, the conclusion is particular.

†D Appealing to the syllogistic rules, prove your answers to the following questions. For all but the first question, adopt an existential viewpoint.

1 Can a syllogism be valid from the hypothetical viewpoint but not from an existential viewpoint?

2 In what syllogisms, if any, is the middle term distributed in both premises?

3 Can an invalid syllogism violate all four rules at once?

4 What is the maximum number of rules that an invalid syllogism can violate at once?

5 How many more occurrences of distributed terms can there be in the premises of a valid syllogism than there are in its conclusion?

6 In what valid syllogism is the major term distributed in the major premise but not in the conclusion? Prove that there is just one such syllogism.

9   TRANSLATING INTO STANDARD FORM

So far, we have been considering arguments that are in standard form. Our rules for the syllogism, for instance, are supposed to apply only to arguments that are strictly in standard syllogistic form. But few of the arguments we meet in ordinary discourse are exactly in standard form. To make our logical rules more widely useful, we need to understand that many arguments which are not quite in standard form can be put into standard form so as to be testable by our rules.

Putting Sentences into Categorical Form

Arguments in ordinary discourse often contain sentences which are not categorical—this is one way in which ordinary arguments can fail to have the standard form that we want. However, any sentence can be translated into an equivalent standard-form categorical sentence, if we exercise ingenuity (indeed, there are always various acceptable ways of doing this, if we do not mind awkwardness, and if all we are looking for is a standard-form sentence equivalent to the original).[13] Let us think about some examples of such translations.

When a sentence fails to be categorical merely because its predicate is an adjective, we can supply a noun. Thus, "All tigers are carnivorous" can become "All tigers are carnivorous animals," and "No realtors are altruistic" can become "No realtors are altruists."

Where a sentence contains a verb other than "are," we can convert the sentence into standard form by moving the old verb into the predicate. Thus, "All cats eat mice" can become "All cats are animals that eat mice" or "All cats are mouse-eaters." "Some Senators seek reelection" can become "Some Senators are seekers of reelection."

Sentences containing the verb "to be" in the past tense or future tense can be put into categorical form by moving the tensed verb into the predicate. Thus "Some Elizabethans are people who were lovers of bear baiting" can replace "Some Elizabethans were people who loved bear baiting." Similarly, "No rich men will enter into the Kingdom of Heaven" can become "No rich men are people who will enter the Kingdom of Heaven." These examples illustrate how, in a categorical sentence, the copula is to be understood in a tenseless sense.

Sentences in which the word order is different from our standard form can be realigned. Thus "Jaguars are all fast cars" can become "All Jaguar cars are fast cars." (Notice that it would be misleading to use the translation "All Jaguar cars are fast things," for here the word "fast" has a meaning that is comparative—Jaguars are fast for cars, though they are not fast compared with jet planes.) As another example, "No lazy workers are the bees" can become "No bees are lazy workers."

Some further examples: "Elephants never are carnivorous" can become "No elephants are carnivorous creatures." And "There are abstemious sailors" can become "Some sailors are abstemious persons." In each case we try to construct in categorical form a new sentence that is equivalent to the original one.

Sentences like "Ohio is a state" and "Caesar conquered Gaul" seem to pose a problem. We cannot translate the former into "All Ohio is a state," because this has the wrong copula and because its subject term is not a general term (it is a proper name instead—a kind of singular term). To translate it into "All parts of Ohio are states" would be wrong because this is not equivalent to the original. The best way is to translate it into "All things identical to Ohio are states." This translation sounds artificial, but it provides a sentence in proper categorical form that necessarily agrees with the original sentence as regards truth and falsity, since one and only one thing is identical to Ohio (that is, Ohio itself). Similarly, "Caesar conquered Gaul" can become "All persons identical to Caesar are people who were conquerors of Gaul." This somewhat cumbersome style of translation is appropriate only for handling singular terms, however; it would be pointless to translate "All Jaguars are fast cars" into "All things identical to Jaguars are fast cars."

Sometimes we meet sentences that contain no specific indication of quantity. Occasionally such sentences are really ambiguous, but often if we think about how they would be used, we can see that they mean one thing rather than the other. Thus, someone who says "Bachelors are unmarried" surely intends to say "*All* bachelors are unmarried persons," while someone who says "Visitors are coming" surely intends to say "*Some* visitors are coming." Similarly, "An elephant is a pachyderm" surely is equivalent to "All elephants are pachyderms," but "A police officer is at the door" is equivalent to "Some police officers are persons at the door."

Another sort of ambiguity can occur when the word "not" is inserted in the middle of a universal sentence. Does it belong to the copula or to the predicate? "All my professors are not boring" might be equivalent to "All professors of mine are people who are not boring," or it might be equivalent to "It is not the case that all professors of mine are people who are boring," that is, "Some professors of mine are not people who are boring." When we meet a sentence constructed in this ambiguous way, we have to try to guess what the speaker means.

Sentences containing the words "only" and "none but" must be handled carefully. "Only Midwesterners attend Calvin Coolidge College" does not mean that all Midwesterners are attenders of C.C.C.; what it means is "All persons who attend C.C.C. are midwesterners." Similarly, "None but the brave deserve the fair" does not mean that all brave persons are deservers of the fair; it means "All persons who deserve the fair are brave persons." In general, "Only S are P" and "None but S are P" both are equivalent to "All P are S."

However, "only some" has a meaning different from "only" by itself. Thus "Only some pigs eat acorns" means "Some pigs are eaters of acorns and some pigs are not eaters of acorns." In a similar vein, "All except employees are eligible" means "All nonemployees are eligible," and it strongly *suggests*, although it does not necessarily *say*, that no employees are eligible—whether it should ever be interpreted as implying that no employees are eligible is arguable. Similarly, "Anyone is eligible unless he is an employee" means "All nonemployees are eligible," and it too suggests, though it does not necessarily say, that no employees are eligible. In general, both "All except S are P" and "Anything is P unless it is S" imply "All nonS are P," and it is ambiguous whether they also imply "No S are P."

Sometimes we may have to devise entirely new terms before we can put a sentence into categorical form. The sentence "Whenever it rains, it pours" does not look like a categorical sentence, but if we think of it as a remark about *times*, we can see that it is equivalent to "All times when it rains are times when it pours." Similarly, "Wherever you go, I will go" can be understood as referring to places, and it can become "All places where you go are places where I will go." However, we have to be alert to the intended meanings of sentences like these. "Wilbur always sleeps in class" probably does not mean "All times are times when Wilbur sleeps in class"; surely the intended meaning is more likely to be "All times when Wilbur is in class are times during which he does some sleeping." Similarly, "She goes everywhere with him" probably does not mean "All places are places to which she goes with him"; much more likely it means "All places he goes are places where she goes with him."

Working out translations such as these will often be necessary as a preliminary to the syllogistic analysis of ordinary reasoning. But it also has an additional intellectual value in that it encourages us to understand more accurately what ordinary sentences are saying.

Translating into Syllogistic Form

Many arguments that are not in syllogistic form as they stand can nevertheless be translated legitimately into syllogisms. That is, their premises and conclusions admit of being translated into equivalent categorical sentences that do form syllogisms, and the validity of the original arguments stands or falls with that of the standard syllogisms into which they are translated. By translating arguments in this way, we make it easier to test their validity by means of Venn diagrams, and we make it possible to test their validity by the rules of the syllogism.

There are two different respects in which an argument that can be translated into a syllogism may at first fall short of being in standard syllogistic form. The argument may at first contain sentences that are not categorical, or it may at first contain more than three terms. How shall we deal with syllogistic arguments that contain too many terms?

Suppose we have an argument that looks like a syllogism, in that it contains three sentences and talks about just three classes of things. However, it contains too many terms, some of these terms being negations (contradictories) of others. When this happens, we can use operations such as obversion or contraposition to eliminate some of the terms, replacing some original sentences by equivalent new ones. For instance, consider the argument "No millionaires are paupers; no stars of television are non-millionaires; therefore no stars of television are paupers." The argument is not in syllogistic form as it stands, because it contains four terms. But two of its terms are contradictories, and so if we obvert the second premise, we can change the argument into the form "No M are P. All S are M. So no S are P." Now it is a standard syllogism (**EAE** in the first figure, and valid).

Notice that it would have been an error to have called the original argument invalid because it contained two negative premises. The rule that an argument with two negative premises is invalid applies only to syllogisms in standard form (and the same goes for all our syllogistic rules). We should not try to apply the rules until after we have got the argument into standard form.

When some terms are contradictories of others, obversion and contraposition can often allow us to reword an argument so as to reduce the number of terms. But sometimes a deeper rewording of an argument is required if we are to put it into syllogistic form. Where this is so, we must be thoughtful about selecting our terms, trying to word the argument so that we have just three terms in all, each of which appears in two different sentences of the argument. For instance, consider the argument "The car doesn't start easily when the temperature is below zero; it will be below zero tomorrow; so tomorrow the car won't start easily." Although this does not look much like a syllogism, we can get it into syllogistic form. One way is this: "All days when the temperature falls below zero are days when the car does not start easily; all days identical to tomorrow are days when the temperature falls below zero; therefore, all days identical to tomorrow are days when the car does not start easily." Here we have **AAA** in the first figure, and it is valid.

EXERCISE 9

*A Translate each sentence into an equivalent sentence in categorical form, trying to interpret it in the way most likely to be intended.
1 All ducks are aquatic.
2 Some concerts are not boring.
3 A Rolls Royce is very costly.
4 Tadpoles never become snakes.
5 There are fortress monasteries.
6 There are no unclimbed mountains.
7 All cashiers are not courteous.
8 Whoever spies for a foreign power commits treason.
9 Only Esquimos live in Greenland.
10 The dinosaurs were made extinct by a change of climate.
11 A fish has scales.
12 Ithaca was the home of Odysseus.
13 Whatever you buy in Paris will be stylish.
14 Nothing but aspirin helps my headache.
15 Wherever there are oaks, acorns will be found.
16 All violators will be prosecuted.
17 Whenever he felt homesick he would get drunk.
18 My car always starts with difficulty.
19 The llama is wooly.
20 The Minotaur was slain by Theseus.
*B Put each argument into syllogistic form, explaining your steps. Name the resulting mood and figure, and test its validity by a Venn diagram and by the rules.

1 A noncitizen is a nonvoter. No resident alien is a citizen. So some resident aliens are not voters.

2 It's not the case that some Brazilians are not South Americans. Uzbeks never are South Americans. So no Uzbeks are Brazilians.

3 No sharks aren't fish. So a hammerhead is a fish, since a hammerhead is a shark.

4 Straight lines never curve. Only straight lines are the sides of triangles. So the sides of triangles never curve.

5 Nothing but ghosts are poltergeists. Hence, no succubus is a ghost, since a succubus never is a poltergeist.

6 There aren't any carthorses that are racehorses. Hence, old Dobbin isn't a racehorse, for he's a carthorse.

7 Africans never are Hindus, since only non-Hindus are Egyptians, and Egyptians always are Africans.

8 Some dictatorships are not nonmonarchies. In a monarchy a king is the head of state. So some states headed by kings are not dictatorships.

9 Some nonoceans are not nonseas. All lakes are nonoceans. So lakes sometimes aren't seas.

10 Whoever isn't a friend of Mil's isn't a friend of Phil's. So, friends of Sal's never are friends of Phil's, since there are no friends of Mil's who are friends of Sal's.

11 There are mice that aren't prolific. No mice are nonrodents. So rodents sometimes are nonprolific.

12 Grandmothers never go in for surfing. Surfers sometimes go in for sunbathing. So no sunbathers are grandmothers.

13 Wherever the soil is very acid, flowers won't grow. But flowers grow in your garden, so the soil can't be very acid there.

14 You can't convict someone of murder just on circumstantial evidence. There is only circumstantial evidence against the butler. So the butler can't be convicted of murder.

15 Anytime the press is free there will be active criticism of the government. You never get active criticism of the government without some of it being unfair. So you can't have a free press without some unfair criticism of the government.

C Translate each sentence into categorical form, trying to interpret as it is likely to be intended.

1 Blessed are the peacemakers.

2 None but the lonely heart can know my sadness.

3 He jests at scars who never felt a wound.

4 Who lives without folly is not so wise as he thinks.

5 Tardiness is reprehensible.

6 There never was a philosopher that could endure the toothache patiently.

7 He cannot become rich who will not labor.

8 No news is good news.

9 No friend is better than a fair-weather friend.

10 Whoever loves me loves my dog.

11 Those who live in glass houses shouldn't throw stones.

12 It is a wise father that knows his own child.

13 None but those who love virtue love angling.
14 Except ye be as little children, ye shall not enter into the kingdom of God.
15 It is sharper than a serpent's tooth to have an ungrateful child.

10 RELATED TYPES OF ARGUMENT

We can make use of what we now know about syllogisms and about Venn diagrams in order to analyze some additional arguments that are a little different from the types we have studied so far.

The Sorites

Sometimes we encounter an argument that can be interpreted as a chain, or sequence, of syllogisms. This means that two premises of the original argument can be combined to form a syllogism, whose conclusion can then be combined with another premise from the original argument to form another, whose conclusion can then be combined with another premise from the original argument to form yet another syllogism, and so on, until we reach the final conclusion. An argument of this type is called a *sorites* (from the Greek word for a pile).

In order to show that a sorites is valid, we must show how it is possible to pass, by a series of valid syllogistic steps, from the premises to the conclusion. We use our ingenuity in order to fit together the links of the chain, testing each link by means of a Venn diagram or by the rules of the syllogism.

For example, consider the argument:

Some prime numbers are integers.	(1)
All rational numbers are real numbers.	(2)
All integers are rational numbers	(3)
Therefore, some prime numbers are real numbers.	(4)

This may be symbolized:

Some *P* are *I*.	(1)
All *Ra* are *Re*.	(2)
All *I* are *Ra*.	(3)
∴ some *P* are *Re*.	(4)

Here (1) and (3) can be combined to make a syllogism of the form **AII** in the first figure; their conclusion, "Some *P* are *Ra*," can then be combined with (2) to make a syllogism again of the form **AII** in the first figure; its conclusion is (4). Thus we show that the original premises validly yield the desired result.

The method just employed is a method for establishing the validity of a valid sorites. Suppose, however, that in a given case we try to pass, by means of syllogistic steps, from the premises to the conclusion but do not find a way to do so. This may lead us to suspect that the sorites is invalid, but just by itself our failure does not definitely *prove* that the sorites is invalid. Perhaps we simply have not been ingenious enough. To prove that the sorites is invalid by using our present method, we would have to investigate *every* possible sequence in which the premises might have been combined, and we would have to show that *none* of these sequences validly yields the conclusion.

Further Uses of Venn Diagrams

Some arguments that cannot be translated into syllogisms or into chains of syllogisms can nevertheless be tested by means of Venn diagrams. Consider the argument "Every student of theology studies Greek or studies Hebrew. Some students of theology do not study Hebrew. So not all who study Greek study Hebrew." We may rewrite this argument in the form:

All *T* are (*G* or *H*).
Some *T* are not *H*.
∴ some *G* are not *H*.

Here we have an argument that is not valid as a syllogism, for if we think of it as containing just three terms, then its premises are not all in categorical form; while if we think of its premises as in categorical form, then there are more than three terms ("*T*," "*H*," "*G*," and "*G* or *H*").

But we would be too hasty if we assumed this argument to be invalid just because it is not a valid syllogism. This kind of argument is not supposed to be a syllogism. It is a kind of argument, however, whose validity can be tested by means of a Venn diagram, since it deals with just three classes of individuals and makes appropriately simple assertions about them. We can test it by making a diagram which shows exactly what the premises say; then we can inspect the diagram to see whether the conclusion follows.

Here our diagram needs three circles, representing those who study theology, those who study Greek, and those who study Hebrew. The first premise declares that all individuals inside the *T* circle are either inside the *G* circle or inside the *H* circle (we interpret the premise as not intending to exclude the possibility that some who are in *T* may be in *G* and *H* both). This means that none who are inside the *T* circle are outside both the *G* and *H* circles (Figure 28). The second premise makes the added claim that some individuals inside the *T* circle are outside the *H* circle (Figure 29). Inspecting the completed diagram, we see that the conclusion that not all who are inside the *G* circle are inside the *H* circle validly follows.

EXERCISE 10

*A Use appropriate methods to deal with these arguments.
  1 Whatever Allie likes, Bud likes. Allie likes nothing that Cal likes. Everything Dan likes, Cal likes. So Bud likes nothing Dan likes.

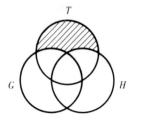

Figure 28

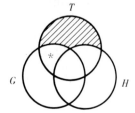

Figure 29

2 No one European is Chinese. Everyone Scandinavian is European. Every-one Swedish is Scandinavian. Some Laplanders are Swedish. So some Laplanders are not Chinese.

3 Derive a valid conclusion that follows only from all three premises to-gether: Feathers of the moa bird cannot be had at any price. Nothing is sold in discount stores except what can be bought cheaply. Nothing that cannot be had at any price can be bought cheaply.

4 Derive a valid conclusion using all these premises: Anyone likely to cause trouble in cramped quarters is dangerous aboard a space capsule. Infants are always noisy. All distracting companions are likely to cause trouble in cramped quarters. No one who would be dangerous aboard a space cap-sule is suitable as an astronaut for the trip to Mars. Any noisy person is a distracting companion.

5 No scientists are both bureaucrats and astronauts. All astronauts are sci-entists. So some astronauts are not bureaucrats.

6 Any Mexican speaks Russian or speaks Spanish. No Russian speakers are either Mexicans or Spanish speakers. So all Mexicans speak Spanish.

7 All high-performance cars that are economical are unsafe. Some econom-ical cars are either high-performance cars or unsafe. So some economical cars are unsafe.

8 Every Cypriot is either Turkish or Greek. There are non-Turkish Cypriots. So some non-Turkish Cypriots are Greek.

9 Would you advise a person who wants to become a doctor to enroll at Calvin Coolige College? Its rules require that: All students must take logic; all premedical students must take physics; no one may take physics with-out taking calculus; only those who do not take calculus may take logic.

10 Anyone who knows either Jan or Dora knows Ken. No one who knows both Jan and Dora knows Ken. So no one who knows Jan knows Dora.

†B Analyze the following arguments.

1 Speculative opinions...and articles of faith...which are required only to be believed, cannot be imposed on any church by the law of the land. For it is absurd that things should be enjoined by laws which are not in men's power to perform. And to believe this or that to be true does not depend upon our will.   JOHN LOCKE, *A Letter Concerning Toleration*

2 Philosophy must possess complete certitude. For since philosophy is a science, its content must be demonstrated by inferring conclusions with legitimate sequence from certain and immutable principles. Now, that which is inferred by legitimate sequence from certain and immutable principles is thereby certain and cannot be doubted....Hence, since there is no room for doubt in philosophy, which is a science, it must possess complete certitude.

CHRISTIAN WOLFF, *Preliminary Discourse on Philosophy in General*

3 Some...have...expressed themselves in a manner...of imagining the whole of virtue to consist in singly aiming according to the best of their judgment, at promoting the happiness of mankind in the present state; and the whole of vice in doing what they foresee, or might foresee, is likely to produce an overbalance of unhappiness in it: than which mistakes, none can be conceived more terrible. For it is certain, that some of the most shocking instances of injustice, adultery, murder, perjury, and even of persecution, may, in many supposable cases, not have the appearance of being likely to produce an overbalance of misery in the present state; perhaps sometimes may have the contrary appearance.

JOSEPH BUTLER, *The Analogy of Religion*

4 The governments, not only the military ones, but the governments in general, could be, I do not say useful, but harmless, only in case they consisted of infallible, holy people....But the governments, by dint of their very activity, which consists in the practice of violence, are always composed of elements which are the very opposite of holy,—of the most impudent, coarse, and corrupted men. For this reason every government...is a most dangerous institution in the world.

LEO TOLSTOI, "Patriotism and Government"

5 The senses never give us anything but instances, that is to say particular or individual truths. Now all the instances which confirm a general truth, however numerous..., are not sufficient to establish the universal necessity of this same truth.... Whence it seems that necessary truths...must...not depend upon instances, nor, consequently, upon the witness of the senses...   LEIBNIZ, *New Essays*

CHAPTER **3**

THE LOGIC OF TRUTH FUNCTIONS

In this chapter we shall study a group of deductive arguments quite different in character from those based on categorical sentences. These arguments will contain compound sentences of a special kind, and will depend for their validity upon the special properties of these sentences.

11 ARGUMENTS CONTAINING COMPOUND SENTENCES

We may think of an argument as having two parts. One part consists of those words which make up its logical skeleton, that is, its logical form, or structure. The other part consists of those words which are the flesh with which the skeleton is filled out. For instance, (1) is an argument, and (2) is its logical skeleton:

All spiders are eight-legged. (1)	All...are ### (2)
No wasps are eight legged.	No *** are ###
∴ no wasps are spiders.	∴ no *** are...

In argument (1) the words "all," "no," and "are" make up the logical skeleton, while the words "spiders," "wasps," and "eight-legged" are the flesh with which the skeleton happens to be clothed. Notice that (1) is a valid argument, and it is valid *because* (2) is a valid kind of skeleton. That is, *any* argument having this same form will have a true conclusion provided that its premises are true.

All the arguments dealt with in Chapter 2 were like (1) in that their logical skeletons had gaps that were to be filled by single words or phrases. However, not all arguments are like this. Consider argument (3) and its skeleton (4):

This is a wasp, or this is a spider. (3)   ### or... (4)
This is not a wasp.   Not ###

∴this is a spider.   ∴....

Argument (3) is deductively valid too, but notice the difference between skeleton (4) and skeleton (2). The gaps in (4) must be filled not by single words or phrases but by whole sentences. In argument (3) the sentences which happen to fill these gaps are the sentences "This is a wasp" and "This is a spider." Notice also that in analyzing this argument we must think of the first premise not as a categorical sentence but rather as a compound sentence. Only by thinking of it in this way can we see what makes the argument valid. We shall now become acquainted with some of the main kinds of arguments that contain compound sentences like this—arguments whose fleshy parts are whole sentences.

Some of them are very simple, trivial forms of argument. You may think that they are pointless or silly. But remember that simple arguments can be combined to form chains of reasoning, and a chain of reasoning may succeed in reaching an interesting conclusion that was not obvious, even if each step in it is trivial and obvious.

Negation

A simple way of forming a compound sentence is by adding at the beginning the words "It is not the case that." The sentence "It is not the case that spiders are insects" is a compound sentence, for it contains within itself the simpler sentence "Spiders are insects." We say that the former sentence is the *negation* of the latter sentence. The negation of a given sentence is *contradictory* to it; that is, it denies just what the given sentence says, no less and no more.

Another way of forming negations is to use the single word "not." "Spiders are not insects" also expresses the negation of "Spiders are insects." But notice that the word "not" is somewhat unreliable as a way of forming negations. "Some spiders are not insects" fails to be the negation of "Some spiders are insects," because these sentences are not contradictories. The negation of the latter sentence is best expressed as "It is not the case that some spiders are insects," and is equivalent to "No spiders are insects."

The negation of a sentence will deny just what the sentence says, no less and no more. Therefore, the negation of the negation of a sentence will have to be equivalent to the original sentence itself. This provides us with two extremely simple forms of argument that involve negation only.

Double negation

Not (not p)	e.g. It is not the case that wasps aren't insects.
∴*p*	Therefore wasps are insects.
p	e.g. Wasps are insects.
∴not (not p)	Therefore it is not the case that wasps aren't insects.

Here, in representing the forms of compound sentences, we have stopped using cumbersome dots, asterisks, and so on; instead, we use the letters "p," "q," and "r," which are to be thought of as doing just the same job—that is, marking places where whole sentences may be filled in. We shall use capital letters when we wish to abbreviate specific sentences—thus we can let "W" be short for "Wasps are insects," and then the two examples we were just considering of double-negation arguments can be abbreviated "not (not W), ∴ W" and "W, ∴ not (not W)."

Notice, however, that we cannot use the principle of double negation to cancel out negations indiscriminately. From "It is not the case both that there will not be rain and that there will not be snow," we are not entitled to infer "There will be rain, and there will be snow." The structure of this mistaken reasoning is:

Not (not p and not q)

∴ p *and* q

This is a misuse of the principle of double negation. Here the mistake is that our premise is the negation of an "and" sentence rather than the negation of a negation. To avoid mistakes like this, we need to pay close attention to the logical forms of the expressions with which we deal. The position of a negation can make a great difference to its meaning.

As another example, we have to distinguish among:

Not (p or q)	e.g. It is not the case that it will either rain or snow.
Not p or q	e.g. It will not rain, or it will snow.
Not p or not q	e.g. It will not rain, or it will not snow.

Here are three different forms of sentences which say three different things. They are not equivalent.

Disjunction

A compound sentence consisting of two simpler sentences linked together by "or" (or by "either...or...," which means just the same) is called a *dis-*

junction (or an *alternation*). A disjunction is symmetrical, in the sense that "*p* or *q*" always is equivalent to "*q* or *p*." We can rewrite our earlier skeleton (4) using letters:

Disjunctive arguments

p **or** *q*	also: *p* **or** *q*	e.g.	It will rain, or it will snow.
Not *p*	Not *q*		It will not rain.
∴ *q*	∴ *p*		∴ it will snow.

These forms of disjunctive arguments are valid because the first premise tells us that at least one component is true, while the second premise tells us that a certain component is not true. It follows that the other component must be true.

In English there are two different ways of using the word "or." Sometimes when we say "*p* or *q*," what we mean is "*p* or *q* but not both." This is called the *exclusive* sense of "or." More often when we say "*p* or *q*," we mean "*p* or *q* and perhaps both." This is the *nonexclusive* sense of "or." In ordinary conversation, if a gentleman says to his girlfriend in a tone of acquiescence, "I'll buy you a Cadillac, or I'll buy you a mink coat," he is surely using "or" in the nonexclusive sense, since one cannot accuse him of having spoken falsely if he then gives her both. Cases of the exclusive sense of "or" occur, though less often. If a father says to his child in a tone of refusal, "I'll take you to the zoo, *or* I'll take you to the beach," then one can accuse him of having spoken falsely if he takes the child both places.

It seems best to adopt the policy of always interpreting the word "or" in the nonexclusive sense except in those cases where we have some positive indication that the exclusive sense is intended. In this way, we can be sure of not taking too much for granted. Therefore, we regard the following two forms of argument as invalid:

Invalid disjunctive arguments

p or *q*	*p* or *q*	e.g.	He's guilty, or she's guilty.
p	*q*		He's guilty.
∴ not *q*	∴ not *p*		Therefore she's not guilty.

These forms would be valid if "or" were understood in the exclusive sense, but they are invalid when "or" is understood in the commoner, nonexclusive sense.

Conjunction

A compound sentence consisting of two simpler sentences linked by the word "and" is called a *conjunction*. Sometimes, as in the sentence "They got married and had a baby," the word "and" may mean "and then," indicating that one event occurred first and the other event occurred later. But other times, as in the sentence "I like cake, and I like candy," the word "and" is simply used to join together two assertions, without indicating any time relationship. This latter sense of "and" is what we are concerned with. When "and" is used in this minimum sense, conjunctions are symmetrical; that is, "p and q" is equivalent to "q and p." In English, various other words, such as "but" and "although," often do essentially the same logical job as "and."   One absurdly simple but perfectly valid form of conjunctive argument is this:

Valid conjunctive argument (simplification)

p and q	Also: p and q	e.g. It rains, and it snows.
∴ p	∴ q	∴ it rains.

If we combine negation with conjunction, we can obtain a slightly less trivial kind of valid conjunctive argument:

Valid conjunctive arguments

Not (p and q) p	e.g. Sue and Kim don't both smoke. Sue smokes.
∴ not q	∴ Kim doesn't smoke.

Not (p and q) q	e.g. Jon and Tim aren't both poor. Tim is poor.
∴ not p	∴ Jon isn't poor.

The following forms are invalid, however:

Invalid conjunctive arguments

Not (p and q) Not p	e.g. Mac isn't both young and wise. Mac isn't young.
∴ q	∴ Mac is wise.

Not (p and q) not q	e.g. Sue doesn't both fish and ride. Sue doesn't ride.
∴ p	∴ Sue fishes.

Conditionals

Consider the sentence, "If tufa floats, then some rocks float." This is a compound sentence consisting of two simpler sentences, "Tufa floats" and "Some rocks float", linked by the words "if" and "then". In order for this compound sentence to be true, the simpler sentences do not necessarily have to be true. Thus, someone who asserts the compound sentence is not committed to believing that tufa floats, or that some rocks float. What such a person is committed to is the claim that the truth of "Tufa floats" would be sufficient to ensure that "Some rocks float" is true. To put it another way, such a speaker is claiming that tufa doesn't float unless some rocks float.

A sentence consisting of two simpler sentences linked by the words "if" and "then" (or just by "if") is called a *conditional* sentence, or a *hypothetical* sentence. The part to which the word "if" is directly attached is called the *antecedent* of the conditional sentence, and the other part is called the *consequent*. Let us consider some forms of arguments containing conditional sentences.

Modus ponens

If p then q	e.g. If tufa floats, some rocks float.
p	Tufa floats.
$\therefore q$	$\therefore$ some rocks float.

Modus tollens

If p then q	e.g. If French is easy, Italian is easy.
Not q	Italian isn't easy.
$\therefore$ not p	$\therefore$ French isn't easy.

Somewhat similar, but not deductively valid, are the following:

Fallacy of affirming the consequent

If p then q	e.g. If profits rise, taxes rise.
q	Taxes rise.
$\therefore p$	$\therefore$ profits rise.

Fallacy of denying the antecedent

If p then q	e.g. If the car runs, it has gas.
Not p	The car doesn't run.
$\therefore$ not q	$\therefore$ the car doesn't have gas.

Another valid form has three conditional sentences, the consequent of the first being the same as the antecedent of the second:

Chain argument (or hypothetical syllogism)

If p then q	e.g. If Fido barks, Rover barks.
If q then r	If Rover barks, Champ barks.
∴ if p then r	∴ if Fido barks, Champ barks.

We can also construct even longer chain arguments with any number of premises. The one requirement for a valid chain argument is that the consequent of the first premise must serve as the antecedent of the next, the consequent of that premise as the antecedent of the next, and so on, while the conclusion must have the first antecedent as its antecedent and the last consequent as its consequent.

Another style of argument involving a conditional premise goes by the name of *reductio ad absurdum* (Latin: "reduction to the absurd"). Suppose we want to prove that there is no largest whole number (integer). We may reason as follows: If there is an integer larger than every other integer, then (because adding 1 to it will yield a still larger integer) it is not an integer larger than every other integer. From this it follows that there is not a largest integer. This reasoning has the form:

Reductio ad absurdum

If p then not p	e.g. If there is a largest integer, then there is not a largest integer.
∴ not p	∴ There is not a largest integer.

This style of reasoning may seem puzzling because one may be inclined to think that a sentence of the form "if p then not p" says something impossible, something necessarily false. This is not so. A sentence of the form "if p then not p" can very well be true, but only if its antecedent is false. This is why the conclusion follows. The premise tells us that the truth of the antecedent will carry with it a consequent inconsistent with the truth of the antecedent. Thus the antecedent is 'reduced to absurdity,' and this entitles us to conclude that the antecedent is false.

Another similar way of reasoning involves reducing an antecedent to absurdity by pointing out that it can have a consequent which is necessarily false. For example:

Reductio ad absurdum (another form)

If p then both q and not q	e.g. If I get home before dark, then I'll both have come at 90 mph and not come at 90 mph
∴ not p	∴ I won't get home before dark.

Here the point perhaps is that I'm 90 miles from home, and it's one hour until darkness; yet if I drive on this road at 90 m.p.h. I'll surely crash. Here the premise is a conditional whose consequent is necessarily false, but this does not prevent the premise as a whole from being a true sentence. The antecedent is 'reduced to absurdity,' and this allows us to infer that it is false.

In ordinary language when we come to put a compound sentence into words the component sentences often are condensed together, to make the whole sentence more manageable. Instead of saying "Ellen is coming, and Fay is coming," we are likely to say "Ellen and Fay both are coming." Instead of saying "John is a baker, or Bill is a baker," we may say "John or Bill is a baker." The shorter sentence is clearly equivalent to the longer one in cases like this. Translations back and forth between the fuller standard form and the shorter colloquial form are easy, and we need not make a fuss about them.

EXERCISE 11

*A Abbreviate each argument using the suggested letters (keep clear what each letter means). Identify the form and say whether it is deductively valid.

1 This concerto is by Bach or by Handel. It isn't by Handel, so it must be by Bach. (*B, H*)

2 Cigarette smoking is a major cause of heart disease and of cancer. So it's a major cause of heart disease. (*H, C*)

3 If it's above zero today, my car will start. But it's not above zero today, so my car won't start. (*A, C*)

4 If the moon is full, the dogs all howl. If the dogs all howl, Mr. Smith calls the police. So, if the moon is full, Mr. Smith calls the police. (*M, D, S*)

5 The suspect wasn't both at the scene of the crime and at his mother's house. He was at his mother's. So he wasn't at the scene of the crime. (*C, M*)

6 Either Jack did well in math or he didn't do well in physics. He didn't do well in math. So he didn't do well in physics. (*M, P*)

7 It's not the case that 3 is both a real number and an imaginary number. It isn't imaginary. So it's real. (*R, I*)

8 If Jill is late for school, she won't learn her lessons today. She isn't going to learn her lessons today. So she will be late for school. (*S, L*)

9 Mary loves either her husband or son. She does love her son. So she doesn't love her husband. (*H, S*)

10 If this creature bites, it isn't a toad. It's not the case that it isn't a toad. So it doesn't bite. (*B, T*)

11 The dog is friendly, if the child approaches it quietly. The child does approach it quietly. So the dog is friendly. (*F, Q*)

12 If the company is to stay profitable, it must raise its prices (to increase unit revenue) and not raise its prices (to preserve market share). So the company isn't going to stay profitable. (*S, R*)

13 We're going to win the game. So it's not the case that we won't win. (*W*)

14 If I join the Navy, I'll go to sea. If I become an admiral, I'll go to sea. So if I join the Navy, I'll become an admiral. (*J, S, A*)

15 If it rains and freezes, then the streets will be wet and slippery. It is raining and freezing. So the streets will be wet and slippery. (Choose your
own letters. How many are needed?)

16 They won't fail to come. So they will come. (C)

17 If Al doesn't sing, Tim and Bo won't dance. Al won't sing. So Tim and Bo
won't dance. (Choose your own letters.)

18 It's not the case that some judges aren't lawyers. So some judges are lawyers. (Choose your own letters.)

19 If these are two different circles each going through three of the same
points, then these are not two different circles each going through three of
the same points. So these aren't two different circles each doing that. (T)

20 His driving licence won't have been revoked if he hasn't violated the law.
But he must have violated the law, as his licence has been revoked. (V, R)

B A pundit predicts that if interest rates fall, the stock market will rise; but if
interest rates don't fall either inflation will accelerate or neither will the stock
market rise nor will inflation accelerate. Which of the following outcomes accord with the prediction?

1 Interest rates fall, the stock market rises, and inflation accelerates.

2 Interest rates hold steady, the stock market rises, inflation accelerates.

3 Interest rates fall, the stock market doesn't rise, inflation accelerates.

4 Interest rates don't fall, the stock market doesn't rise, but inflation accelerates.

5 Interest rates fall, the stock market rises, inflation does not accelerate.

6 Interest rates rise, the stock market rises, inflation decelerates.

7 Interest rates fall, the stock market crashes, inflation stops dead.

8 Interest rates rise, the stock market falls, inflation ceases.

12 TRANSLATING INTO STANDARD FORM; DILEMMAS

Many ordinary arguments admit of being translated into the kind of standard forms we have just been discussing. We have already noticed some
ambiguities and misunderstandings that can arise when we try to interpret
sentences involving negation, disjunction, and conjunction. However, translations involving them usually are comparatively straightforward. With the
conditional, though, the situation is more complicated.

Consider the following ways in which a conditional may be formulated:

If he's a senator, then he's over thirty.	If p then q
if he's a senator, he's over thirty.	If p, q
He's over thirty if he's a senator.	q if p
He's over thirty provided he's a senator.	q provided p
He's a senator only if he's over thirty.	p only if q
He's not a senator unless he's over thirty.	Not p unless q
Unless he's over thirty, he's not a senator.	Unless q not p

All these sentences are equivalent to one another. In each sentence "He's a
senator" may be regarded as the antecedent and "He's over thirty" as the

consequent. Each of these conditional sentences claims that the antecedent expresses a sufficient condition for the consequent—his being a senator is sufficient to guarantee his being over thirty. Also, each claims that the consequent expresses a necessary condition for the antecedent—his being over thirty is necessary to his being a senator.

An important point to notice about conditionals is that "if p then q" is not in general equivalent to "if q then p." Thus, "If he's a senator, then he's over thirty" is not equivalent to "If he's over thirty, then he's a senator." These two sentences express independent thoughts, and the truth of one does not guarantee the truth of the other.

Because of this, we have to be on our guard. It is easy to make the mistake of supposing that "if" means the same as "only if"; and this would lead one to suppose that "He's a senator only if he's over thirty" means the same as "He's a senator if he's over thirty." But this is quite wrong. The general rule is that "p only if q" is always equivalent to "if p then q" but not to "if q then p."

Similarly, when we translate an "unless" sentence into "if-then" form, we must be careful to distinguish correctly between antecedent and consequent, and not get them in the wrong positions. A general rule for translating "unless" sentences is: negate either part of the "unless" sentence and make it the antecedent of your conditional. Thus, "p unless q" can become either "if not p then q" or "if not q then p." For example, "He's an admiral unless he's a general" is equivalent to "If he isn't an admiral, then he's a general" and to "If he isn't a general, then he's an admiral." But it is not equivalent to "If he's an admiral, then he isn't a general" or to "If he's a general, then he isn't an admiral."

When the antecedent and consequent trade places in a conditional sentence, we obtain what is called the *converse* of the original sentence. Thus, "If he's over thirty, then he's a senator" is the converse of "If he's a senator, then he's over thirty." In general, "if q then p" is the converse of "if p then q." As we have already noticed, the converse is a new and different sentence which need not agree with the original as regards truth and falsity.

In a conditional sentence, if the antecedent and consequent trade places and also each of them is negated, we obtain what we call the *contrapositive* of the original sentence. Thus, "If he's not over thirty, then he's not a senator" is the contrapositive of "If he's a senator, then he's over thirty." And in general, "if not q then not p" is the contrapositive of "if p then q." The contrapositive always is equivalent to the original sentence. This is because the original sentence says in effect that the truth of p ensures the truth of q, while its contrapositive says that the falsehood of q ensures the falsehood of p—which amounts to the same thing.

Understanding these relationships can help us to deal with arguments which are not stated in standard form. Suppose we are wondering about whether a given argument is valid, but as it stands, it is not in any one of our standard forms. If its premises and conclusion can be translated into equivalent sentences that do form an argument of a standard type, then we can use what we know about the validity of the standard type to evaluate the validity of the given argument. Our method here permits two sorts of moves: We may replace any premise or conclusion by a new sentence equivalent to it; and we may change the order of the premises. Such moves will have no effect on the validity or invalidity of the argument. Our aim in dealing with a non-standard argument will be to get it into some familiar standard form so that we can reliably tell whether it is valid.

For instance, we may handle an example as follows:

Mica sinks only if tufa doesn't sink. ⟶ If M then not T
Mica does sink. ⟶ M
Hence tufa doesn't sink. ⟶ Therefore not T

Here the arrows merely connect each original sentence with its translation, to indicate our moves. We use capital letters to abbreviate the sentences, and it is important always to keep clearly in mind what sentence a given capital letter is short for. (We shall not use the small letters "p," "q," and "r" to abbreviate particular sentences; they will be reserved for use when we are representing general logical forms.) The above argument is translated into a case of modus ponens, because the first premise becomes a conditional whose antecedent is the same as the second premise and whose consequent is the same as the conclusion. Since the original argument can be translated into modus ponens, we know that the original argument is valid.

Here is another example:

If argon burns, neon burns. ⟶ If X then A
If argon doesn't burn, xenon doesn't burn. ⟶ If A then N
So xenon does not burn unless neon does. ⟶ If X then N

Here we have replaced the second premise by its contrapositive, letting the double negations cancel out; this is permissible because our new sentence is strictly equivalent to the original one. Also, we have changed the order of the premises, as we are permitted to do. Since this new argument that we obtain is a valid chain argument, we know that our original argument is valid also.

We shall conclude this section by considering one further group of standard forms for arguments containing compound sentences. Arguments of this group are called *dilemmas*, and they combine conditional and disjunctive sentences in a special way.

Simple constructive dilemma

If p then q   e.g. If he gives her mink, he loves her.
If r then q   If he gives her a Rolls, he loves her.
p or r   He gives her mink or a Rolls.
_____   _____

∴ q   ∴ he loves her.

Simple destructive dilemma

If p then q	e.g. If he graduates, he'll have passed physics.
If p then r	If he graduates, he'll have passed biology.
Not q or not r	He won't pass physics or won't pass biology.
∴ not p	∴ he isn't graduating.

Complex constructive dilemma

If p then q	e.g. If she shot intentionally, she's guilty of murder.
If r then s	If she shot unintentionally, she's guilty of manslaughter.
p or r	She shot intentionally or unintentionally.
∴ q or s	∴ she's guilty of murder or manslaughter.

Complex destructive dilemma

If p then q	e.g. If he's smart, he earned profits.
If r then s	If he's honest, he paid taxes due.
Not q or not s	He didn't earn profits or didn't pay taxes due.
∴ not p or not r	∴ he isn't smart or isn't honest.

A valid constructive dilemma is like a double use of modus ponens, while a valid destructive dilemma is like a double use of modus tollens. A dilemma is invalid if it resembles the fallacy of affirming the consequent or of denying the antecedent.

Invalid dilemma

If p then q	e.g. If he gets all the answers right, he'll pass the test.
If r then not q	If he gets all the answers wrong, he'll fail the test.
q or not q	He'll either pass or fail.
∴ p or r	∴ he'll get all the answers right or all the answers wrong.

Dilemmas have often been used by debaters, and they were a formidable weapon in the rhetoric of the ancients. Often dilemmas whose overall logical form is valid nevertheless contain logical flaws that prevent them from being good arguments (we shall return to this point in Chapter 6).

If your opponent in a debate presents a dilemma which you do not know how to find fault with but whose conclusion you do not wish to accept, then you are said to be 'caught on the horns of a dilemma.' If you succeed in showing that his argument is unsatisfactory by pointing out that the disjunctive premise is not true, then you 'escape between the horns of the dilemma.'

EXERCISE 12

*A Abbreviate each argument, using the suggested letters, translate it into some standard form, name the form, and say whether it is valid.

1 Ed knows Latin if he knows Greek. He does know Latin. So he knows Greek. (L, G)

2 Sue will perform if Rod requests it. If Jon requests it, Sue will perform. Rod or Jon will request it. So Sue will perform. (S, R, J)

3 The music is baroque if it's by Vivaldi. It's not baroque unless it's not romantic. So if the music is by Vivaldi, it's not romantic. (B, V, R)

4 Cara will drive unless she flies. She won't fly. So she'll drive. (D, F)

5 If Jack approved it, the loan was made. If Ellen approved it, the loan was made. But either Jack didn't approve it or Ellen didn't approve it. So the loan wasn't made. (J, L, E)

6 Matt will have eaten, if Jane cooked. Matt didn't eat unless Bob ate too. So Bob ate only if Jane cooked. (J, M, B)

7 The sale will not be completed unless financing is found. But the sale will be completed. So financing is being found. (S, F)

8 Jill will go running only if it isn't going to be hot. She isn't going to run. So it won't be hot. (J, H)

9 This cylinder is square only if it's both round and not round. So this cylinder isn't square. (S, R)

10 If interest rates rise, retail prices will rise. Interest rates will rise only if unemployment rises. But either retail prices won't rise or unemployment won't. So interest rates won't rise. (I, R, U)

11 If the cylinder is empty, the pump will operate. If the vapor pressure is excessive, the pump won't operate. So if the vapor pressure is excessive, the cylinder isn't empty. (C, P, V)

12 If mice sing, some rodents sing. Fleas dance only if some insects dance. Either it's not the case that some rodents sing or it's not the case that some insects dance. So either mice don't sing or fleas don't dance. (M, R, F, I)

13 Ellen will come if Bill does. Donna will come unless Chris doesn't. Either Ellen or Donna will come. So either Bill or Chris will come too. (E, B, D, C)

14 Unless clubs were not led, I can take this trick. I have a good hand if spades are trump. Either clubs were led or spades are trump. So either I can't take this trick or I have a good hand. (C, T, S, G)

15 The landlord may evict the tenant only if the tenant has not fulfilled the terms of the lease. If the rent is overdue, the tenant has not fulfilled the terms of the lease. So if the rent is overdue, the landlord may evict the tenant. (E, L, R)

B Which of the following sentences are equivalent to "If Al knows calculus, then he knows algebra"?

1 Al knows calculus only if he knows algebra.

2 Al doesn't know algebra without knowing calculus.

3 Al doesn't know algebra only if he doesn't know calculus.

4 Al knows algebra only if he knows calculus.

5 Al doesn't know calculus without knowing algebra.

6 Al doesn't know calculus only if he doesn't know algebra.

7 Al knows calculus unless he doesn't know algebra.

  8 Al doesn't know algebra provided that he doesn't know calculus.
  9 Al knows algebra only if he knows calculus.
  10 Al knows calculus unless he doesn't know algebra.
  11 Al knows calculus if he doesn't know algebra.
  12 If Al doesn't know algebra, then he doesn't know calculus.
  13 Al doesn't know calculus unless he knows algebra.
  14 Al knows calculus if he knows algebra.
  15 Al knows algebra if he knows calculus.
  16 Al knows calculus unless he knows algebra.
  17 Al doesn't know algebra if he doesn't know calculus.
  18 Al knows calculus provided that he knows algebra.
  19 Al doesn't know algebra unless he knows calculus.
  20 Al doesn't know calculus unless he knows algebra.
  21 Al doesn't know calculus if he doesn't know algebra.
  22 Al knows algebra if he doesn't know calculus.
  23 Al knows algebra unless he doesn't know calculus.
  24 Al knows algebra unless he knows calculus.

13 TRUTH FUNCTIONS AND THEIR GROUPING

To say that a compound sentence is *truth-functional* is to say that whether it is true or false is strictly determined by (is a function of) the truth or falsity of the shorter sentences of which it is composed. That is, settling the truth or falsity of each of its component sentences enables us to settle whether the compound sentence is true or false. Not all compound sentences are truth-functional; for instance, in order to discover whether "Ted is going because Jim is coming" is true or whether it is false, we need to know more than just whether "Ted is going" is true and whether "Jim is coming" is true. However, most sentences of the kinds considered in the preceding section are truth-functional, and this allows us to develop further methods for testing arguments which involve such sentences.

Negation

How is a sentence that is a negation related to its component sentence? The relation is that they must be opposite as regards truth and falsity. We can use the following little table to show the relationship. Here we use the dash as our symbol for negation, writing "$-p$" as short for "It's not the case that p."

p	$-p$
True	False
False	True

This "truth table" has two lines, covering the two cases that arise here. If p is true, its negation is false (first line). If p is false, its negation is true (second line). We may interpret "*p*" as short for whatever sentence we please, and the table will show how our chosen sentence and its negation are related.

In using the dash symbol for negation, we shall always interpret the dash as governing as little of what follows as would make sense. Thus, in "–*p* and *q*" the negation sign is to be regarded as governing only "*p*," not "*p* and *q*." That is, "–*p* and *q*" means "(–*p*) and *q*" rather than "–(*p* and *q*)."

For the purposes of symbolic logic, when we speak about *the negation* of a sentence, we shall understand this in a special, restricted way. The negation of any sentence will be just that very sentence, with a negation sign written in front of it so as to apply to the whole of it. Thus, the negation of "*p*" is "–*p*", the negation of "*p* or *q*" is "–(*p* or *q*)", the negation of "–*p*" is "– –*p*", and so on.

In order to write down the negation of a given sentence, we must place our negation sign properly, and not just stick it in anywhere. If we want the negation of "*p* and *q*", for instance, we must not carelessly wrote down "–*p* and *q*", or "–*p* and –*q*". Neither of these versions is the negation of the given sentence; its negation is "–(*p* and *q*)", and these versions are not even equivalent to that.

Moreover, even if we do succeed in writing down something that is equivalent to the negation of the given sentence, we may still not have written down its negation. Thus, "– –*p*" is the negation of "–*p*", and "*p*" is equivalent to "– –*p*", but this does not make "*p*" the negation of "–*p*" (although of course "*p*" is a *contradictory* of "–*p*").

Conjunction

How is a sentence that is a conjunction related to its two component sentences? The answer is that the conjunction is true when both its parts are true, and otherwise it is false. Here too we can draw up a truth table to show the relationship. Let us use "T" to abbreviate "true" and "F" to abbreviate "false."

p	*q*	*p* & *q*
T	T	T
F	T	F
T	F	F
F	F	F

We use the ampersand as our symbol for truth-functional conjunction, writing "*p* & *q*" as short for "*p* and *q*." Our truth table needs four lines to cover the possible situations. Thus, for instance, the sentence "It will rain, and it will get colder" is true if it both rains and gets colder, but is false if either one of these things fails to happen or if both fail to happen.

As we noticed earlier, "and" is sometimes used in English to mean "and then," as in "They got married and had a baby." Such a sentence is not truth-functional. Merely knowing whether they got married and whether they had a baby does not enable you to know whether "They got married and (then) had a baby" is true—you also need to know which happened first. Since we are using the ampersand to mean just "and," not "and then," it would be misleading to symbolize "They got married and had a baby" as "*M & B.*" However, when we are analyzing an argument, often it is all right to replace a premise that is a non-truth-functional "and" sentence by a truth-functional conjunction. The truth-functional conjunction, though it says less, may well express that part of the meaning which is relevant to the validity of the argument.

Disjunction

What is the relation between a disjunctive sentence and its component sentences? A nonexclusive disjunction is true whenever at least one of its components is true, and it is false otherwise. Here our table must have four lines, as there are four possible situations to be considered. Using the wedge as our symbol for nonexclusive disjunction, we can abbreviate "*p* or *q*" as "*p* ∨ *q*."

p	*q*	*p* ∨ *q*
T	T	T
F	T	T
T	F	T
F	F	F

Here we may replace "*p*" and "*q*" by any sentences we please, and the table will show how they are truth-functionally related to their disjunction.

Conditionals

Conditional sentences present a difficulty, because the words "if-then" are often used in ways that are not truth-functional. However, let us consider some cases where "if-then" is truth-functional.

Suppose a petulant mother exclaims, "If I've told you once, then I've told you a thousand times." She means this in a sense in which it is equivalent to denying that she has told you once without telling you a thousand times. If we write "*O*" for "I told you once" and "*T*" for "I told you a thousand times," then the mother's original remark may be expressed "If *O* then *T*." And it is equivalent to "−(*O* & −*T*)." This compound sentence is false if "*O*" is true but "*T*" is false (if she told you once but did not tell you a thousand times), and it is true otherwise. Construed in this way, the sentence is truth-functional, since its truth or falsity is strictly determined by the truth or falsity of its component parts.

Let us take another example and see exactly what the truth function is which "if-then" expresses. Suppose someone says, "If the Cavaliers lose today, then I'm a monkey's uncle." What he is saying can be reworded as "It's not the case both that the Cavaliers lose today and that I'm not a monkey's uncle." We can draw up a table for this:

C	M	–M	C & –M	–(C & –M) If C then M
True	True	False	False	True
False	True	False	False	True
True	False	True	True	False
False	False	True	False	True

The four horizontal lines (rows) of this truth table represent the four possible combinations of truth and falsity for "C" and "M." Since we are dealing with specific sentences here, just one of these combinations must represent the actual situation; but we are interested in all four possibilities, for we are studying the meaning of the conditional. The first two columns of the table show these possibilities and form the starting point. In the first line, where "C" and "M" both are true, "–M" must be false. Hence "C & –M" has to be false too. Its negation "–(C & –M)" must therefore be true; and "If C then M" which means the same will be true too. In the second line, the reasoning is just the same. In the third line, since "M" is false, "–M" will be true, and "C & –M" will be true too. Thus "–(C & –M)" will be false. In the fourth line, since "C" is false, "C & –M" must be false too, and so "–(C & –M)" must be true.

What has been said in this particular case holds good in general. The rule is: a truth-functional conditional is false when its antecedent is true and its consequent false, and is true otherwise. We represent the truth-functional conditional by means of the horseshoe symbol. Thus "p ⊃ q" will be our way of writing it, and here is its truth table:

p	q	p ⊃ q
T	T	T
F	T	T
T	F	F
F	F	T

We have defined the horseshoe symbol in such a way that "p ⊃ q" has to be equivalent to "–(p & –q)." Therefore, the negation of "p ⊃ q," that is, "–(p ⊃ q)," has to be equivalent to "p & –q." Now, you might have thought that "–(p ⊃ q)" would be equivalent to "p ⊃ –q." But this is not so. You see, "p ⊃ q" and "p ⊃ –q" are not contradictories. They might both be true, as will happen when "p" is false. We can illustrate these relationships this way:

p	q	−q	p ⊃ q	−(p ⊃ q)	p & −q	p ⊃ −q
T	T	F	T	F	F	F
F	T	F	T	F	F	T
T	F	T	F	T	T	T
F	F	T	T	F	F	T

In this table the first two columns define the starting point. The third column is an auxiliary column, to be used when we fill in the last two columns. The fourth column is for a conditional, and its four lines are filled in on the basis of the first two columns in the way we just discussed. The fifth column is for the negation of the conditional, and so in each line it must be opposite to the fourth column, as regards truth or falsity. In the sixth column we consider "p & −q," and we fill in the column by looking back at the first and third columns. It will be true when "p" and "−q" both are true (the third line), and it will be false otherwise. Now we can see that the fifth and sixth columns are alike in every line, thereby showing that "−(p ⊃ q)" and "p & −q" are equivalent—alike as regards truth or falsity in every possible case. Our last column is for "p ⊃ −q." This conditional is false when its antecedent is true and its consequent is false (first line), and is true otherwise. We can see that "p ⊃ −q" and "−(p ⊃ q)" are not equivalent, as they differ with regard to truth and falsity in the second and fourth lines.

We can draw up a truth table for a conditional only when it is a truth-functional conditional. In English, however, the words "if-then" are often (perhaps much more often) used in ways that are not truth-functional. Suppose someone says, "If you drop this vase, then it will break." The speaker means to assert *more* than merely that it is not the case that you will drop it without its breaking. Over and above this, the speaker is saying that dropping it *would cause* it to break. Here we may know the truth or falsity of the component sentences "You will drop it" and "It will break" (perhaps we agree that you are not going to drop it and that it is not going to break), and yet still we may disagree or be in doubt about the truth or falsity of "If you drop it, it will break." A conditional sentence understood in this way is not truth-functional, and we lose part of its meaning if we replace it by the weaker sentence "D ⊃ B."

However, if we make it our practice to use the truth-functional horseshoe to symbolize conditional sentences, we can usually test arguments very adequately. For the truth-functional horseshoe expresses that part of the meaning of conditional sentences which normally is important as regards the validity of arguments in which conditional sentences occur.[14]

Biconditionals

A compound sentence is called a *biconditional* when it consists of two simpler sentences linked by the words "if and only if." When these words are understood in a truth-functional sense, "p if and only if q" is symbolized "p

≡ q." Of course, "p if and only if q" is equivalent to "p if q and p only if q". That is, "p ≡ q" is equivalent to "(q ⊃ p) & (p ⊃ q)." Let us draw up a truth table for the latter expression in order to see what the truth table for the former should be.

p	q	(q ⊃ p)	(p ⊃ q)	(q ⊃ p) & (p ⊃ q)	p ≡ q
T	T	T	T	T	T
F	T	F	T	F	F
T	F	T	F	F	F
F	F	T	T	T	T

The third and fourth columns of this table are obtained from the first two columns, in light of the rule that a conditional is always true except when its antecedent is true and its consequent false. The fifth column is obtained from the third and fourth, in light of the rule that a conjunction is true when and only when both its parts are true. The last column is copied from the fifth; it shows us that the biconditional is true whenever its components are alike as regards truth and falsity, and it is false whenever they differ.

A biconditional says something stronger than does a single conditional. Thus "You'll be promoted if and only if you pass the examination" promises that passing the examination is necessary *and* sufficient for being promoted. In contrast, the single conditional "If you pass the examination, then you'll be promoted" merely says that passing the examination is sufficient, while the other conditional "You'll be promoted only if you pass the examination" merely says that passing the examination is necessary.

Summary

Looking back over what we have learned about various types of truth functions, we can formulate these rules:

> A *negation* always is opposite to the sentence negated, as regards truth or falsity.
> A *conjunction* is true when and only when both parts are true.
> A *disjunction* is true when and only when at least one part is true.
> A *conditional* is false when its antecedent is true and its consequent is false; otherwise it is true.
> A *biconditional* is true when and only when its parts are alike as regards truth or falsity.

Grouping

When we deal with expressions containing several symbols, it is important to pay attention to the grouping of the parts. This is because changing the grouping of its parts sometimes can entirely change the meaning of an expression. Therefore, if we are to avoid misunderstanding when we write down truth-functional compounds, we always need to make clear what grouping is intended. We shall use parentheses for this purpose.

Notice, for instance, the difference between "p & (q v r)" and "(p & q) v r." The former is a conjunction, one part of which is a disjunction. The latter is a disjunction, one part of which is a conjunction. They are not equivalent, for they can differ as regards truth and falsity.

To see that this is so, suppose we replace "p" by the sentence "I'm going to Paris," and replace "q" by the sentence "I'm going to Quebec," and replace "r" by "I'm going to Rome." Suppose that in fact I am not going to Paris or Quebec but am going to Rome. Then the compound sentence "I'm going to Paris and either to Quebec or to Rome"—which is of the form "p & (q v r)"—is false, since I'm not going to Paris. But the corresponding sentence, "Either I'm going both to Paris and to Quebec or I'm going to Rome"—which is of the form "(p & q) v r"—is true, since I am going to Rome.

Our example shows that "p & (q v r)" is not equivalent to "(p & q) v r." For this reason it would be improper to write the expression "p & q v r" without parentheses. This expression is ambiguous, because it might have either of two quite different meanings. One cannot tell whether it is supposed to be a conjunction, one part of which is a disjunction, or a disjunction, one part of which is a conjunction.

Carelessly written sentences in ordinary language, such as "I'm going to Paris and Quebec or Rome," are ambiguous in just the same confusing way. But if we word the sentence more carefully and use a comma, the meaning can be made clear. Thus, "I'm going to Paris, and I'm going to Quebec or Rome" has the logical structure "p & (q v r)." And "I'm going to Paris and Quebec, or to Rome" has the logical structure "(p & q) v r." In addition to the comma and other forms of punctuation, we can use pairs of words such as "both-and" and "either-or" to prevent ambiguity and make our meanings clear.

EXERCISE 13

A For each pair of formulas: (a) Is the first the negation of the second? (b) Is the second the negation of the first? (c) If neither is the negation of the other, are they nevertheless contradictories?

1. $-q$; q	**2.** $--r$; r
3. $--r$; $-r$	**4.** $---p$; $--p$
5. p & q; $-p$ & q	**6.** $-(p$ & $q)$; p & q
7. $p \supset q$; $-(p \supset q)$	**8.** $p \supset q$; $p \supset -q$
9. $-p \supset q$; $-(-p \supset q)$	**10.** q v r; $-q$ v $-r$
11. p v q; $-(q$ v $p)$	**12.** $r \supset q$; $-q \supset -r$
13. $-(r$ & $q)$; q & r	**14.** $p \equiv q$; $-p \equiv q$
15. q v r; $-q$ v r	**16.** $-(p \supset q)$; $p \equiv q$

17. $p \equiv q; -(p \equiv q)$ **18.** $p; -(p \vee q)$

19. $p \mathbin{\&} (q \vee r);$

     $-p \mathbin{\&} -(q \vee r)$

20. $(q \supset p) \mathbin{\&} (p \supset q);$

     $-[(q \supset p) \mathbin{\&} (p \supset q)]$

B   Let "W" mean "It gets warmer," let "M" mean "The snow melts," and let "O" mean "The sun comes out." Match each sentence of the first group with the one from the second group that most closely corresponds to it.

Group I

  1 If it doesn't get warmer, the snow doesn't melt.

  2 It's not the case that it gets warmer, or the snow melts.

  3 It gets warmer if and only if the snow melts.

  4 It gets warmer only if the snow melts.

  5 It's not the case that the snow melts if it gets warmer.

  6 Neither does it get warmer nor does the snow melt.

  7 It's not the case either that it gets warmer or the snow doesn't melt.

  8 It's not the case that it gets warmer if and only if the snow melts.

  9 Unless it doesn't get warmer, the snow doesn't melt.

10 It's not the case both that it gets warmer and the snow melts.

11 It gets warmer if and only if the snow doesn't melt.

12 It's not the case both that it doesn't get warmer and the snow melts.

13 It gets warmer or the snow doesn't melt.

14 It gets warmer unless the snow melts.

15 It doesn't get warmer and the snow doesn't melt.

Group II

1. $W \supset M$	**2.** $W \supset -M$
3. $-W \supset M$	**4.** $-W \supset -M$
5. $-W \vee M$	**6.** $W \vee -M$
7. $-W \mathbin{\&} -M$	**8.** $W \equiv M$
9. $W \equiv -M$	**10.** $-(W \vee M)$
11. $-(W \vee -M)$	**12.** $-(W \mathbin{\&} M)$
13. $-(-W \mathbin{\&} M)$	**14.** $-(W \equiv M)$
15. $-(W \supset M)$	

C   Letting "W" and "M" mean the same as before, and letting "O" mean "The sun comes out," match each sentence from the first group with its closest kin in the second group.

Group I

  1 It gets warmer, only if the snow melts and the sun comes out.

  2 If the sun comes out, it gets warmer and the snow melts.

  3 If it gets warmer the snow melts, and the sun comes out.

  4 It gets warmer, or the sun comes out if the snow melts.

  5 If it gets warmer, then the snow melts only if the sun comes out.

  6 If it gets warmer only if the snow melts, then the sun comes out.

  7 It gets warmer, and the snow melts if and only if the sun comes out.

  8 It gets warmer, if and only if the sun comes out if the snow melts.

  9 The sun comes out, if either it doesn't get warmer or the snow doesn't melt,

10 It's not the case that, if it gets warmer, either the snow melts or the sun comes out.

11 If it gets warmer if and only if the snow melts, then the sun comes out.

12 It gets warmer if and only if both the snow melts and the sun comes out.

13 Either the snow melts or the sun doesn't come out, if it doesn't get warmer.

14 That it gets warmer only if the snow melts, is the case if and only if the sun comes out.

15 It's not the case that if either it doesn't get warmer or the snow melts, the sun comes out.

Group II

1. $W \equiv (M \& O)$

2. $W \& (M \equiv O)$

3. $(W \supset M) \& O$

4. $(W \supset M) \equiv O$

5. $W \supset (M \supset O)$

6. $(W \equiv M) \supset O$

7. $W \supset (M \& O)$

8. $W \equiv (M \supset O)$

9. $-[W \supset (M \lor O)]$

10. $-[(-W \lor M) \supset O]$

11. $(W \supset M) \supset O$

12. $O \supset (W \& M)$

13. $W \lor (M \supset O)$

14. $(-W \lor -M) \supset O$

15. $-W \supset (M \lor -O)$

D Let "A" be short for "Australia is not in Africa," let "B" be short for "Bulgaria is in Europe," let "M" be short for "Manila is in China,", and let "N" be short for "New Delhi is in Russia." Determine whether each sentence is true.

1. $A \& B$

2. $A \& M$

3. $M \lor N$

4. $M \lor B$

5. $A \supset B$

6. $M \supset N$

7. $A \supset M$

8. $A \equiv B$

9. $B \equiv N$

10. $M \lor -N$

11. $-(N \equiv A)$

12. $-(M \supset A)$

13. $A \& (M \& B)$

14. $M \lor (N \lor A)$

15. $M \lor (M \supset N)$

16. $N \lor (M \equiv N)$

17. $A \supset (M \supset B)$

18. $N \supset (M \& -A)$

19. $-N \supset (-M \lor -B)$

20. $-M \& (A \lor N)$

21. $N \lor (B \supset -A)$

22. $-[A \supset (M \lor N)]$

23. $-B \equiv -(A \& N)$

24. $-[(M \supset A) \supset B]$

E Let "C" mean "Canada is larger than England," let "D" mean "Denmark is smaller than India," let "O" mean "Omaha is the capital of Spain," and let "P" mean "Philadelphia is in Cuba." Determine whether each sentence is true.

1. $(C \& D) \lor (O \& P)$

2. $(O \lor P) \& (C \lor D)$

3. $(C \& D) \supset (O \& P)$

4. $(O \lor P) \supset (D \lor C)$

5. $C \supset [D \lor (O \& P)]$

6. $(O \supset C) \lor (P \supset D)$

7. $(D \supset P) \supset (C \& O)$

8. $(O \equiv C) \supset (P \equiv D)$

9. $(O \& P) \equiv -(C \lor D)$

10. $(D \equiv O) \supset (P \& O)$

11. $(C \supset P) \& (D \lor O)$

12. $-[P \supset (C \& D)] \supset O$

13. $[(C \& C) \lor (O \& P)] \lor D$

14. $(O \lor -O) \supset [(D \& C) \& P]$

15. $(O \supset -O) \supset [P \supset (C \lor D)]$

16. $(P \& -P) \supset [(C \lor D) \supset D]$

17. $(C \lor -C) \supset [(O \& -O) \& D]$

18. $(O \supset C) \& [D \equiv (P \& D)]$

19. $-(O \& P) \supset -[C \& (D \lor P)]$

20. $-[(P \& C) \lor (O \& C)] \& D$

21. $[(O \equiv P) \& (C \equiv D)] \lor D$

22. $(P \equiv C) \supset [(D \equiv O) \lor P]$

23. $-[O \& (P \equiv C)] \equiv (P \supset B)$

24. $P \supset -[(C \lor O) \& (D \equiv P)]$

14 TRUTH TABLES

In light of the rules concerning truth functions that we learned in the preceding section, we shall be able to construct truth tables for more complex sentences—truth tables that will enable us to answer several kinds of logical questions.

A complete truth table for a compound sentence must have lines representing all possible cases—all the different combinations of truth and falsity that could arise for its basic component sentences. The number of possible situations that must be considered (the number of horizontal lines in the truth table) depends on the number of different basic components.

In the second section of this chapter we wrote a truth table for "$-p$," which needed only two lines. Similarly, a truth table for "$(p \vee -p)$ & p" would need only two lines. Where only one basic component is present (in this case there is only "p"), the only possibilities to be considered are its truth and its falsity. However, a truth table for "$p \vee q$" has to have four lines, and so does a truth table for "$(q$ & $p) \vee (q \vee p)$." Here "p" and "q" are the basic components. Thus "p" may be either true or false when "q" is true, and may be either true or false when "q" is false, making four possibilities. If we were dealing with a compound containing three different basic components, there would be eight possibilities to consider and so eight lines in the truth table. In general, each additional basic component doubles the number of lines required in the truth table.

In constructing a truth table, we need to be sure to take account of just the proper possibilities; using a systematic procedure will help. In drawing up the initial columns, let us follow the practice of alternating the entries in the first column ("T" in the first line, "F" in the second line, etc.), pairing the entries in the second column ("T" in the first and second lines, "F" in the third and fourth lines, etc.), alternating by fours the entries in the third column, and so on.

When we are dealing with complicated compounds, it often helps to use auxiliary columns, working step by step to reach the final column in which we are interested. For instance, suppose we want a truth table for "$(r$ & $q) \supset (p \equiv r)$." Since this contains three basic components, we require eight lines. The compound as a whole is a conditional, one part of which is a conjunction and the other part a biconditional. Here it will be wise to use two auxiliary columns, one for the conjunction and one for the biconditional. Then it will be easier to draw up the final column for the conditional as a whole. The table will look like this:

p	q	r	r & q	p ≡ r	(r & q) ⊃ (p ≡ r)
T	T	T	T	T	T
F	T	T	T	F	F
T	F	T	F	T	T
F	F	T	F	F	T
T	T	F	F	F	T
F	T	F	F	T	T
T	F	F	F	F	T
F	F	F	F	T	T

Here three initial columns have been drawn up in a systematic fashion so as to take account of exactly the right possibilities. The fourth and fifth columns are auxiliary columns drawn up by looking at the first three columns. Then from the fourth and fifth columns we get the sixth column, the one we are seeking. The sixth column tells us, in each of the eight possible cases, whether the compound is true or false. From the table we obtain the information that the compound is false only if "*p*" is false and "*q*" and "*r*" are both true.

Logicians have also devised various other methods for working out the answers to questions about truth-functional compounds. Some of them yield their answers more quickly and with less writing than this truth-table method does. But this truth-table method has the advantage of being easy to explain and to understand.

Truth-Functional Implication and Validity

When one sentence (or group of sentences) implies another and the relationship depends solely upon the truth-functional forms of the sentences concerned, we call this a *truth-functional implication*. Truth tables provide a method for telling whether truth-functional implications hold. The method is this: we construct a truth table containing a column for each sentence involved in the implication. Then we inspect the table line by line to see whether there is any line in which the supposedly implying sentences are all true and the supposedly implied sentence is false. If there is such a line, then the implication does not hold. If there is no such line, the implication does hold.

An argument whose premises truth-functionally imply its conclusion is said to be *truth-functionally valid*. We can use a method similar to the one above for telling whether an argument is truth-functionally valid. We construct a truth table containing a column for each premise of the argument and a column for the conclusion. Then we inspect the table line by line to see whether there is any line in which all the premises are true and the conclusion is false. If there is such a line, the argument is not truth-functionally valid; otherwise it is.

All valid arguments of the forms discussed in the first section of this chapter are truth-functionally valid. Each of them can be shown to be truth-functionally valid in this way. As an example, let us consider modus ponens. A truth table for a particular argument of this form will contain columns for the two premises, say, "$A \supset B$" and "A" and a column for the conclusion "B." Or we can make the headings more general in style by expressing the premises as "$p \supset q$" and "p" and the conclusion as "q." When we do it this latter way, the understanding is that the truth table represents *any* argument of this form.

Premise *p*	Conclusion *q*	Premise *p* $\supset$ *q*
T	T	T
F	T	T
T	F	F
F	F	T

Since just two basic letters occur in the argument, we need four lines in the table; we have a column for each premise and one for the conclusion. Now, what does the table show? We see that the first line is the only line in which both premises are true, and in the first line the conclusion is true too. There is no possibility of having the premises all true and the conclusion false. This demonstrates that the premises truth-functionally imply the conclusion, that is, that modus ponens is truth-functionally valid.

As another example, let us consider arguments of the form "p, therefore p ∨ q." This is a simple type of disjunctive argument which we have not discussed so far; it is called *disjunctive addition*.

Premise p	q	Conclusion p ∨ q
T	T	T
F	T	T
T	F	T
F	F	F

Here the table shows that whenever "p" is true, "p ∨ q" must be true also, and so this form of argument is valid. Of course, it is a very trivial form of argument. Someone who argued "It is raining; therefore it is raining or snowing" would not be offering us interesting food for thought. However, the argument is strictly valid, and it might be of value as one step in the middle of some longer chain of reasoning.

As another example, let us treat the simple destructive dilemma. Can we show by means of a truth table that this form of argument is valid? Here we need columns for the premises "p ⊃ q," "p ⊃ r," and "−q ∨ −r," and we need a column for the conclusion "−p." Since there are three letters, the table must have eight lines. The work is easier if we use some auxiliary columns to help us reach the final ones.

p	q	r	Premise p ⊃ q	Premise p ⊃ r	−q	−r	Premise −q ∨ −r	Concl. −p
T	T	T	T	T	F	F	F	F
F	T	T	T	T	F	F	F	T
T	F	T	F	T	T	F	T	F
F	F	T	T	T	T	F	T	T
T	T	F	T	F	F	T	T	F
F	T	F	T	T	F	T	T	T
T	F	F	F	F	T	T	T	F
F	F	F	T	T	T	T	T	T

Here the fourth and fifth columns are for the first two premises, and we get them from the three initial columns by using the rule for the conditional. The sixth and seventh columns are auxiliary ones taken from the initial columns by using the rule for negation. The eighth column is for the third premise, and we derive it from the sixth and seventh, using the rule for disjunction. Then we add a column for the conclusion. Inspection of the completed table shows that only in the fourth, sixth, and eighth lines are all premises true, and in each of these lines the conclusion is true. Hence the table shows this form of argument to be truth-functionally valid.

As a final example of this procedure, let us consider the particular argument:

> If matter exists, Berkeley was mistaken.
> If my hand exists, matter exists.
> Therefore, either my hand exists or Berkeley was mistaken.

We may symbolize it:

$M \supset B$
$H \supset M$
$\therefore H \vee B$

Let us test the validity of this argument by means of a truth table.

M	B	H	Premise $M \supset B$	Premise $H \supset M$	Conclusion $H \vee B$
T	T	T	T	T	T
F	T	T	T	F	
T	F	T	F		
F	F	T	T	F	
T	T	F	T	T	T
F	T	F	T	T	T
T	F	F	F		
F	F	F	T	T	F

We are concerned only with the question whether it is possible for the premises both to be true and the conclusion false, and so any parts of the table that do not help to answer that question may be left blank. Thus we leave the fifth column blank in the third and seventh lines, for we are interested only in lines where both premises are true. We leave the last column blank in the second, third, fourth, and seventh lines for the same reason. The eighth line finally gives a definite answer to our question, for in that line both premises are true and the conclusion is false. This demonstrates that the argument is not truth-functionally valid.

Truth-Functional Equivalence

To say that two sentences are equivalent to one another is to say that they necessarily are alike as regards truth and falsity. When they are equivalent simply because of their truth-functional form, we say that they are *truth-*

functionally equivalent. Truth tables provide a method for determining whether sentences are truth-functionally equivalent. Consider a sentence of the form "–(p & q)" and a corresponding sentence of the form "–p & –q." Are these truth-functionally equivalent? We can establish the answer by constructing a truth table containing a column for each compound. Then we compare these columns, line by line. If they are alike in every line, this shows that the equivalence holds, while if the columns differ in any line, the equivalence does not hold. (Notice that it would not make sense to say that the compounds are equivalent in some lines but not in others. Being equivalent means being alike as regards truth and falsity in *all* possible cases.)

Continuing with this example, let us draw up a table with a column for each of the two compounds. Let us also include a column for "–p ∨ –q" so that it can be compared with the others.

p	*q*	*p & q*	*–(p & q)*	*–p*	*–q*	*–p & –q*	*–p ∨ –q*
T	T	T	F	F	F	F	F
F	T	F	T	T	F	F	T
T	F	F	T	F	T	F	T
F	F	F	T	T	T	T	T

Here the third column is obtained from the first two and serves as an auxiliary column from which we get the fourth column. The fifth and sixth columns come from the first and second; from them we obtain the seventh and eighth. With the table complete, we look at it line by line, and we observe that in the second and third lines "–(p & q)" differs from "–p & –q," the former being true and the latter false. This shows that these two compounds are not truth-functionally equivalent to one another. However, "–(p & q)" and "–p ∨ –q" are just alike in each line, which shows that they are equivalent. Thus "–(p & q)" and "–p & –q" are not equivalent, while "–(p & q)" and "–p ∨ –q" are.

Not only is "–(p & q)" equivalent to "–p ∨ –q," but also "–(p ∨ q)" is equivalent to "–p & –q," as could be shown by another truth table. These two equivalences are known as *De Morgan's laws,* after the nineteenth-century logician De Morgan.

All the various equivalences mentioned earlier in this chapter also can be demonstrated by means of truth tables. We can show by truth tables that "p" and "–(–p)" are equivalent, that "p & q" and "q & p" are equivalent, that "p ⊃ q" and "–q ⊃ –p" are equivalent, and so on.

When two sentences are truth-functionally equivalent, each implies the other, and so either may be validly inferred from the other. This is one way in which knowing about equivalences can help us to understand certain kinds of steps in reasoning.

Another slightly more complicated principle concerning truth-functional equivalence also is useful in connection with reasoning. This principle may be illustrated as follows: A sentence of the form "r ⊃ –(p & q)" has to be equivalent to a corresponding sentence of the form "r ⊃ (–p ∨ –q)," because these two compounds are exactly alike except that where the first contains the component "–(p & q)" the second contains "–p ∨ –q," which is equivalent to it. Since the two short compounds are necessarily alike as regards truth and falsity, replacing one by the other in the longer expression cannot alter the truth table for the longer expression. Hence the altered longer expression necessarily agrees with the original longer expression, as regards truth and falsity. This principle holds in general: Any two longer truthfunctional compounds are bound to be equivalent if they are exactly alike except that in one of them a component present in the other has been replaced by something equivalent to that component.

Tautology and Contradiction

When we draw up a truth table for a truth-functionally compound sentence, usually we find that it comes out true in some lines and false in other lines. But occasionally we meet extreme cases: for instance, we may meet a compound that comes out true in every line of its truth table. Such a compound is called a *tautology*. Also, occasionally we meet a compound that is false in every line of its truth table. Such a compound is a truth-functional *contradiction*. (Notice the difference between a contradiction, an expression that is bound to be false, and contradictories, sentences that are necessarily opposite in truth or falsity.)

A sentence that is a tautology is bound to be true in every possible situation. Thus, it is a kind of necessarily true sentence, whose necessary truth results from its truth-functional form. One well-known type of tautology has the form "p ∨ –p." This is sometimes called the "law of excluded middle," because it reflects the fact that any given sentence must be either true or false, there being no third alternative. Another well-known type of tautology has the form "–(p & –p)." This is sometimes called the "law of contradiction," because it reflects the fact that a sentence cannot be both true and false. Some other tautologies that do not have special names are "p ⊃ p" and "p ≡ p." There are an unlimited number of tautologies, for we can always keep inventing longer and longer ones.

A sentence that is a truth-functional contradiction is necessarily false, because of its truth-functional form. Some examples are "p & –p," "–(p ∨ –p)," and "p ≡ –p." And there are an unlimited number of other truth-functional contradictions.

To every valid truth-functional argument there corresponds a conditional that is a tautology. The conditional will have as its antecedent the conjunction of the premises of the argument, and it will have as its consequent the conclusion of the argument. For example, the tautology "[(p ⊃ q) & p] ⊃ q" corresponds to modus ponens.

To say that a form of argument is valid is to say that if its premises are true, then its conclusion must be true. Under such circumstances the corresponding conditional cannot have a true antecedent and a false consequent, and so will necessarily be true, a tautology. Thus we can say that a truth-functional argument is valid if and only if its corresponding conditional is a tautology. Hence, another way of testing the validity of a truth-functional argument would be to form a conditional whose antecedent is the conjunction of the premises and whose consequent is the conclusion, and draw up a truth table for the conditional. If the conditional is a tautology, this shows that the argument is valid; if not, the argument is invalid. However, the method described in the preceding section is slightly simpler.

EXERCISE 14

*A In each case, use a truth table to show whether the argument is truth-functionally valid.

1 Cows moo, and horses whinny. So horses whinny.
2 Cows moo, and horses whinny. So cows moo, or horses whinny.
3 If horses whinny, cows moo. So if cows don't moo, horses don't whinny.
4 If cows moo, horses whinny. So cows moo if horses whinny.
5 Horses whinny if and only if cows moo. So cows moo if horses whinny.
6 Cows moo, and horses whinny. So horses whinny if and only if cows moo.
7 Horses whinny if and only if cows moo. So horses whinny and cows moo.
8 It's not the case both that cows moo and horses whinny. So it's not the case that either horses whinny or cows moo.
9 Horses don't whinny and cows don't moo. So, if horses whinny, cows moo.
10 Horses whinny, or cows don't moo. So it's not the case that cows moo if horses whinny.

B In each case, use a truth table to show whether a sentence having the first form would truth-functionally imply a sentence having the second form.

1. $p \& q; q$		**2.** $q; q \lor p$	
3. $p \& r; p \lor r$		**4.** $p; q \lor q$	
5. $p; p \supset p$		**6.** $p \supset p; p$	
7. $q; q \equiv q$		**8.** $q \equiv q; q$	
9. $p \lor q; p \supset q$		**10.** $p \& q; p \supset q$	
11. $-p; p \supset q$		**12.** $-p; p \equiv p$	
13. $-(p \lor q); -q$		**14.** $-(p \& q); -q$	
15. $-(p \supset q); p$		**16.** $-(p \supset q); -q$	
17. $p \& q; p \equiv q$		**18.** $p \lor q; p \equiv q$	
19. $p \lor q; p \& q$		**20.** $p \equiv q; p \supset q$	

C In each case, use a truth table to show whether a pair of sentences having the given forms would be truth-functionally equivalent.

1. $p; p \lor p$		**2.** $p \& p; p$
3. $p; p \supset p$		**4.** $p \equiv p; p$

5. p ∨ q; q ∨ p

7. p; p ∨ q

9. p ⊃ q; q ⊃ p

11. p & –q; q & –p

13. –(p ∨ q); –p ∨ –q

15. –p & –q; –(p ∨ q)

17. p ⊃ –q; –(p ⊃ q)

19. –(p ≡ q); (p & –q)
  ∨ (–p & q)

6. p & q; q & p

8. p & q; q

10. p ≡ q; q ≡ p

12. p ∨ –q; –p ∨ q

14. –(p & q); –p & –q

16. –p ∨ –q; –(p & q)

18. p ≡ –q; –(p ≡ q)

20. –(p ⊃ q); p & –q

D Which of the following are tautologies, which are truth-functional contradictions, which are neither?

1. p

3. q ∨ –q

5. p ⊃ p

7. q ⊃ –q

9. p ≡ q

11. –(p & –p)

13. p & (q & –p)

15. p ∨ (q ⊃ q)

17. (p & q) ⊃ q

19. (p & –p) ∨ q

2. p & –p

4. q ∨ q

6. –p ⊃ –p

8. p ≡ p

10. p ∨ q

12. p ⊃ (p ∨ q)

14. p ⊃ (p ∨ p)

16. q ≡ –q

18. (p ≡ –p) & q

20. (p & –p) ∨ (q & –q)

†E Which statements are true, which are false? Explain each answer.

1 The negation of any truth-functional contradiction is a tautology.

2 The negation of any tautology is a tautology.

3 The disjunction of any tautology with itself is a tautology.

4 Any disjunction, one component of which is a contradiction, is a tautology.

5 Any conjunction, one component of which is a contradiction, is a contradiction.

6 The disjunction of any sentence with itself is equivalent to the given sentence.

7 The conjunction of any sentence with a contradiction is equivalent to the given sentence.

8 Any truth-functional conditional whose antecedent is a tautology is a tautology.

9 Any truth-functional conditional whose consequent is a tautology is a tautology.

10 The conjunction of any sentence with itself is equivalent to the given sentence.

11 Any tautology is implied by any sentence.

12 Any truth-functional contradiction implies any sentence.

13 The disjunction of any tautology with any truth-functional contradiction is a contradiction.

14 Any argument whose conclusion is a tautology is valid.

15 Any argument all of whose premises are tautologies is valid.

15   FORMAL DEDUCTIONS

Truth tables provide a perfectly general method for testing the validity of all truth-functional arguments. However, when an argument is a lengthy one, and especially if it contains many different basic components, the truth-table method may be long and tedious. It is valuable to have a short-cut method to deal more efficiently with longer, more complex arguments. We shall now develop a method that involves breaking up long arguments into simpler steps (this method will also be useful in Chapter 4 in connection with another type of problem). If we can show how it is possible to pass, by means of simple valid steps, from the premises to other sentences that follow from them, and then from these to the conclusion, we shall have succeeded in showing that the conclusion does follow validly from the original premises.

Suppose we have the argument: "If he is both vacationing at Sun Valley this year and buying a Porsche, then he has inherited money. He will have inherited money only if his rich grandmother has died. He is buying a Porsche, but his grandmother is hale and hearty. Therefore, he is not vacationing at Sun Valley." Since this argument contains four different basic component sentences, its truth table would require sixteen lines and would be rather tedious. Let us try to pass to the conclusion from the premises by familiar steps. Writing "S" for "He vacations at Sun Valley," "P" for "He buys a Porsche," "I" for "He inherits money," and "G" for "His rich grandmother has died," we can symbolize our starting point as follows:

1 $(S \& P) \supset I$ Premise
2 $I \supset G$ Premise
3 $P \& -G$ Premise

We can make a useful first move by separating one part of the conjunction of line 3:

4 $- G$ From 3 by *conjunctive simplification*

Next we can put together lines 4 and 2 by using modus tollens:

5 $- I$ From 2, 4 by *modus tollens*

Then we can use modus tollens again:

6 $- (S \& P)$ From 1, 5 by *modus tollens*

And from this we can get the desired conclusion:

7 P From 3 by *conjunctive simplification*
8 $- S$ From 6, 7 by *conjunctive argument*

Here we have broken up the involved argument into a particular sequence of simple valid steps. Thus we succeed in showing that the conclusion follows from the premises. When arranged in a coherent order like this, the steps are said to constitute a deduction. Each line in the deduction must either be a premise or be clearly justified by means of some standard principle. We call it a *formal deduction* when the rules are strictly observed and no steps are permitted except the ones explicitly sanctioned by the rules.

In more advanced studies of symbolic logic, it is usual to select some very small group of standard principles for justifying steps and then to insist upon using no others. In that way, greater elegance and economy are achieved, thereby enhancing the theoretical interest of the deductions that are constructed. For our elementary purposes, however, that sort of elegance is not so important. Let us therefore include among our principles for use in deduction all those principles with which we have so far become acquainted, and also a few new ones. This broad though inelegant approach will mean that our deductions will be comparatively easy to construct; it will spare us some of the irritation sometimes felt by beginners using elegantly economical deductive rules when they find that certain moves, which they see to be perfectly valid, nevertheless are not directly sanctioned by their rules.

Let us arrange our principles under three headings. First are our standard elementary forms of valid argument; we always may write any new line in a deduction if that new line follows from earlier lines by one of these forms of argument. Next are equivalences; we always are justified in adding a new line if it is equivalent to some preceding line. Finally, we shall draw up a short list of especially useful forms of tautology, and we shall allow ourselves to add as a new line any sentence having one of the forms on our list. Tautologies have to be true, and cannot lead us astray. The underlying idea is that adding a tautology to your set of premises cannot ever change the set of conclusions that are implied by those premises.

Truth-Functional Principles for Use in Deduction

Elementary forms of valid argument

Modus ponens:	p ⊃ q, p; therefore q
Modus tollens:	p ⊃ q, –q; therefore –p
Chain argument:	p ⊃ q, q ⊃ r; therefore p ⊃ r
Disjunctive arguments:	p v q, –p; therefore q
	p v q, –q; therefore p
	p; therefore p v q (*disjunctive addition*)
	q; therefore p v q (*disjunctive addition*)
Conjunctive arguments:	–(p & q), p; therefore –q
	–(p & q), q; therefore –p
	p & q; therefore p (*simplification*)
	p & q; therefore q (*simplification*)
	p, q; therefore p & q (*adjunction*)
Reductio ad absurdum:	p ⊃ –p; therefore –p
	p ⊃ (q & –q); therefore –p

Dilemmas:	p ⊃ q, r ⊃ q, p ∨ r; therefore q
	(simple constructive)
	p ⊃ q, p ⊃ r, –q ∨ –r; therefore –p
	(simple destructive)
	p ⊃ q, r ⊃ s, p ∨ r; therefore q ∨ s
	(complex constructive)
	p ⊃ q, r ⊃ s, –q ∨ –s; therefore –p ∨ –r
	(complex destructive)

Equivalences Any expression may validly be inferred from any other that is equivalent to it, according to the following principles:

"p" and "p ∨ p" and "p & p" all are equivalent.
"p ⊃ q" and "–p ∨ q" and "–(p & –q)" all are equivalent.
"p ≡ q" and "(q ⊃ p) & (p ⊃ q)" are equivalent.
"–(p ⊃ q)" and "p & –q" are equivalent.

Double negation:	"p" and "– –p" are equivalent.
Contraposition:	"p ⊃ q" and "–q ⊃ –p" are equivalent.
Commutation:	"p ∨ q" and "q ∨ p" are equivalent.
	"p & q" and "q & p" are equivalent.
Association:	"p ∨ (q ∨ r)" and "(p ∨ q) ∨ r" are equivalent.
	"p & (q & r)" and "(p & q) & r" are equivalent.
Distribution:	"p & (q ∨ r)" and "(p & q) ∨ (p & r)" are equivalent.
	"p ∨ (q & r)" and "(p ∨ q) & (p ∨ r)" are equivalent.
De Morgan's laws:	"–(p ∨ q)" and "–p & –q" are equivalent.
	"–(p & q)" and "–p ∨ –q" are equivalent.
Exportation:	"(p & q) ⊃ r" and "p ⊃ (q ⊃ r)" are equivalent.

Tautologies The following list includes a number of forms of tautologies. Our rule will be that any sentence having one of these forms may be written down as a new line in a formal deduction.

p ∨ –p	–(p & –p)
p ⊃ p	p ≡ p
p ⊃ (p ∨ q)	(p & q) ⊃ p
(p & –p) ⊃ q	p ⊃ (q ∨ –q)

When we want to write down a tautology as a new line, we must of course make sure that it conforms *exactly* to one of these forms. We shall limit our list to just these eight forms.[15]

This list of principles perhaps looks tediously long, but the advantage of having a good many principles is that they make deductions easier to construct; all the principles in this list are standard logical principles worth being acquainted with. We have already met the elementary valid forms of argument; if any of them seems strange or dubious, its validity can be proved by means of truth tables. Disjunctive addition and conjunctive adjunction are new principles. We did not discuss them earlier because they are so absurdly simple that they don't look like serious forms of argument at all—but they can provide useful steps in formal deductions. Under the heading of equivalences are some principles that we have met and also some new ones. If any of these seems strange or dubious, again truth tables can be used. (It is also illuminating to invent sentences illustrating these principles.)

Notice that our forms of valid argument are to be used only for deriving one whole line from other whole lines in the deduction, not from parts of lines. For example, by disjunctive addition from "p" we may derive "$p \lor q$," where these occupy whole lines. But suppose we have a line which is of the form "$p \supset r$." It would be a misuse of the rules to rewrite this, replacing "p" in it by "$p \lor q$," thus obtaining a new line of the form "$(p \lor q) \supset r$." This does not follow and is not the right way to apply the rule.

The situation is different with regard to principles of equivalence, however. These may be applied to whole lines or to parts of lines. For instance, if we have a line of the form "$p \lor q$," we may use the principle of commutation to derive "$q \lor p$," thus dealing with the line as a whole. But also from a line of the form "$r \supset (p \lor q)$" we may obtain "$r \supset (q \lor p)$" by commutation, dealing with only part of the line. The underlying justification of this is that two longer truth-functional compounds have to be equivalent if they are alike except that where one contains a certain part the other contains something else equivalent to it. Equivalence of the parts to each other guarantees that the entire compounds will be equivalent to each other.

In constructing our deductions, let us try to proceed in a strict manner, always using one and only one of our principles to justify each line that we write down. In considering whether a particular move is or is not an exact instance of one of our principles, we should ask whether there is some way of getting the instance from the principle by replacing each letter in the principle ("p," "q," "r," etc.) wherever it occurs by some sentence or other, simple or compound. It is permissible to put the same sentence for more than one letter; thus, from "$(A \& B) \supset (C \lor D)$" and "$(C \lor D) \supset (A \& B)$" it would be all right to derive "$(A \& B) \supset (A \& B)$" by the principle of the chain argument—here the same thing has replaced both "p" and "r" in the principle of the chain argument, but this is permissible.

Now let us examine another example of a deduction in which more of these principles are employed. Let us suppose that we are given an argument having three premises, which we shall symbolize as lines 1, 2, and 3, and a conclusion, "C," to be derived through a deduction (we do not know at first that the conclusion will be the thirteenth line; we know that only after finishing the deduction).

1. $A \lor (B \& C)$ *Premise*
2. $A \supset D$ *Premise*
3. $D \supset C$ *Premise*

4.	$A \supset C$	*From 2, 3 by chain argument*
5.	$-- A \vee (B \,\&\, C)$	*From 1 by equivalence of "p" to " $-- p$"*
6.	$- A \supset (B \,\&\, C)$	*From 5 by equivalence of " $- p \vee q$" to "p $\supset$ q"*
7.	$- C \supset -A$	*From 4 by contraposition*
8.	$- C \supset (B \,\&\, C)$	*From 7, 6 by chain argument*
9.	$(B \,\&\, C) \supset C$	*Tautology*
10.	$(B \,\&\, C) \supset -- C$	*From 9 by equivalence*
11.	$- C \supset -- C$	*From 8, 10 by chain argument*
12.	$-- C$	*From 11 by reductio ad absurdum*
13	C	*From 12 by double negation*

In constructing the deduction, our strategy could have been the following: Looking at the premises, we see that the second and third can be put together to form a chain argument, yielding line 4. Wondering how to combine line 4 with anything else, we notice that line 1 might possibly combine with line 4. If line 1 is rewritten as a conditional instead of a disjunction, it will be more likely to combine with line 4, and so we make use of the fact that "–p ∨ q" is equivalent to "p ⊃ q." Now, if line 4 is replaced by its contrapositive, we obtain a standard chain argument whose conclusion is line 8. This is close to what we want, but we still need to separate out the "C" which is contained in the consequent of line 8. If we choose an appropriate tautology, we can do this; and so we write line 9 and then get line 11 by another chain argument. Line 11 gives the desired conclusion by way of *reductio ad absurdum*. However, this is not the only way of getting from these premises to this conclusion (for instance, a shorter, more elegant deduction can be constructed using a simple constructive dilemma).

In order to construct a proof such as this, we must use a little ingenuity; we have not mastered any mechanical method that will automatically tell us what steps we should take to get from premises to conclusion. But if we are familiar with the main types of elementary forms of valid argument, with the main types of equivalences, and with simple sorts of tautologies, we find that only very little ingenuity is required to proceed step by step.

Some tactics that often are useful are these: Try working backward from the conclusion, seeking lines that the conclusion could be derived from. Always be alert for opportunities to apply modus ponens, modus tollens, disjunctive arguments, or the chain argument. Often when you have a conjunction, it is helpful to break it up by conjunctive simplification. When you have a negated conditional, it usually is wise to rewrite it as a conjunction making use of the fact that "–(p ⊃ q)" is equivalent to "p & –q."

EXERCISE 15

  *A In each of the following deductions the first two lines are premises. State the justification for each of the other lines that are not premises. Say what specific principles are used, and what earlier lines, if any, are involved.

<table>
<tr><td>

1 1. $A \supset B$
   2. $C \supset A$
   3. $C \supset B$
   4. $-B \supset -C$

3 1. $A \& B$
   2. $B \supset C$
   3. B
   4. C

5 1. $C \supset A$
   2. $-(A \& B)$
   3. $-A \vee -B$
   4. $A \supset -B$
   5. $C \supset -B$

7 1. $G \supset -H$
   2. $-G \supset K$
   3. $G \vee -G$
   4. $-H \vee K$
   5. $H \supset K$

9 1. $(A \supset B) \& (C \supset D)$
   2. $-B \vee -D$
   3. $-A \vee -C$
   4. $-C \vee -A$
   5. $C \supset -A$

</td><td>

2 1. $B \vee (A \& -C)$
   2. $-B$
   3. $A \& -C$
   4. $-C$

4 1. $(E \& F) \& D$
   2. $(E \& F) \supset H$
   3. $E \& F$
   4. H

6 1. $(E \vee F) \supset (A \& B)$
   2. $-(A \& B)$
   3. $-(E \vee F)$
   4. $-E \& -F$
   5. $-F$

8 1. $K \vee (C \supset K)$
   2. $-K$
   3. $C \supset K$
   4. $-C$
   5. $-C \& -K$

10 1. $H \supset J$
   2. H
   3. J
   4. $J \supset (J \vee K)$
   5. $J \vee K$

</td></tr>
</table>

*B Construct deductions to establish validity.

   1 $-K \& -J, K \vee H, \therefore H$
   2 $J \& K, -(K \& H), \therefore -H$
   3 $-E \vee F, G \supset E, \therefore G \supset F$
   4 $A \& D, C \vee C, \therefore D \& C$
   5 $C \supset D, -D \supset D, \therefore D$
   6 $J, A \supset K, -(K \& J), \therefore -A$
   7 $-H \vee J, -J \vee -J, \therefore -H$
   8 $A \supset B, A \supset -B, \therefore -A$
   9 $J \supset K, -(H \& -H) \supset -K, \therefore -J$
  10 $A, C \supset D, -(D \& A), \therefore -C$

C Construct deductions to establish validity.

   1 $E \supset J, -J \supset -H, -(-H \& -E), \therefore J$
   2 $B \supset (A \& -A), C \supset B, \therefore -C$
   3 $-A \supset D, B \vee B, -D, \therefore (B \& A) \vee (B \& D)$
   4 $(K \vee -K) \supset -J, (E \& F) \supset J, \therefore -E \vee -F$
   5 $G \supset (K \& J), -(H \vee H), (J \& K) \supset H, \therefore -G$
   6 $-C \supset -D, C \supset D, -C \supset -A, C \supset A, \therefore D \equiv A$
   7 $-(D \vee -E) \equiv -F, F, \therefore E \supset (D \vee G)$
   8 $H \& H, K \supset -K, -(G \& H), \therefore -(G \vee K)$
   9 $E \supset D, -B \supset -D, B \equiv A, \therefore E \supset A$
  10 $(E \& F) \supset G, H \supset E, \therefore F \supset (H \supset G)$

D Symbolize each argument, using the suggested letters. Then construct a deduction to show that it is valid.

1 If the patient had no fever, then malaria was not the cause of his illness. But malaria or food poisoning was the cause of his illness. The patient had no fever. Therefore, food poisoning must have caused his illness. (F, M, P)

2 The centrifuge is to be started if the specimen remains homogenous. Either the specimen remains homogeneous, or a white solid is precipitated. A white solid is not being precipitated. So the centrifuge is to be started. (C, S. W)

3 Had Franklin D. Roosevelt been a socialist, he would have been willing to nationalize industries. Had he been willing to nationalize industries, this would have been done during the Depression. But no industries were nationalized during the Depression. Hence Roosevelt must not have been a socialist. (R, W, D)

4 If either the husband or the wife paid the premium that was due, then the policy was in force and the cost of the accident was covered. If the cost of the accident was covered, they were not forced into bankruptcy. But they were forced into bankruptcy. Therefore, the husband did not pay the premium that was due. (H, W, P, C, B)

16 THE INDIRECT METHOD; SHOWING INVALIDITY

In this section we shall supplement our method of truth-functional deduction, first by considering an alternative way of arranging deductions, and then by noting a short-cut way of establishing that an argument is invalid.

The Indirect Method of Deduction

The method of formal deduction which we have been considering is a 'direct' method: in establishing the validity of an argument, the deduction starts from the premises and moves directly toward the conclusion. However, there is another way of organizing deductions which also is worth noticing. This is the 'indirect,' or *reductio ad absurdum*, approach. It proceeds by showing that a contradiction can be deduced from the combination of the premises with the negation of the conclusion. Let us see how this would work. Suppose we have the argument "A, A ≡ B, C ⊃ –B, therefore –C." Let us construct a deduction whose premises are the premises of the original argument plus the negation of its conclusion. Then let us try to deduce an outright contradiction from this set of assumptions. Such a deduction can be drawn up as follows:

1. A   *Premises*
2. A ≡ B   *Premises*
3. C ⊃ –B   *Premise*
4. – –C   *Premise*
5. C   *From 4 by double negation*
6. –B   *From 5 and 3 by modus ponens*

7. $(B \supset A)$ & $(A \supset B)$ *From 2 by equivalence*
8. $A \supset B$ *From 7 by simplification*
9. $-A$ *From 8 and 6 by modus tollens*
10. A & $-A$ *From 1 and 9 by adjunction*

What this deduction shows is that an obvious contradiction of the form "p & $-p$" follows from the combined four premises of the deduction. This means that those four premises cannot all be true; if the first three are true, then the fourth cannot be. But the fourth was the negation of the conclusion of our original argument, while the first three were the premises of our original argument. So what we have shown is that if the premises of the original argument are true, then the conclusion of the original argument cannot be false. This establishes that the original argument is valid.

In general, then, if we want to set up a deduction using this *reductio ad absurdum* method, we proceed as follows: Suppose that what we want to show is that a certain sentence q follows validly from certain other sentences $r_1 \ldots r_n$. We take as our premises $r_1 \ldots r_n$ together with the negation of q. And the conclusion of this deduction should be some outright contradiction, preferably of the most obvious form, "p & $-p$." If we can construct such a deduction, getting by valid steps from such premises to such a conclusion, then we shall have succeeded in showing that q does follow validly from $r_1 \ldots r_n$.

This indirect method is usually no better or quicker for handling truth-functional arguments than is the direct method. However, if you have trouble figuring out how to complete a direct deduction, it may be worthwhile to try constructing your deduction in this indirect style instead; sometimes an indirect deduction is easier to put together.

Showing Invalidity

Naturally, the method of formal deduction, whether direct or indirect, will work only for arguments that are deductively valid. If an argument is not valid, of course it will not be possible to construct a deduction that moves step by step from the premises to the conclusion. But the fact that we have failed to construct a deduction for an argument by no means demonstrates that it is invalid; perhaps we have not worked intelligently enough. Suppose we work on an argument, trying unsuccessfully to construct a deduction for it; we may eventually suspect that perhaps the argument is not valid. In such a situation we could resort to a truth table. But it is valuable also to have a short-cut method of demonstrating that an argument is invalid.

To say that an argument is invalid is to say that it is possible for the premises all to be true yet the conclusion false. This gives us the clue to a short-cut method of demonstrating invalidity. If we can find a way of assigning truth and falsity to the constituent letters so that the premises all will be true but the conclusion false, this will demonstrate that the argument is invalid (or, at any rate, that it is not valid in virtue of its truth-functional form, which usually means that it is invalid; we shall discuss this point further in Chapter 8).

Suppose we have an argument whose three premises are symbolized "$A \supset (B \vee C)$," "$(C \& D) \supset E$," and "$-E$," and whose conclusion is symbolized "$-A$." We shall not be able to pass, by valid steps, from these premises to this conclusion. Let us try instead to show that the argument is invalid. We want to see whether it is logically possible for the premises all to be true and the conclusion false. If the conclusion is false, "A" must be true; if "A" is true, then either "B" or "C" (or both) must be true in order that the first premise be true. Also, in order that the third premise be true "E" must be false; if "E" is false, "C" and "D" cannot both be true, in order that the second premise be true. Let us try letting "A" be true, "E" false, "B" and "C" both true, and "D" false. This proves to be one satisfactory way of assigning truth and falsity to the constituent letters, for this is a way of making the premises all true and the conclusion false. Thus we have shown that there is a logically possible way for the premises all to be true while the conclusion is false; hence the argument is shown to be invalid. This method is like finding in the truth table for the argument one single line that suffices to show that the argument is invalid.

EXERCISE 16

A Go back to part **A** or **B** of Exercise 15 and rework those formal deductions, now using the indirect method.

*B For each of the following arguments, use the short-cut method to show that it is invalid.

    1 $C \supset D, D, \therefore C$

    2 $F \vee G, F, \therefore -G$

    3 $-(A \& B), -A, \therefore B$

    4 $A \supset -B, -A \equiv B, -A, \therefore -B$

    5 $D \supset E, E \supset G, F \supset G, \therefore D \supset F$

    6 $C \supset D, -C \supset -A, -D \supset -B, \therefore -B \supset -A$

    7 $A \supset B, C \supset D, B \vee D, \therefore A \vee C$

    8 $F \supset G, H \supset K, -F \vee -H, \therefore -G \vee -K$

    9 $A \supset (C \& D), (B \vee C) \supset D, \therefore D \supset A$

    10 $K \supset (L \supset M), F \supset (G \vee H), G \supset (K \vee L), -(F \& M), \therefore F \equiv H$

C For each argument, choose an appropriate method, and show either that the argument is valid or that it is invalid.

    1 If the seal has not been broken and the routine servicing has been performed, the guarantee is in effect. The owner is responsible for the damage only if the routine servicing has not been performed or the seal has been broken. Hence, the guarantee is in effect unless the owner is responsible for the damage.

    2 Either Thales said nothing moves and Parmenides didn't say it, or else Parmenides said it and Heraclitus denied it. If Thales said it, his thought didn't conform to the Milesian pattern. Thales' thought did conform to the Milesian pattern. Therefore, Heraclitus denied that nothing moves.

3 If either revenues increase or debt and costs decrease, the firm's profitability will improve. Costs won't decrease unless debt decreases. It's not the case both that revenues will increase and that profitability will improve. Therefore, either debts won't decrease or profitability will improve.

4 If Locke had denied the existence of spiritual substance, he would have been a materialist; if he had denied the existence of physical substance, he would have been an idealist. If he had been either an idealist or a materialist, he would not have been a dualist. But Locke was a dualist. Therefore, he did not deny the existence of either spiritual or physical substance.

5 If Moses and Abraham were patriarchs, then Samuel and Jeremiah were prophets. If Abraham was a patriarch, Samuel was a prophet. Therefore, either Moses was not a patriarch or Jeremiah was not a prophet.

D A set of sentences is consistent if and only if it is possible for all of them to be true together. You can show that a set is consistent by finding a way of assigning truth and falsity to the basic letters so as to make all the compound sentences true. You can show that a set is inconsistent by deducing a contradiction from them. Show whether sets of sentences having the following forms are consistent.

1 $p \supset q, q \supset p$

2 $p, p \supset q, -q$

3 $-(p \mathbin{\&} q), p, q$

4 $p \vee q, -q, p$

5 $p \equiv q, q \equiv r, -(p \equiv r)$

6 $p \supset q, q \supset r, p \mathbin{\&} -r$

7 $p \supset -q, r \supset -p, r \mathbin{\&} -q$

8 $p \equiv (q \vee r), r \equiv -q$

9 $p \supset q, q \supset r, p \mathbin{\&} r$

10 $p \supset (q \mathbin{\&} r), s \supset (q \mathbin{\&} r), s \equiv -p$

†E Analyze the structure of each of the following truth-functional arguments. Watch for unstated premises.

1 "I hope, Marianne," continued Elinor, "you do not consider Edward as deficient in general taste. Indeed, I think I may say that you cannot, for your behavior to him is perfectly cordial, and if that were your opinion, I am sure you could never be civil to him."

JANE AUSTEN, Sense and Sensibility

2 Murder and treachery cannot be good without regret being bad: regret cannot be good without treachery and murder being bad. Both, however, are supposed to have been foredoomed; so something must be fatally unreasonable, absurd, and wrong in the world. It must be a place of which either sin or error forms a necessary part. From this dilemma there seems at first sight no escape.

WILLIAM JAMES, "The Dilemma of Determinism"

3 With respect to every reality external to myself, I can get hold of it only through thinking it. In order to get hold of it really, I should have to be able to make myself into the other, the acting individual, and make the foreign reality my own reality, which is impossible. For if I make the foreign reality my own, this does not mean that I become the other through knowing his reality, but it means that I acquire a new reality, which belongs to me as opposed to him.

SÖREN KIERKEGAARD, *Concluding Unscientific Postscript*

4   Either to disinthrone the King of Heav'n
We war, if war be best, or to regain
Our own right lost: him to unthrone we then
May hope, when everlasting Fate shall yield
To fickle Chance, and *Chaos* judge the strife:
The former vain to hope argues as vain
The latter: for what place can be for us
Within Heav'n's bound, unless Heav'n's Lord supreme
We overpower?   JOHN MILTON, *Paradise Lost*

5   If man lacked free judgment of will, how would that be good for which justice itself is commended when it condemns sins and honors deeds rightly done? For that which was not done by the will would be neither sinfully nor rightly done. And according to this if man did not have free will, both punishment and reward would be unjust. However, there must have been justice in both punishment and reward since it is one of the goods which are from God. Therefore, God must have given man free will.

ST. AUGUSTINE, *De Libero Arbitrio*

6   The universe, then, has no circumference, for, if it had a center and a circumference, it would thus have in itself its beginning and its end, and the universe itself would be terminated by relation to something else; there would be outside the universe another thing and a place—but all this contains no truth.   NICHOLAS OF CUSA, *Of Learned Ignorance*

17   LOGIC AND COMPUTERS

Nowadays digital computers are rapidly altering many aspects of our lives. They have developed enormous power to perform elaborate calculations quickly, to store and sort vast amounts of information, and to control intricate machinery. Many tasks that we formerly did by hand are now being performed far more efficiently by computers, and many tasks that formerly could not be done at all are being accomplished through use of these machines.

Logic is related to computers in various ways. Some of these have to do with computer programming (the planning out of the series of steps by means of which computers are to perform specific tasks). There a knowledge of logical distinctions can sometimes be most helpful, enabling the computer programmer who is acquainted with logic to avoid mistakes and find short cuts. However, we shall consider a more fundamental connection between logic and computers, having to do with the basic electric structure of the digital computer, which is strongly analogous to the logic of truth functions.

A digital computer is built up of various types of basic units, each of which can be regarded as a kind of switching circuit. By a switching circuit we mean a device having one or more 'input' terminals and one or more 'output' terminals; and the device is built in such a way that the voltage at the output terminals is related to the voltage at the input terminals according to some regular, definite pattern—so that the input voltages determine the output voltages. (When we speak of "input" and "output" here we do not mean that any palpable thing is put in or taken out; it is just that the voltage at the so-called input terminals will correspond to some initial information, while the voltage at the output terminals will correspond to some other information calculated from the initial information.)

The computer as a whole is a network of these basic units wired together. The network has its overall electrical input and its overall electrical output. It is designed so that its overall output will depend upon the overall input in a desired fashion; but the relationship between input and output will be far more complicated for the network as a whole than it is for any one basic unit. For example, in a computer that does addition, the network will be designed so that when there are electrical inputs corresponding to two numbers, the electrical output will correspond to the number that is the sum of these two numbers (this output can then light up a display panel to show the answer).

In very early computers, the basic units contained electric relays—actual switches, opened or closed by electromagnets. Because the units were bulky and expensive, consumed considerable power, and were slow and unreliable, networks composed of them could not be very complicated. Then vacuum tubes came to be used, and later, transistors. In recent decades printed circuits have been devised where many basic units can be put on a single small wafer of material such as silicon. By making the basic units increasingly small, inexpensive, economical of power, and quick in their operations, it has become practical to devise more and more intricate networks which can adjust outputs to inputs in very complicated ways.

In thinking about a network of this kind, let us suppose that only two different voltages can occur at points in it. If we are using a 9-volt battery as our power supply, then these can be +9 volts and 0 volts; each point in the network will be at one or the other of these two voltage levels. Let us consider now some representative types of basic units of which our network may be composed.

Suppose we have a unit with one input point and one output point, whose operation is shown in the following table:

Input	Output
+	0
0	+

That is, the unit is constructed so that whenever its input voltage is positive, its output voltage will be zero; and whenever its input voltage is zero, its output voltage will be positive. Let us call this type of unit an "N" unit, because of its analogy with negation.[16]

Next let us consider basic units having two inputs and one output each. One such unit would operate like this:

Input 1	Input 2	Output
+	+	+
0	+	0
+	0	0
0	0	0

That is, the output is always zero except when both inputs are positive. Let us call this type of unit a "C" unit, because of its analogy with conjunction.[17]

Another type of basic unit would function like this:

Input 1	Input 2	Output
+	+	+
0	+	+
+	0	+
0	0	0

That is, the output is always positive except when both inputs are negative. Let us call this type of unit a "D" unit, because of its analogy with disjunction.[18]

There is a striking analogy between these tables and the tables we drew up for truth-functional compounds. The first table of this section has exactly the same type of pattern as negation, the second has exactly the same type of pattern as conjunction, and the third has the same type of pattern as disjunction. The difference is that instead of truth and falsity as features of sentences, here we are dealing with two different levels of voltage as features of points in electric circuits. Nevertheless, the structural analogy between truth functions and these basic computer units is exact. As a result, we can apply what we know about truth functions to answer certain kinds of questions about computer networks.

In order to be able to do this, we need to correlate truth-functional formulas with combinations of basic units in the network. To see how this may be done, consider this arrangement of units:

Here we may think of the inputs as corresponding to two sentence letters, say, "p" and "q"; and we may write the formula "–p ∨ –q" to correspond to the whole pattern of the circuitry—the whole circuit is analogous to the disjunction of two negations. The truth or falsity of the compound formula depends in a certain way upon the truth or falsity of its component sentences; analogously, in the circuit, whether the voltage at the output is positive or zero depends in a certain way upon the voltages at the inputs. The pattern of dependence has exactly the same structure in both the logical formula and the electric circuit.

As another example, consider the circuit:

Input 1 ○─[C]─[N]──────○   Output *B*
Input 2 ○─

We may think of this circuit as corresponding to the formula "–(p & q)." In this circuit the output voltage again depends on the input voltages, but the circuit is not built in the same way or of the same basic units as was the previous circuit.

However, the question may arise: Are these two circuits equivalent in their functioning? That is, considering every possible situation, will there be the same pattern of relationship between inputs and output in both circuits? As it happens, in this case the answer is yes. If you work through the definitions, you can see that the following table is correct.

Input 1	Input 2	Output A	Output B
+	+	0	0
0	+	+	+
+	0	+	+
0	0	+	+

These two circuits are equivalent in their functioning, in that they both yield the same output for each possible combination of inputs. For us, a more direct way of detecting that these two circuits function equivalently is to notice that the formulas corresponding to them are truth-functionally equivalent, according to De Morgan's law.

In designing circuits, usually we want to avoid using any more basic units than are needed. That way, the circuit will be less expensive to build and may be more reliable in operation. Therefore, it is good to be able to recognize situations where one circuit, or portion of a circuit, can be replaced by something else more economical that will do the same job. Because of the exact analogy between switching circuits and truth functions, truth-functional symbolism can often be helpful in enabling us to tell about this. We can write down a truth-functional formula corresponding to the given circuit, and then we ask ourselves whether the formula is equivalent to some simpler truth-functional formula. If it is, then the simpler formula will indicate to us how to construct a simpler circuit.

EXERCISE 17

A Draw a diagram of a circuit composed of "N", "C", or "D" units that will perform the desired function, and write a truth-functional formula corresponding to it. In each case there are to be two inputs and one output.

    1 Output is always the opposite of input 1.

    2 Output is always the opposite of input 2.

    3 Output is always positive.

    4 Output is always zero.

    5 Output is positive when and only when both inputs are positive.

    6 Output is positive when and only when both inputs are zero.

    7 Output is positive when and only when at least one input is positive.

    8 Output is positive when and only when at least one input is zero.

    9 Output is positive except when input 1 is positive and input 2 is zero.

  10 Output is zero except when input 1 is positive and input 2 is zero.

  11 Output is positive when and only when inputs are alike.

  12 Output is positive when and only when inputs differ.

B In each case, are the two circuits equivalent in their functioning? Make use of what you know about truth functions to establish your answers. Inputs are on the left and outputs on the right.

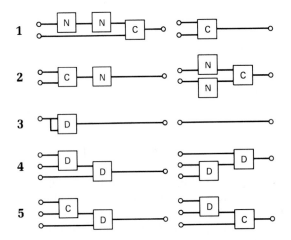

C In each case, is there any way to simplify the circuit without altering its overall functioning? Use truth functions to establish your answers.

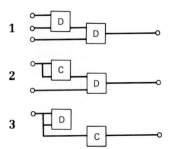

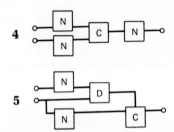

D   For each formula, draw a circuit consisting of "N", "C", and "D" units that will exhibit the same structure. Note that the number of basic letters determines the number of inputs.

1. −p   2. p ∨ −p
3. p ∨ q   4. p ⊃ q
5. q & −q   6. p ∨ (q & r)
7. q ≡ p   8. (q ⊃ p) & (p ⊃ q)
9. (p ∨ q) & (q ∨ r)   10. (p & q) ⊃ (r & s)
11. (p & r) ≡ (q & r)   12. −[p ⊃ (r & s)] ⊃ q

CHAPTER 4

MONADIC QUANTIFICATION

In Chapter 2 we met the quantifiers "all" and "some," in categorical sentences. Now we shall see how to use symbols in place of quantifier words. We shall also see how these quantifier symbols can be combined with truth-functional symbols to provide a powerful symbolic language, which enables us to analyze a wider range of sentences and arguments. In this chapter we shall introduce quantification; in the next chapter we shall extend our quantificational symbolism to its full generality.

18 THE SYMBOLISM OF QUANTIFICATION

Let us begin with a sentence in ordinary language and see how it can be expressed in the symbolism of quantification. Consider the sentence:

There exists at least one unclimbed mountain. (1)

We can reword this as:

There exists at least one thing such that it is unclimbed and it is a mountain. (2)

and as:

There exists at least one thing x such that x is unclimbed and x is a mountain. (3)

The letter "x" in (3) is called a *variable*. There is nothing mysterious about its significance, however, for it functions as a pronoun, the way "it" did in

(2), enabling us to see that in the different parts of the sentence the speaker is talking about the same thing rather than about different things. Now we introduce the symbol "($\exists$x)," which is called an *existential quantifier* and which corresponds to the words "There exists at least one thing x such that."[19] This enables us to rewrite (3) in the form:

$$(\exists x)(x \text{ is unclimbed \& } x \text{ is a mountain}) \tag{4}$$

This sentence is called an *existential quantification,* because it starts with an existential quantifier which is attached to the whole of the rest of the sentence. Sentence (4) can be read in various equivalent ways besides (1), (2), and (3). All the following readings are also permissible:

There is something such that it is unclimbed and is a mountain.
Something is unclimbed and is a mountain.
Some unclimbed things are mountains.
There are unclimbed mountains.
Unclimbed mountains exist.

Next let us look at a different kind of sentence and see how it can be expressed using another quantificational symbol. Consider the sentence:

$$\text{Each thing is either solid or not solid.} \tag{5}$$

We can reword this as:

$$\text{Each thing is such that either it is solid or it is not solid.} \tag{6}$$

and as:

$$\text{Each thing x is such that either x is solid or x is not solid.} \tag{7}$$

Again the variable "x" is merely doing the job of a pronoun. Now we introduce the symbol "(x)," which is called a *universal quantifier* and which corresponds to the words "Each thing x is such that." This enables us to rewrite (7) in the form:

$$(x)(x \text{ is solid v } x \text{ is not solid}) \tag{8}$$

This sentence is called a *universal quantification,* because it starts with a universal quantifier which is attached to the whole of the rest of the sentence. Sentence (8) can be read in various equivalent ways; besides (5), (6), and (7), all the following readings are possible:

Each thing is solid or not solid.
Anything is solid or not solid.
Everything is either solid or not solid.
All things are either solid or not solid.

So far, we have used just the letter "x" as a variable. But other variables, such as "y" and "z," can equally well be used in quantifications. The sentence "($\exists$y)(y is unclimbed & y is a mountain)" is equivalent to (4). Both say that there is something such that it is an unclimbed mountain. The sentence "(z)(z is solid ∨ z is not solid)" is equivalent to (8). Both of them say that each thing is such that *it* is solid or *it* is not solid. When the quantifier is "(∃x)" or "(x)," we say that "x" is the *variable of quantification;* when the quantifier is "(∃y)" or "(y)," we say that "y" is the variable of quantification; and so on.

In the cases that we have considered thus far, the quantifier has been attached to the whole of the rest of the sentence. In these cases we put parentheses around all the rest of the sentence to show that it all falls within what we call the *scope* of the quantifier. Attaching the quantifier to the whole remainder of the sentence means that every occurrence of the variable of quantification within the rest of the sentence has to be thought of as a pronoun referring to that quantifier.

However, quantifiers are not always attached in this way; sometimes we have a quantifier that is attached only to a portion of the sentence. For example, the sentence:

Either something is solid or everything is liquid.

can be reworded:

Either there is something x such that x is solid or each thing x is such that x is liquid.

and can be put into quantificational symbolism as:

$$(\exists x)(x \text{ is solid}) \lor (x)(x \text{ is liquid}) \tag{9}$$

Here sentence (9) considered as a whole is not a quantification; rather it is a disjunction whose components are quantifications. The parentheses show us that the "x" within "(x is solid)" is to be thought of as a pronoun referring to the first quantifier, while the "x" in "(x is liquid)" is to be thought of as a pronoun referring to the second quantifier. Thus the scope of the first quantifier does not overlap that of the second quantifier, and the two quantifications that form parts of the disjunction are completely separate. Therefore it would be equally correct to write sentence (9) in the following equivalent form:

$$(\exists y)(y \text{ is solid}) \lor (z)(z \text{ is liquid}) \tag{10}$$

Because each quantification is self-contained, we get equivalent results whether we use different variables in the two quantifications, as in (10), or use the same variable throughout, as in (9).

All the variables we have considered so far have been functioning as pronouns referring to quantifiers. Variables are said to be *bound* by their quantifiers when they occur in this way. A variable can be bound by (or 'governed by') only one quantifier at a time. A variable that does not refer to any quantifier is said to be *free.* Consider the expressions:

x is solid ∨ x is liquid
(∃x)(x is solid) ∨ x is liquid
(y)(y is solid ∨ x is liquid)

There are two free occurrences of the letter "x" in the first expression, and there is one in each of the others. Expressions like these are neither true nor false, so long as nothing has been decided about what these free occurrences of "x" are supposed to refer to. The letter "x" here is like a pronoun that does not refer to anything. An expression is not a true or false sentence so long as it contains any such free occurrences of variables. We shall not be making any use of free variables as we symbolize sentences and test quantificational arguments. We consider free variables only in order to notice that they are not supposed to occur in our work.

Now let us notice some basic relations of equivalence and non-equivalence that hold between certain kinds of quantificational sentences. This will help us understand better how quantifiers work. Here we shall be concerned especially with how much of what follows the quantifier falls within the scope of the quantifier.

To say that two sentences are equivalent is to say that they are necessarily alike as regards truth and falsity. Consider the sentences:

Something is liquid and is solid. (11)

Something is liquid, and something is solid. (12)

These are definitely not equivalent, as is shown by the fact that (11) is false but (12) is true. In the symbolism of quantification, we use parentheses to indicate the distinction:

$(\exists x)(x$ is liquid & x is solid) (13)

$(\exists x)(x$ is liquid) & $(\exists x)(x$ is solid) (14)

Here (13) is a way of symbolizing (11), and (14) is a way of symbolizing (12). Each of these quantifiers governs just what is enclosed within the parentheses that immediately follow it. In (13) the quantifier embraces within its scope all that follows, and the whole expression is the existential quantification of a conjunction. In (14) we have two separate quantifiers each with a briefer scope; here the whole thing is a conjunction of two existential quantifications.

Similarly, with universal quantifiers we must distinguish between:

$(x)(x$ is solid $\lor$ x is not solid) (15)

$(x)(x$ is solid) $\lor$ $(x)(x$ is not solid) (16)

These sentences are not equivalent. Sentence (15) is the universal quantification of a disjunction, and it truly says that each thing is solid or not solid; sentence (16) is the disjunction of two universal quantifications, and it falsely says that either everything is solid or everything is nonsolid.

We must also pay attention to the positions of negation signs. It makes a difference whether a negation sign occurs outside or within the scope of a quantifier, and we must distinguish between:

$-(x)(x$ is solid) (17)

$(x)-(x$ is solid) (18)

Sentence (17) is the negation of a universal quantification, and thus it truly says that not everything is solid. Sentence (18) is the universal quantification of a negation, and it falsely says that everything is nonsolid.[20]

Furthermore, we must not assume that negation signs flanking a quantifier will merely cancel out; we must distinguish between:

–(∃x)–(x is solid ∨ x is liquid) $\qquad$ (19)

(∃x)(x is solid ∨ x is liquid) $\qquad$ (20)

These are not equivalent. Sentence (19) falsely says that nothing is neither solid nor liquid, while sentence (20) truly says that something is either solid or liquid.

However, some simple and important equivalences involve pairs of negation signs. Consider the existential quantification "(∃x)(x is liquid)." Is there any equivalent way in which this thought can be expressed? To say that there is at least one liquid amounts to denying that everything is such as not to be liquid. Thus "(∃x)(x is liquid)" is equivalent to "–(x)–(x is liquid)." And the underlying principle is perfectly general: If an existential quantifier is replaced by a universal quantifier flanked with negation signs, the new sentence is equivalent to the old one.

Next consider the sentence "(x)(x is solid)." Is there any equivalent way in which this can be expressed? To say that each thing is solid amounts to denying that there exists even one thing that is not solid. Thus "(x)(x is solid)" is equivalent to "–(∃x)–(x is solid)." The underlying principle is perfectly general: whenever a universal quantifier is replaced by an existential quantifier flanked with negation signs, the new sentence is equivalent to the old one.

By similar reflection, we can see that "–(x)(x is solid)" is equivalent to "(∃x)–(x is solid)" and that "–(∃x)(x is liquid)" is equivalent to "(x)–(x is liquid)." Here too the principles involved are perfectly general. When a negation sign immediately followed by a universal quantifier is replaced by an existential quantifier immediately followed by a negation sign, the new sentence is equivalent to the old. And when a negation sign immediately followed by an existential quantifier is replaced by a universal quantifier immediately followed by a negation sign, again the new sentence is equivalent to the old. These two principles of equivalence can be summarized by saying that a negation sign may be 'passed through' a quantifier, either forward or backward, provided that the type of quantifier is changed (i.e., from universal to existential, or vice versa).

These various kinds of elementary quantificational equivalence also have some further consequences. We remember that it is a basic fact about truth-functionally compound sentences that any two such sentences have to be equivalent if they are exactly alike except that in one of them a component present in the other has been replaced by something equivalent to it. This means that, for instance, we can employ our knowledge of the equivalence of "–(x)(x is liquid)" to "(∃x)(x is liquid)" in order to conclude that a longer sentence such as "(∃y)(x is solid) ⊃ –(x)(x is liquid)" must be equivalent to "(∃y)(x is solid) ⊃ (∃x)–(x is liquid)." Here the latter two sentences are truth-functional compounds (both are conditionals) and are exactly alike except that a component of one has been replaced in the other by something equivalent to it. Since the two longer sentences are alike in their overall form and since each component of the former necessarily agrees with the corresponding component of the latter as regards truth or falsity, the two longer sentences must agree as regards truth or falsity (i.e., they are equivalent). We shall make use of these principles of equivalence in a later section.

EXERCISE 18

*A Match each sentence in the first group with its translation in the second group.

Group I

1 Everything is physical.
2 Nothing is mental.
3 Everything is both physical and mental.
4 Everything is physical, and not everything is mental.
5 Each thing is either physical or mental.
6 Something is mental.
7 Something is physical or something is mental.
8 Something is such as to be either physical or mental.
9 Something is physical and everything is mental.
10 If something is physical, then nothing is mental.
11 If nothing is physical, then everything is mental.
12 Everything is physical, or everything is mental.

Group II

1 (x)(x is physical & x is mental)
2 (y)–(y is mental)
3 (x)(x is physical)
4 (∃x)(x is physical) ∨ (∃x)(x is mental)
5 (∃y)(y is mental)
6 (x)(x is physical) & –(y)(y is mental)
7 (x)(x is physical ∨ x is mental)
8 (x)(x is physical) ∨ (x)(x is mental)
9 (∃x)(x is physical) ⊃ (y)–(y is mental)
10 (∃x)(x is physical) & (x)(x is mental)
11 (∃y)(y is physical ∨ y is mental)
12 (x)–(x is physical) ⊃ (x)(x is mental)

*B Translate each sentence into the symbolism of quantification. Use "G" to mean "is a ghost" and "P" to mean "is physical".

1 There are ghosts.
2 No ghosts exist.
3 Not everything is physical.
4 Something is not physical.
5 There are ghosts which aren't physical.
6 It's not the case that physical ghosts exist.
7 There are physical ghosts and there are nonphysical ghosts.
8 Something is physical, and something is a ghost.

9 If there are ghosts, not everything is physical.

10 If there are ghosts, there are nonphysical ghosts.

11 Everything is physical, if there are physical ghosts.

12 Anything is a ghost if and only if it isn't physical.

C   Which of these expressions are true-or-false sentences? Which occurrences of variables are free, which are bound?

1 $(x)(x$ is in motion $\lor x$ is at rest$)$

2 $(x)(x$ is in motion$) \lor y$ is at rest.

3 x is in motion $\lor y$ is at rest.

4 $(x)(x$ is in motion$) \lor x$ is at rest.

5 z is at rest & $(\exists y)(y$ is in motion$)$

6 $(\exists y)(y$ is in motion & z is at rest$)$

7 $(\exists z)(z$ is in motion & z is at rest$)$

8 $(x)–(x$ is in motion$) \supset (\exists y)(y$ is at rest$)$

9 $–(y$ is at rest$)$

10 $(x)(x$ is in motion $\supset y$ is at rest$)$

11 $(\exists z)(x$ is in motion $\supset z$ is at rest$)$

12 $(\exists z)(z$ is at rest$) \supset (y)(y$ is in motion$)$

D   Translate each sentence into good English. Which are equivalent to one another? (Hint: They form at most four groups.)

1 $(\exists x)(x$ is ancient $\lor x$ is modern$)$

2 $(\exists x)(x$ is ancient$) \lor (\exists y)(y$ is modern$)$

3 $(x)(x$ is ancient $\lor x$ is modern$)$

4 $(y)(y$ is ancient$) \lor (x)(x$ is modern$)$

5 $–(y)–(y$ is ancient $\lor y$ is modern$)$

6 $–(\exists z)–(z$ is ancient $\lor z$ is modern$)$

7 $–(\exists x)–(x$ is ancient$) \lor (z)(z$ is modern$)$

8 $–(x)(x$ is not ancient & x is not modern$)$

9 $–(\exists z)(z$ is ancient$) \supset (\exists x)(x$ is modern$)$

10 $–(\exists z)(z$ is not ancient & z is not modern$)$

11 $(x)(x$ is ancient$) \lor –(\exists x)(x$ is not modern$)$

12 $(y)(y$ is not ancient$) \supset –(x)(x$ is not modern$)$

19   SYMBOLIZING CATEGORICAL SENTENCES

The four traditional forms of categorical sentence can each be translated into quantificational symbolism. Practicing this will help us develop skill at using this symbolism.

Consider the **A** sentence "All sedums are perennials." This can be understood as a sentence concerning each thing, and it can be written as a universal quantification. What does it say about each thing? It says of each thing that *if* it is a sedum, *then* it is a perennial. Thus the **A** sentence can be expressed in symbols as:

$$(x)(Sx \supset Px) \tag{A}$$

Here we write "Sx" as short for "x is a sedum", and we write "Px" as short for "x is a perennial". (Here "Px" can also be read "x is perennial" or "x grows perennially"; we can get equivalent results whether we use noun, adjective, or verb.) The **E** sentence "No sedums are perennials" can also be understood as speaking about each thing. What it says concerning each thing is that *if* it is a sedum, *then* it is not a perennial. So it can be written in symbols as:

$(x)(Sx \supset -Px)$ **(E)**

The **I** sentence "Some sedums are perennials" can be understood as saying that there is at least one thing of a certain kind, so it can be symbolized as an existential quantification. It says that there exists at least one thing which is both a sedum and a perennial. We can write it:

$(\exists x)(Sx \ \& \ Px)$ **(I)**

The **O** sentence "Some sedums are not perennials" also can be understood as an existential quantification. It says that there is at least one thing which is both a sedum and not a perennial. So it may be written as:

$(\exists x)(Sx \ \& \ -Px)$ **(O)**

Thus, for each of the four categorical forms, we have found a way—the most straightforward way—to put it into quantificational symbolism.

However, we remember that the **A** and **O** sentences are contradictories, as are the **E** and **I**. This indicates that an equivalent way of symbolizing the **A** sentence would be to write the **O** preceded by a negation sign. That is, "(x) $(Sx \supset Px)$" and "$-(\exists x)(Sx \ \& \ -Px)$" are equivalent. If you think about what the symbols mean, you can see that this makes sense, for "$(Sx \supset Px)$" is truthfunctionally equivalent to "$-(Sx \ \& \ -Px)$" in virtue of the definition of the horseshoe, and so "$(x)(Sx \supset Px)$" will be equivalent to "$-(\exists x)(Sx \ \& \ -Px)$" in virtue of the principle about passing a negation sign through a quantifier. Similarly, an equivalent way of symbolizing the **E** would be to write the **I** preceded by a negation sign. That is, "$(x)(Sx \supset -Px)$" is equivalent to "$-(\exists x)(Sx \ \& \ Px)$."

It is necessary to avoid the mistake of supposing that "Some *S* are *P*" could be rendered as "$(\exists x)(Sx \supset Px)$." Remembering how the conditional is related to disjunction, we can see that "$(Sx \supset Px)$" is equivalent to "$(-Sx \ v \ Px)$"; so the existential quantification of either of these merely claims that there is at least one thing that is either a nonsedum or a perennial. But this is a very weak statement; the existence of at least one stone would be enough to make it true (for stones are nonsedums). This shows that "$(\exists x)$ $(-Sx \ v \ Px)$", and with it "$(\exists x)(Sx \supset Px)$", mean something far weaker than what "Some *S* are *P*" means.

A kindred mistake would be to suppose that "No *S* are *P*" could be rendered as "$(x)-(Sx \supset Px)$." To see that this is a mistake, let us rewrite "$-(Sx \supset Px)$" in terms of disjunction, getting "$-(-Sx \ v \ Px)$." By De Morgan's law (and double negation), this becomes "$Sx \ \& \ -Px$". The universal quantification of this says that each thing is both an *S* and a non*P*. This is a very strong statement, far stronger than what "No *S* are *P*" says. Thus "$(x)-(Sx \supset Px)$" is not equivalent to "No *S* are *P*".

So far in our treatment of quantificational symbolism, we have been taking for granted that when we talk about 'each thing' or about 'at least one thing' we mean among all the things there are. Thus the universal quantification "(x)(x is physical)" is understood to mean that among all the things there are, each one is physical; and the existential quantification "(∃y)(y is mental)" is understood to mean that among all the things there are, at least one is mental.[21]

However, it sometimes is desirable to pick a more specific universe of discourse, and we may do so if we choose. To accomplish this, we merely stipulate what universe of discouse is to be employed, and then we interpret all our quantifications accordingly. That is, we interpret a universal quantification as speaking of each thing in our specified universe of discourse; and we interpret an existential quantification as speaking of at least one thing in our specified universe of discourse.

Sometimes spelling out just what universe of discourse is intended will help to avoid unclarity. Suppose someone asserts that there are no carniverous marsupials, and symbolizes the assertion as "(x)(x is carniverous ⊃ x is not a marsupial)." We may be puzzled how to interpret this. Perhaps we think of the Tasmanian tiger, but since it is extinct we do not know whether to count it as a counterexample against what the speaker intends to say. Does the speaker intend to say that, among the things there are at present, there are no carniverous marsupials; or does the speaker intend to say that among things past, present, and future there are none? The speaker could remove this unclarity by stipulating what universe of discourse is intended.

Another reason why it can be helpful to restrict the universe of discourse is that doing so sometimes enables us to shorten and simplify our symbolic formulas. For example, suppose we are told to symbolize the argument:

> Anyone over 7 feet tall is a giant.
> No one who is an Eskimo is a giant.
> Therefore no one who is an Eskimo is over 7 feet tall.

And suppose we are told to use "S" as short for "is over 7 feet tall," "G" for "is a giant," and "E" for "is an Eskimo." Let us consider two ways of symbolizing this, first without limiting the universe of discourse, then doing so. If we do not limit our universe of discourse, we shall need to introduce an additional letter, say "P," as short for "is a person." Then the argument may be symbolized:

> (x)[Px ⊃ (Sx ⊃ Gx)]
> − (∃x)[Px & (Ex & Gx)]
> ∴ −(∃x)[Px & (Ex & Sx)]

Here the first formula says that each thing is such that if it is a person, then if it is over 7 feet tall it is a giant. The second formula says that nothing is both a person and both an Eskimo and a giant. And the third formula says that nothing is both a person and both an Eskimo and over 7 feet tall. We get a simpler symbolization, however, if we explicitly limit the universe of discourse to *persons*; then the argument can be formulated:

(x)(Sx ⊃ Gx)
 − (∃x)(Ex & Gx)
∴ −(∃x)(Ex & Sx)

Here the first formula tells us that, among persons, each that is over 7 feet tall is a giant. The second formula tells us that, among persons, none is both an Eskimo and a giant. And the third formula tells us that, among persons, none is both an Eskimo and over 7 feet tall. This second way of symbolizing the argument is more convenient, and will be slightly easier to test for validity.[22]

EXERCICE 19

A Which symbolic formulas are equivalent to the original? Let "F" mean "is a fish" and "C" mean "can fly."

1. Some fish can fly.
(a) (∃x)Fx & Cx
(b) (∃y)(Fy ⊃ Cy)
(c) (∃z)(Fz & Cz)
3. Not all fish can fly.
(a) (y)(Fy ⊃ −Cy)
(b) −(z)Fz ⊃ Cz
(c) −(x)(Fx ⊃ Cx)
5. Some fish can fly, some can't.
(a) (∃x)Fx & Cx & −Cx
(b) (∃y)[(Fy & Cy) & (Fy & −Cy)]
(c) (∃z)(Fz & Cz) & (∃z) (Fz & −Cz)
6. If no fish can fly, no flyers are fish.
(a) −(y)(Fy ⊃ Cy) ⊃ −(z) (Cz ⊃ Fz)
(b) (y)Fx ⊃ −Cy ⊃ (z)Cz ⊃ −Fz
(c) (x)(Fx ⊃ −Cx) ⊃ (x)(Cx ⊃ −Fx)
7. If every fish can fly, some flyers aren't fish.
(a) (x)(Fx & Cx) ⊃ (∃y)Fy & −Cy
(b) (y)(Fy ⊃ Cy) ⊃ (∃z)Cz & −Fz
(c) (z)(Fz ⊃ Cz) ⊃ (∃x)(Cx & −Fx)
8. All and only nonfish can fly.
(a) (x)[(F & −Fx) ⊃ (Cx & −Cx)]
(b) (y)(−Fy ⊃ Cy) & (y)(Cy ⊃ −Fy)
(c) (∃z)−Fz ≡ (∃z)Cz

2. No fish can fly.
(a) −(x)(Fx & Cx)
(b) (x)Fx ⊃ −Cx
(c) (x)(Fx ⊃ −Cx)
4. Some nonfish can fly.
(a) (∃)x (−Fx & Cx)
(b) (∃x)(−Fx ⊃ Cx)
(c) (∃y)−Fy & (∃y)Cy

B Translate the following formulas into good English, letting "E" mean "is an ellipse," "H" mean "is a hyperbola," and "C" mean "is a conic section."

1. (x)(Ex ⊃ Cx)
2. (∃y)(Ey & Cy)
3. (z)(Hz ⊃ −Hx)
4. (∃x)(Ex & −Hx)
5. −(∃y)(Ey & Hy)
6. −(z)(Ez ⊃ Hz)

7. (∃x)(–Ex & Cx)
9. (y)(–Cy ⊃ –Ey)
11. (x)[(Ex v Hx) ⊃ Cx]
13. (∃x)Ex ⊃ (∃y)Cy
15. –(∃x)(Ex v Hx) ⊃ –(∃y)Cy
17. (z)[(Cz & Ez) ⊃ –Hz]
19. (x)[Cx ⊃ (Ex v Hx)]

8. (∃x)(–Ex & –Cx)
10. –(∃z)(Hz & –Cz)
12. (y)[–Cy ⊃ (–Ey & –Hy)]
14. (x)(Ex ⊃ Cx) ⊃ (∃y)Cy
16. (x)[(Ex & Hx) ⊃ Cx]
18. (∃y)[(Cy & Ey) & –Hy]
20. (y)[(Ey v Hy) ≡ Cy]

C Translate into quantificational symbolism, using "T" to mean "is a theist," "M" to mean "is a materialist," and "P" to mean "is a philosopher."
1 Some philosophers are materialists.
2 Some materialists are not theists.
3 All materialists are philosophers.
4 No theists are materialists.
5 Some nontheists are materialists.
6 All materialists are nontheists.
7 There are materialists, or there are theists.
8 Some philosophers are theists, some aren't.
9 Someone is a philosopher, if there are theists.
10 Someone is a philosopher, if he's a theist.
11 No theistic materialists are philosophers.
12 Some philosophers are neither materialists nor theists.
13 All materialistic philosophers are nontheists.
14 There are theists if and only if there are nonmaterialists.
15 Some materialistic theists are not philosophers.

D Translate the first six formulas into English, limiting the universe of discourse to chemical elements. Then translate the second six formulas into English, letting the universe of discourse be unlimited. Finally, say which examples among the first six are equivalent to which examples among the second six. Interpret "A" as "is an acid," "R" as "is radioactive," "I" as "has isotopes," and "C" as "is a chemical element."
1. (∃x)Rx
3. (x)(Rx ⊃ Ix)
5. (x)(Ix ⊃ –Ax)
7. –(∃y)(Cy & Ay)
9. (∃y)[Cy & (Iy & –Ry)]
11. (y)[(Cy & Ry) ⊃ Iy]

2. –(∃x)(Ax & Rx)
4. (∃x)(Ix & –Rx)
6. –(∃x)Ax
8. (∃y)(Cy & Ry)
10. –(∃y)[Cy & (Ay & Ry)]
12. (y)[(Cy & Iy) ⊃ –Ay]

E Symbolize each of the following arguments. Consider in each case whether it is appropriate to limit the universe of discourse. Explain the meanings you are assigning to the capital letters you use.
1 Not all whole numbers are even. Every whole number is either odd or even. Hence some whole numbers are odd.
2 No Marxists are Zoroastrians. All Trotskyites are Marxists. Hence, no Zoroastrians are Trotskyites.
3 All germs are either viruses or bacteria. No germs that are viruses can be fought with antibiotics. So some germs cannot be fought with antibiotics.
4 Square roots of negative numbers are not real numbers. There are numbers that are square roots of negative numbers. So not all numbers are real numbers.

5 All cycads are gymnosperms. Angiosperms are either dicots or monocots. Gymnosperms are not angiosperms. So there are no cycads that are angiosperms.

6 Kiwis are birds that are toothless, solitary, nocturnal, and flightless. So there are flightless nocturnal birds.

7 All copperheads are pit vipers. No rattlesnakes are pit vipers. So no rattlesnakes are copperheads.

8 No good table wines are produced in Iceland. All champagnes are good table wines. There are Icelandic wines. So some Icelandic wines are not champagnes.

9 All ancient astronomers worked without telescopes, but some of them were able to predict eclipses accurately. So not all astronomers who have predicted eclipses accurately have had telescopes.

10 Any truck or bus weighs over 2 tons and is not permitted in the park. All moving vans are trucks. So no moving van is permitted in the park.

20 PROVING THE VALIDITY OF ARGUMENTS

In this chapter we are studying the logic of quantification, but we are limiting our attention to "monadic" quantification—that is, to sentences which can be symbolized using capital letters followed by only one variable at a time.

The symbolism of monadic quantification is able to deal with all the categorical sentences of traditional logic, and also with other types of sentences which traditional logic did not treat. As a result, the range of arguments which the logic of monadic quantification has to consider is broader than the range of arguments dealt with by traditional logic; it includes all the arguments that involve categorical sentences, and others besides.

If we are to deal adequately with the logic of monadic quantification, we need to learn a method for establishing the validity of all valid arguments in this area. Venn's diagrams and the rules of the syllogism work for some of these arguments, but not for all. We need a method which goes beyond those techniques. The method we shall now consider will be sufficient for establishing the validity of any valid argument in the area of monadic quantification (and it will easily be extended in Chapter 5 to deal with all other quantificational arguments).

Suppose we are interested in a specific quantificational argument. We think it is valid, but we wish to demonstrate that this is so. Now, to claim that an argument is valid is to claim that it is impossible for the premises all to be true but the conclusion false. This amounts to the same thing as claiming that the premises in combination with the negation of the conclusion form an inconsistent set. If we can find a way of showing that a set of quantificational sentences is an inconsistent set, we shall thereby have a way of showing that our original argument is valid.

How can we show that a set of quantificational sentences is an inconsistent set? The *reductio ad absurdum* reasoning employed in Chapter 3 gives a hint. Suppose we can show that from a set of sentences some other sentence that is obviously a contradiction validly follows. This will mean that the set of sentences is an inconsistent set—the sentences cannot all be true. We shall now develop some rules of quantificational deduction which will enable us to do this. Our use of the *reductio ad absurdum* approach means that we shall need special rules only for removing quantifiers from our formulas; we shall not need any rules for adding quantifiers to formulas. Consequently, our method will not have to be as complex to explain as rules for direct proof would be.

Let us introduce the letters "*a*," "*b*," "*c*," etc., which we shall employ as *names* for particular things in the universe. We must regard each letter as naming just one thing, at least during the course of any one deduction (although a letter might name different things in different deductions). By a universal quantification, we mean an expression that starts with a universal quantifier whose scope is all the rest of the expression. A universal quantification such as "(*x*)(*x* is physical)," which we might write "(*x*)*Fx*," says that everything is physical; thus from the universal quantification we are entitled to infer "*Fa*," "*Fb*," "*Fc*," etc. Here we are simply making use of the idea that what is true of everything must be true of each particular thing.

Here the singular sentence "*Fa*" is called an *instance* of the universal sentence "(*x*)*Fx*." In general, an instance is anything that we get from a quantification by removing the quantifier and inserting a name in place of the variable of quantification wherever it occurred governed by the quantifier. Even if we do not know what the various letters mean, we still can tell that "*Ha*" is an instance of "(*x*)*Hx*," that "*Fa* ⊃ *Ga*" is an instance of "(*y*)(*Fy* ⊃ *Gy*)," and that "*Kb* & (*y*)*Hy*" is an instance of "(*z*)[*Kz* & (*y*)*Hy*]." However, "*Fa* ⊃ *Gx*" is not an instance of "(*x*)(*Fx* ⊃ *Gx*)," for the name has not replaced all occurrences of the variable of quantification.

This rule of *universal instantiation* is perfectly general: It says that from any universal quantification we may validly deduce any instance of it. Notice, however, that the rule does not entitle us from "(*x*)*Fx* ⊃ *P*" to infer "*Fa* ⊃ *P*." This case is improper and does not accord with the rule because the expression with which we start is not a universal quantification; the quantifier does not govern the whole of the expression. (Here "*P*" is to be thought of as a letter of the kind we used in the preceding chapter; it is short for some whole sentence.) To see that this case is improper, think of the sentence "If everything is physical, Plato was mistaken," which may be symbolized "(*x*)*Fx* ⊃ *P*," and think of the sentence "If this book is physical, Plato was mistaken," which may be symbolized "*Fa* ⊃ *P*." The first could be true even if the second is false, which shows that the second cannot follow validly from the first.

An expression is called an existential quantification if it starts with an existential quantifier whose scope is all the rest of the expression. An existential quantification "(∃*x*)*Fx*" says that there is at least one thing that is an

F. Now let us take the letter "*a*" and arbitrarily use it as a name to refer to this thing (or to one of these things) that is supposed to be an *F*. If we understand "*a*" in this way, we may derive "*Fa*" from "(∃x)*Fx*." Here too we can employ the notion of an instance: Anything is an instance of an existential quantification if it can be derived from the quantification by dropping the initial quantifier and inserting a name in all the places where the variable of quantification occurred governed by the quantifier.

The rule of *existential instantiation* tells us that from any existential quantification we may infer any instance of it. However, if we are to avoid fallacious reasoning, this rule has to be hedged with a restriction. We shall formulate the restriction as follows: When the instance is inferred by means of existential instantiation, the name being introduced into the instance must be one that has not previously been used in the deduction. Before we discuss this restriction more fully, let us first see how the rules are used.

To start with, let us choose a simple example, the argument "All Burmans are Asians, and so no non-Asians are Burmans." This can be symbolized "(x)(*Bx* ⊃ *Ax*), therefore (x)(−*Ax* ⊃ −*Bx*)." (To be sure, we do not need a new method to analyze this kind of argument; the methods of Chapter 2 would suffice. But we use this simple example here to start illustrating our new method, which is going to be more powerful than were the methods of earlier chapters.)

We want to show that this argument is valid, and we intend to do this by showing that its premise and the negation of its conclusion form an inconsistent set. So we set up a deduction using that set of two sentences as its premises. From them we shall derive an obvious contradiction, thereby showing that they do form an inconsistent set. In justifying steps of the deduction we shall use our two quantificational rules, the quantificational equivalences from earlier in this chapter and also the truth-functional principles from Chapter 3. Our deduction can look like this:

1 (x)(*Bx* ⊃ *Ax*)	Premise
2 −(x)(−*Ax* ⊃ −*Bx*)	Premise
3 (∃x)−(−*Ax* ⊃ −*Bx*)	2, Q.E. *(quantificational equivalence)*
4 −(−*Aa* ⊃ −*Ba*)	3, E.I. *(existential instantiation)*
5 −*Aa* & −−*Ba*)	4, T.F.E. *(truth-functional equivalence)*
6 *Ba* ⊃ *Aa*	1, U.I. *(universal instantiation)*
7 −*Aa*	5, c.s. *(conjunctive simplification)*
8 −*Ba*	6, 7, m.t. *(modus tollens)*
9 −−*Ba*)	5, c.s. *(conjunctive simplification)*
10 −*Ba* & −−*Ba*)	8, 9, c.a. *(conjunctive adjunction)*

Looking at the deduction as a whole, we see that in the last line we have derived a definite contradiction of the form "*p* & −*p*." Conclusions of this form are the clearest and most obvious of contradictions, and so we shall use them as the standard type of contradiction, always trying to obtain a conclusion of this form as the last line of a quantificational deduction. In this deduction the contradiction was validly derived from the first lines, and so they must be an inconsistent set of sentences. This shows that our original argument was valid. Here then is our method for showing the validity of valid quantificational arguments.

Going back now to the rule of existential instantiation, let us consider why there must be some kind of restriction upon it. A sentence such as "(∃x)Fx" says at least one thing is F, and if we think of the letter "a" as naming such a thing, then we may infer "Fa." But clearly it is important here that "a" be a name which has not previously been assigned some other special sense elsewhere in the same deduction. Invalid reasoning can easily occur if we neglect this restriction and allow a single letter to be assigned to name more than one thing in the course of a deduction.

For example, the formulas "(∃x)Fx" and "(∃x)–Fx" do not form an inconsistent set, but the following deduction purports to show that they do:

1	(∃x)Fx	Premise
2	(∃x)–Fx	Premise
3	Fa	From 1 by E.I.
4	–Fa	From 2 by E.I.
5	Fa & –Fa	From 3, 5 by c.a.

This deduction claims to show that a contradiction follows from the first two lines and therefore that they form an inconsistent set. But that is not so, and the deduction is illegitimate. The fallacy is that in getting line 3 we have chosen to think of "a" as naming a particular thing that is F, but in line 4 we think of the same letter "a" as naming a particular thing that is nonF. It is illegitimate to assume that the thing that was the F is the thing that is the nonF; there is no reason why they need be the same thing. The mistake lies in line 4, where the name introduced into the instance ought to have been a name that had not occurred before in the deduction.

Let us look at another example. Suppose we wish to use our new method to demonstrate the validity of a syllogism whose form is "(x)(Mx ⊃ –Px), (∃x) (Sx & Mx), therefore (∃x)(Sx & –Px)." We shall want to show that the two premises in combination with the negation of the conclusion form an inconsistent set. And we do this by constructing a deduction which starts from those three sentences as its premises, and validly derives from them an obvious contradiction. Our deduction can look like this:

1	(x)(Mx ⊃ –Px)	Premise
2	(∃x)(Sx & Mx)	Premise
3	–(∃x)(Sx & –Px)	Premise
4	Sa & Ma	2, E.I.
5	Ma ⊃ –Pa	1, U.I.

6 $(x)-(Sx \& -Px)$ 3, Q.E.
7 $-(Sa \& -Pa)$ 6, U.I.
8 Ma 4, c.s.
9 $-Pa$ 5, 8, m.p. (modus ponens)
10 $-Sa$ 7,9, conj. arg.
11 Sa 4, c.s.
12 $Sa \& -Sa$ 11, 10, c.a.

How do we figure out what steps to take when we are constructing such a deduction? There are going to be various correct ways of doing it, various sequences of steps that will accomplish the task. Our general strategy must be to use the rules of existential instantiation and universal instantiation to remove quantifiers, and then use truth-functional rules to get our obvious contradiction. It is usually wise to perform E.I. before performing U.I. (this is because of the restriction on E.I.). For simple problems like this, we want to use only one name as we perform instantiations; otherwise, we are not likely to get a contradiction. And we want to be alert and use our ingenuity, so as to keep the deduction as short as we can.

Principles for Use in Quantificational Deductions

I. Truth-functional inference We may use any of the principles of truth-functional deduction that were listed in Chapter 3.

II. Quantificational rules of inference *Universal instantiation* (U.I.): From any universal quantification we may validly infer any instance of it.
Existential instantiation (E.I.): From an existential quantification we may validly infer any instance of it, provided that the name being introduced into the instance is new to the deduction.

III. Quantificational equivalences (Q.E.) From a sentence we may validly infer any sentence that is equivalent to it according to these rules:

1 Two sentences are equivalent if they are exactly alike except that where one contains a negation sign immediately followed by a universal quantifier, the other contains an existential quantifier immediately followed by a negation sign; e.g., "$-(x)Fx$" is equivalent to "$(\exists x)-Fx$."

2 Two sentences always are equivalent if they are exactly alike except that where one contains a negation sign immediately followed by an existential quantifier, the other contains a universal quantifier immediately followed by a negation sign; e.g., "$-(\exists x)Fx$" is equivalent to "$(x)-Fx$."

Two more quantificational equivalences will be added later.

A word of explanation about truth-functional inference. We are entitled to write down any new line that can be justified by the purely truth-functional rules of Chapter 3. For instance, if we have previous lines that read "(∃x)Fx ⊃ (y)Gy" and "(∃x)Fx," then by modus ponens we may derive "(y)Gy." Although these lines contain quantifiers, their overall structure is exactly that of modus ponens, and the move is purely truth-functional. However, the principles of Chapter 3 do not justify us in making changes within the scopes of quantifiers. Suppose we tried to go from "(x)(Fx ⊃ Gx)" and "(x)Fx" to "(x)Gx." It would be a mistake to suppose that mere modus ponens justifies this move; here the move does not have the exact structure required by modus ponens, for the first line is not a conditional (instead, it is a universal quantification). Nor would it be correct to go from "(x)[(Fx ⊃ Gx) & Fx]" to "(x)Gx" merely by modus ponens. Such a move may be valid, but it is not justified by modus ponens as such. In constructing our deductions, we want to keep strictly to those moves which we know are justified by the standard rules we have become familiar with; that is the whole point of the game. Were we to start relying upon our special feelings as to what is valid, our deductions would cease to be reliable.

In connection with the quantificational rules of inference, it is important to keep in mind that one has to start with a universal quantification or an existential quantification before one can use these rules. That is, for U.I. one must start with a line that has a universal quantifier at the very beginning, and the scope of the quantifier must be all the rest of the line. And for E.I. one must start with a line having an existential quantifier at the very beginning, and the scope of the quantifier must be all the rest of the line. It would be a misuse of U.I. to try to use it to justify a move from "−(x)Fx" to "−Fa," because here the first is not a universal quantification; it is the negation of one. Also, it would be a mistake to try to go by E.I. from "(∃x)Gx ⊃ Fy" to "Ga ⊃ Fy"; the first one is not an existential quantification.

Also, we must take care that the final line in a deduction is really a contradiction of the form "p & −p." It would be inappropriate to terminate a deduction with "(Fa & Ga) & (−Fa & −Ga)"; this is a contradiction, but not as obvious and clear-cut a specimen as we want. It would be much worse to try to end a deduction with "(Fa ⊃ Ga) & (Fa ⊃ −Ga)," which is not a contradiction at all.

EXERCISE 20

*A Each of the following is a correct deduction; the first two lines are premises. Explain the justification for each further step, and say what the deduction shows.

1.
   1. (∃x)Fx
   2. (x)−Fx
   3. Fa
   4. −Fa
   5. Fa & −Fa

2.
   1. (y)Hy
   2. −(∃y)Hy
   3. (y)−Hy
   4. Hb
   5. −Hb
   6. Hb & −Hb

3. 1. $(z)(Hz \supset Kz)$
2. $-(\exists z)(Hz \supset Kz)$
3. $Ha \supset Ka$
4. $(z)-(Hz \supset Kz)$
5. $-(Ha \supset Ka)$
6. $(Ha \supset Ka)$ & $-(Ha \supset Ka)$

5. 1. $-(\exists x)Hx$
2. $-[-(x)Hx]$
3. $(x)-Hx$
4. $-Ha$
5. $(x)Hx$
6. Ha
7. Ha & $-Ha$

7. 1. $(z)(Hz \supset -Fz)$
2. $(\exists z)(Hz$ & $Fz)$
3. Ha & Fa
4. $Ha \supset -Fa$
5. Ha
6. $-Fa$
7. Fa
8. Fa & $-Fa$

9. 1. $(x)(Hx \equiv Gx)$
2. $(\exists z)(Hz$ & $-Gz)$
3. Ha & $-Ga$
4. $Ha \equiv Ga$
5. $(Ga \supset Ha)$ & $(Ha \supset Ga)$
6. $Ha \supset Ga$
7. Ha
8. Ga
9. $-Ga$
10. Ga & $-Ga$

4. 1. $(x)Gx$
2. $-(z)Gz$
3. $(\exists z)-Gz$
4. $-Gb$
5. Gb
6. Gb & $-Gb$

6. 1. $(y)(Hy$ & $Gy)$
2. $-(\exists y)Gy$
3. $(y)-Gy$
4. Ha & Ga
5. $-Ga$
6. Ga
7. Ga & $-Ga$

8. 1. $(y)(Fy \supset Hy)$
2. $(\exists y)(Fy$ & $-Hy)$
3. Fb & $-Hb$
4. $Fb \supset Hb$
5. Fb
6. Hb
7. $-Hb$
8. Hb & $-Hb$

10. 1. $(y)(Hy \supset Fy)$ & $(\exists z)Hz$
2. $(x)(Hx \supset -Fx)$
3. $(y)(Hy \supset Fy)$
4. $(\exists z)Hz$
5. Ha
6. $Ha \supset -Fa$
7. $Ha \supset Fa$
8. $-Fa$
9. Fa
10. Fa & $-Fa$

B Find all incorrect steps. Explain whether the deduction can be revised so as to reach the same final result correctly. The first three lines are premises.

1. 1. $(\exists x)(Ax$ & $Bx)$
2. $(y)(Ay \supset -Cy)$
3. $-(\exists x)(Bx$ & $-Cx)$
4. $Ay \supset -Cy$ (2)
5. $(\exists x)Ax$ (1)
6. $-(\exists x)-Cx$ (3)
7. $--Ca$ (6)
8. Ca (7)
9. $Aa \supset -Ca$ (4)
10. $-Aa$ (8, 9)
11. $(\exists x)Ax$ & $-Aa$ (5, 10)

2. 1. $(y)(Cy \supset By)$
2. $(\exists x)(Ax$ & $-Cx)$
3. $-(\exists x)(Ax$ & $Bx)$
4. $-(Aa$ & $Ba)$ (3)
5. $(\exists x)Ax$ (2)
6. Ab (5)
7. $-Aa$ (4)
8. Ab & $-Aa$ (6, 7)

C Construct deductions to show that each of the following is an inconsistent set.

1. $(\exists x)Hx$; $-(\exists x)Hx$
2. $(\exists z)(Hz$ & $Fz)$; $-(\exists x)Fx$
3. $(x)Gx$; $(\exists x)-Gx$
4. $-(\exists y)-Gy$; $-(x)Gx$
5. $(\exists z)Hz$; $(x)-Hx$
6. $(x)(Hx \supset Fx)$; $(\exists x)(-Fx$ & $Hx)$

7. $(x)Fx; (x)-Fx$
9. $-(\exists x)Hx; -(y)-Hy$

8. $(x)(Gx \supset -Hx); (\exists y)(Hy \,\&\, Gy)$
10. $(\exists y)(Gy \vee Hy); (x)-Gx; (y)-Hy$

21 USING THE METHOD

When a set of quantificational sentences is inconsistent, our method of quantificational deduction enables us to demonstrate this by showing that from the sentences there validly follows an obvious contradiction of the form "$p \,\&\, -p$." As we have already seen, this method can be used to answer questions about the validity of arguments, because any question about the validity of an argument can be rephrased as a question about whether its premises when combined with the negation of its conclusion form an inconsistent set.

Questions about implication can be handled in a similar way. To ask whether a certain quantificational sentence (or group of sentences) implies another amounts to asking whether the former and the negation of the latter make an inconsistent set.

The question whether a single quantificational sentence is a contradiction can be dealt with even more simply by our method. To show that a given sentence is a contradiction, we validly derive from it an obvious contradiction—this settles the matter.

Another question we can handle is whether a quantificational sentence is necessarily true. This question can be rephrased as a question about a contradiction, since the given sentence is necessarily true if and only if its negation is a contradiction. So, for instance, if we want to find out whether a sentence of the form "$(x)(Fx \supset Fx)$" is necessarily true, we investigate whether its negation, of the form "$-(x)(Fx \supset Fx)$," is a contradiction. This provides a way of demonstrating the necessary truth of a quantificational sentence: we form its negation and then show that from this negation an obvious contradiction can be validly derived.

Also our method can be used to show that two quantificational sentences are equivalent. To say that two sentences are equivalent is to say that each implies the other. So to establish the equivalence of two sentences A and B, we first construct a deduction to show that A follows from B, and then we construct another deduction to show that B follows from A.

When we use our method of quantificational deduction to answer questions of these various kinds, we sometimes may need to construct fairly complex deductions. In figuring out how to finish them, it will be helpful to keep in mind certain points of strategy.

One point has to do with how to avoid being balked by the restriction on the rule of existential instantiation. The restriction requires that any name introduced by means of E.I. must be a new name. We should not let this restriction prevent us from getting the legitimate results that we want. For example, suppose we are trying to show by deduction that a syllogism of the type **AII** in the first figure is valid. Symbolizing the premises and the negation of the conclusion, we have the following:

1 $(x)(Mx \supset Px)$ *Premise*
2 $(\exists x)(Sx \ \& \ Mx)$ *Premise*
3 $-(\exists x)(Sx \ \& \ Px)$ *Premise*

We might then attempt to derive a contradiction from this by proceeding as follows:

4 $Ma \supset Pa$ *From 1 by U.I.*

But now we are in trouble. We would like to obtain "$Sa \ \& \ Ma$" from line 2 by E.I., but we cannot do this, for the name "a" has already been used in the deduction. An instance obtained from line 2 using a new and different name would not combine with line 4 to yield a contradiction. So we seem to be blocked.

Here the solution is to take our steps in a different order. We perform E.I. first and then U.I. The deduction as a whole can look like this:

1 $(x)(Mx \supset Px)$ *Premise*
2 $(\exists x)(Sx \ \& \ Mx)$ *Premise*
3 $-(\exists x)(Sx \ \& \ Px)$ *Premise*
4 $Sa \ \& \ Ma$ *From 2 by E.I.*
5 $Ma \supset Pa$ *From 1 by U.I.*
6 $(x)-(Sx \ \& \ Px)$ *From 3 by Q.E.*
7 $-(Sa \ \& \ Pa)$ *From 6 by U.I.*
8 Ma *From 4 by c.s.*
9 Pa *From 5, 8 by m.p.*
10 Sa *From 4 by c.s.*
11 $-Sa$ *From 7, 9 by conj. arg.*
12 $Sa \ \& \ -Sa$ *From 10, 11, by c.a.*

Here we get the contradiction we want by arranging the sequence of steps so that we do not violate the restriction. As was mentioned before, it is always wise to perform E.I. before U.I., insofar as that is possible.

Another point of strategy: Usually to complete a deduction we shall need to derive only one instance from each quantification that we encounter. However, we should keep in mind that our rules do permit us to derive two or more different instances from one and the same quantification. Occasionally we may run into deductions which are complicated in such a way that they can be completed only by deriving two or more instances from the same quantification. We need to be prepared to do this when it is necessary.

There is a further slight extension of our symbolism which will be useful to us in handling some kinds of arguments that contain singular terms. A sentence containing a proper name or other phrase that purports to apply to exactly one individual is called a singular sentence. Such sentences can be translated into categorical form, as we saw in Chapter 2. But quantificational symbolism offers a better way of treating them, for we can use the letters "a," "b," "c," etc., as names. Thus, for instance, "All philosophers are wise; Socrates is a philosopher; therefore Socrates is wise" can be symbolized as "$(x)(Px \supset Wx)$, Pa, therefore Wa." Here "a" refers to Socrates. We can demonstrate the validity of the syllogism thus:

1 $(x)(Px \supset Wx)$	*Premise*	
2 Pa	*Premise*	
3 $-Wa$	*Premise*	
4 $Pa \supset Wa$	*1, U.I.*	
5 Wa	*4, 2, m.p.*	
6 $Wa \,\&\, -Wa$	*5, 3, c.a.*	

EXERCISE 21

*A Construct a deduction to show that the first sentence implies the second.
   1 Nothing is perfect. Something is not perfect.
   2 Nothing is perfect. Nothing human is perfect.
   3 Everything is perfect. Everything human is perfect.
   4 Everything is perfect. Everything human is perfect or everything superhuman is perfect.
   5 Something is perfect. It's not the case that nothing is perfect.
   6 The Mona Lisa is perfect. Something is perfect.
B Construct a deduction to show that the sentence is necessarily true.
   1 Everything that moves, moves.
   2 Something is such that if it moves, then it moves.
   3 Either the magnetic pole moves or it doesn't move.
   4 Either something moves, or everything that is at rest is at rest.
   5 If the equator both moves and doesn't move, then nothing moves.
   6 If everything moves, then the equator moves.
C Construct deductions to show that the two sentences are equivalent.
   1 Something is not indestructible. Not everything is indestructible.
   2 Each thing is either in motion or at rest. It's not the case that something both isn't in motion and isn't at rest.
   3 The equator is in motion or it isn't. Either everything is at rest or not everything is at rest.
   4 Nothing indestructible is in motion. Everything indestructible is such as not to be in motion.
   5 Everything is either indestructible and at rest or indestructible and not at rest. Everything is indestructible
   6 The Mona Lisa is indestructible and not indestructible. The Mona Lisa is valuable and not valuable.
†D Construct deductions to show that the syllogisms of the following moods are valid.

   1. EAE, 1   **2.** EIO, 2   **3.** OAO, 3
   4. IAI, 4   **5.** AEO, 2   **6.** AAI, 4

22 EXTENDING THE METHOD

Our method of quantificational deduction is not yet complete. So far, we have seen how to establish the inconsistency of a set of premises when each premise is either a universal quantification, an existential quantification, a negation of one of the preceding, or a conjunction both components of which are the preceding kinds. But we do not yet have any way of dealing with premises that are disjunctions, conditionals, or biconditionals containing quantifications.

For example, consider the sentence "Either everything is solid and not solid or everything is liquid and not liquid," which can be symbolized "$(x)(Sx \& -Sx) \lor (y)(Ly \& -Ly)$." This is a fairly obvious contradiction. However, it is the disjunction of two quantifications, and so far we do not have any way of proving it to be a contradiction, because we cannot derive any instances from it. Our rule U.I. permits us to derive an instance only when the quantifier occurs at the beginning of a sentence and has all the rest of the sentence within its scope—and in this example neither quantifier governs the whole sentence. And because it is a disjunction, we are not permitted to separate off one of the quantifications, as we would be able to do if it were a conjunction.

Our rules need to be extended so that we can handle this and similar problems. We shall extend them by adding a pair of further principles of quantificational equivalence.

First consider the two sentences:

Either each thing is mental or Berkeley's philosophy is mistaken.
Each thing is such that either it is mental or Berkeley's philosophy is mistaken.

Writing "M" for "is mental" and "B" for the complete sentence "Berkeley's philosophy is mistaken," we can symbolize the two sentences thus:

$(x)Mx \lor B$
$(x)(Mx \lor B)$

The first sentence is a disjunction one component of which is a universal quantification, while the second sentence is a universal quantification of a disjunction. The two sentences are equivalent, however, for each is true if and only if either everything is mental or Berkeley's philosophy is mistaken. The underlying principle of equivalence here can be stated in more general terms: Any disjunction, one part of which is a universal quantification, may be rewritten in the equivalent form of a universal quantification of a disjunction.[23]

Returning now to the example we were considering in the second paragraph of this section, we can carry out the desired deduction fairly easily.

1 $(x)(Sx \& -Sx) \lor (y)(Ly \& -Ly)$

2 $(x)[(Sx \ \& -Sx) \vee (y)(Ly \ \& -Ly)]$ 1, Q.E.
3 $(Sa \ \& -Sa) \vee (y)(Ly \ \& -Ly)$ 2, U.I.
4 $-(Sa \ \& -Sa)$ Tautology
5 $(y)(Ly \ \& -Ly)$ 3,4, disj. arg.
6 $La \ \& -La$ 5, U.I.

Here we make use of our new principle of quantificational equivalence in line 2, taking a universal quantifier that governed only one component of a disjunction and moving it so that it governs the whole disjunction.

Still another kind of example that our method does not yet enable us to handle is illustrated by the sentence "Either something is liquid and is not liquid or something is solid and is not solid," which may be symbolized "$(\exists x)(Lx \ \& -Lx) \vee (\exists y)(Sy \ \& -Sy)$." This sentence is a contradiction, but here again we cannot show that it is so, for our rules do not yet enable us to take any useful step beyond the first line. We need one more principle of equivalence.

To understand this last principle of equivalence, consider these sentences:

Either something moves or Zeno's philosophy is correct.
Something is such that either it moves or Zeno's philosophy is correct.

Writing "M" for "moves" and "Z" for the complete sentence "Zeno's philosophy is correct," we can symbolize these as follows:

$(\exists x)Mx \vee Z$
$(\exists x)(Mx \vee Z)$

The first sentence is a disjunction one component of which is an existential quantification, while the second sentence is an existential quantification of a disjunction. They are equivalent, however, for each is true if and only if either at least one thing moves or Zeno's philosophy is correct. The underlying principle of equivalence here can be stated in general terms: Any disjunction, one part of which is an existential quantification, may be rewritten in the equivalent form of an existential quantification of a disjunction.[24]

Returning to our example, we now can complete the desired deduction.

1 $(\exists x)(Lx \ \& -Lx) \vee (\exists y)(Sy \ \& -Sy)$
2 $(\exists x)[(Lx \ \& -Lx) \vee (\exists y)(Sy \ \& -Sy)]$ 1, Q.E.
3 $(La \ \& -La) \vee (\exists y)(Sy \ \& -Sy)$ 2, E.I.
4 $(\exists y)[(La \ \& -La) \vee (Sy \ \& -Sy)]$ 3, Q.E.
5 $(La \ \& -La) \vee (Sb \ \& -Sb)$ 4, E.I.
6 $-(Sb \ \& -Sb)$ Tautology
7 $La \ \& -La$ 5, 6 by disj. arg.

Here we twice make use of our newest principle of quantificational equivalence, first in line 2 and again in line 4. In each case we take an existential quantifier that governed only one component of a disjunction and move it so that it governs the whole disjunction.

These two new principles of quantificational equivalence involve disjunction, and it alone, and so by themselves they do not tell us how to deal with lines in which quantifications are linked by the conditional or biconditional. However, the conditional or any other truth-functional compound can be equivalently expressed using nothing but conjunction, negation, and disjunction; thus we are able to take the steps we need. For example, the sentence "If everything is liquid or not liquid, then something is solid and not solid" is shown to be a contradiction in the following manner:

1	$(x)(Lx \lor -Lx) \supset (\exists x)(Sy \& -Sy)$	Premise
2	$-(x)(Lx \lor -Lx) \lor (\exists y)(Sy \& -Sy)$	1, T.F.E.
3	$(\exists y)[-(x)(Lx \lor -Lx) \lor (Sy \& -Sy)]$	2, Q.E.
4	$-(x)(Lx \lor -Lx) \lor (Sa \& -Sa)$	3, E.I.
5	$(\exists x)-(Lx \lor -Lx) \lor (Sa \& -Sa)$	4, Q.E.
6	$(\exists x)[-(Lx \lor -Lx) \lor (Sa \& -Sa)]$	5, Q.E.
7	$-(Lb \lor -Lb) \lor (Sa \& -Sa)$	6, E.I.
8	$(Lb \lor -Lb) \supset (Sa \& -Sa)$	7, T.F.E.
9	$Lb \lor -Lb$	Tautology
10	$Sa \& -Sa$	8, 9, m.p.

This deduction starts with a first line that is a conditional, and our rules do not allow us to remove quantifiers from within such a line. So our first step has to be to rewrite the conditional as a disjunction; then we can use our new quantificational equivalences to move the quantifiers to the front of the whole formula, and from there we can remove them. In this deduction it turns out that we need to use two different names, because we have to perform E.I. twice.

In light of what has been said, we can now add two further principles of quantificational equivalence to the list. These additional principles belong under heading III of the list.[25]

Additional principles of quantificational equivalence

3 Any disjunction, one component of which is a universal quantification, may be rewritten in the equivalent form of a universal quantification of a disjunction; for example, "$(x)Mx \lor B$" is equivalent to "$(x)(Mx \lor B)$."

4 Any disjunction, one component of which is an existential quantification, may be rewritten in the equivalent form of an existential quantification of a disjunction; for example, "$(\exists x)Mx \lor Z$" is equivalent to "$(\exists x)(Mx \lor Z)$."

EXERCISE 22

A Construct a deduction showing that the sentence is a contradiction.

    1 $(x)-(Hx \supset Hx) \lor (\exists y)-(Hy \supset Hy)$

    2 $(\exists x)(Fx \& -Fx) \lor (\exists y)(Gy \& -Gy)$

    3 $(x)(Fx \lor -Fx) \supset (\exists y)(Gy \& -Gy)$

    4 $(\exists x)(Fx \supset Fx) \supset (y)-(Gy \supset Gy)$

    5 $-[(x)(Fx \lor -Fx) \& (\exists y)(Gy \supset Gy)]$

B Construct deductions to show that the arguments of Exercise 19, part **E**, are valid.

C Symbolize each argument and construct a deduction to show that it is valid.

    1 If there is something with mass, there is something with weight. Everything has mass. So something has weight.

    2 Everything is either mental and indestructible or physical and corruptible. Therefore, whatever is incorruptible is indestructible.

    3 Everything is physical and destructible. Therefore, everything is physical, and everything is destructible.

    4 No corrosive liquids are potable. Therefore, if there are corrosive liquids, there are liquids which are not potable.

    5 Something is either solid or gaseous. Therefore, either there are solid things or there are gaseous things.

    6 Access must be restricted to any chemical in the supply room that is explosive or poisonous. There is a chemical in the supply room which is poisonous if it has a warning label. Therefore, there is a chemical in the supply room to which access must be restricted, if it has a warning label.

    7 Not all carnivores are quadrupeds. There are no carnivorous marsupials. Therefore, some carnivores are neither quadrupeds nor marsupials.

    8 All bank robberies are crimes. Any crime or misdemeanor is punishable. Therefore, all bank robberies are punishable.

    9 A substance is chemically inert if and only if it does not alter other substances and is not altered by them. Therefore, any chemically inert substance does not alter other substances.

    10 All Moslems are monotheists. Therefore, if there are Moslems, there are monotheistic Moslems.

    11 All these diamonds are valuable. Whatever gets lost will have to be paid for. Therefore, if everything valuable gets lost, then all these diamonds will have to be paid for.

    12 All radioactive atoms are unstable. Therefore, either no large radioactive atoms are stable or no radioactive atoms that are not large are stable.

D Construct a deduction to show that the sentence is a contradiction, or that the set of sentences is inconsistent.

    1 $(\exists y)(Gy \& -Gy) \lor (z)(Hz \equiv -Hz)$

    2 $-(\exists y)(Fy \equiv Fy) \lor (y)(Gy \equiv -Gy)$

    3 $(\exists z)Hz \supset (y)-Hy; (z)-Hz \supset (\exists y)Hy$

    4 $(x)Fx \supset (\exists y)-Fy; (\exists x)-Fx \supset (y)Fy$

    5 $(y)(Fy \supset Hy) \equiv (\exists x)(-Hx \& Fx)$

CHAPTER 5

GENERAL
QUANTIFICATION

In the previous chapter we studied how quantificational symbolism can be used to analyze sentences and arguments, where these can be symbolized so that capital letters are followed by variables only one at a time. Now we shall remove that restriction. We shall allow capital letters to be followed by two or more variables at a time; and in connection with that change, we shall also allow quantifiers to occur within the scope of other quantifiers. This enables us to use the symbolism of quantification with its full generality.

23 SYMBOLIZING WITH MULTIPLE VARIABLES

Often we talk about *relations* which hold between two or more things at a time. For example, if we say that one thing *exceeds another in size,* we are claiming that a certain relation holds between the first thing and the second. We could symbolize this relation by using the capital letter "E." Then, letting "a" name the first thing and "b" name the second, we could write "Eab" to mean "a exceeds b in size."

Here it is important to notice that the order of the names "a" and "b" in the sentence "Eab" is in one respect of no significance: "Eab" can be equally well put into words either as "a exceeds b in size" or as "b is exceeded in size by a." But in another respect the order does make an essential difference: "Eab" is not equivalent to "Eba," for the former sentence says that a is the bigger, whereas the latter sentence says to the contrary that b is the bigger.

Let us continue to use "*E*" with this same meaning, but now let us introduce a variable and a quantifier to govern it. This enables us to formulate sentences such as these:

$$(\exists x)\text{–}Exx \tag{1}$$
$$(x)\text{–}Exx \tag{2}$$

Here sentence (1) says that there is at least one thing which does not exceed itself in size; in other words, something is not larger than itself. Sentence (2) says that each thing is such that it does not exceed itself in size; in other words, nothing is larger than itself.

Also we can use two different variables at once, and we can allow one quantifier to occur within the scope of another. Then we can formulate sentences such as:

$$(\exists x)(\exists y)Exy \tag{3}$$
$$(x)(y)Exy \tag{4}$$

Here sentence (3) says that at least one thing exceeds at least one thing in size; that is, something is larger than something. Sentence (4) says that everything is such as to exceed everything in size; that is, everything is larger than everything (of course this sentence is false, whereas the previous sentences were true).

Notice that example (4) does not say merely that each thing is larger than each *other* thing; it says that each thing is larger than each thing, *including itself.*

Because we are allowing one quantifier to occur within the scope of another, we must notice that sometimes the order of the quantifiers can affect the meaning of a sentence. Thus, "$(y)(\exists x)Exy$" says that each thing is such that there is at least one thing exceeding it in size; whereas "$(\exists x)(y)Exy$" says that there is at least one thing which exceeds everything in size. These two sentences are not equivalent. To see that they are different in what they say, notice that the second sentence is utterly false, for it implies that something exceeds itself in size. In contrast, the first sentence could be true—it will be true if the universe is infinite in size and contains no largest thing, and if we limit our universe of discourse to things of finite size. The situation is this: the second sentence makes a more extreme statement and logically implies the first; the first sentence makes a less extreme statement and could be true even if the second is not.

Let us now get some further practice in translating words into quantificational symbolism. In doing this, especially at this stage, let us not try to do the whole job of translating a sentence all in a single step; it is better to proceed toward the symbolic formulation by a series of gradual steps. For example:

There is something that influences everything.

(∃x)(x influences everything)
(∃x)(y)(x influences y)
(∃x)(y)Ixy

Everyone fears someone.
Each person fears someone.
(x)(Px ⊃ x fears someone)
(x)(Px ⊃ there is a person x fears)
(x)[Px ⊃ (∃y)(y is a person & x fears y)]
(x)[Px ⊃ (∃y)(Py & Fxy)]

There is someone who loves everyone.
There is a person who loves every person.
(∃x)(Px & x loves every person)
(∃x)[Px & (y)(y is a person ⊃ x loves y)]
(∃x)[Px & (y)(Py ⊃ Lxy)]

Every elephant outweighs any mouse.
(x)(x is an elephant ⊃ x outweighs any mouse)
(x)[Ex ⊃ (y)(y is a mouse ⊃ x outweighs y)]
(x)[Ex ⊃ (y)(My ⊃ Oxy)]

These are not the only correct ways of symbolizing the original sentences, but they are the easiest ways. Notice that when a true-or-false sentence is properly symbolized, every occurrence of a variable in it must fall within the scope of the proper quantifier; free variables never occur in sentences like these.

The following is an argument of medieval vintage and is an example of a valid argument whose validity cannot be established either by syllogistic or by truth-functional methods:

All circles are figures.
Therefore, whoever draws a circle draws a figure.

We are not yet in a position to show that the argument is valid, but we can now symbolize its premise and conclusion. The premise becomes:

(x)(Cx ⊃ Fx)

Symbolizing the conclusion is more difficult and is best done step by step. Two initial steps can be:

Each thing is such that if it is a person who draws a circle, then it is a person who draws a figure.
(x)(x is a person who draws a circle ⊃ x is a person who draws a figure)

In order to exhibit the connection between the premise and the conclusion of the argument, we must introduce into our version of the conclusion the letters "C" and "F" that we used in the premise. Otherwise we would not bring out those aspects of the logical structure which are germane to the validity of the argument. We can do this by taking the following steps:

(x)[(x is a person who draws something that is a circle) ⊃ (x)(is a person who draws something that is a figure)]

(x)[(something is a circle & x is a person who draws it) ⊃ (something is a figure & x is a person who draws it)]

(x)[(∃y)(Cy & x is a person who draws y) ⊃ (∃y)(Fy & x is a person who draws y)]

Now if we use "*D*" to express "is a person who draws," we have:

(x)[(∃y)(Cy & Dxy) ⊃ (∃y)(Fy & Dxy)]

Thus we have symbolized both the premise and the conclusion of the argument in such a way as to exhibit the logical structure involved in the reasoning. In the next section we shall discuss how our method of quantificational deduction can establish the validity of an argument like this.

So far we have used capital letters followed by variables only two at a time. But there are other, more complicated relations which may need to be symbolized by using a capital letter followed by three or more variables at once. Consider, for instance, the relation among three things when one is *between* the other two. We can write "*Bxyz*" to mean "x is between y and z." Then the expression "(x)(∃y)(∃z)Bxyz" will mean that each thing is between something and something (this will be true if we are thinking about points in euclidean space). It is even permissible to use a capital letter followed by four or more variables at once, but we shall not have any need to do that.

EXERCISE 23

*A Symbolize the following sentences, using "Ixy" as short for "x influences y". Are any of them contradictories of each other? Are any equivalent?
1 Something influences something.
2 Everything influences everything.
3 There is something which everything influences.
4 Everything is influenced by something or other.
5 Nothing influences everything.
6 Nothing influences anything.
7 Nothing influences nothing.
8 There is something which does not influence everything.
9 Everything influences something or other.
10 Something does not influence anything.
11 Everything influences itself.
12 Anything that influences itself, influences something.
13 Anything that influences nothing, doesn't influence itself.
14 If nothing influences anything, nothing influences itself.
15 Whatever influences everything, influences itself.

B Let "D" be short for "is a dog," let "R" be short for "is a rabbit," and let "C" be short for "chases." Translate the following into English.
   1 $(x)(Rx \supset -Dx)$
   2 $(\exists x)(Dx \& -Rx)$
   3 $(\exists x)[Dx \& (\exists y)Cxy]$
   4 $(\exists x)[Rx \& (y)-Cxy]$
   5 $(\exists x)[Dx \& (\exists y)(Ry \& Cxy)]$
   6 $(\exists x)[Dx \& (y)(Ry \supset Cxy)]$
   7 $(x)[Dx \supset (\exists y)(Ry \& Cxy)]$
   8 $(y)[Dy \supset (x)(Rx \supset Cyx)]$
   9 $(\exists x)[Rx \& (\exists y)(Dy \& Cxy)]$
   10 $-(\exists x)[Rx \& (y)(Dy \supset Cxy)]$
   11 $-(\exists x)[Rx \& (y)(Dy \supset Cyx)]$
   12 $(y)[Ry \supset (\exists x)(Dx \& Cxy)]$
   13 $(\exists x)(Dx \& Cxx)$
   14 $(x)[(Dx \& Cxx) \supset -(\exists y)(Ry \& Cxy)]$
   15 $(x)[(Dx \& Cxx) \supset -(y)(Ry \supset Cxy)]$

C Symbolize by means of quantifiers, making clear the meanings of the capital letters you use.
   1 There is a city to which all roads lead.
   2 There is a courthouse in every town.
   3 There is a human being from whom all later humans are descended.
   4 If something has been stolen, someone will be unhappy.
   5 If something has been stolen, someone will have to pay for it.
   6 Someone will have to pay for everything that has been stolen.
   7 If any automobiles are solid gold, some automobiles are expensive.
   8 If any automobiles are solid gold, they are expensive.
   9 If all teachers are perfectionists and no students are hardworking, then some teachers will be frustrated by some students.
   10 If any student is careless, and if all teachers are perfectionists, then that student will be criticized by some teachers.

D Symbolize so as to bring out the logical structure that is relevant to the validity of each argument.
   1 There is a trouble that any mechanic can correct. Therefore, every mechanic can correct some trouble or other.
   2 There is a woman to whom everyone listens. Therefore, there is a woman who listens to herself.
   3 No one is cheating anyone. So no one is cheating everyone.
   4 Everyone is afraid of someone. So no one is afraid of no one.
   5 Everything resembles itself. So each thing resembles something.
   6 Everything physical attracts everything physical. So something attracts something.
   7 Burglars are criminals. So those who are friends of burglars are friends of criminals.
   8 Every physical event is determined by some earlier physical event. Some events are not determined by anything. So some events are not physical events.
   9 When one organism is descended from another it never is the case that the latter is descended from the former. Therefore, no organism is descended from itself.

    10 Whenever A is an ancestor of B and B is an ancestor of C, A is an ancestor of C. Nothing is an ancestor of itself. Therefore, whenever A is an ancestor of B, B is not an ancestor of A.

†E Each of the following sentences is at least somewhat ambiguous in English. Symbolize each in two ways that are not equivalent.

  1 Everything is created by someone.
  2 There is a travel agency in every city.
  3 Everyone does not respect anyone.
  4 Does anyone love no one?
  5 Everyone refuses to admire someone.
  6 Does anyone fail to understand anything?
  7 Whoever loves anyone, loves everyone.
  8 A man who fears everyone fears himself.
  9 Is everything pleasing to no one?
 10 Someone who admires no one is admired by no one.

24 DEDUCTIONS AGAIN

The method of deduction which we employed in the preceding chapter is adequate for handling problems in the broader area of general quantification with which we are now concerned. However, we must expand our explanation of the notion of an instance of a quantification. This is necessary in order to allow for the possibilities that arise with the use of capital letters followed by two or more variables.

    The general idea of an instance remains the same as before. An instance has to come from a sentence which, at its beginning, has a quantifier whose scope is all the rest of the sentence. And an instance is obtained from that sentence by dropping its initial quantifier and then putting in a certain name ("a," or "b," or "c," etc.) in place of every occurrence of the variable of quantification.

    Here are a few examples of instances of quantifications.

Quantification	Sample instances of it
$(x)(\exists y)Rxy$	$(\exists y)Ray$, $(\exists y)Rby$
$(x)Hxb$	Hab, Hbb, Hcb
$(\exists z)(x)(Hzx \supset Kxzx)$	$(x)(Hax \supset Kxax)$, $(x)(Hbx \supset Kxbx)$

The point is that the instance must be exactly like the original quantification except that the initial quantifier is dropped and a name now occurs at all places at least where the variable of quantification occurred in the quantification.

    Now let us see how the method of deduction works.

    In order to establish the validity of the argument "$(\exists x)(y)Cxy$, therefore $(y)(\exists x)Cxy$," we want to derive an obvious contradiction from the premises "$(\exists x)(y)Cxy$" and "$-(y)(\exists x)Cxy$." We are now in a position to do this. Let us draw up our work in the form of a deduction. We shall use our two quantificational rules and the quantificational equivalences from Chapter 4, and also the truth–functional principles from Chapter 3. Our deduction can go as follows.

1	(∃x)(y)Cxy	*Premise*
2	−(y)(∃x)Cxy	*Premise*
3	(y)Cay	*From 1 by E.I.*
4	(∃y)−(∃x)Cxy	*From 2 by Q.E.*
5	−(∃x)Cxb	*From 4 by E.I.*
6	Cab	*From 3 by U.I.*
7	(x)−Cxb	*From 5 by Q.E.*
8	−Cab	*From 7 by U.I.*
9	Cab & −Cab	*From 6, 8 by c.a.*

As another example, let us return to the medieval argument symbolized at the end of the preceding section. We now are able to demonstrate its validity by means of a deduction.

1	(x)(Cx ⊃ Fx)	*Premise*
2	−(x)[(∃y)(Cy & Dxy) ⊃ (∃y)(Fy & Dxy)]	*Premise*
3	(∃x)−[(∃y)(Cy & Dxy) ⊃ (∃y)(Fy & Dxy)]	*2, Q.E.*
4	−[(∃y)(Cy & Day) ⊃ (∃y)(Fy & Day)]	*3, E.I.*
5	(∃y)(Cy & Day) & −(∃y)(Fy & Day)	*4, T.F.E.*
6	(∃y)(Cy & Day)	*5, c.s.*
7	Cb & Dab	*6, E.I.*
8	−(∃y)(Fy & Day)	*5, c.s.*
9	(y)−(Fy & Day)	*8, Q.E.*
10	−(Fb & Dab)	*9, U.I.*
11	Cb ⊃ Fb	*1, U.I.*
12	Cb	*7, c.s.*
13	Fb	*11, 12, m.p.*
14	Dab	*7, c.s.*
15	Fb & Dab	*13, 14, c.a.*
16	(Fb & Dab) & −(Fb & Dab)	*15, 10, c.a.*

Looking back over this deduction, we see that the steps obey our rules and that the deduction establishes the validity of the original argument. It should be emphasized that there can also be other correct series of steps that could establish the desired result.

But you may wonder how the deduction was invented. The rules of deduction present the many kinds of steps that we *may* perform, but they do not tell us what we *must* do to finish the deduction; for that, some trial-and-error work will be needed. The aim in constructing the deduction is to reach a last line of the form "*p* & −*p*"; anything of that form will do. Now, if we are to obtain that sort of obvious contradiction here, it is likely that we shall need different instances, some of which contain the same names. (If we introduce a new name into each new instance, we are not likely to obtain any contradiction.) For this reason, it is wise, insofar as possible, to perform E.I. before we perform U.I. Doing so allows us to introduce into the U.I. instance the same name that previously we introduced into the E.I. instance, thus improving the chances of obtaining a contradiction. This is why in the earlier lines of the deduction we elect to deal first with premise 2, upon which we can perform E.I., rather than with premise 1, upon which we would have to perform U.I. Then in lines 10 and 11, when we finally perform U.I., we choose the previously used name "b," which seems to offer the most promise of yielding a contradiction.

In inventing these deductions, we may sometimes wonder what names to choose to put into our instances. When a deduction contains one or more different relations (capital letters followed by more than one variable at a time), we usually have to use two or more distinct names, in order to obtain our contradiction. But the best strategy is to use comparatively few names, and to choose them so as to maximize our chances of finding the contradiction.

As an example where the choice of names is momentarily puzzling, consider the argument "$(x)(y)Cxy$, therefore $(\exists x)(y)Cxy$." We start the deduction as follows.

1	$(x)(y)Cxy$	Premise
2	$-(\exists x)(y)Cxy$	Premise
3	$(x)-(y)Cxy$	2, Q.E.
4	$(x)(\exists y)-Cxy$	3, Q.E.
5	$(\exists y)-Cay$	4, U.I.
6	$-Cab$	5, E.I.

From this point, we might be inclined to continue as follows:

7	$(y)Cby$	1, U.I.
8	Cba	7, U.I.
9	$Cba \ \& \ -Cab$	6,8, c.a.

But this will not do. What we have reached is not a contradiction at all, and we have no way to go on from line 5 toward any contradiction. Bad strategy has been followed. We should go back and replace the last three lines by others, making a different selection of names.

7	$(y)Cay$	1, U.I.
8	Cab	7, U.I.
9	$Cab \ \& \ -Cab$	8,6, c.a.

In inventing deductions like these, we have to use trial and error, experimenting with various possibilities until we find a combination of steps that will yield the needed result.

As yet another example of strategy, let us consider how we would show that the sentence "There is something such that if something is physical then it is physical" is necessarily true. We may symbolize it "(∃x) [(∃y)Py ⊃ Px]". To show that it is necessarily true, we must derive a contradiction from its negation. We can start this way:

1 –(∃x) [(∃y)Py ⊃ Px]   Premise
2 (x)–[(∃y)Py ⊃ Px]   1, Q.E.
3 –[(∃y)Py ⊃ Pa]   2, U.I.
4 (∃y)Py & –Pa   3, T.F.E.
5 (∃y)Py   4, c.s.

At this point in the deduction we are prevented from reaching "Pa" as the next line, for that would violate the restriction. And here we cannot perform the existential instantiation first, because the existential quantifier is buried within the scope of the universal quantifier. (The rule of existential instantiation allows removal of an existential quantifier only when it stands at the beginning of the expression and governs the whole.) Here the problem of strategy is momentarily puzzling. The solution is to use another name and then go back and obtain a second instance from the universal quantification so as to produce a contradiction.

6 Pb   5, E.I.
7 –[(∃y)Py ⊃ Pb]   2, U.I.
8 (∃y)Py & –Pb   7, T.F.E.
9 –Pb   8, c.s.
10 Pb & –Pb   6,9, c.a.

Here the example at first looks like a very simple one, but it surprises us by requiring more strategy than we might have expected.

EXERCISE 24

*A Each of the following is a correct deduction; the first two lines are premises. Explain the justification for each line after the first two, and say what the deduction shows.

1. **1.** (x)(∃y)Hyxy
   2. (∃x)–(∃y)Hyxy
   3. –(∃y)Hyay
   4. (∃y)Hyay
   5. (∃y)Hyay & –(∃y)Hyay

2. **1.** (∃x)(∃w)Fxw
   2. (z)(w)–Fzw
   3. (∃w)Fbw
   4. (w)–Fbw
   5. –(∃w)Fbw
   6. (∃w)Fbw & –(∃w)Fbw

3. **1.** (∃z)(w)–Fwz
   2. (z)(∃w)Fwz
   3. (w)–Fwb
   4. (∃w)Fwb
   5. Fab
   6. –Fab
   7. Fab & –Fab

4. **1.** (∃y)–(x)Jxy
   2. (y)–(∃x)–Jxy
   3. –(x)Jxc
   4. (∃x)–Jxc
   5. –(∃x)–Jxc
   6. (∃x)–Jxc & –(∃x)–Jxc

5. **1.** $-(\exists x)(\exists z)-Hxz$
  2. $(\exists x)(z)-Hxz$
  3. $(z)-Hbz$
  4. $(x)-(\exists z)-Hxz$
  5. $-(\exists z)-Hbz$
  6. $(z)--Hbz$
  7. $-Hba$
  8. $-(-Hba)$
  9. $-Hba$ & $--Hba$

6. **1.** $(y)(z)Kyz$
  2. $-(y)(\exists z)Kyz$
  3. $(\exists y)-(\exists z)Kyz$
  4. $-(\exists z)Kaz$
  5. $(z)-Kaz$
  6. $-Kab$
  7. $(z)Kaz$
  8. Kab
  9. Kab & $-Kab$

B   Use quantificational deductions to establish the answers to these questions.

 1 Is "Everything influences itself, and nothing influences anything" a contradiction?

 2 Is "Not everything attracts something, and everything attracts everything" a contradiction?

 3 Does "Everyone loves someone or other" imply "Someone loves someone"?

 4 Does "Everything repels something or other" follow from "Everything repels everything"?

 5 Does "Someone admires someone" follow from "Everyone is a self-admirer"?

 6 Is "If everything affects everything, then there is something that affects each thing" necessarily true?

 7 Is "If no one hates anyone, then not everyone is a self-hater" necessarily true?

 8 Is "Either someone admires someone or no one admires anyone" necessarily true?

 9 Is "There is something which everything affects" equivalent to "It's not the case that for each thing there is something or other such that the latter doesn't affect the former"?

 10 Is "Whenever something influences something, it changes it" equivalent to "It's not the case that something influences something but the former doesn't change the latter"?

C   In each case construct a quantificational deduction to show that the reasoning is valid. Also do the same for each argument in Exercise 23, part D.

 1 No person who's a girl is prettier than everyone, because no girl is prettier than herself.

 2 A king reigns over Sweden. Sweden is a democracy. So some kings reign over democracies.

 3 No sincere person engages in self-deception. Therefore, anyone who deceives everyone is not sincere.

 4 Any person who eats people is a cannibal. Englishmen are people. So any person who eats Englishmen is a cannibal.

 5 Every eruption is preceded by a tremor. Some eruptions are not preceded by earthquakes. So some tremors aren't earthquakes.

 6 All the music that Bach wrote is baroque music. So whoever enjoys any music that Bach wrote enjoys some baroque music.

 7 No country adjoins every country. So, if each country trades only with countries it adjoins, some countries do not trade together.

8 Infinity is larger than any countable number. No number is larger than itself. So infinity is not a countable number.

9 There is a subject that is liked by any student who likes any subject at all. Every student likes some subject or other. Therefore, there is a subject liked by all students.

10 The regulations of a certain ship require that any barber aboard that ship is to shave all and only those aboard the ship who do not shave themselves. So (according to these regulations) there is to be no barber aboard the ship.

D Show by quantificational deduction that each set is inconsistent.

1 $(\exists x)-(\exists y)Gxy;\ -(\exists x)(y)-Gxy$

2 $(\exists x)(y)-Fxy;\ (x)(\exists y)Fxy$

3 $(z)-(x)-Kzx;\ (\exists z)(x)-Kzx$

4 $(x)[Fx \supset (\exists y)Gxy];\ (\exists x)[Fx\ \&\ (y)-Gxy]$

5 $(\exists y)[Fy\ \&\ -(\exists w)Hyw];\ (x)(y)\{(Fx \lor Gy) \supset [(\exists z)Hxz\ \&\ (\exists w)Hyw]\}$

6 $(\exists x)[Kx\ \&\ -(\exists y)Fxy];\ (x)(\exists y)[Kx \supset Fxy]$

7 $-(\exists y)Hyyy;\ (\exists y)(x)(w)Hyxw$

8 $(\exists x)[Gx\ \&\ (z)Hzx];\ (x)(Gx \supset Kx);\ -(\exists w)(Kw\ \&\ Hww)$

9 $(x)(y)(Gxy \supset Fyx);\ (\exists x)[Jx\ \&\ (y)Gyx];\ -(\exists x)(y)Fxy$

10 $(\exists x)[Hx\ \&\ (z)-Gxz];\ (y)[Hx \equiv (\exists z)Gyz]$

25 NEGATIVE DEMONSTRATIONS

The method of quantificational deduction that we have been using is basically a method for showing that a quantificational sentence is a contradiction, or that a set of quantificational sentences are inconsistent. We have been using the method to establish the validity of valid quantificational arguments and to establish quantificational implications, equivalences, and necessary truths.

But can this method be used to demonstrate that a quantificational sentence is *not* a contradiction? Can it be used to show that an argument is *not* valid, or that a pair of sentences are *not* equivalent?

Notice that when we fail to discover a quantificational deduction showing a given sentence to be a contradiction, this does not necessarily mean that the sentence is *not* a contradiction. Perhaps we have not been ingenious enough. Of course, if we try hard and carefully to find such a deduction and do not succeed, this should make us *suspect* that perhaps the sentence we are working with is not a contradiction. But our failure to find a deduction is not a *proof* of anything, one way or the other. Our method of quantificational deduction simply does not provide a general way of demonstrating the negative fact that a quantificational sentence is not a contradiction. As a result, we so far have no general way of proving that one sentence does not imply another, or is not equivalent to another, etc.

Consider the sentence "There is something that is a unicorn only if it is herbivorous, and all unicorns are nonherbivorous." It may be symbolized "$(\exists x)(Ux \supset Hx)\ \&\ (x)(Ux \supset -Hx)$." Suppose we want to learn whether it is a contradiction. If we try to use our method of deduction, we find that even after working long and hard we do not deduce a truth-functional contradiction. But this lack of success means merely that we have established nothing. Can we show more definitely that the sentence is not a contradiction?

If a sentence of the form "(∃x)(Ux ⊃ Hx) & (x)(Ux ⊃ –Hx)" is not a contradiction, this means that some sentences of this form are true. If we find at least one sentence of this form that is definitely true, we shall thereby demonstrate that our original sentence is not a contradiction on account of having this quantificational form.[26]

Let us try then to discover a sentence of this same form that is very clearly true. This can best be done if we seek a sentence dealing with things concerning which very clear and definite assertions can be made. Numbers are probably the best subject matter for this purpose. Let us see whether we can discover a way of reinterpreting the letters "U" and "H" so that "(∃x)(Ux ⊃ Hx) & (x)(Ux ⊃ –Hx)" becomes a true sentence about numbers. Let us reinterpret "U" to mean "odd" and "H" to mean "even," and limit our universe of discourse to numbers. Under this reinterpretation, "(∃x)(Ux ⊃ Hx) & (x)(Ux ⊃ –Hx)" turns into the sentence "There is at least one number such that if it is odd then it is even, and every number is such that if it is odd then it is not even." This sentence is a conjunction, and its first component is definitely true since there is at least one number, for instance 2, such that if it is odd then it is even. (Remember that this is the truth-functional sense of "if-then.") The second component of the conjunction is definitely true too, since no odd numbers are even. Thus the sentence as a whole is definitely true. This shows that our original sentence is not a contradiction (at least, not on account of its quantificational form).

So far, we have discussed a procedure for showing that a quantificational sentence is not a contradiction. This same procedure can be employed to show that an argument is not valid in virtue of its quantificational form. For example, suppose the question is whether the argument "Everything attracts something; therefore something is attracted by everything," symbolized as "(x)(∃y)Axy, therefore (∃y)(x)Axy," is valid. We can show that it is an invalid argument if a reinterpretation of "A" can turn the premise into a definitely true sentence and turn the conclusion into a definitely false one.

To do this, let us again talk about numbers, limiting our universe of discourse to numbers. Let us reinterpret "A" to mean "is smaller than." Then "(x)(∃y)Axy" comes to mean "Each number is smaller than some number," while "(∃y)(x)Axy" becomes "There is a number than which every number is smaller." The former sentence is definitely true, whereas the latter is definitely false. This shows the invalidity of the original argument; or, to speak more precisely, it shows that the original argument is not valid on account of its quantificational form.

Finally, we shall note one further sort of negative result that can be established by this procedure of reinterpreting quantificational sentences. Suppose the question now is whether two quantificational sentences are equivalent. Consider, for example, the sentences:

If something is not for the best, then Leibniz's philosophy is mistaken.

Something is such that if it is not for the best, then Leibniz's philosophy is mistaken.

Writing "B" for "is for the best" and "L" for the sentence "Leibniz's philosophy is mistaken," we can symbolize these:

(∃x)–Bx ⊃ L
(∃x)(–Bx ⊃ L)

Perhaps we would start by trying to demonstrate that the two sentences are equivalent. To say that two sentences are equivalent is to say that they are necessarily alike as regards truth and falsity. This means that each must validly follow from the other. We could attempt to construct two deductions, one showing that the first sentence validly follows from the second, and another showing that the second sentence validly follows from the first. In this case, however, we would not be able to complete both deductions. Encountering difficulty, we could change our approach and seek to show instead that the two sentences are not equivalent. How can we do this?

One way of showing that they are not equivalent is to reinterpret the letters "B" and "L" so that we obtain two new sentences having the very same forms but definitely differing as regards truth and falsity. In doing this, let us again work with numbers. Reinterpret "B" to mean "is even" and reinterpret "L" to mean "2 is smaller than 1." Then we obtain two new sentences:

If something is not an even number, then 2 is smaller than 1.

Something is such that if it is not an even number, then 2 is smaller than 1.

The first sentence is definitely false, because it is a conditional with true antecedent and false consequent. The second sentence is definitely true, because there is at least one thing, say the number 4, such that if it is not an even number then 2 is smaller than 1. (Here again we recall the truth-functional sense of "if-then.") Thus we have found two sentences definitely different as regards truth and falsity but having the very same forms as the original two sentences. This shows that our original two sentences are not equivalent; or, to put the point more guardedly, it shows that they are not equivalent in virtue of their quantificational form.

EXERCISE 25

*A Use the method of this section to show that sentences of the following forms are not contradictions on account of their forms.

1 (x)(Gx ⊃ Hx)
2 (y)(Hy ⊃ –Hy)
3 P ⊃ –P
4 (∃x)Gx & (∃y)–Gy

5 (∃y)(Gy & Hy) & (∃y)(Gy & –Hy)
6 (∃x)(Fx ⊃ –Fx)
7 P ⊃ (Fa & –Fa)
8 (∃y)(∃z)Kyz & (∃y)(∃z)–Kyz
9 (∃x)(Fx ⊃ P) ≡[(∃x)Fx ⊃ P]
10 (x)Fxx & –(∃z)(x)Fxz
11 (y)(∃z)Gyz & –(∃z)(y)Gyz
12 (∃x)(∃y)Fxy & –(x)(∃y)Fxy

B   Show that arguments of the following forms are not valid on account of their forms.

1 (x)Gx ⊃ (∃z)Gz; therefore Fa ⊃ (∃y)Gy
2 (z)Hz ⊃ Ja; therefore (z)(Hz ⊃ Ja)
3 (y)[(Hy & Jy) ⊃ Ky]; therefore (z) [(Hz v Jz) ⊃ Kz]
4 (x)Gx ⊃ (∃z)Fz; therefore (z)[Gz ⊃ (∃x)Fx]
5 (∃y)[(Ky v Jy) ⊃ P]; therefore (∃y)(Ky v Jy) ⊃ P
6 (y)(Fy ⊃ Gy) & (z)(Fz ⊃ Hz); therefore (∃x)(Gx & Hz)
7 (∃z)(∃y)Fyz; therefore (z)(y)Fyz
8 (y)(∃z)Fyz; therefore (∃z)(y)Fyz
9 (x)(y)(∃z)Fxzy; therefore –(x)(y)(z)Fxzy
10 (z)[Fz ⊃ (∃x)Gzx]; therefore (∃y)[Fy & (x)Gyx]
11 (y)–Gyy; therefore (y)(z)(w)[(Gyz & Gzw) ⊃ Gyw]
12 (x)(y)(z)[(Gxy & Gyz) ⊃ Gxz]; therefore (x)–Gxx

C   Show that each statement is correct.

1 Sentences of the forms "(x)(∃y)Fxy" and "(x)(∃y)–Fxy" do not make an inconsistent set.
2 Sentences of the forms "(∃y)(z)Fzy" and "(∃y)–(z)Fzy" do not make an inconsistent set.
3 Sentences of the forms "(y)(z)Hyz" and "(y)(z)–Hyz" are not contradictories of each other.
4 Sentences of the form "(∃z)(w)Fzw v (∃z)(w)–Fzw" are not necessarily true.
5 Sentences of the form "(x)[(∃y)Fxy v (∃y)Fyx]" are not necessarily true.
6 Sentences of the forms "(y)(z)(Fy ⊃ Gyz)" and "(y)(z)(Fy ⊃ Gzy)" are not equivalent.
7 Sentences of the forms "–(y)(∃z)Hyz" and "(y)(∃z)–Hyz" are not equivalent.
8 Even if each thing has a purpose, it does not follow that there is a purpose which all things have.
9 Even if each trail reaches some places, it does not follow that each place is reached by some trail or other.
10 It is not necessarily true that either some viruses attack every organism or some organisms are attacked by every virus.
11 It is not inconsistent to say that something physical influences nothing, but that everything physical is influenced by something.
12 Even if everyone prefers some persons to some persons, it does not follow that there is anyone whom everyone prefers to everyone.

D   For each argument, show that it is valid or show that it is invalid.

1 Any miracle is a violation of some natural law. Anything that is violated is not a natural law. So there are no miracles.

2 Any railway unit that carries a payload is propelled by something. A railway unit is a locomotive if and only if it propels itself and does not carry a payload. Therefore, every railway unit that carries a payload is propelled by a locomotive.

3 A woman who envies everyone is not liked by anyone. Hence, if a woman likes herself, there is someone whom she does not envy.

4 No Hondas are German cars. Therefore, no one who owns a Honda owns a German car.

5 The guards have been careless if there was a checkpoint which was unattended at all times or if there were some times at which all checkpoints were unattended. So if all checkpoints were unattended at all times, the guards have been careless.

6 Some vampires aren't werewolves. So anything that protects us against all vampires won't protect us against all werewolves.

7 Among the Yahoos, if A admires B, B never admires A. Therefore, among them, no one is a self-admirer.

8 Anyone who has seen all Bill's friends admires some of them. Joan doesn't admire any friends of Bill's. So some friends of Bill's haven't seen Joan.

26 IDENTITY AND ITS LAWS

Earlier in this chapter we saw how relations can be symbolized using capital letters, and how our method of quantificational deduction can be used to establish the validity of arguments involving relations. Now we shall consider one specific relation that is of special importance to logic, the relation of identity.

Think of the sentences "Boise is the capital of Idaho," "12 is the sum of 5 and 7," and "Firenza is Florence." Each of these sentences says that something is identical with something. But what is it to say this? What, for instance, does it mean to say that Boise is the capital of Idaho? It does not mean merely that Boise and the capital of Idaho are alike in some respect, or equivalent in some respect. No, it means more than that; it means that they are one and the same. It says they are identical in the strong sense that Boise is the very same individual city as the capital of Idaho. It tells us that if one mentions Boise and also mentions the capital of Idaho then one has mentioned only one city, not two. (Identical twins are not identical in this strong sense, for a pair of identical twins, despite their close similarity, are two separate individuals, not one.)

In English we use forms of the verb "to be," especially "is," to express identity in this strong sense. However, this is by no means the only job that the word "is" (and other forms of "to be") has to do. More frequently the word "is" is used for *predication*, as when we say "Bread is starchy," or "Algebra is difficult." Here a property is attributed to (or "predicated of") something, but the relation of identity is not involved.

In logic it is customary to use the equals sign from mathematics to express identity. Thus, we can write "Boise = the capital of Idaho," "12 = the sum of 5 and 7," and "Firenza = Florence." Letting "b" be short for "Boise" and letting "c" be short for "the capital of Idaho," we can abbreviate the first of these as "b = c."

Moreover, we can also use variables along with identity, and this will enable us to express certain kinds of general statements. For instance, limiting our universe of discourse to persons and letting "P" be short for "is a parent of," we can write,

$(x)(y)[Pxy \supset -(x = y)]$ (1)
$(x)(\exists y)[Pyx \ \& \ -(x = y)]$ (2)
$(x)(\exists y)(\exists z)[(Pyx \ \& \ Pzx) \ \& \ -(y = z)]$ (3)
$(\exists x)(y)(z)[(Pyx \ \& \ Pzx) \supset z = y]$ (4)
$(\exists x)(\exists y)[Pxy \ \& \ (z)(Pxz \supset z = y)]$ (5)

Here sentence (1) says that whenever someone is a parent of someone, they are not identical; in other words, no one is his or her own parent. Sentence (2) says that everyone has at least one parent not identical to himself or herself. Sentence (3) says that everyone has at least two parents. Sentence (4) says that someone is such that any parents of his or hers are identical; in other words, someone has at most one parent. Sentence (5) says that someone is a parent of someone and that anyone of whom the former is a parent is identical to the latter; in other words, someone has one and only one offspring.

As these examples illustrate, use of identity enables us to formulate many sentences concerning whether things being spoken of are identical or distinct. Moreover, it enables us to formulate sentences about the existence of at most one thing, exactly one, at least two, at most two, exactly two, and so on.

Now that we have a symbol for identity, we are able to symbolize some sentences using only symbols of logic (that is, not using any letters such as "F" or "a," which will need to be interpreted before they can enter into true-or-false sentences). Among such sentences there are some that are necessary truths just because of what the identity sign means. Here are a few of them.

$(x)(x = x)$ (1)
$(x)(y)(x = y \supset y = x)$ (2)
$(x)(y)(z)[(x = y \ \& \ y = z) \supset x = z]$ (3)

Sentence (1) says that each thing is identical to itself. Sentence (2) says that the relation of identity is symmetrical: whenever it holds in one direction, it holds also in the reverse direction. Sentence (3) says that identity is a transitive relation; whenever it holds between a first thing and a second, and between the second and a third, it holds also between the first and the third.

We also can use our symbolism to pick out an important family of necessary truths involving identity. The sentences of this family all have the general form:

$(x)(y)[(Fx \ \& \ x = y) \supset Fy]$ (4)

Here (4) is not a sentence, because we have not yet assigned any meaning to the letter "F" in it. But the point is that whatever meaning we do assign to the letter "F" in (4), we shall obtain a truth.[27] Thus expression (4) yields us a whole family of necessary truths—all those that can be obtained by interpreting (4).[28] Among these would be included, for example,

$(x)(y)[(x$ is physical $\& x = y) \supset y$ is physical]
$(x)(y)[(x$ is human $\& x = y) \supset y$ is human]
$(x)(y)[(x$ likes $x \& x = y) \supset y$ likes $y]$
$(x)(y)[(x$ likes $x \& x = y) \supset y$ likes $x]$
$(x)(y)[(x = x \& x = y) \supset y = x]$

Notice that in our last three examples here we have more than one occurrence of "x" in the part of the sentence which corresponds to "Fx" in (4). This is permissible. The point is that the phrase that we interpret "Fx" as being short for must be exactly like the phrase that we interpret "Fy" as being short for, except that the former contains "x" at some or all the places where the latter contains "y."

Our method of quantificational deduction, by itself, is not able to establish the necessary truth of identity sentences such as those we have just been considering. In order to use our method of deduction for solving problems involving identity, we have to expand it by adding some further logical laws dealing with identity. Two laws will be enough for our purposes. The first of them is closely akin to (1), and involves the idea that each thing is identical to itself. The second is closely akin to (4), and involves the idea that when a first thing is identical to a second, whatever is true of the first must also be true of the second.

First Law of Identity (I–1)

Sentences of the form "$a = a$" are necessarily true. Here any other name may be substituted for "a." Examples: "$b = b$," "$c = c$."

Second Law of Identity (I–2)

Sentences of the form "$(Fa \& a = b) \supset Fb$" are necessarily true. Here other names may be substituted for "a" and "b". Moreover, in place of "F" may be substituted any meaningful expression. Examples (let "F" mean "is French" and "G" mean "is German"):

$(Fb \& b = c) \supset Fc$
$(Ga \& a = b) \supset Gb$
$[(Fa \lor Ga) \& a = b] \supset (Fb \lor Gb)$
$(b = a \& b = c) \supset c = a$
$(a = a \& a = b) \supset b = a$

How do these examples, especially those for the second law, come from the laws? Some further explanation is needed of what counts as *substitution*.

This is not difficult to explain with the first law. If we are substituting another name for "*a*" in the first law, the new name must appear in the sentence we are obtaining at *both* the places where "*a*" appeared in the law, not just at one of them. Thus it would be a mistake to think that we could derive "*a* = *b*" from the first law by replacing "*a*" by "*b*" just on the right-hand side of the identity sign.

With the second law, we must similarly take care to make substitutions for "*a*" and "*b*" only in a uniform way. In our first example of the second law, "*b*" replaces "*a*" throughout, and "*c*" replaces "*b*." In the fourth example, "*b*" replaces "*a*," "*c*" replaces "*b*," and "*a*" replaces "*c*."

Moreover, with the second law, we must see to it that we substitute for "*F*" in the same way at both places where it occurs. This substitution must be made in such a way that the new part corresponding to "*Fa*" shall be just the same as the new part corresponding to "*Fb*," except for containing the name corresponding to "*a*" at some or all places where the latter contains the name corresponding to "*b*."

Notice that in the last of our examples of the second law, the part corresponding to "*Fb*" in the law contains the variable corresponding to "*b*" (here it happens to be "*b*" itself) only at some and not at all the places where the part corresponding to "*Fa*" contains the variable corresponding to "*a*" (here this happens to be "*a*" itself). This is all right; the sentence says that if being-identical-to-a characterizes a, and if a is the very same thing as b, then being-identical-to-a will characterize b.

Now let us see how to use these two laws of identity in deductions. Suppose that we want to show by deduction that "*a* = *b*" implies "*b* = *a*." Our deduction can look like this:

1	$a = b$	P
2	$-(b = a)$	P
3	$(a = a \ \& \ a = b) \supset b = a$	I-2
4	$a = a$	I-1
5	$a = a \ \& \ a = b$	TF
6	$b = a$	TF
7	$b = a \ \& \ -(b = a)$	TF

To show that our first sentence implies the second, we show that the first together with the negation of the second yields a contradiction of the form "*p* & –*p*". Our third and fourth lines are instances of the laws of identity. The remaining steps are truth-functional (for simplicity, we now group together all truth-functional moves under the justification "TF").

EXERCISE 26

    A Symbolize each sentence, and tell what you mean by the letters you use. Your formulation should make clear whether you are interpreting the sentence as an identity sentence or as a predicative sentence.

    1 Beijing is Peking.
    2 Mohammed is The Prophet.
    3 Coffee is addictive.
    4 Cicero is Tully.
    5 Gold is valuable.
    6 Venus is the evening star.
    7 Socrates is the teacher of Plato.
    8 Socrates is a wise man.
    9 The product of 3 and 7 is 21.
    10 The square root of 2 is an irrational number.

B Translate each formula into English. Let "L" mean "loves," let "W" mean "is a woman," let "d" name "Darby," and let "j" name "Joan." Limit the universe to persons.

    1 $(x)(Ldx \supset x = j)$
    2 $(x)[-(x = d) \supset -Ljx]$
    3 $Ldj \& (x)(Lxj \supset x = d)$
    4 $Ljd \& (x)(Lxd \supset x = j)$
    5 $(x)[(Wx \& Ldx) \supset x = j]$
    6 $(\exists x)[(Wx \& Lxj) \& -(x = j)]$
    7 $(\exists x)[Lxd \& (y)(Lyd \supset y = x)]$
    8 $(x)[(Wx \& (\exists y)Lxy) \supset x = j]$
    9 $(x)[(Wx \& (y)Lxy) \supset -(x = j)]$
    10 $(x)(y)\{[(Wx \& Wy) \& (Ldx \& Ldy)] \supset x = y\}$

C Symbolize, using the same letters as in the previous part.

    1 Darby and Joan are two distinct persons.
    2 At least one person loves Darby.
    3 Joan loves at most one person.
    4 Exactly one person loves Darby.
    5 More than one person loves Joan.
    6 Darby loves Joan but no one else.
    7 Joan loves herself and at least one other person.
    8 Some persons love no one other than themselves.
    9 Some persons love everyone other than themselves.
    10 Exactly two persons love Joan.

D Show by deduction that each statement is correct.

    1 "$(y)(y = y)$" is true.
    2 "$(\exists z)(z = z)$" is true.
    3 "$(x)(y)(x = y \supset y = x)$" is true.
    4 "$(x)[(\exists y)(y = y) \supset x = x]$" is true.
    5 Any sentence of the form "$(x)(Fx \supset x = x)$" is true.
    6 Any sentence of the form "$(z)[-(z = z) \supset Fz]$" is true.
    7 "Fa, therefore $(\exists x)(Fx \& x = a)$" is valid.
    8 "$a = b \& b = c$, therefore $a = c$" is valid.
    9 Any sentence of the form "$Fa \& a = b$" implies the corresponding sentence of the form "Fb."
    10 Any argument of the form "$(\exists y)(\exists z)[(Fdy \& Fdz) \& -(y = z)]$, therefore $(\exists w)Fdw$" is valid.

6

CHAPTER

FALLACIES

If we want to become more skillful at playing chess, or football, or any other game, it is a good idea to study not only the shrewd moves that experts make, but also the poor moves that less experienced players make—we can learn from their mistakes. Similarly, as we try to improve our ability to reason logically, we should not confine our attention to specimens of good reasoning; we should also consider plenty of tempting examples of bad reasoning. By becoming more aware of how these bad arguments are bad, we strengthen our ability to distinguish between good and bad reasoning.

27 INCONSISTENCY, *PETITIO,* AND THE PURE *NON SEQUITUR*

In ordinary talk the term "fallacy" is often loosely applied to any sort of mistaken belief or untrue sentence. "It's a fallacy to believe that handling a toad causes warts," people say. Here the thing being called a fallacy is just a belief, not a piece of reasoning. But in logic the term "fallacy" is restricted to mistakes in reasoning: a *fallacy* is a logical mistake in reasoning, especially one that it is tempting to make. There is a logical fallacy only when there are premises and a conclusion which is erroneously thought to be proved by them.

Many types of fallacies have been given special names, especially those types that are rather tempting and likely to deceive people. The great advantage of having a name for something is that it enables us to keep the thing clearly in mind so that we can recognize it when we meet it. In this sense, knowing the name gives us a sort of power over the thing. By learning the names of some of the main kinds of fallacies and by having a general scheme for classifying them, we shall be able to recognize fallacies more readily and think more clearly about them.

At the same time, however, we should recognize that names for fallacies can easily be misused. When they are misused, they become very destructive weapons in debate. Suppose you accuse your opponent of "*ad hominem* reasoning," of "begging the question," or the like; your opponent probably will feel quite intimidated, and the audience will be impressed by your effectiveness as a debater—especially if they do not know what these phrases really mean. If you yourself do not understand what you are saying either, then you are really blowing the debate off the rails in a most harmful way.

Unfortunately, it takes quite a lot of good judgment to apply the terminology of fallacies responsibly and wisely. This is a part of logic where maturity and understanding are especially needed, if the logical apparatus is not to do more harm than good. So here we must take special care to avoid glib superficiality and be sure we are understanding the reasoning we try to appraise.

Classification of Fallacies

In order to have a definite scheme in which to think about fallacies, we shall classify them in terms of the headings shown in the following table. The table presents some of the traditional terminology for fallacies, but in reorganized form. This classification covers fallacies in both deductive and inductive reasoning, although for the present we shall limit our examples to deductive fallacies.

In thinking about the classification of fallacies, let us recall that the purpose of constructing arguments is to establish conclusions that are in some way unknown or doubtful, or that have been challenged or called into question. In order that a speaker's argument should have a chance of establishing its conclusion, its premises must have the following three features. (1) They must be logically capable of all being true together—if they are not, then no one should be convinced by the argument. (2) They must be such that those to whom the argument is addressed can know them to be true without being aware of whether the conclusion is true—if this is not so, then those whom the argument is supposed to convince should not be convinced by it. (3) They must support the conclusion to the required degree—with deductive arguments the premises must strictly guarantee the conclusion. These three necessary conditions for a successful argument give rise to three separate categories of fallacies, each category involving the neglect of a different condition.

Neglect of the third requirement gives rise to the fallacies of *non sequitur* (Latin: "it does not follow"). These fallacious arguments are fallacies in the

Classification of Fallacies

General type			Some specific forms
Inconsistency			. . .
Petitio principii			Fallacy of complex question . . .
Non sequitur	Pure fallacies	Formal fallacies in deduction	Undistributed middle Illicit process Affirming the consequent Denying the antecedent . . .
		Pure inductive fallacies	Forgetful induction Hasty induction Slothful induction . . .
	Fallacies of ambiguity	Equivocation	Fallacy of four terms Composition, division . . . . . .
		Amphiboly	. . .

	Fallacies of irrelevance (ignoratio elenchi)		ad hominem abusive
			                   circumstantial
			                   tu quoque
			ad baculum
			ad verecundiam
			ad misericordiam
			black-and-white thinking
			. . .

most obvious sense of the term, for their logical defect is that they have an insufficient link between premises and conclusion.

Neglect of the second requirement gives rise to reasoning that is fallacious in a more subtle sense. If the premises are related to the conclusion in such an intimate way that the speaker and listeners could not have less reason to doubt the premises than they have to doubt the conclusion, then the argument is worthless as a proof, even though the link between premises and conclusion may have the most cast-iron rigor. Fallacies of this second category are called fallacies of *petitio principii* (Latin: "begging of the question").

Finally, neglect of the first requirement gives rise to the remaining category of fallacies. If someone uses as premises sentences that are logically related in such a way that they necessarily could not all be true at once, then such reasoning certainly cannot establish the conclusion, even though the link between premises and conclusion is as rigorous as can be. Someone who reasons from such a set of premises is committing a fallacy of *inconsistency*.

Using our scheme for classifying fallacies, we shall have to keep in mind that sometimes a fallacious argument may allow of being interpreted in more than one way so that its fallacy can be classified in more than one way. Perhaps when interpreted in one fashion it commits one fallacy, while under some other legitimate interpretation it would be regarded as committing some different fallacy. (We shall meet examples of this sort presently.) But every fallacious argument should admit of being classified in at least one place in our scheme. Also we should note that an argument may fall under some general heading without being an example of any specifically named form of fallacy under that heading; the dots at various places in the table indicate where there are further specific types of fallacies, many of them without special names.

Although we have been concentrating so far on deductive reasoning, it should be noted that inductive reasoning can be subject to fallacies of inconsistency, of begging the question, of ambiguity, and of irrelevance, just as deductive reasoning can. Only with regard to the pure fallacies do we need to treat induction and deduction separately, as we shall see.

Inconsistency

Suppose someone reasons in the following way: "Franklin is 20 miles due north of Jefferson. There is a straight road that starts at Franklin and goes through Adamston to Sperryville. Jefferson is 20 miles due west of Adamston. Sperryville is northeast of Adamston. Therefore, Jefferson is nearer to Adamston than to Sperryville."

Something is wrong with this argument, even though the speaker may not have noticed it. The trouble here is not that there is any insufficiency about the link between premises and conclusion; instead, the trouble is with the premises themselves. They cannot all be true. Now, to use premises that are not all true is always a mistake, but it is not always a logical mistake. In this case, however, the premises do not merely happen to be not all true; they necessarily cannot all be true, and so we may say that here a logical error is being committed and thus a fallacy is occurring. In this example, one can see that something is logically wrong if one notices that the stated premises imply pairs of consequences that are contradictories; for example, they imply both "Sperryville is southeast of Adamston" and "Sperryville is not southeast of Adamston." Thus one would be committing oneself to inconsistency if one accepted all four of these premises. To use this argument is to commit a logical error, a fallacy of inconsistency. And in general, anyone commits a fallacy of inconsistency who reasons from premises that necessarily could not all be true.

Sometimes inconsistency in the premises of an argument is brought about by the logical forms of the premises. For example, if you have one premise of the form "p" and another of the form "$-p$," you have a formal inconsistency; if you have one premise of the form "p & q" and another of the form "$p \equiv -q$," again you have a formal inconsistency; and so on. However, not all inconsistency results merely from logical form. In the geographical example of the first paragraph, the mere logical forms of the premises do not give rise to an inconsistency; the inconsistency results from the special meanings of particular nonlogical words ("straight," "north," "west," etc.) occurring as they do in the premises.

Usually it is a clear-cut matter whether the premises of an argument are inconsistent on account of their logical form. But in less formal cases the matter sometimes is far from clear-cut. Suppose someone argues that abortion is wrong because it violates the respect that we owe to life; while at the same time this speaker also argues that capital punishment is permissible, because the guilty deserve to pay for their crimes. Is such a person being inconsistent? An opponent might say that this position is inconsistent, urging that if respect for life prohibits abortion, then it must prohibit capital punishment as well. But is the first speaker being inconsistent? That depends on whether there is any sound distinction between abortion and capital punishment, from the point of view of respect for life. Perhaps a distinction should be drawn: perhaps respect for life means respect for *innocent* life, not for *guilty* life, so that abortion is very different from capital punishment, and there is no inconsistency. There is no cut-and-dried way of settling which side is correct in a controversy such as this. In thinking the matter through, we have to weigh the considerations on each side and reach our own best judgment about whether there is inconsistency or not.

Should we say that arguments are invalid when their premises are inconsistent? No, for the following reason. If the premises form an inconsistent set, this means either that one premise is the negation of another or that there is some consequence which follows from the premises but whose negation also follows from them. So either among the premises or implied by them, we have two sentences of the forms "p" and "$-p$." If we have both "p" and "$-p$," what else can be deduced? Consider the following deduction.

1	p	Premise
2	$-p$	Premise
3	$p \lor q$	From 1, by disjunctive addition
4	q	From 2, 3 by disjunctive argument

Here each step is strictly legitimate, according to our principles of truth-functional deduction. The conclusion "q" can be any new sentence we please. And what this deduction illustrates is that *any* sentence deductively follows from a pair of contradictory sentences. Thus, if we have both "*p*" and "*–p*" either among our premises or implied by them, any conclusion whatsoever validly follows. Thus arguments which commit the fallacy of inconsistency at any rate have the virtue of being valid—although this is not enough to make them good arguments.

The Petitio Principii

An argument is called a *petitio principii* (or begging of the question) if the argument fails to prove anything because it somehow takes for granted what it is supposed to prove. Suppose a man says "Jones is insane, you know," and we reply "Really? Are you sure?" and he responds, "Certainly, I can prove it. Jones is demented; therefore he is insane." This is a valid argument in the sense that if the premise is true, the conclusion must be true too; but the argument is unsatisfactory, for it does not really prove anything. The premise is merely another statement of the conclusion, so that practically anyone who doubts the truth of the conclusion ought to be equally doubtful about the truth of the premise, and the argument is useless for the purpose of convincing us of the truth of the conclusion.[29] Thus the argument takes for granted just what it is supposed to prove; it begs the question.

Consider a longer chain of reasoning:

"We must not drink liquor."
"Why do you say that?"
"Drinking is against the will of Allah."
"How do you know?" "The Koran says so."
"But how do you know that the Koran is right?"
"Everything said in the Koran is right."
"How do you know that?"
"Why, it's all divinely inspired."
"But how do you know that?"
"Why, the Koran itself declares that it is divinely inspired."
"But why believe that?"
"You've got to believe the Koran, because everything in the Koran is right."

This chain of reasoning is a more extended case of begging the question; the speaker is reasoning in a large circle, taking for granted one of the things that is supposed to be proved.[30]

One specific form of *petitio principii*, or begging of the question, has a special name of its own: the fallacy of *complex question*. This is the fallacy of framing a question so as to take for granted something controversial that ought to be proved.

Suppose Mr. White is trying to prove that Mr. Green has a bad character, and White asks Green the famous question "Have you stopped beating your wife yet?" If Green answers "Yes" to this question, White will argue that Green is admitting to having been a wife-beater; if he answers "No," then White will argue that Green is admitting to still being a wife-beater. The questioner has framed his question in such a way as to take for granted that Green has a wife whom he has been beating. The fallacy is that this is a controversial proposition that is at least as doubtful as is the conclusion (that Green has a bad character) supposedly being established. It is not proper in this debate to take for granted this controversial proposition; it needs to be proved if White is to make use of it at all.

However, it would also be legitimate to regard the fallacy of complex question as a kind of fallacy of ambiguity. In the example we could say that the answer no is ambiguous, for it could mean either "No, I'm still beating my wife" or "No, I haven't stopped because I never started." We shall consider fallacies of ambiguity in the next section.

The Non Sequitur: Pure Fallacies

We call an argument a *non sequitur* if its conclusion does not follow from its premises. The fallacies of *non sequitur* form the largest category, which we shall subdivide into three types. First we shall consider what, for want of a better name, we shall call *pure* fallacies. These are *non sequitur* fallacies in which the source of the error is purely some misunderstanding of specific logical principles themselves. The principles of deductive reasoning are distinctly different from those of inductive reasoning. Therefore, in treating this type of fallacy, we need to classify the deductive and the inductive cases separately; this is not necessary with regard to the other sorts of fallacy. For the present, we shall not discuss the inductive cases of pure fallacies but shall focus our attention upon the deductive cases.

The specific logical principles with which deductive logic deals are principles that have to do with the logical forms of sentences. Therefore, pure fallacies in deduction are *formal* fallacies. That is, they are *non sequiturs* because of defects in their logical form. The victim of such a fallacy commits a logical error through mistakenly supposing that the form is valid. The victim symbolizes the argument correctly (if symbols are being used); the mistake is not that of misinterpreting what logical form the argument has (as would be the case if it had been symbolized incorrectly). Instead, the mistake is that of believing the logical form to be deductively valid when it is not. Thus, for example, when people are taken in by the fallacy of affirming the consequent, the likeliest source of their confusion is failure to notice that this form, unlike modus ponens, is invalid.

A more complicated situation arises when someone argues: "If men are not evil, then it is unnecessary to have police to prevent crime. And if men are evil, then police will be ineffectual in preventing crime. Now, either men are not evil or they are evil. Therefore, police are either unnecessary or ineffectual." The argument is in the form of a valid dilemma, but even though the dilemma is valid, there is something amiss with the thinking here. The trouble is that the third premise is an absurd oversimplification; it is absurd to believe that either all men are evil or all men are not evil. But what would lead anyone to accept a premise like this? By what sort of reasoning would one arrive at the premise itself? The line of thought leading to the third premise probably involved committing a formal fallacy. The fallacy would lie in thinking that from the necessary truth "Every man is such that either he is evil or he is not evil" we may validly infer "Either every man is evil or every man is not evil." It is the formal fallacy of supposing that from a universal sentence whose parts are disjunctions, we may infer a corresponding disjunction both of whose parts are universal. This is a mistake arising from misunderstanding a specific principle about logical form.

Notice that fallacies of inconsistency do not arise in this way. A person who uses inconsistent premises simply has not noticed that one premise contradicts another; the mistake results from an oversight, rather than from intentionally employing some incorrect logical principle. Similarly, fallacies of begging the question also result from sheer oversight, rather than from intentionally employing some incorrect logical principle.[31]

EXERCISE 27

A Identify and explain any fallacies present in the following examples.

1 Any application is invalid if the fee hasn't been paid. Your application is invalid, and so your fee must not have been paid.

2 Under all circumstances it is wrong to tolerate censorship, since censorship violates the principle that everyone ought to be guaranteed total freedom of expression.

3 Nothing is both deceitful and honest. Hence, nothing is deceitful, and nothing is honest.

4 You say that your cat plays Frisbee? I don't believe you. No cats ever play Frisbee, and so yours certainly doesn't.

5 Platinum is worth more per gram than gold is. Therefore, platinum is more valuable than gold.

6 We interviewed 147 local voters. One hundred thirteen of them approved of how the President is handling domestic affairs, eighty-nine approved his handling of foreign affairs, and fifty-one approved of both. We conclude that these voters are more favorable than unfavorable in their views of how the President is handling his job.

7 No friends of mine are friends of yours. All friends of mine are schoolmates of mine. So no schoolmates of mine are friends of yours.

8 You think Elaine is going to become a successful lawyer? Certainly not, for no one in her family has ever amounted to anything, and none of them ever will.

9 Libertarians aren't socialists. Anarchists aren't socialists. So anarchists must be libertarians.

10 I support individual rights to life, liberty, and property. So I favor free enterprise in the economic area. However, I believe there should be military

conscription, because the policy of all-volunteer armed forces doesn't yield enough good recruits in the long run.

11 All noncommissioned officers are former enlisted men. So all former enlisted men are noncommissioned officers.

12 It will rain if and only if it won't snow. It either won't rain or will snow. It won't both snow and not rain. So if it doesn't snow, it will rain.

13 Of course she likes me. She told me that she does, and she wouldn't lie to me about it, for she always tells the truth to people she likes.

14 We ought never to tell lies. Of course, politeness requires us to tell white lies sometimes, but they almost aren't lies at all.

15 Whoever likes dancing will adore the Hotel Olympus. But I don't like dancing, and so I wouldn't like it there.

16 If everyone comes, we'll have too little food, and if no one comes, we'll have too much. Each person will either come or not come, and so either everyone will come or no one will. Hence, we'll either have too much food or too little.

17 I'm against any legislator who doesn't give first priority to working for a balanced budget. I'll vote for Senator Boeing, though, since he's interested only in maintaining defense expenditures, and we have to do that.

18 Men are better drivers than women are. The proof of this is that men are more capable than women at managing cars on the road.

19 The poet must be allowed complete freedom to express whatever wells up creatively out of the unconscious, because only thus can great poetry be written. Obscenity cannot be allowed to intrude into poetry, of course, and so indecent poems must be banned.

20 Tan ah Tiat, forty-nine years old, a native of Kuala Lumpur, Malaysia, was charged with possession of opium. Arguing for acquittal, he told the judge that his opium habit did no harm, as he was to old to work anyway. Asked how he lived, he replied that he lived on the earnings of his grandmother.

†B Discuss any fallacies.

1 God, may He be exalted...existed alone, and nothing else....Afterwards, through His will and His volition, He brought into existence out of nothing all the beings as they are, time itself being one of the created things. For time is consequent upon motion, and motion is an accident of what is moved. Furthermore, what is moved...is itself created in time....

  MOSES MAIMONIDES, *The Guide of the Perplexed*

2 Everything that is in motion must be moved by something else. If therefore the thing which causes it to move be in motion, this too must be moved by something else, and so on. But we cannot proceed to infinity in this way, because in that case there would be no first mover, and in consequence neither would there be any other mover; for secondary movers do not cause movement except they be moved by a first mover, as, for example, a stick cannot cause movement unless it is moved by the hand. Therefore it is necessary to stop at some first mover which is moved by nothing else. And this is what we all understand God to be.

  ST. THOMAS AQUINAS, *Summa Theologica*

28 FALLACIES OF AMBIGUITY AND IRRELEVANCE

So far, we have considered fallacies of *non sequitur* in which the logical form is at fault. A quite different sort of *non sequitur* occurs when we make the mistake of incorrectly interpreting what logical form an argument has. The language in which the argument is expressed leads us to misunderstand the logical structure of the argument; we incorrectly translate the argument into a valid form when actually its form is invalid. We shall distinguish between two different ways in which the language of an argument may tempt us to make this mistake.

Ambiguity

Perhaps some one word or phrase in the argument is used in two different senses. In this case, if we do not notice these different senses, we may carelessly assume that they are the same; thus we misinterpret the logical form of the argument. It is called a fallacy of *equivocation* if some definite word or phrase is ambiguous.

Some fallacies of equivocation have special names of their own. In an argument that is intended to be a syllogism but that really contains four terms instead of three, we have the *fallacy of four terms*. For example, the argument "No designing persons are to be trusted; architects are people who make designs; therefore, architects are not to be trusted" is a crude specimen of this fallacy. Here the terms "designing person" and "person who makes designs" are used by the speaker as if they meant the same, but of course they do not have the same sense at all; the first term refers to people who hatch evil schemes, while the second refers to people who draw blueprints. The argument is intended to be a syllogism but is not really one, for it has no middle term. In this example the equivocation is very obvious and the fallacy easy to detect, but sometimes fallacies of this sort are more hidden and insidious.

The fallacies of *composition* and *division* are two special forms of equivocation that involve an improper sort of reasoning from part to whole or from whole to part. This may occur in syllogisms or in other kinds of argument.

Suppose someone reasons: "No man can sing as loud as an organ plays; the glee club are men; therefore, the glee club cannot sing as loud as an organ plays." This is intended to be a syllogism of the form **EAE** in the first figure. If it really were **EAE** in the first figure, it would have to be valid. Since it certainly is not valid, something is wrong. The second premise talks about the glee club *distributively*; that is, it says something about individual members of the glee club considered singly (that each individual member is a man). The conclusion, however, talks about the members of the glee club *collectively*; that is, it says something about the members of the glee club considered as a whole unit, not about each of them considered singly.

This argument cannot correctly be translated into a syllogism, for we cannot word it so as to consist of categorical sentences containing just three terms. If we put the premises correctly into categorical form, they become "No men are singers louder than organs" and "All groups identical to the glee club are groups consisting of men," with more than three terms. And if we use just three terms, there is no correct way of putting the premises into categorical form. The equivocation between "the glee club" understood distributively and "the glee club" understood collectively causes the speaker to reason fallaciously from a fact about individual members of the group to a conclusion about the group as a unit. This is called the *fallacy of composition.*[32]

A kindred example is this: "Accidents are frequent; getting struck by lightning is an accident; therefore getting struck by lightning is frequent." Here again we have an argument probably intended to be a valid syllogism, but it is invalid, and the mistake most likely is a case of equivocation. The trouble is that the first premise talks about accidents collectively; it says that the whole class of accidents is a class such that during most time periods some of its members are occurring. The second premise, however, talks about accidents distributively, for it says that each individual case of getting struck by lightning is an individual case of an accident. Here equivocation arises because the word "accident" is used in these two senses, collective and distributive. This equivocation causes the speaker to reason fallaciously from a fact about the whole to a conclusion about a part. This is called the *fallacy of division.*[33]

Notice, however, that it is not always fallacious to reason from part to whole or from whole to part. Valid syllogisms and quantificational arguments do this legitimately. For instance, the syllogism "All people are mortal and all Greeks are people, so all Greeks are mortal" validly reasons from information about the whole class of people to a conclusion about Greeks, who form a part, or subclass, of it. And the syllogism "All Greeks are humans and some Greeks are not wise, and so some humans are not wise" validly reasons from information about the subclass to a conclusion about the whole class.

Let us move on to another fallacy of equivocation which may be called *illicit obversion.* It arises when terms that are not really negations of one another are used as though they were. Someone who reasons "All child-murderers are inhuman; therefore no child-murderers are human," is guilty of this fallacy. The example purports to be obversion, but it is not correct obversion, for the predicate has not really been negated. The term "human" is not the contradictory of the term "inhuman," for "inhuman" means cruel rather than nonhuman. If we correctly obverted the sentence "All child-murderers are inhuman" we would get "No child-murderers are noninhuman." It would be the same type of fallacy if someone were to argue "No rocks are alive; therefore all rocks are dead." Here again the obversion is incorrect, for "alive" and "dead" are not contradictory terms; instead they are merely contraries.

In general, two terms are *contradictories* of each other if and only if one or the other but not both of the terms must apply to each thing; while two terms are *contraries* of each other if and only if at most one of them applies to each thing and neither applies to some things. The terms "alive" and "dead" are contraries rather than contradictories because there are some things, such as rocks, that are neither alive nor dead. (To call a thing dead is to imply that it once was alive.) The proper contradictory of "alive" is "lifeless," and so the sentence "No rocks are alive" has as its correct obverse "All rocks are lifeless."

A different kind of equivocation arises from confusion between words and what they stand for. Suppose someone were to argue: "Much ancient history is contained in the Bible; the Bible is a phrase of eight letters; therefore, much ancient history is contained in a phrase of eight letters." The argument is ridiculous, but what mistake does it contain? In order for the first premise to be true it must talk about (mention) the Bible, a lengthy book; whereas in order for the second premise to be true it must talk about (mention) the words "the Bible," a short phrase. Only if we fail to notice this distinction will we be tempted to think that the argument is good. The argument tends to be confusing because it is written in such a way as to use the very same two-word expression to mention the book and to mention the name of the book—thereby inviting us to confuse the thing with its name. We can reduce this sort of confusion in our own writing if we form the habit of always using quotation marks when we want to mention words. Let us always write:

"The Bible" is a phrase of eight letters.

instead of:

The Bible is a phrase of eight letters.

If we follow this practice, we shall be less likely to confuse the name of a thing with the thing itself.

There are far too many kinds of equivocation for us to discuss them all, but we shall consider one more kind, which arises from confusion among the various senses of the verb "to be." Suppose someone were to reason as follows: "Time is money; time is measured in seconds; and so money is measured in seconds." This argument is intended to be a case of identity reasoning, and so it has a confusing air of correctness about it. But the fallacy arises because the first occurrence of "is" in this argument is not the true "is" of identity. When we say "Time is money," we do not mean that time is just the same thing as money; we mean only that time is as good as money or that time can be exchanged for money. Here the word "is" is used in a metaphorical sense which is neither strictly the "is" of predication nor the "is" of identity.

Again, suppose that someone argues: "God is love; love is an emotion; therefore God is an emotion." Again the argument apes identity reasoning.

Here too the fallacy is one of equivocation, for the premise "God is love" probably is not meant as an identity sentence. People who say "God is love" probably mean that God personifies love or exhibits love; again the "is" is used in some metaphorical sense. The moral of this is that we must be alert against fallacies arising from confusion among the different senses of "to be."

So far in this section, we have been considering equivocation, the type of ambiguity arising when a single word or phrase is used in more than one sense. We shall conclude our discussion of ambiguity by noting that sometimes the logical form of an argument is misinterpreted not because any single word is ambiguous but because the grammar of a whole sentence is ambiguous and allows of more than one interpretation. This type of ambiguity traditionally has been called *amphiboly*. An example occurs in Shakespeare's *Henry VI* when the spirit prophesies "The Duke yet lives that Henry shall depose." Henry infers from this prophecy that he is going to depose a duke. However, the correct interpretation was that a duke was going to depose Henry. (It is easier for a prophet to stay in business if the predictions made are amphibolous.)

Throughout this section we have been considering logical mistakes that can arise from ambiguity. It would be incorrect, however, to conclude that ambiguity is always bad, or that it is always a logical error to use ambiguous language. Ambiguous language sometimes has a vivid flavor which can be admirable, if we are not misled by it. Ambiguity, like vagueness, is objectionable only insofar as it confuses people and causes them to commit fallacies in reasoning.

Irrelevance

The third kind of *non sequitur* arises when something about an argument tempts us simply to overlook the fact that there really is no connection between the premises and the conclusion. The argument excites us somehow, and we are misled into thinking that the premises support the conclusion, when actually they have nothing to do with the point supposedly being proved. Fallacies of this sort are called *fallacies of irrelevance*, or fallacies of *ignoratio elenchi* (Latin and Greek: "ignorance of what is to be refuted").

One important type of fallacy of this kind is the *ad hominem* fallacy. An argument is *ad hominem* (Latin: "to the man") if it is directed at an opponent in a controversy rather than being directly relevant to proving the conclusion under discussion. Such arguments are often, but not always, fallacious. For example, suppose someone argues: "Of course Karl Marx must have been mistaken in maintaining that capitalism is an evil form of economic and social organization. Why, he was a miserable failure of a man who couldn't even earn enough money to support his family." This is an *ad hominem* argument, for it attacks Marx the man instead of offering direct reasons why his views are incorrect. And it is a fallacy because the premise does not really establish the conclusion at all. This is the *abusive* form of the *ad hominem* argument.

Another form of the *ad hominem* argument occurs if a speaker produces reasons why his opponent might be expected to believe the conclusion, rather than reasons why the conclusion is true. Suppose members of Congress are debating whether the United States should permit localities to tax church buildings at their fair market value. Senator Brown happens to be religious but supports the proposal as a fund-raising measure, while Senator Green, who is not religious, opposes it because it displeases his constituents. Suppose Senator Green argues with Senator Brown, saying, "This proposal would harm religion, which you support, so that ought to prove to you that it's a bad proposal." Here Green is appealing to religious principles in which he himself does not believe; he has not offered any direct reason why the proposal is bad but instead has given a reason why Brown might have been expected to regard the proposal as bad. This is called the *circumstantial* form of the *ad hominem* argument.

A third form of the *ad hominem* argument occurs when a speaker, trying to show that he is not at fault, argues that his opponent has said or done things just as bad as those of which he, the speaker, is accused. For example, suppose White has accused Green of driving a car that is not safe, because it has no brakes. Green, aiming to refute the accusation, might reply "Who are you to talk? On your car the doors won't even latch, and you tie them shut with bits of string." This is the *tu quoque* (Latin: "you're another") form of the *ad hominem* argument.

Not all *ad hominem* arguments are fallacious. The abusive form of the *ad hominem* argument says that because a man has some weakness or defect, his views are incorrect. This is often but not always a worthless line of reasoning; sometimes it can be quite a good argument and not a fallacy at all. For instance, the fact that Professor Smith is a stupid, maladjusted man of paranoid tendencies increases the probability that his views on economic theory are unsound, for we know from past experience that economic theory is a difficult subject and that intelligent people of balanced judgment are more likely to have sound views about it. Perhaps we still ought to read Professor Smith's books, if we have time, before we definitely dismiss his views, but this information about his personality certainly is not irrelevant to the question whether his views are correct. We have here an inductive argument, which is not conclusive but is logically respectable (unlike the argument concerning Karl Marx, which is silly, for we have no reason to think there is a correlation between a man's earning power and the soundness of his views on social philosophy).

The circumstantial form of the *ad hominem* argument also can be of some value, though never as a direct proof of the conclusion. Pointing out to Senator Brown that his views on legislation are inconsistent with his religious principles may be worthwhile, for if his views contradict one another, they cannot both be right. To point this out does not show which view is mistaken, but it may show that Senator Brown needs to change at least one opinion or the other. Even the *tu quoque* form of *ad hominem* reasoning is not always worthless; it can be of real intellectual value in helping us form a consistent view of the comparative depravity of different individuals. It is fallacious only if it is supposed to be something more than that.

Another quite different fallacy of irrelevance is the appeal to unsuitable authority (the argument *ad verecundiam*). We commit this fallacy when we appeal to some admired or famous person as if that person were an authority on the matter being discussed—but when we have no good reason for thinking that the person is a genuine authority on it. Of course it is not always fallacious to appeal to authorities, but we are not entitled to appeal to persons as authorities unless there are good reasons for believing them to be authorities, and we should not trust an authority outside his or her special proven field of competence. A famous guitarist may be an expert on one type of music, but this does not make her an authority on philosophy of life. A movie star may be an authority on how to look attractive to the opposite sex, but is not likely to be an authority on which pain reliever is most healthful or which toothpaste tastes best.

The appeal to force is another fallacy of irrelevance (also called the *ad baculum* argument—"appeal to the stick"). By threatening a person we may succeed in winning that individual over to our point of view, but we must not think that a threat constitutes a logically valid argument. Usually a threat is not presented as an argument at all. We have the *ad baculum* fallacy only when the threat is treated as if it were a proof. A robber who says "Give me your money or I'll blow your brains out" is not committing the fallacy of appeal to force. The robber is not reasoning and is not committing any fallacy; an order is being given and an intention stated; that is all. However, a dictator who says "My opinions are right, because I'll imprison anyone who disagrees with me" perhaps would be committing the fallacy, by making the mistake of regarding a threat as though it were a logical reason in favor of a conclusion.

Even if cases in which anyone really thinks that a threat can serve as a logical reason are very rare, the traditional phrase "*ad baculum* argument" is a good phrase to have in our vocabulary. We can use it to refer to the procedure of people who abandon reasoning and resort to force, or threats of force, in trying to get their way. In this loose sense, the *ad baculum* 'argument' is not really an argument and is not a fallacy in reasoning; instead, it is an abandonment of reasoning. (And it is often but not always wrong to abandon reasoning in favor of force.)

The appeal to pity, or appeal for mercy (*ad misericordiam* argument), is the fallacy of arguing that a certain conclusion must be true because otherwise someone who deserves pity will be made more miserable. An appeal to pity or a plea for mercy is not a fallacy unless it is claimed to be a logical reason for believing some conclusion. The *ad misericordiam* fallacy is committed by the employee who argues "Please, Boss, you can see that my work is worth higher wages; I've got many hungry wives and children to feed." And a defendant would be committing this fallacy who tried to offer information about an unhappy childhood as if it were evidence showing innocence of crime. (However, it might not be fallacious to offer evidence about one's unhappy childhood in trying to show that one deserves to be treated leniently.)

We conclude with what is perhaps the most common of all fallacies of irrelevance, the fallacy of *black-and-white* thinking. A wife may say to her husband "So you think the soup is too cold, do you? Well, I suppose you would like to have had it scalding hot then, instead." The second remark is presented as if it followed logically from the first, and yet there is no logical connection whatever. But people find it very easy to fall into this sort of thinking in extremes, especially in the heat of controversy. Various causes could have induced the wife to reason this way; possibly ambiguity or a formal fallacy may be involved. But frequently this type of thinking is just a fallacy of irrelevance.

EXERCISE 28

A In each case discuss whether the second speaker is offering a good criticism.

1 **Al**: You grant me that no fishes have feathers and that all sharks are fishes. So you've got to grant that no sharks have feathers.
Betty: Invalid. You are committing the fallacy of division, by reasoning from whole (fishes) to part (sharks).

2 **Cindy**: If your girlfriend is mad, you can't have a pleasant evening. And she is mad. So if you want a pleasant evening, don't spend it with her.
Don: That's invalid thinking, because the word "mad" can have two meanings, "angry" and "insane."

3 **Earl**: If you were rich, you could afford a skiing vacation in Switzerland. But I see you can't afford that. So you must not be rich.
Fran: Your argument is no good, because the way you use the word "rich" is vague. Just how much money does a person have to have to be rich?

4 **Gail**: Surely there must be something unsound about the current indeterministic theory of quantum mechanics, for Einstein himself opposed it, saying that he could not believe that God would play dice with the universe.
Hal: You are appealing to authority. This is the fallacious argument *ad verecundiam*.

5 **Ian**: I'm having a serious attack of illness, so you should help get me to a hospital.
Jan: Certainly not. You are making an appeal to pity, and that's fallacious.

6 **Kay**: You tell me that these Baffin Island real estate shares you're selling are a good investment. But I know you earn a sizeable commission on whatever shares you sell, so I don't think I can trust what you tell me.
Lou: My friend, you accuse me of having a selfish motive instead of disproving what I said. You've committed the *ad hominem* fallacy.

7 **Mark**: It will be to your advantage to get off my land, since, if you don't leave at once, I'll have you arrested.

Nan: That's faulty reasoning. You've committed the fallacy of appealing to force.

8 Olga: You'd better get completely off the railway track. Otherwise, you'll be hit by the oncoming train.

Paul: That is black-and-white thinking. You are making the error of supposing that there are only two extreme possibilities.

B Identify and explain any fallacies.

1 We want our children to be normal, not abnormal. Now, the normal child doesn't start reading until age seven. So we don't want our children to read before they're seven.

2 Congressman Pink is an atheist and a libertine, so we can disregard what he says about the consequences of the government's fiscal policy.

3 There are some real bargains listed in the advertising for a sale at Rose's department stores. But it says, "All items not available at all stores." So I guess one can't actually buy these bargains at any of their stores.

4 Fairness requires that we dockworkers get much higher pay. After all, if we strike, we can close this port down until half the city goes bankrupt.

5 Please, Mr. Dean, don't think that I set fire to the dormitory. I'm underprivileged, and my old mother has been slaving for years to send me to college. It would kill her if you decided that I was the one who did it.

6 Each article of clothing that she is wearing is very stylish. So she must be very stylishly dressed.

7 You're quite mistaken when you call me dishonest. I did falsify my income tax some, but that's nothing. You yourself pad your expense account all the time.

8 There are people who, just by touching with their fingertips, can detect colors they can't see with their eyes. It's true, because my hairdresser told me about it.

9 Even though you're not a pacifist, as I am, you ought to agree with me that our intercontinental missiles should be scrapped. You belong to the Flat Earth Society. If the earth is flat, as you believe, then our missiles, which are designed to navigate around a spherical earth, cannot reach their intended targets, and so are worthless.

10 All roads going west from here lead to California. This road goes south; therefore, it doesn't lead to California.

11 There are beetles as much as 4 inches long. I haven't seen them myself, but my friend who has a Ph.D. in entomology says it's so.

12 This is a hijacking. Fly the plane to Libya, or I'll set off my bomb.

13 Of course I haven't been dealing in narcotics. How could you believe that of me when you know that I'm a person who has had a very hard life and suffered much?

14 These stomach tablets do cost twice as much as the ones you've been using, but they're really worth it. Each tablet dissolves 50 percent more stomach acid.

15 You mustn't evict me and my little children just because I'm behind with the rent. There's no place we can go. My little ones mustn't be cast out into the street.

16 Senator Gray says too much is being spent on national defense. He must be one of those pacifists who advocates disbanding our armed forces.

17 I deserve a better grade on this test, professor, because getting low grades makes me feel awful. I can't stand it.

18 A larger allowance? Surely you realize that money doesn't bring happiness. So if I increased your allowance, it would only increase your unhappiness.

19 Members of the jury, you must convict the defendant, if not of murder, then of manslaughter. For when I asked her, "Did you intentionally kill the deceased?" she answered, "No." Thus she herself confesses that she killed unintentionally.

20 I'm tempted to say that the number of Roman emperors during the republican era was none at all, that is, zero. But this can't be right, as zero wasn't invented until later, by the Arabs.

21 You think I ought to study more, instead of averaging sixty hours a week at parties? That's absurd, because one can't get an all-around education by spending one's every waking hour grinding away at those dreary textbooks.

22 To call you an organism is to speak the truth. To call you a swine is to call you an organism. So to call you a swine is to speak the truth.

23 You didn't come out to join our march against repression. Why are you supporting repression?

24 Bugs are everywhere this summer. But praying mantises aren't everywhere this summer. So they aren't bugs.

25 It would be a good idea for each college student to spend every second year working at a job away from school. Thus, what is now a four-year undergraduate program would require eight years to complete, which would automatically reduce the undergraduate enrollment by 50 percent.

26 Anyone who works for the company can understand an English sentence. The instructions for operation of this computer are just English sentences. So anyone who works for the company can understand the instructions for operation of this computer.

27 All the works of Dickens cannot be read in a week. Therefore, *A Christmas Carol*, which is one of his works, cannot be read in a week.

28 Basketball players are people. So a short basketball player is a short person.

29 Amphetamines are perfectly safe for diet control. Swami Mananda told me so, and he really knew all about hygiene. That was before he was committed, of course.

30 We want to make education joyful, humane, responsive, and warm. Yet how can this be accomplished in a society which is racist, hierarchical, competitive, violent, repressive, narrow-minded, and selfish? It follows that the only sure way to reform education is to abolish capitalism.

†C Discuss whether fallacies occur in each of these examples.

    1 There is a compelling logic for Rolls-Royce ownership. Of all the Rolls-Royce cars built since 1904, more than half are still cruising the world's highways. Total up the purchase prices of all the ordinary cars you have owned, or plan to own, subtracting their trade-in values. Now match this figure against the purchase price of a Rolls Silver Shadow. This remarkable value cannot go unheeded.

    2 See how absurd and stupid it is to say: I should prefer non-existence to miserable existence. He who says, I prefer this to that, chooses something.

> Non-existence is not something; it is nothing. There can be no real choice when what you choose is nothing. ST. AUGUSTINE, *On Free Will*

3 If a friend of yours requests you on his deathbed to hand over his estate to his daughter, without leaving his intention anywhere in writing...or speaking of it to anybody, what will you do? You no doubt will hand over the money; perhaps Epicurus himself would have done the same....Do you not see that...even you Epicureans, who profess to make your own interest and pleasure your sole standard, nevertheless perform actions that prove you to be really aiming not at pleasure but at duty...?
CICERO, *De Finibus*

4 From the moment when private property in movable objects developed, in all societies in which this private property existed there must be this moral law in common: Thou shalt not steal. Does this law thereby become an eternal moral law? By no means. In a society in which the motive for stealing has been done away with, in which therefore at the very most only lunatics would ever steal, how the teacher of morals would be laughed at who tried solemnly to proclaim the eternal truth: Thou shalt not steal! FRIEDRICH ENGELS, *Anti-Dühring*

5 We are what we all abhor, *Anthropophagi* and Cannibals, devourers not only of men but of our selves; and that not in an allegory, but a positive truth; for all this mass of flesh which we behold, came in at our mouths; this frame we look upon, hath been upon our trenchers; in brief, we have devour'd our selves. SIR THOMAS BROWNE, *Religio Medici*

6 But, say you, surely there is nothing easier than to imagine...books existing in a closet, and nobody by to perceive them....But what is all this, I beseech you, more than framing in your mind certain ideas, which you call books...and at the same time omitting to frame the idea of anyone that may perceive them? But do not you yourself perceive or think of them all the while? This therefore...only shows you have the power of imagining or forming ideas in your mind; but it does not show that you can conceive it possible the objects of your thought may exist without the mind. To make out this, it is necessary that you conceive them existing unconceived or unthought of, which is a manifest repugnancy.
GEORGE BERKELEY, *Principles of Human Knowledge*

29 AVOIDING AMBIGUITY; DEFINITIONS

When we encounter words that cause confusion because their meanings are ambiguous, it is often helpful to define them. A traditional way of characterizing the definition of a word is to say that the definition is a verbal formulation of its meaning. However, the word "meaning" itself is ambiguous. Thus a general term may be said to mean each individual thing to which it applies (for example, the general term "man" means Socrates, Caesar, and each other man). This is called *extensional* meaning, and the totality of things to which the general term applies is called the extension of the term.

But also a general term may be said to mean those characteristics which anything must possess in order that the term correctly apply to it (for example, the term "bachelor" means being a man and being unmarried). This is called *intensional* meaning, and the totality of characteristics which anything would have to possess in order that the term apply to it is called the intension of the term. A definition of a general term tries to specify the intension; the definition does not tell us what the extension is.

From another point of view, however, we can characterize definitions without employing the term "meaning." We may say that a definition of a word is a recipe for eliminating the word by paraphrasing, that is, for transforming sentences containing the word into equivalent sentences that contain other expressions instead. Recipes of this kind are of especial practical value when they tell us how to eliminate ambiguous, confusing, or unfamiliar words by paraphrasing—replacing them with clearer or more familiar words.

The most fundamental way of explaining a word is to give examples. Sometimes we do this by pointing to visible examples. When a child asks "What's a dog?" we respond by pointing to Fido, Rover, and Bruno. Some philosophers have called this procedure "ostensive definition," but it is better to call it merely ostensive teaching of words. This ostensive procedure differs from definition in that it gives no recipe for paraphrasing the word. Although explaining a word by giving examples often can be indispensably valuable, it is not the same as giving a definition. Sometimes a definition is much more helpful than a list of examples.

In ordinary discourse we often express definitions in ways that do not clearly show that they are definitions. Wishing to define the word "dormouse," a speaker may say, "A dormouse is a small hibernating European rodent resembling a squirrel." The hearer is then expected to realize that the speaker is intending to define the word "dormouse," rather than intending to make an ordinary statement about dormice (as he would be doing if he said, "Dormice are rather prolific animals"). A careful speaker can make his intention clearer by stating his definition in such a way as to leave no doubt that it is a definition. If he says "The word 'dormouse' means 'small hibernating European rodent resembling a squirrel,'" then he has made it perfectly clear that he is defining the word. Moreover, here he has given what is called an *explicit* definition, that is, a definition in which the *definiendum* (the expression being defined) is declared to be replaceable by another explicitly given expression, the *definiens* (that which does the defining.)[34]

Definitions that are useful in preventing ambiguity may be subdivided into two types. Some of them serve the purpose of describing the meaning that a word already has in language. We might call these *analytical* definitions. In giving this kind of definition of a word, the speaker does not aim to change its meaning; he aims only to characterize the meaning it already has. Dictionary definitions are of this type. When a definition has this purpose, we can properly ask whether the definition is correct or incorrect.

In order to be correct in its description of the meaning of a word, an analytical definition must not be *too broad*; that is, it must not embrace things that do not really belong. (To define "pneumonia" as "disease of the lungs" would be too broad, for there are many lung diseases besides pneumonia.) Also, in order to be correct in its description of the meaning of a word, an analytical definition must not be *too narrow*; that is, it must not exclude things that really belong. (To define "psychosis" as "schizophrenia" would be too narrow, for there are other kinds of psychoses.) Sometimes an incorrect definition errs by being too broad in one respect and also too narrow in some other respect (for instance, defining "liberalism" as "the view that the power of the government should be increased").

Furthermore, analytical definitions should be clear enough to be understood by those for whom they are intended; otherwise they are of little use. When in his dictionary Dr. Johnson defined a net as "any thing made with interstitial vacuities," his readers would not have understood the definiens as well as they already understood the definiendum; the definition uses murky works to explain a relatively clear one and so is not helpful.

Finally, a definition cannot serve much useful purpose if it is circular, that is, if the definiendum occurs within the definiens in such a way that no one could understand the definiens who did not already understand the definiendum. For example, to define "straight line" as "the line along which a ray of light travels when it goes straight" is circular and uninformative.

Traditional logic used to prescribe additional rules for definitions, including the rule that definitions should be given by genus and species and the rule that a definition ought not to be negative. However, these rules need not always be obeyed. Granted, in giving a definition it often is helpful to proceed by genus and species, that is, first saying what general kind of thing the word means and then saying what the specific form is. But not all legitimate definitions follow this pattern. Also, it is often wise to avoid definitions couched in negative terms ("A lion is a big cat; not a tiger, not a leopard, not an ocelot"), for such definitions are likely to be too broad. But some negative definitions are perfectly legitimate.

A second type of definition useful in preventing ambiguity is the *stipulative* definition, whose purpose is to declare how a speaker intends that a certain word, phrase, or symbol shall be understood ("Let 'S' mean 'Samoans' "; "Let 'heavy truck' mean 'truck that can carry a load of 5 tons or more' "; etc.). Perhaps the expression being defined is one that previously had no meaning, or perhaps it had a different or a vaguer meaning. At any rate, the point of the stipulative definition is that the expression now is deliberately endowed with a particular meaning. Obviously, a stipulative definition cannot be of much use if it is unclear or circular. However, we do not have to worry about whether it is too broad or too narrow, for that sort of correctness cannot pertain to stipulative definitions. A stipulative definition is arbitrary, in that it expresses only the speaker's intention to use the word in the stipulated manner, and the speaker is, after all, entitled to use it in any desired way, so long as it does not cause confusion.

In order to avoid causing confusion, however, a stipulative definition should not assign to a word that already has an established meaning some new meaning that is likely to be confused with it. Consider the following dialogue:

Smith: General Green is insane, you know. He ought to be dismissed.

Jones: He is? I agree that we should not have insane persons serving in the Army. But how do you know he's insane?

Smith: It's obvious. He says he believes in extrasensory perception, and according to my definition—surely I'm entitled to use words as I please—anyone who does that is insane.

Here the stipulative definition is used to promote ambiguity rather than to prevent it. In the ordinary sense of the term "insane," Jones agrees with Smith that insane persons ought not to be generals. But Smith offers no evidence that General Green is insane in this sense. All that Smith shows is that the general is 'insane' in a special, idiosyncratic sense of the word. From that, nothing follows about whether he ought to be dismissed. Smith is causing confusion by failing to keep distinct these two very different senses of the word; this happens because he fails to recognize the difference here between a stipulative and an analytical definition.

Confusion can be caused in another way by a stipulative definition if a word or symbol that purports to name some individual thing (such a word or symbol is a singular term) is introduced even though it is not known that there is any such thing. Suppose I say "let 'n' stand for the largest whole number." And then I go on to use this symbol "n" in making supposed assertions about this largest whole number. Here I am guilty of constructing a confused definition, for there is no largest whole number; hence, I have no right to introduce and use a singular term for this nonentity.[35] I may become badly confused if I assume that this definition is enough to entitle me to start talking about this largest whole number as if it existed. There is no such number, and a mere definition cannot create a number or any other object.

The two kinds of definitions mentioned so far both aim to inform us about verbal usage. The stipulative definition expresses a speaker's intention henceforth to use his definiendum in a certain way, and the analytical definition describes the way in which the definiendum already is used in language. These two kinds of definitions are valuable in helping to prevent ambiguity.

It would be a mistake, however, to suppose that everything called a definition belongs to one of these two kinds. In fact, the profoundest and most valuable definitions usually do not fit tidily into either kind. When Newton defined force as the product of mass times acceleration, when Einstein defined simultaneity of distant events in terms of the transmission of light rays, and when Whitehead and Russell defined zero as the class of all empty classes, these important definitions expressed stipulations about how Newton, Einstein, and Whitehead and Russell proposed to use their terms. But these definitions did not merely do this; they also reflected previously established usage. What these definitions did was to propose new verbal usages growing out of the previously established usages. It was felt that these new usages perfected tendencies of thought implicit in the old usages and offered more insight into the subject matter being treated.

We might give the name *revelatory* definitions to definitions like these, which do not fit into either of the two categories of stipulative and analytical. Revelatory definitions constitute a third category. Further examples of revelatory definitions can be found in other, diverse fields. For example, when a nineteenth-century writer defined architecture as frozen music, he was not trying to describe how the word "architecture" is used in our language. (He took it for granted that his readers would know what kinds of constructions are considered architecture.) Nor was he proposing some arbitrary new usage. We should not censure his definition on the ground that it is unhelpful for the purpose of preventing ambiguity; that is not the purpose of this kind of definition. This definition is a metaphor, and it suggests a new way of looking at architecture, comparing the structural organization of the parts of a building with the structural organization of the parts of a musical composition. In trying to decide whether the definition is a good one or not, we must reflect about the extent and validity of this comparison between music and buildings; the definition is a good one if and only if the comparison is revealing.

Or again, when a writer on psychoanalysis says that man is to be defined as the neurotic animal, this definition does not have the purpose of explaining the meaning of the word "man" to someone unfamiliar with it. Instead, its purpose is to call attention to something about human beings that the writer thinks is of fundamental importance in making humans what they are and in explaining the differences between the life of humans and the life of animals. The definition is a good one if it achieves this. These revelatory definitions have no relation to the elimination of ambiguity; they are mentioned merely to indicate that analytical and stipulative definitions are not the only kinds of definitions.[36]

How frequently are definitions needed? People sometimes think that one always should define one's terms at the beginning of any discussion. But this idea becomes absurd if carried too far. Suppose that we as speakers did undertake to define all our terms in noncircular ways. However far we proceeded, we would always still have at least one definiens containing as yet undefined terms; therefore this task is an impossible one to complete. Moreover, we do have a fairly adequate understanding of the meanings of many words that we have never bothered to define and also of many words that we would not know how to define satisfactorily even if we tried. Thus, it would be foolish to try indiscriminately to define all or even most of our terms before proceeding with our thinking. What we should do at the beginning of a discussion is seek definitions of those particular words which are especially likely to make trouble in the discussion because they are harmfully ambiguous, obscure, or vague.

This is especially true with regard to discussions in which confusion is caused by failure to notice the different meanings of a term. A *verbal dispute* is a dispute arising solely from the fact that some word is being used with different meanings; this kind of dispute can be settled merely by giving the definitions that clarify the situation (though to say this is not to say that such disputes always are *easy* to settle).

The American philosopher William James gives a classic example of such a verbal dispute (*Pragmatism*, Lecture II). Suppose there is a squirrel on the trunk of a tree, and a man walks around the tree. The squirrel moves around the tree trunk so as to stay out of sight, always facing the man but keeping the tree between them. Has the man gone around the squirrel or not? Some of James's friends disputed hotly for a long time about this question. Here is a purely verbal dispute; it can be settled by pointing out that in one sense the man has gone 'around' the squirrel, for he has moved from the north to the west and then to the south and east of the squirrel's location, but in another sense the man has not gone 'around' the squirrel, for the squirrel has always been facing him. Once we have pointed out these two different senses of the word, we have done all that can reasonably be done; there is nothing more worth discussing (though this does not ensure that discussion will cease). With a verbal dispute like this, giving definitions is the way to resolve the dispute. But it would be utterly wrong to assume that all disputes are verbal in this way. There are many serious problems for the settling of which definitions are not needed, and there are many other problems where if definitions help, they mark only the beginning of the thinking needed to resolve the issue.

EXERCISE 29

A For each example, explain the main ambiguity and discuss whether definitions would be helpful.

1 John sent Mary the dog from Ireland.
2 The skies are not cloudy all day.
3 This is a wild horse.
4 She lacks broad vision.
5 Nothing is too good for him.
6 She got high on the mountain.
7 No man can walk while sitting.
8 How many pints of beer has she drunk? An irrational number.
9 The grand jury issued an illegal gambling indictment.
10 A pint of heavy cream isn't heavier than a pint of light cream.
11 I had been driving for 40 years when I fell asleep at the wheel and had an accident.

12 The guy was all over the road. I had to swerve a number of times before I hit him.

13 The government of France is now facing declining public confidence that their economic program is failing.

14 He is the forty-five-year-old son of a West Virginia coal miner and an ordained minister of the United Church.

15 They were found murdered in the blood-spattered apartment they shared in northwest Washington.

16 Headline: "Mining Company Picks Cave-in Survivor's Brain."

17 How did this group of adolescent mothers make out? Eventually, two-thirds of the sample married, and 70 percent married the fathers of their children.

18 A woman who had just had triplets was visited by a friend, who said how wonderful it was. "Yes," answered the mother, "the doctor tells me it happens only once in 167,000 times." "Goodness," said the friend, "how did either of you ever find time to do your housework?"

19 Tony ate cold steak and kidney pie. EVELYN WAUGH

20 Both the oracles agreed in the tenor of their reply, which was in each case a prophecy that if Croesus attacked the Persians, he would destroy a mighty empire...Croesus was overjoyed,...feeling sure now that he would destroy the empire of the Persians. HERODOTUS

C In each case, discuss the definitions being employed and the nature of the disagreement, and explain whether there is purely verbal confusion.

 1 Alice: The law says "No trucks over 1 ton on this street." You're driving your van on this street, and your van weighs 2 tons. So you're violating the law.
 Bob: No, that's unsound reasoning. My van has a payload of only 1 ton, and so it's a 1-ton truck.

 2 Cal: The price of gold has fluctuated dreadfully in recent years.
 Donna: That's only the dollar price of gold. Actually, gold is the most stable thing there is, because it is the standard of value. It is the value of the dollar that fluctuates, not gold.

 3 Ellen: Corporations pay heavy taxes.
 Frank: No, they don't pay taxes. They merely collect taxes from their customers in the form of higher prices. It is the consumer who ultimately pays the taxes.

 4 Gene: How dare you tell everyone that I stole this car? You know I bought it.
 Helen: You bought it for a ridiculously low price, and according to my definition that's stealing. So when people ask me about you, I tell them you're a thief.

 5 Ilsa: What fine, solid furniture!
 Joe: It's not solid at all. It consists of swarms of atoms whirling through mostly empty space. It's no more solid than a swarm of bees.

 6 Ken: People are less religious than they used to be.
 Lana: Religion is best defined as "ultimate concern"; whatever a man's ultimate concern is, that is his religion. Perhaps nowadays more people have television, making money, or taking drugs as their religions; but people are not less religious now.

7 Mary: The universe is infinitely old.

Norm: Impossible. Let *e* be the earliest event in the history of the universe. Now, there cannot have been any happening earlier than *e*, since *e* is by definition the earliest event. As every two points in time are separated by only a finite interval, *e* must have occurred only a finite length of time ago.

8 Owen: Brown is a barbarian. He never bathes or changes his clothes.

Pam: He's no barbarian. He reads Proust in French and plays the viola da gamba.

†D Discuss the adequacy of the definition involved in each example.

1 A few years ago a German-born woman appeared before a federal district judge in Los Angeles, seeking to become a citizen of the United States. In order to be granted citizenship, she would have to take an oath of allegiance, the wording of which expresses belief in a supreme being. She testified that she considered herself an atheist, because she did not believe in a supreme being; however, under questioning by the judge, she agreed that she regarded the universe as ordered and not created by any human beings or animals. "That qualifies as religion," the judge said, swearing her in. "That's the same as believing in a supreme being."

2 By *Original Sin*, as the phrase has been most commonly used by divines, is meant the *innate, sinful depravity of the heart.*

> JONATHAN EDWARDS, *Doctrine of Original Sin*

3 Evil, as we have said, is nothing else but *the privation of what is connatural and due to anyone;* for the term *evil* is used in this sense by all.

> ST. THOMAS AQUINAS, *Summa Contra Gentiles*

4 By pleasure we mean the absence of pain in the body and of trouble in the soul.

> EPICURUS

5 Time is our consciousness of the succession of ideas in our mind....If a mind be conscious of a hundred ideas during one minute, by the clock, and of two hundred during another, the latter of these spaces would actually occupy so much greater extent in the mind as two exceed one in quantity. If, therefore, the human mind, by any future improvement of its sensibility, should become conscious of an infinite number of ideas in a minute, that minute would be eternity....Perhaps the perishing ephemeron enjoys a longer life than the tortoise.

> PERCY BYSSHE SHELLEY, *Queen Mab*

6 We were never more free than under the German Occupation. We had lost all our rights...Since we were hunted, each gesture had the weight of a commitment. The often frightful circumstances of our struggle enabled us finally to live, undisguised and unconcealed, that anxious, unbearable situation which is called the human predicament.

> JEAN-PAUL SARTRE, *Situations*

7 We must first be clear on what is meant by "the people" and what is meant by "the enemy."...At the present stage, the period of building socialism, the classes, strata and social groups which favor, support and work for the cause of socialist construction all come within the category of the people, while the social forces and groups which resist the socialist revolution and are hostile to or sabotage socialist construction are all enemies of the people.

MAO-TSE-TUNG, *On the Correct Handling of Contradictions*

8 We reject the subjectivist view that to call an action right, or a thing good, is to say that it is generally approved of, because it is not self-contradictory to assert that some actions which are generally approved of are not right, or that some things which are generally approved of are not good. A. J. AYER, *Language, Truth and Logic*

9 They are not being tried by a jury of their peers, for these two defendants are black, young, and inmates of California's penal institutions—segments of society from which jury panels are not drawn.

SOLEDAD BROTHERS LEGAL COMMITTEE

10 Now you might ask: When is the will right? The will is unimpaired and right when it is entirely free from self-seeking, and when it has forsaken itself and is formed and transformed into the will of God, indeed, the more it is so, the more the will is right and true.

MEISTER ECKHART, *Treatises and Sermons*

CHAPTER 7

INDUCTIVE REASONING

So far, we have been concentrating on deductive arguments. But a great many of the arguments we encounter in ordinary thinking are inductive in character. Let us now turn to a fuller consideration of inductive reasoning.

30   INDUCTION AND PROBABILITY

A valid deductive argument is demonstrative; that is, if the premises are true, the conclusion must necessarily be true also. Because of this, the conclusion cannot embody conjectures about observable reality that do not follow deductively from what the premises say. In this sense the conclusion of a valid deductive argument must be 'contained in' its premises. Inductive arguments are not like this, however.

An inductive argument (as we defined induction) has to have a conclusion embodying empirical conjectures about the world that do not follow deductively what its premises say—in an inductive argument the conclusion is not wholly 'contained in' its premises. Consequently, in an inductive argument the truth of the premises cannot absolutely ensure the truth of the conclusion, and the argument cannot be demonstrative in the way that valid deduction is. But if the premises of an inductive argument are true and the reasoning is good, then it is reasonable to believe the conclusion; the conclusion is *probably* true.[37]

Inductive reasoning is of great importance because so many of our beliefs about the world cannot be proved by deduction alone. If they are to be proved at all, the reasoning in support of them must include inductive reasoning. Now, it is not being suggested here that everything one believes needs to be proved (this issue will be discussed in Section 42). But beliefs which are doubtful or controversial do often need to be justified by reasoning—and deductive reasoning alone is insufficient.

For example, it is a very ordinary belief that a person will be nourished by eating bread for lunch, whereas eating arsenic will be poisonous. What reasoning can we employ in justification of these beliefs? Fundamentally, the belief that bread will nourish and that arsenic will poison is supported by past experience—by our observation of past cases in which these effects occurred. Thus, the straightforward way of reasoning here is to infer that bread will nourish us if we eat it today, since bread that we know of has usually nourished, and that if we eat arsenic today it will poison us, since arsenic that we know of in the past has usually poisoned. This reasoning is clearly inductive in character.

Granted we could reason deductively that since bread always nourishes, it will nourish us today, and that since arsenic always poisons, it will poison us if we eat it today. But this deductive reasoning depends on major premises that are more dubious than the conclusions we are trying to justify. How do we know that bread always nourishes and that arsenic always poisons (not just in the past, but always)? In the end, if we know this at all, our knowledge of it has to be based on induction—on our realizing that in the past this is what happened, and so probably it is what always happens. In justifying beliefs like these about how things happen in the world, we must sooner or later resort to inductive inference, for deduction alone would not suffice for completing a proof. Because our actions are so largely based upon beliefs arrived at by induction, Bishop Butler, an English philosopher, declared, "Probability is the very guide to life."

With inductive arguments, just as with deductive ones, we have to distinguish between the truth of the conclusion and the logical validity of the reasoning. However, with inductive reasoning the situation is more complicated, since we must allow for variations in the degree of probability the speaker claims that the premises confer on the conclusion. A speaker who says "My past experience is such-and-such; therefore it is practically certain that arsenic is always poisonous" is claiming a high degree of probability for the conclusion. A speaker who says "My past experience is such-and-such, and so it is rather likely that arsenic is always poisonous" is claiming a much lower degree of probability for it.

What then should we mean by calling an inductive argument valid? An inductive argument is a valid argument if the degree of probability claimed for its conclusion is indeed a reasonable degree of probability to attribute to that conclusion, relative to the available evidence. The argument is a *non sequitur* if it claims for its conclusion a degree of probability that it is unreasonable to attribute to that conclusion, relative to the available evidence. Thus, an inductive argument that can be valid and perfectly legitimate when a moderate degree of probability is claimed for the conclusion (e.g.,

"He's a Hindu, and so quite likely he's a vegetarian") can become invalid and fallacious if an unduly high degree of probability is claimed for the conclusion (e.g., "He's a Hindu, and so he's bound to be a vegetarian").

Keeping this in mind, we can see that an inductive argument may happen to reach a true conclusion without being a logically good argument. (In this respect, induction is like deduction.) For instance, suppose a man sees a black cat cross his path and infers that bad luck is probably imminent; soon after he is struck by lightning. Here his conclusion happens to have been true, but his reasoning may well have been invalid all the same; relative to what he knew at the time he made the inference, it may not have been very probable that he was going to have bad luck. The conclusion accidentally turned out to be true, but the reasoning was logically bad.

Also, an inductive argument may reach a false conclusion even though the reasoning involved is logically good and starts from true premises. (In this respect, induction is unlike deduction.) For instance, suppose there has been a thunderstorm every afternoon at five o'clock for the past week, and I infer that there will rather likely be one tomorrow too. Here my data are true and my reasoning may well be perfectly logical, and yet it is possible that my conclusion is false; perhaps no storm occurs on the morrow. Here it was reasonable for me to make this inference, even though the conclusion turned out not to be true.

To grasp this character of inductive reasoning, we must understand the notion of probability. When we speak of the degree of probability of a conclusion, we are referring to the degree to which it is reasonable to believe the conclusion; probability here is the same thing as rational credibility. We take for granted that there can be such a thing as the degree to which it is reasonable to believe a conclusion on the basis of given evidence. To hold that this is so is not to claim that such degrees of belief, or probabilities, always are so definite as to be numerically measurable—perhaps they will sometimes be rather indefinite ranges, where stronger or weaker degrees of belief within that range are equally reasonable (in Section 33 we shall discuss further the question of numerical values for probabilities). But some degrees of belief in a conclusion are reasonable, while others are not, relative to given evidence. This difference is not merely a matter of personal taste, but is a matter of logic which all thinkers ought to respect if they want to think reasonably.

Thinking of probability as rational credibility is not the only legitimate way of understanding probability, however. A quite different sense of the term "probability" is involved when a physicist speaks of the probability of decay of a uranium atom; what is meant there is the *relative frequency* with which uranium atoms do, in fact, disintegrate. Probabilities in this sense must have definite numerical values. This notion of probability is widely used in science, and can be an entirely legitimate notion. However, it has no especial relevance to logical reasoning, and is not the notion of probability that we want in connection with inductive reasoning.

But now we must notice that probability when understood as rational credibility is a *relative* matter, in this respect: the degree to which it is reasonable to believe something depends upon how much we know. The very same conjecture takes on different degrees of probability relative to different amounts of evidence. For example, if all we know about Hugo is that he is twenty years old, then, relative to this evidence, the conjecture that he will be alive next year is highly probable and very reasonable to believe (for we know that most twenty-year-olds survive). But if we learn that young Hugo loves fast driving and has already had several accidents, the probability is distinctly diminished. And if we learn in addition that he has just collided with a concrete abutment at 90 miles per hour, then, relative to this augmented evidence, the probability of his being alive next year is very much further reduced. Relative to our original information, the conjecture that he will survive was highly probable; relative to our augmented information, it has only a low degree of probability. This illustrates how changes in available evidence can change the degree to which it is reasonable to believe a conclusion. And it illustrates how probability is something quite different from truth, for the conjecture could be highly probable without being true or could be true without being very probable.

Probabilities always are relative to evidence, and yet often we speak of the probability of something without specifically stating to what evidence this probability is related. When we speak of the probability of a sentence, we mean its probability relative to *all* the information available to us. If someone asks, "What is the probability that there is life on Mars?" the questioner means, "What is the probability, relative to all the evidence now available?" The degree of probability may have been different in times past when there was less evidence, and it will surely be different in the future when more evidence is gathered.

This brings us to another basic difference between deductive and inductive reasoning. Deductive arguments are *self-contained* as regards validity in a way that inductive arguments are not. Thus, the question whether it is deductively valid to argue "No deciduous trees are conifers; all fig trees are deciduous; therefore no fig trees are conifers" is a question whose answer depends solely upon the logical relation of the stated premises to the conclusion. No further information about botany or anything else (excepting logic, of course) is required. Indeed, there exists no other sentence (excluding sentences that express principles of logic) the truth or falsity of which has any decisive bearing upon whether this reasoning is deductively valid.

Because of this, when we are determining whether a deductive argument is valid, we may limit our attention strictly to the stated premises, except for deductive arguments having suppressed premises (which we shall discuss in Chapter 8); even with them the unstated premises always are limited in number and can, in principle, be stated in full.

Inductive arguments are not self-contained in this way. Consider the argument: "Hugo is twenty; most twenty-year-olds survive another year, and so probably Hugo will reach twenty-one." The person who presents this argument is not just claiming that the conclusion *would* be probable *were* the stated premises *all* our relevant evidence; if he were making only that very uninteresting, milksop claim, his remark would be a mere conditional sentence, not an inference at all. The arguer is claiming something more significant: What is being claimed is that the conclusion is reasonable to believe in the light of all that we now know. The conclusion is being claimed to be probable relative to all the directly and indirectly relevant evidence that we possess. How much evidence is this? A great deal—indeed, indefinitely much, for so many of the things we know about the world have at least indirect bearings on the question of Hugo's survival. (Our knowledge of the longevity of other people, our knowledge of the longevity of other animals, and our knowledge of the general regularity of nature are all indirectly relevant.) If we tried to list all the empirical sentences we know to be true that are at least indirectly relevant to the question of young Hugo's survival, we would find that we had embarked upon a task that we could not complete, or at any rate that we could never be sure we had completed. There are indefinitely many such sentences, and we always seem to be able to keep on adding more of them to our list.

In an inductive argument the explicitly stated premises are only a tiny part, although usually the most noteworthy part, of the indefinitely vast amount of information about the world upon which the conclusion depends. Each bit of this known but unstated information has a bearing upon whether the argument is inductively valid. But where reasoning involves relevant premises so rich that we cannot even state them definitively, we cannot expect to be able to impute to the premises and conclusion any logical form specific enough to settle whether the argument is valid or invalid. Thus, we cannot rely on considerations of logical form for judging the validity of inductive reasoning. Because inductive arguments are not 'self-contained' in the way that deductive arguments are, their whole logic is profoundly different, and so formal rules cannot play the central role in inductive logic that they do in deductive logic.

EXERCISE 30

  *A Criticize each of the following comments.

    1 On Friday, all the indications were we would have fair weather for sailing on the weekend; the barometer was high, and there was no report of storm systems moving in our direction. But by Saturday afternoon a fierce squall had blown up, capsizing our boat. How wrong we had been to think that the weather would probably stay fair!

    2 The argument "He's a Hindu, and so quite likely he's a vegetarian" isn't valid. His being a Hindu doesn't strictly guarantee that he's a vegetarian—so the argument can't possibly be a valid one.

    3 All that Jane knows about Hugo is that he's twenty, and so she thinks it's probable he'll survive until next year. Molly saw him heading into a bad

automobile crash, and so she thinks it's not very probable he'll survive until next year. But this shows that probability is just a matter of subjective opinion. There's no such thing as the real probability that he'll survive.

4 When all I know about Hugo is that he's a twenty-year-old American male, I have very little evidence about whether he'll survive another year. My evidence certainly isn't "indefinitely much."

B Discuss the following comments.

1 A sentence is either true or false. If it's true, then it's pointless to call it probable (when you're assuming that it's true, it's a silly understatement to say merely that it is probable), and wrong to call it improbable (when you admit that it's true, you're accepting it, and so you've no right to call it improbable, which amounts to rejecting it). On the other hand, if it's false, it's wrong to call it probable (you'd be both rejecting and accepting it) and pointless to call it improbable (this is a silly understatement). So probability and improbability are notions that are of no use whatever.

2 No reasonable person needs proofs that bread is nourishing and arsenic is poisonous. These facts are just obvious. Anyone who doubts or questions them has got to be irrational, and in need of psychiatric help rather than logical refutation.

3 To me, probability means the relative frequency with which a given characteristic occurs in a population. If 9 out of 10 Swedes are blue-eyed, then the probability that a Swede will be blue-eyed is 90 percent. As I see it, probabilities always are objective facts about populations. They never are some hazy kind of weak logical links.

4 Every inductive argument is really just a deductive argument in disguise. Take that argument about arsenic, for example. It starts from the premise that the available data show arsenic to have poisoned in the past; we can add as another premise that whatever has happened in the past probably will happen in the future; and then we can deductively derive the conclusion that arsenic probably will poison in the future.

31 INDUCTIVE GENERALIZATION

Suppose we have met some swans and observed each of them to be white. This information is not enough to enable us to prove deductively that all swans are white, or even that the next swan we meet will be so. But here we might construct an inductive argument of the form:

Inductive generalization

a, b, c...each has been observed to be S and P.
Nothing has been observed to be S without being P.

Therefore, probably, all S are P.

Here the conclusion is an "all" sentence and is called a generalization. In terms of our example, a, b, c...would be the individual swans that have been observed; "S" would be interpreted to mean "swans," and "P" would be interpreted to mean "white things." This is the simplest form of inductive generalization. Notice, however, that some arguments of this form are logically good, while others are not. The form alone does not settle this.

A kindred but slightly more complicated form of reasoning would start from evidence that a certain percentage of observed S are P, and it would pass to the conclusion (a statistical generalization) that probably approximately the same percentage of all S are P. For example, from the fact that 20 percent of the birds I have seen today were robins, I might infer that probably about 20 percent of the birds now in my part of the country are robins.

In trying to judge what the degree of probability is with which the conclusion follows from the evidence in an inductive generalization, we need to take account of various factors. These factors have to do with how reasonable it is to suppose that the things observed constitute a 'fair sample' of S in general, with regard to being P. How reasonable is it to suppose that the particular swans that we have observed constitute a 'fair sample' of swans in general, with regard to color? Five factors should be considered.

1 The degree to which a, b, c...have been observed to be alike (besides the mere fact that each is both S and P) is important. This is called the *positive analogy*. For instance, suppose that all the observed swans were female and American. Then our argument would be relatively weak, for we would not have excluded the possibility that it is only female swans, or perhaps only American swans, that are white. In general, the greater the positive analogy among the observed instances, the weaker the argument, other things being equal.

2 Also important is the degree to which a, b, c...have been observed to differ one from another. This is called the *negative analogy*. For instance, if we have observed swans in winter and in summer, in the wilds and in captivity, young and fully grown, then our argument is strengthened. We have increased the probability that the sample is representative as regards color, for we have excluded the possibilities that it is only swans in winter, or only wild swans, or only young ones that are white. In general, the greater the negative analogy among the observed instances, the stronger the argument. (Notice that the extent of the positive analogy and the extent of the negative analogy are two quite independent matters. Having much positive analogy need not entail having little negative analogy.)

3 Also we should consider the *character of the conclusion*; we must take account of how much it says. The more sweeping the generalization that we seek to establish, the less is its probability relative to our evidence, and the weaker is our argument. For example, "All swans are white" is a generalization that says more than "All American swans are nonblack." The less specific the subject term and the more specific the predicate term, the more a universal generalization says. Statistical conclusions too can differ in how much they say; that at least 10 percent of the birds in this wood are robins is a statistical generalization that says less than does the generalization that between 19 and 21 percent of birds in this wood are robins.

In addition to these three factors, there are two others, perhaps less fundamental but also deserving notice.

4 We should consider the *number of observed instances* ($a, b, c \ldots$). An increase in the number of observed instances normally means an increase in the strength of the argument. Here a rather abstract question may be raised: Does an increase in the number of observed instances, just as such, necessarily increase the probability of the generalization? Or does the conclusion become more probable only because additional observed instances ordinarily mean an increase in the extent of the negative analogy among the observed instances? Suppose that the number of observed instances was increased without the negative analogy thereby being increased. Would this strengthen the argument, or would this leave the probability of the conclusion unchanged? Philosophers disagree in their views about this abstract question. Fortunately, the matter is very academic, for in actual practice when we increase the number of observed instances we practically always also increase the extent of the negative analogy among the observed instances.

5 Finally, we should consider the *relevance* of S to P. How probable is it that there would be a connection between the property of being a swan and the property of being white? Are these properties that may reasonably be expected to be correlated? Here we must rely upon the background of knowledge we already possess. In our example we might reasonably suppose that being a swan is relevant to being white, since we know (from previous inductions) that birds of the same species usually have the same coloring.

In practice, we should take all five of these factors into account, weighing them together, when we seek to decide whether a specific inductive generalization attains a relatively strong or relatively weak degree of probability. We need to use common sense as we ask ourselves whether we are entitled to suppose that our observed instances constitute a 'fair sample' of the whole class about which we are generalizing.

As we try to weigh the strength of an inductive argument, three main types of mistakes should be avoided. We shall call these the fallacies of forgetful induction, hasty induction, and slothful induction. All three are mistakes that can arise in inductive reasoning of any type, but we shall consider them now just in connection with inductive generalization. First there is the mistake that arises from neglecting some of the relevant empirical information that we possess. Let us call this the fallacy of *forgetful induction*. Where the conclusion is a generalization, we may speak of the fallacy of forgetful generalization.

For example, suppose a woman wishes to estimate how many polo players there are in a given city. She visits a golf club there and interviews the first 500 people she meets, of whom 10 percent say that they play polo. She then concludes that it is highly probable that just about 10 percent of the people in this city are polo players. This is an example of very faulty reasoning. Her mistake lies in forgetting that people met in a golf club are usually sportsmen and relatively well-to-do; sportsmen and the well-to-do play polo more than other people do, as polo is a sporty and expensive game. These are facts that she knows, if only she would stop to think. Thus there is positive reason to believe that this sample is not representative of the population of the city at large, with respect to polo playing. Under the circumstances, this woman's conclusion is not highly probable, as she imagines, but really has a very low degree of probability.

A second type of mistake in inductive reasoning is the fallacy of leaping to a conclusion when the evidence is too slight to make the conclusion very probable. Let us call this the fallacy of *hasty induction*. With regard to inductive generalization, this had traditionally been called the fallacy of hasty generalization. For example, suppose a young man for the first time meets a young woman from Carrie Nation College. He finds that she talks rather firmly about women's rights, and so the next day he tells his friends that all the young women from Carrie Nation are fierce female liberationists. Here his reasoning is illogical, for he has based a sweeping generalization upon very slight evidence. The probability of the conclusion relative to his data is rather low, and yet he states his conclusion as though it were highly probable. His mistake is that he leaps to a conclusion on the basis of very little evidence. This is somewhat different from the mistake made by the woman who visited the country club; she collected a considerable amount of evidence but, in evaluating it, forgot about other relevant information that was available to her.

The third type of mistake is the mistake of treating a conclusion as though it were less probable than it is. If a conclusion is something that, for one reason or another, we would prefer not to believe, all too often we refuse to accept it even after the evidence has piled up strongly; we persist in believing that the conclusion is improbable when it is not. Let us call this the fallacy of *slothful induction*. When it arises in connection with inductive generalization, it is the fallacy of slothful generalization.

Suppose the question is whether Hugo is a driver who will have relatively few accidents in the long run. In March the Buick he was driving ran into a tree. His father then bought him a Chrysler, but in April it collided with a telephone pole. His indulgent father then bought him a Pontiac, but in May it struck a stone wall. His still-indulgent father then bought him a Ford, but in June it plunged into a river. The father, thinking back over the available evidence, begins to wonder whether it does not perhaps point toward the generalization that if young Hugo is allowed to continue driving, he will comparatively often have accidents. But Hugo insists that it is just a series of unfortunate coincidences; after all, a person can have some accidents without necessarily having a bad record in the long run. He urges his father to buy him a Cadillac so that he can show how safe a driver he really is. Here is an instance of slothful generalization. Hugo is refusing to face the facts, for the evidence is sufficient to make it very probable that he is not a safe driver. The probability, which a prudent father ought to recognize, is that if Hugo is given more cars, he will smash them soon.

EXERCISE 31

*A Inside an ancient Egyptian tomb, Dr. Gray finds a tightly sealed parcel. It contains many seeds, all of which look alike. She plants five dozen, and is surprised when ten of them sprout. They grow into plants very like modern barley, but only half as tall. She infers that all the seeds are of ancient barley, and that ancient barley plants were only half as big as modern ones. Consider whether this inference would be made stronger or weaker by each of following changes (explain each answer).

   1 Suppose the planted seeds were grown under various conditions of moisture, soil, and temperature.

   2 Suppose all the planted seeds came from the top of the parcel.

   3 Suppose she merely infers that all the seeds in the parcel are barley.

   4 Suppose the seeds that were planted came from parcels found in several different Egyptian tombs.

   5 Suppose 1,000 seeds were planted, but still only 10 sprouted.

   6 Suppose all five dozen seeds that were planted sprout.

   7 Suppose the parcel was accidentally exposed to a heavy dose of radiation when other objects in the tomb were x-rayed.

   8 Suppose the tomb was opened on Halloween.

   9 Suppose she infers that most ancient crops were only half the size of modern ones.

   10 Suppose the plants grow to very different sizes, but their average size is half that of modern barley.

B Discuss any fallacies committed in the following examples.

   1 I've questioned all the adults on my block, and half of them say they're going to vote next Tuesday. So I guess about half the people in the city will vote on Tuesday.

   2 You lost a job last year, and now you're losing your present job. It just seems that you can't ever hold any job at all.

   3 A cupful of water from the reservoir was tested and was found safe to drink. The authorities concluded that all the water in the reservoir was safe to drink.

   4 Using a finely calibrated steel tape, I measured the length of the bridge on several of the hottest and several of the coldest days of the year, finding no difference. So probably the bridge does not expand or contract with changing temperatures.

   5 You introduced me to your friend Ed, and he just talked about baseball. You introduced me to your friend Phil, and he just talked about the theater. All your friends are so boring!

   6 Since I started teaching in this school last week, I've found three pupils in my morning class smoking pot; several during recess were taking strangely colored pills; some in my afternoon class were fooling around with spoons and needles; and then the principal offered me some unfamiliar white powder. Is it possible that there is drug activity going on here?

7 Texas has a very wet climate. I know, because I visited Galveston last August, and it had 3 inches of rain in a single day.

8 Murders are always discovered, sooner or later. Just think back: When did you ever hear of a murder that wasn't discovered?

9 Oh, yes, I'm glad to recommend him. He was always an excellent employee. I never had reason to question his honesty. True, he did take money out of the till quite a few times, and what he had told me about his past experience wasn't true—but I don't believe in setting unreasonable standards of conduct for people I employ.

10 From dawn to dusk we tramped the woods, looking for owls, but without finding any. So probably hardly any owls live in these woods.

32 INDUCTIVE ANALOGY

An analogy is a parallel or a resemblance between two different things. Sometimes we use literal language to talk about analogies, and when we use figurative language, we nearly always employ analogies. To use language in a *figurative* way is to stretch words beyond the bounds of their normal literal uses. Figurative language often is used for description, though sometimes as a basis for argument. Simile and metaphor are the two most familiar forms of figurative language.

A *simile* is a statement that one thing is *like* something else of a very different type, or that one thing *does* something as if it were something else of a very different type. A metaphor states that one thing *is* something else of a very different type, or that it *does* something very different from what it literally does do. In Shakespeare's account of Cleopatra on the Nile we find a combination of forms of description:

The barge she sat in, like a burnished throne,
Burned on the water; the poop was beaten gold.

Here the claim that the barge was like a burnished throne is a simile; to say that it burned on the water is to use a metaphor; and to say that its poop was beaten gold is literal, nonfigurative description. A simile or metaphor says something which, if taken literally, would be false or even absurd; when we understand that it is intended to be figurative, we see that it rests upon an analogy of a kind not ordinarily noticed, an analogy that may be vivid and illuminating.

Often we use analogies in our discourse just for purposes of description, but sometimes we employ them also as a basis for reasoning. In connection with inductive generalization, we have already noted the importance of the positive and negative analogies among the observed instances; but we shall see that there are other inductive inferences in which analogy plays a still more prominent role. This happens when an arguer points out an analogy between two things for the purpose of proving something about one of them.

Suppose the postman once met a boxer dog and found that it had a bad temper and a tendency to bite. If he now meets another boxer dog, he may reason by analogy that this dog also is likely to have a bad temper and a tendency to bite. Here his reasoning rests upon analogy. From the fact that the present dog resembles the past one in breed, he infers that probably it resembles it in temperament as well. Moreover, his reasoning is inductive, since the conclusion (that this new dog has a bad temper and will bite) expresses an empirical conjecture going beyond the evidence then available to the postman.

We can describe this type of reasoning in more general terms if we notice that sometimes there may be more than one past instance upon which the inductive analogy is based. For example, suppose that we have observed a number of swans in the past (call them a, b, c) and have observed each of them to be white. Now we learn of another swan (call it k) whose color we have not yet had opportunity to observe. We may reason by analogy that since this new bird resembles the already observed ones in species, probably it will resemble them in color as well. Here the reasoning rests upon an analogy drawn between the present bird and a number of previously observed ones.

Inductive analogy

a, b, c...each has been observed to be S and P.
k is an S.

Therefore, probably, k is P.

The form of this reasoning is closely akin to that of inductive generalization, but the difference is that here the conclusion is a singular sentence rather than a universal generalization.[38]

In judging the strength of an argument of this type, we need to take account of the five factors discussed in connection with inductive generalization and also of one additional factor:

1 We must consider the extent of the positive analogy among the observed instances, a, b, c..., that is, the respects (not counting being S and being P) in which the previously observed instances are known to be alike. In the example of the postman, there was only one past instance; there the question of positive analogy among the previously observed instances does not arise.

2 Also we must consider the extent of the negative analogy among the observed instances, that is, the respects in which they are known to differ from one another. The greater the extent of these differences, the stronger the argument.

3 We must consider how much the conclusion says. Does it make a very informative claim, or is it comparatively vague? The more the conclusion says, the weaker is the argument. For example, the conclusion "This dog will bite" says more than does "This dog will bark or bite."

4 We should consider the number of observed instances, a, b, c, etc.; the more of them there are, the stronger is the argument.

5 We should consider what our past experience tells us about the probable relevance of S to P.

6 The additional very important factor that must be taken into account is the degree of analogy between the new thing k on the one hand and the previously observed instances a, b, c, etc., on the other hand. If it is known that k has properties that none of a, b, c, etc., possesses, or if it is known that all a, b, c, etc., possess properties that k lacks, then the argument is weaker than it would otherwise be. For example, if we know that a, b, c, etc., are all European swans but that k is an Australian swan, then our argument is weakened. But if k, to the best of our knowledge, is very like a, b, c, etc., then the argument may be quite strong.

When an argument by analogy is weak, sometimes a good way of showing that it is weak is to show that the available evidence permits us to construct other arguments by analogy that are no weaker but that reach an opposite conclusion. If I think that the postman is unduly worried about the analogy between the present boxer dog and the one he met in the past, I may try to oppose his reasoning by constructing an argument in support of the conclusion that this dog will not bite which is no weaker than his. I remind the postman that this new boxer belongs to old Mrs. Jones, who is well known for her amiable pets; the postman is forgetting that her cats are very friendly, so is her goat, and so is her pet crow. By analogy, since this dog resembles the cats, goat, and crow in being a pet of good old Mrs. Jones, probably it resembles them also in being friendly. Here I am able to use a *counter-analogy* in order to combat the original argument by analogy.

EXERCISE 32

*A The director of the city airport is accustomed to receiving telephoned bomb threats. He has had five so far, but no bomb has ever exploded at the airport. This Monday morning there is another threat: the gruff caller says, "There's a bomb at your airport," and hangs up. The director decides not to close the airport, for he concludes that the threat is a hoax. Consider whether (and why) the probability of his conclusion would be strengthened or weakened by the following changes.

  1 The previous threats occurred at various seasons of the year.

  2 Today's caller insisted on speaking to the director in person, while the previous callers had talked to the phone operator.

  3 On several of the previous occasions bombs were found that did not explode.

  4 The airport's first strike has just begun, as airline mechanics walk out.

  5 The previous threats have all been on Monday mornings.

  6 The director concludes merely that no bomb will go off within the next half hour.

  7 Today is April Fool's Day.

  8 All the previous threats were telephoned in by a voice which sounded the same as today's voice.

9 The director concludes that threats like this are always hoaxes.

10 Today is the director's birthday.

B In each case explain what items are being compared and in what respects. Is the analogy being used as the basis for an argument? If there is an argument, discuss its strength.

1 As when a lion has worsted a tireless boar in conflict, when, with high hearts, they battle for some scant spring upon a mountain's peaks and both would drink, and the lion with his might overcomes the quickly panting boar, so Hector, Priam's son, deprived Menoetius' brave son of his life with the spear, from close at hand, after he had slain many.

HOMER, The Iliad

2 The old couple were left alone in a home that looked suddenly shrunken and decrepit too.... Then Arina Vlasyevna went up to him, and, laying her gray head to his, said: "It can't be helped, Vasya! A son is like a severed branch. He's like the falcon that comes when it wants and goes when it wants; and you and I are like mushrooms on a tree stump, sitting side by side forever on the same spot. Only I will remain the same to you always, and you to me."

IVAN TURGENEV, Fathers and Sons

3 Existential philosophy and the psycho-therapists... demonstrate to secure, contented, and happy mankind that it is really unhappy and desperate and simply unwilling to admit that it is in a predicament about which it knows nothing, and from which only they can rescue it. Wherever there is health, strength, security, simplicity, they scent luscious fruit to gnaw at or to lay their pernicious eggs on.

DIETRICH BONHOEFFER, Letters and Papers from Prison

4 Justice is the first virtue of social institutions, as truth is of systems of thought. A theory however elegant and economical must be rejected or revised if it is untrue; likewise laws and institutions no matter how efficient and well-arranged must be reformed or abolished if they are unjust.... The only thing that permits us to acquiesce in an erroneous theory is the lack of a better one; analogously, an injustice is tolerable only when it is necessary to avoid an even greater injustice.

JOHN RAWLS, A Theory of Justice

5 Mistresses are like books. If you pore upon them too much they doze you and make you unfit for company; but if used discreetly, you are the fitter for conversation by 'em.   WILLIAM WYCHERLEY, The Country Wife

6 Why then should the education of apes be impossible? Why might not the ape, by dint of great pains, at last imitate after the manner of deaf mutes, the motions necessary for pronunciation? I do not dare decide whether the ape's organs of speech, however trained, would be incapable of articulation. But because of the great analogy between ape and man and because there is no known animal whose external and internal organs so strikingly resemble man's, it would surprise me if speech were absolutely impossible to the ape.   JULIEN OFFRAY DE LA METTRIE, Man a Machine

7 Every one who really thinks for himself is like a monarch. His position is undelegated and supreme. His judgments, like royal decrees, spring from his own sovereign power and proceed directly from himself. He acknowledges authority as little as a monarch admits a command; he subscribes to nothing but what he has himself authorized. The multitude of common minds, laboring under all sorts of current opinions, authorities, prejudices, is like the people, which silently obeys the law and accepts orders from above.   ARTHUR SCHOPENHAUER, *The Art of Literature*

8 "Do you think," said Candide, "that men have always massacred each other, as they do today, that they have always been false, cozening, faithless, ungrateful, thieving, weak, inconstant, mean-spirited, envious, greedy, drunken, miserly, ambitious, bloody, slanderous, debauched, fanatic, hypocritical, and stupid?"

"Do you think" said Martin, "that hawks have always eaten pigeons when they could find them?"

"Of course I do," said Candide.

"Well," said Martin, "if hawks have always had the same character, why should you suppose that men have changed theirs?"

VOLTAIRE, *Candide*

9 Words are like leaves; and where they most abound,
Much fruit of sense beneath is rarely found.

ALEXANDER POPE, "Essay on Criticism"

10 Johnson told me, that he went up thither without mentioning it to his servant, when he wanted to study, secure from interruption; for he would not allow his servant to say he was not at home when he really was. "A servant's strict regard for truth (said he) must be weakened by such a practice. A philosopher may know that it is merely a form of denial; but few servants are such nice distinguishers. If I accustom a servant to tell a lie for *me*, have I not reason to apprehend that he will tell many lies for *himself*."   JAMES BOSWELL, *Life of Johnson*

33 HYPOTHESES ABOUT CAUSES

Some inductive arguments aim to establish conclusions about relations of cause and effect. These are important to us, because much of our thinking about the world involves questions of causes and effects. We need to know not merely what phenomena occur, but also which phenomena cause which others. A sentence saying that one thing is cause of another thing—e.g., "Arsenic causes death"—normally has to be an empirical sentence.[39] If such sentences are shown to be true, there must be some appropriate procedure for establishing them. Let us consider the sort of evidence and the sort of reasoning that are required.

A fallacy related to causes occurs often in political speeches and in other common kinds of careless thinking. Suppose someone argues, "There was a decrease in unemployment soon after President Smith took office. So Smith deserves credit for getting people back to work." This is an inductive argument, an argument whose conclusion is a hypothesis about cause and effect (that decreased employment was an effect caused by Smith). But it is a very bad argument. It commits the fallacy of *post hoc, ergo propter hoc* (Latin: "after this, therefore on account of it"). This fallacy is a special case of the general fallacy of hasty induction. Here the speaker has leaped from the evidence that unemployment declined soon after Smith took office to the conclusion that unemployment declined because Smith had taken office. This is too hasty a leap. To be sure, the fact that unemployment declined soon afterward may, if there is no contrary evidence, make it faintly probable that perhaps Smith was the cause; but this fact is utterly insufficient to make it strongly probable. We would need much more evidence before we could reasonably attach any strong probability to the conclusion.

In order to know that one thing is the cause of another, we need to know that the first thing happened or existed earlier than the second, but we need to know a great deal more besides. (In most ordinary cases a cause certainly must precede its effect; whether there are some cases in which a cause may merely be simultaneous with its effect is a point disputed by philosophers.)

What is involved in saying that one thing causes another, beyond the claim that the former thing happens earlier? Let us consider another case: A doctor gives an experimental drug to a patient suffering from a serious disease; the next day the patient's symptoms are lessened, and the patient gradually recovers. What would it mean to say that taking the drug caused the cure in this particular case? We can discuss this matter without worrying about the inner biochemical processes occurring in the patient's bloodstream, for it is possible to know that x causes y without knowing the intervening steps by means of which x causes y (the Indians knew that taking quinine causes relief from malaria, although they did not know how or why it does so).

But what does it mean to say that taking the drug caused the cure? For one thing, it means that taking this drug was somehow *sufficient* to ensure this patient's cure. If the patient had not taken the drug, then the cure would not have occurred when it did. This still is not very clear. But it can be explained as follows: what has happened in this patient's case is an instance of some general regularity, whereby anyone whose case is appropriately similar to that of this patient will cease to have the ailment after taking the drug. Notice that the claim that taking the drug cured this patient would be made improbable if we discovered that other, similar patients are not cured after taking it.

• For another thing, to claim that this dose cured this patient surely is to claim that in such cases, taking the drug is *necessary* in order for the cure to occur when it does. That is, if the patient had not had the drug, the cure would not have occurred (at least, not when it did). Yet someone may object: What sense does it make to talk about what would have occurred if something that did happen had not happened? We cannot go back and change the past; how could we ever find out whether the patient would have recovered without the drug? We must answer this objection by pointing out that talk about what would have happened to this patient derives its sense from its implicit reference to what does happen to other, appropriately similar patients on other sufficiently similar occasions. When we say that if this patient had not had the dose, the cure would not have occurred, we are implicitly claiming that other patients with the same ailment, whose cases are appropriately similar to that of this patient except that they do not get the drug, are not usually cured.

Putting together these points and generalizing them, we may say that a sentence of the form "x causes y" by its very meaning normally implies not only that x occurs earlier than y but also that, in cases of some appropriate kind, x always is present if y is, and only if y is. This is a central part, though to be sure not all, of what is meant by speaking of causes.[40]

The nineteenth-century English philosopher John Stuart Mill described several fundamental ways of detecting causes. These are known as *Mill's methods*. When properly understood and not overrated, these methods are useful in guiding our thinking about causes. We shall consider three of these methods, discussing them first in connection with a concrete example.

Suppose that some of the students who eat in the Coolidge College cafeteria are taken ill after lunch. We investigate a few of the cases and gather the following data:

Student *a* ate soup, ate fish, ate salad, and got ptomaine.
Student *b* ate soup, ate no fish, ate salad, and got ptomaine.
Student *c* ate no soup, ate fish, ate salad, and got ptomaine.

These data will enable us to reach a conclusion about the cause of the food poisoning, provided that we may make a certain assumption. We must be entitled to assume that one and only one of the factors listed (eating of soup, eating of fish, eating of salad) is the cause of the food poisoning. If we assume that, we can use what Mill called the *method of agreement*: We reason that the cause must be present in each case where the effect is present. Here eating salad must have been the cause of the ptomaine, since it is the factor with regard to which all the cases agree.

On another occasion, students again are taken ill. This time we collect the following data:

Student *a* ate meat, ate pie, ate ice cream, and got ptomaine.
Student *b* ate no meat, ate pie, ate no ice cream, and got no ptomaine.
Student *c* ate meat, ate no pie, ate no ice cream, and got no ptomaine.

Again, before we can draw any definite conclusion, we must be entitled to assume that the cause is some one of the factors on the list. But if we make this assumption, we can use what Mill called the *method of difference*: We reason that any factor present in cases in which the effect is absent cannot be the cause. Thus, by process of elimination, we see that eating ice cream must have been the cause of the food poisoning on this occasion.

On still another occasion we again find students being taken ill after eating in the cafeteria. This time we collect the following data:

Student *a* ate one hamburger and got ptomaine with fever of 101°.
Student *b* ate two hamburgers and got ptomaine with fever of 102°.
Student *c* ate three hamburgers and got ptomaine with fever of 103°.

Here we are concerned not with the simple presence or absence of cause and effect but rather with the degree to which cause and effect are present. When we infer from these data that the hamburgers caused the ptomaine, we are employing what Mill called the *method of concomitant variation*. If a factor is present in all and only those cases in which the effect is present, then the more closely its variations in degree are correlated with the variations in degree of the effect, the greater is the probability that this factor is the cause.

Mill regarded these three[41] methods as useful both as a guide in collecting data and planning new experiments to discover causes and as a guide in reflecting about the strength of arguments that try to prove conclusions about cause and effect. His methods are useful in both these ways: for planning further inquiries and for evaluating results that have been obtained. However, we must not make the mistake of assuming that these simple methods provide an infallible way of detecting causes. Far from it, for in any overall piece of inductive reasoning within which we make use of Mill's methods, we always must evaluate the probability that we have actually included the cause among the factors of which we take account. Unless we are entitled to think it probable that we have done this, use of these methods is not legitimate.

Fallacies involving Mill's methods occur frequently. A crude example is this: Suppose that one day a man eats popcorn while watching television and suffers indigestion; the next day he eats pizza while watching television and suffers indigestion; the next day he eats cheesecake while watching television and suffers indigestion. Using the method of difference, he argues that neither popcorn nor pizza nor cheesecake caused his indigestion, and he concludes that watching television caused it (he thinks perhaps the electrical radiations are to blame). Here the reasoning is very poor, for he omitted overeating from the list of factors of which he took account. It certainly ought to have been considered as a possible cause. Here the cause in general may have been overeating, with eating too much popcorn being the specific cause on the first day, eating too much pizza being the specific cause on the second day, and so on.

As another example, suppose it is found that in a certain town those young people who regularly attend church relatively seldom get into trouble with the police, while those who do not attend church relatively more often get into trouble with the police. Using the method of difference, the local religious leaders point to these facts as proof that religion causes improvement in the moral fiber of the young. Is this a reasonable conclusion? Not if it is being claimed that these data by themselves confer any very high degree of probability upon the conclusion. There are certainly other factors that should be taken into account before we could say that any strong proof had been given. Is it not very possible, for instance, that a certain kind of family environment causes some young people both to be religious and to be law-abiding, whereas the lack of that kind of family environment causes others to be neither religious nor law-abiding? If this suggestion is correct, sending young people to church would not be likely to make them more law-abiding, in the absence of that special kind of family environment.

EXERCISE 33

*A Are Mill's methods being employed in the following examples, and if so, which of them? Discuss the soundness of the reasoning.

1 Wanda, Tony, and Mona each smokes heavily and has a chronic cough. Apparently heavy smoking gives people chronic coughs.

2 Jan, June, and Millie each sings a lot but has no chronic cough. So singing probably doesn't cause chronic coughs.

3 Tom doesn't smoke and hardly ever coughs. Sean smokes a pack a day and has a slight chronic cough. Alec smokes two packs a day and has a bad chronic cough. Sheila smokes three packs a day and hacks constantly. Apparently smoking causes coughing.

4 Bill smokes heavily, drinks heavily, sings a lot, and has a chronic cough. Mary doesn't smoke, doesn't drink, sings a lot, and has no cough. Phil doesn't smoke, drinks a lot, doesn't sing, and has no cough. What appears to cause coughs?

5 Rover is always scratching himself; he has fleas, ticks, and a tight collar. Fido doesn't scratch himself; he has ticks but no fleas, and a loose collar. Rex doesn't scratch himself; he has no fleas, no ticks, and a tight collar. What seems to make such dogs scratch?

6 At the party May drank martinis, drank whiskey, ate peanuts, and was taken ill. Monroe drank vodka, drank whiskey, ate peanuts, and was taken ill. Zara drank rum, drank gin, ate peanuts, and was taken ill. It looks as though the peanuts caused the illness.

B In each example, what method is being employed? How sound is the reasoning?

1 A Stanford research team has calculated that the 3 million American males between the ages of twenty-five and thirty-four who have failed to complete high school will earn $237 billion less in personal income over their working lifetimes than will be earned by an equal number of high school graduates. They estimate that it would have cost only $40 billion to put these men through high school. "Each dollar of social investment for this purpose would have generated about $6 per capita of national income, over the lifetime of the group," they stated.

2 According to a study sponsored by the National Institute of Human Development, more teenage girls who obtained abortions than teenage girls who gave birth were practicing contraception at the time they became pregnant. This indicates that teenagers are not using abortion as a substitute for contraception.

3   In Glasgow a German shepherd lifted his leg in the natural fashion, but his target was a city electricity junction box, and the resulting short circuit blew him into the street. Soon he grew grumpy and distrustful, and bit his master. The owner sued the city for damages, saying that he was off work for eight weeks because of the bite. But the sheriff rejected his claim, declaring that the injury was inflicted by the dog, not by the city.

4   An insurance company's study showed that among 3300 automobile-insurance policyholders the accident frequency for those who said they were nonsmokers was 3.75 per 100 car-years, compared with 6.59 for those who said they were smokers. The company concluded that non-smokers are significantly better insurance risks.

5   On the average, children born between May and October seem to get slightly higher scores in intelligence tests than children born from November to April. Is it the season of conception or birth that somehow affects the intelligence of children, in so far as these tests can measure it, or is it the intelligence of the parents that influences the season of conception of the child? The second must surely be the explanation: for example, when one compares the average scores of winter and summer children who are brothers and sisters, the difference between them almost completely disappears.   P. B. MEDAWAR, *The Future of Man*

6   It cannot be assumed that economic motives are the only ones which determine the behavior of men in society. The unquestionable fact that different individuals, races and nations behave differently under the same economic conditions in itself proves that the economic factor cannot be the sole determinant.
     SIGMUND FREUD, "Thoughts for the Time on War and Death"

34 NUMERICAL PROBABILITIES

We have been using the word "probability" in a sense that has to do with inductive arguments, identifying the degree of probability with the degree to which it is reasonable to believe the conclusion on the basis of the evidence. Probability is always a relative matter, in that it makes sense to call a conjecture probable only relative to some evidence, never just in and of itself. A conjecture, whether true or false, may have a high degree of probability relative to one body of evidence and a low degree of probability relative to some other body of evidence.

Various symbols can be used to represent probability, but we shall employ a pair of slanting strokes:

We shall use strokes between two sentences to form an expression that names the probability of the first sentence relative to the second. Thus, if we let "H" be one sentence and "E" another, we write "H // E" as a name for the probability of the former relative to the latter, that is, the degree to which it would be reasonable to believe the former if the latter was the evidence one had.

In the expression "H // E," "H" is the hypothesis (the conclusion) whose probability we are weighing, and "E" is the evidence (the premise, or conjunction of premises) upon which the probability is based. If we let "H" represent the sentence "All swans are white," "H'" represent "The next swan we meet will be white," and "E" symbolize our evidence regarding swans that we have observed to be white, then we can write:

$H' \mathbin{/\!/} E > H \mathbin{/\!/} E$

That is, the probability that the next swan will be white is greater than is the probability that all swans are white, relative to our evidence. Here we make a comparison between two degrees of probability, although we have not assigned a definite numerical value to either.

One small reservation is necessary. We shall speak of the probability of a hypothesis relative to the evidence only where the evidence can be expressed in a sentence that is not a contradiction. If "E" represents a contradiction, other sentences cannot have any sort of probability, high or low, relative to it, as we are interested in considering the probabilities of hypotheses relative only to evidence that might possibly be true. To put it another way, when an inductive argument is found to have inconsistent premises, we must reject the argument completely; there is no point in thinking that the conclusion possesses any sort of probability, high or low, relative to inconsistent premises.

There is a maximum possible degree of probability. Knowing that a sentence is true occasionally puts one in a position of being equally certain of another sentence. Then the probability of the second sentence relative to the first has the maximum possible value. This happens when (and only when) the first sentence deductively implies the second. For instance, the probability of "Some white things are swans" relative to the evidence "Some swans are white" has this maximum value. It is conventional to correlate the number 1 with this maximum degree of probability. Writing "W" for the first sentence and "S" for the second, we have:

$W \mathbin{/\!/} S = 1$

There is also a minimum possible degree of probability. Knowing that "Some swans are white" is true, one is in a position to assign the minimum degree of probability to the sentence "All swans are black" ("B" for short); that is, relative to the known data, the degree to which it is reasonable to believe "B" has hit rock bottom. It is conventional to correlate the number zero with this minimum degree of probability. Thus we say:

$B \mathbin{/\!/} S = 0$

This minimum degree of probability arises when (and only when) the hypothesis is contradicted by the evidence.

All other degrees of probability fall between these two extremes. Degrees of probability falling between these extremes sometimes are comparable with one another and sometimes are not. We can say that relative to the historical evidence we now possess, it is more probable that there was such a man as Plato than that there was such a man as Homer, and it is more probable that there was such a man as George Washington than that there was such a man as Plato. But it does not make sense to ask for an exact measure of how much more probable one of these hypotheses is than another. Moreover, suppose someone asks whether, relative to present evidence, the hypothesis that there was such a man as Homer is more or less probable than is the hypothesis that there is no life on Mars. Perhaps we cannot answer. The two hypotheses are very different, and there may be no basis upon which to make any comparison of their degrees of probability.

If there is no reason for calling one probability greater than another, we cannot maintain that they must be equal, for that view would lead to absurdities. For instance, it would lead us to say that the probability that there was such a man as Homer is equal to the probability that there is no life on Mars (since we have no reason for calling one probability greater than the other). It would also lead us to say that the probability that there was such a man as George Washington is equal to the probability that there is no life on Mars (since we again have no reason for calling one probability greater than the other). This would imply that the probability that Homer existed equals the probability that Washington existed; yet these probabilities are not equal. Thus we must conclude that it is not always possible to make comparisons of degrees of probability of this kind.

In certain special but important kinds of cases, however, we not only can compare probabilities, but can compare them so fully that numbers between 0 and 1 can be assigned to represent their degrees. Use of numbers means that every numerical probability is comparable with every other (either greater, smaller, or equal). Also, we can go further and introduce arithmetical operations such as addition and subtraction. In what sort of situation may numbers be used to measure probabilities? The most straightforward kinds of cases in which this is possible are ones like those involved in some gambling games, where the events in which we are interested can be analyzed into certain fundamental possibilities that are equally reasonable to expect.

Consider the rolling of dice. If someone shows us a pair of dice and we have no positive reason for thinking them irregular, the reasonable thing to suppose is that these dice, when rolled, will behave generally as do most other dice. That is, we believe that the various faces of each die will come up just about equally often in the long run, although their sequence will be unpredictable, and there will be no detectable correlation, in the long run, between the sequence in which faces come up on one die and on the other.

Granting this, what is reasonable to expect regarding the outcome of the next roll of these two dice? It is certain that on the next roll each die must show one and only one of its six faces. (Otherwise a genuine roll would not have been achieved.) We have for each die six mutually exclusive and exhaustive alternatives, which are equally reasonable to expect; therefore, each of these outcomes must be assigned a probability of ⅙. Then what is the probability of getting, say, a total of 7 with the two dice? Here we must reason as follows: With two dice, each of which can land in just one of six equally probable ways, there are thirty-six equally probable outcomes. We write "1–1" to represent the first die landing with one dot up and the second die landing with one dot up, etc. Of these outcomes there are six (underlined in the list) that yield the result in which we are interested, that is, showing a total of seven dots.

1–1	1–2	1–3	1–4	1–5	<u>1–6</u>
2–1	2–2	2–3	2–4	<u>2–5</u>	2–6
3–1	3–2	3–3	<u>3–4</u>	3–5	3–6
4–1	4–2	<u>4–3</u>	4–4	4–5	4–6
5–1	<u>5–2</u>	5–3	5–4	5–5	5–6
<u>6–1</u>	6–2	6–3	6–4	6–5	6–6

Thus the probability of rolling a 7 equals 6 divided by 36, or ⅙. Here we are following the general principle that the numerical probability of a result is equal to the number of outcomes favorable to that result divided by the total number of possible outcomes. Of course this principle makes sense only when we use an exhaustive list of mutually exclusive and equally probable outcomes.

Once we have obtained some numerical probabilities, we can make use of certain elementary laws for deriving further numerical probabilities from ones already known. First there is the law relating the probability of a sentence to the probability of its negation.

Law of Negation

$(-p \mathbin{/\!/} q) = 1 - (p \mathbin{/\!/} q)$

The probability of the negation of a sentence, relative to given evidence, is equal to 1 minus the probability of the sentence itself relative to the same evidence. Notice here that the short dash symbolizes negation—a sentence can have a negation, but a number cannot. The long dash is the subtraction sign—only numbers can be subtracted from one another, not sentences. The strokes are our probability sign, which must not be confused with a division sign, for only sentences are probable relative to one another, and only numbers can be divided by one another.

Let us apply this law of negation to the case of rolling dice. What is the probability of not rolling 7 on the next roll of the dice? This must be 1 minus ⅙ (the probability of rolling 7), that is, ⅚. We can see the correctness of this answer if we look at the list and count the number of ways in which the two dice could fall so as to yield a total different from 7. There are 30 out of 36, and so the probability is indeed ⅚.

Another law is designed for calculating the probability of a conjunction.

Law of Conjunction

$$(p \;\&\; q \;//\; r) = (p \;//\; r) \times (q \;//\; r \;\&\; p)$$

This law tells us that the probability relative to given evidence that two things both will come true equals the probability of the first multiplied by the probability of the second when we assume that the first is true. What is the probability that on the next roll of the dice we will obtain a total greater than 4 and less than 7? Using the law of conjunction, we reason as follows: The probability of getting a total greater than 4 and less than 7 equals the probability of getting a total greater than 4 (30 divided by 36, since 30 possible outcomes are favorable out of the total of 36) multiplied by the probability of getting a total less than 7, on the assumption that our total is greater than 4 (9 divided by 30, since there are 30 possibilities where the total is greater than 4; of these, 9 are favorable to its being less than 7). Thus we have $^{30}\!/_{36} \times {}^{9}\!/_{30} = {}^{9}\!/_{36} = \frac{1}{4}$. If we look at the total list of possible outcomes (Table 1), we see that the law of conjunction has given us the correct result. Table 1 is drawn up to indicate how the law of conjunction has led us to the proper answer in this case.

Table 1

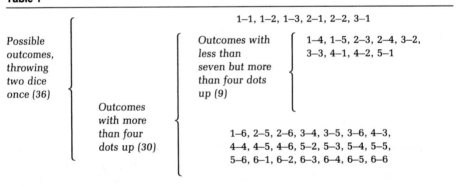

Possible outcomes, throwing two dice once (36)		
	Outcomes with less than seven but more than four dots up (9)	1–1, 1–2, 1–3, 2–1, 2–2, 3–1 1–4, 1–5, 2–3, 2–4, 3–2, 3–3, 4–1, 4–2, 5–1
	Outcomes with more than four dots up (30)	1–6, 2–5, 2–6, 3–4, 3–5, 3–6, 4–3, 4–4, 4–5, 4–6, 5–2, 5–3, 5–4, 5–5, 5–6, 6–1, 6–2, 6–3, 6–4, 6–5, 6–6

We can apply the law of conjunction in a simpler way in cases where the happenings that concern us are *independent*; that is, where the probability of q is unaltered by the assumption that p is true. Suppose we want to calculate the probability of getting heads on the first toss of a coin and getting heads also on the second toss. Here we must multiply the probability of getting heads on the first toss (which is ½, when there is no reason to think the coin abnormal) times the probability of getting heads on the second toss (which is again ½). The probability is simply ½ times ½, or ¼, because here the two events are independent in the sense that what happens on the first toss does not alter the probability of getting heads on the second toss. Where the happenings are independent in this way, we can use the law of conjunction in the simple form:

$$(p \ \& \ q \ /\!/ \ r) = (p \ /\!/ \ r) \times (q \ /\!/ \ r)$$

We also have a law designed for calculating the probability of a disjunction; that is, the probability that at least one of two things will come true.

Law of Disjunction

$$(p \lor q \ /\!/ \ r) = (p \ /\!/ \ r) + (q \ /\!/ \ r) - (p \ \& \ q \ /\!/ \ r)$$

This law tells us that the probability of a (nonexclusive) disjunction equals the sum of the separate probabilities of its components, minus the probability of their conjunction. For instance, with two dice, what is the probability either that both dice will read alike or that the total will be less than 6? The law tells us that this must equal the probability that both dice will read alike (6 divided by 36), plus the probability that their total will be less than 6 (10 divided by 36), minus the probability that both dice will read alike and have a total less than 6 (2 divided by 36). Thus the probability equals $\frac{7}{18}$. We can confirm the correctness of this result by looking at the complete list of outcomes in Table 2.

Table 2

	Outcomes when both dice read alike (6)	3–3, 4–4, 5–5, 6–6
Possible outcomes, throwing two dice once (36)		1–1, 2–2
	Outcomes with less than six dots up (10)	1–2, 1–3, 1–4, 2–1, 2–3, 3–1, 3–2, 4–1
	1–5, 1–6, 2–4, 2–5, 2–6, 3–4, 3–5, 3–6, 4–2, 4–3, 4–5, 4–6, 5–1, 5–2, 5–3, 5–4, 5–6, 6–1, 6–2, 6–3, 6–4, 6–5	

We can calculate the probability of a disjunction in a simpler way if the components cannot both be true. What is the probability that a single die will land with five dots up or with six dots up on a single throw? Here the probability is $\frac{1}{6}$ plus $\frac{1}{6}$ minus zero. We subtract nothing, since the die cannot show two different faces on a single throw. Thus, in cases where the outcomes are mutually exclusive, we merely add the separate probabilities in order to get the probability of the disjunction.

One of the practical uses of these rules for calculating probabilities is deciding whether a gamble is a reasonable one. Suppose that someone invites you to draw two cards from a well-shuffled bridge deck, the first card to be returned and the deck reshuffled before the second card is drawn. He bets you even money that you will not get a spade on either drawing. Would it be reasonable to accept such a bet?

In order to answer, we must calculate your probability of winning. To win, you must draw a spade either on the first trial or on the second trial. There are thirteen spades in the deck of fifty-two cards, and so your probability of succeeding on the first draw is $^{13}\!/_{52}$, or $\frac{1}{4}$; your probability of succeeding on the second draw is the same. But to obtain the probability of your succeeding the first time or the second time, we cannot simply add these two fractions and call that the answer. (According to that fallacious procedure of reckoning, it would be absolutely certain that you would succeed at least once in four drawings—an absurd result.) By the law of disjunction, we must add the two probabilities and then subtract the probability of succeeding both times, which, according to the law of conjunction, is $^{13}\!/_{52} \times {}^{13}\!/_{52}$, or $\frac{1}{16}$. Thus the probability of winning the bet is $\frac{1}{4}$ plus $\frac{1}{4}$ minus $\frac{1}{16}$, or $^{7}\!/_{16}$. Your opponent's probability of winning, according to the law of negation, is 1 minus $^{7}\!/_{16}$, or $^{9}\!/_{16}$. Your opponent has a greater probability of winning than you have, and if you and your opponent have equal amounts of money at stake, it would not be wise for you to accept such a bet.

If your opponent concedes advantage to you as regards the amounts to be wagered, and does so at least in proportion as the probabilities differ, then it becomes reasonable for you to accept the bet. Such a conceded advantage is called "odds." Suppose your opponent offers to pay you $9 if you win, whereas you need pay him only $7 if you lose. That is, here odds of 9 to 7 in your favor are being offered. The bet is now a reasonable one to accept, both from your point of view and from your opponent's; since it is reasonable from both points of view, we call it a *fair bet*.

The result of multiplying a probability by an amount of gain or loss is called a *mathematical expectation*.[42] In the bet just described, your probability of winning ($^{7}\!/_{16}$), multiplied by the amount you stand to win ($9), equals your probability of losing ($^{9}\!/_{16}$), multiplied by the amount you stand to lose ($7). Thus, your mathematical expectation of gain equals your mathematical expectation of loss. It is reasonable to accept a bet when one's mathematical expectation of gain at least equals one's mathematical expectation of loss. To call a bet a fair one is to say that the bet is reasonable from the point of view of each person wagering; in effect, this means that each person's mathematical expectation of gain must equal his or her mathematical expectation of loss.

Now, to say, for instance, that the probability is $\frac{1}{6}$ that a pair of dice will land with a total of seven spots up does not mean that we can definitely expect this outcome to occur once in every six rolls of the dice. Far from it; there is only a moderate probability that this will occur exactly once in a given sequence of six throws. And the probability is very low indeed that in a long series of throws every sixth one will yield this particular outcome. What we can say, however, is that it is highly probable that in the long run just about one-sixth of the outcomes will yield a total of seven spots up. The larger the number of throws, the higher the probability that the fraction of them yielding the outcome 7 will differ from ⅙ by less than any specified percentage. The longer the run, the more probable it is that the relative frequency with which an outcome occurs will closely approximate the probability of that outcome. This principle, which is sometimes referred to as the *law of large numbers,* or the *law of averages,* is fundamental to statistical inference.[43]

Misunderstanding of this principle leads to a common and insidious fallacy, the *Monte Carlo fallacy.* Suppose that a man is playing roulette, and he notices that a certain number has not come up for a long time. He reasons that, because this number has not come up for a long time, there is an increased probability that it will come up on the next spin of the wheel. Or suppose a woman is rolling dice, and she notices that 7 has not been thrown as often lately as was to have been expected; she therefore decides to accept at poorer odds than 1 to 5 a bet that 7 will be thrown on the next roll of the two dice. In both these cases a fallacy is being committed. Both these people are confused in their thinking and are laying their bets foolishly. The law of large numbers does not tell us anything about the probability of what will happen on the next throw; it tells us only about a long-run probability.

It is a complete mistake to think that in this kind of case the relative infrequency of an outcome in the past makes it more probable that it will occur in the future. This kind of thinking runs directly contrary to the whole basic idea of inductive reasoning: the idea that we should expect for the future the *same* sort of thing that we have observed in the past. Those who commit the Monte Carlo fallacy make the mistake of expecting for the future the opposite of what they have observed in the past, because of their misunderstanding of the meaning of the principle about long-run probabilities.

The Monte Carlo fallacy perhaps is best classified as a fallacy of ambiguity. The arguer assumes that "It is improbable that a certain number will fail to come up in n trials" means "Relative to the evidence that the wheel has spun n − 1 times without stopping on that number, it is probable that it will stop there the nth time." Whereas in fact what the sentence means is "Relative to our general evidence about roulette wheels, it is improbable that a wheel will spin n times without ever stopping on that number." Confusion between these two meanings engenders the fallacy.

EXERCISE 34

   *A A standard deck of cards consists of fifty-two cards, comprising four suits of thirteen each. The suits are clubs and spades (black cards), and hearts and diamonds (red cards).

1   From a standard deck, well-shuffled, one card is to be drawn. What is the probability that it will be the Queen of Hearts? That it will not be the Queen of Hearts? That it will be either the Queen of Hearts or the Ace of Spades?

2   From a standard deck, well-shuffled, one card is to be drawn. What is the probability that it will be red? That it will be black? That it will be either red or black? That it will be both red and black?

3   From a standard deck, well-shuffled, one card is to be drawn. At what odds would it be reasonable to bet that the card will be black? That it will be a club? That it will be the Two of hearts?

4   From a standard deck, well-shuffled, one card is to be drawn. It will then be replaced, the deck reshuffled, and another card will be drawn. What is the probability that both cards will be red? That both will be diamonds? That at least one will be a diamond? That at most one will be a diamond?

5   One card will be drawn, but not put back in the deck, and another card will be drawn. What is the probability that both cards will be black? That both will be spades? That at least one will be a spade? That at most one will be a spade?

B   Answer each question, explaining how you reach your result.

1   In a single rolling of a pair of dice, what is the probability of getting an outcome of twelve? Of five? Of eight? Of nine?

2   A coin is to be tossed three times. Not to get heads at least once would be the same as getting tails all three times. Calculate this probability in two different ways.

3   Three cards will be drawn from a standard deck, and not returned to the deck. What is the probability that at least one will be a heart? That all three will be hearts?

4   Two dice are to be rolled. Lisa wins if the total is even. Marie wins if the total is odd. At even odds, is this a fair bet?

5   Two dice are to be rolled. Jack wins if the outcome is six, seven, eight, or nine; Will wins with any other outcome. At even odds, is this bet fair? If not, at what odds would it be a fair bet?

6   Dapper Dan has one chance in four of winning the Kentucky Derby; but he has an even chance of winning the Preakness if he has won the Kentucky Derby. What is the probability that he will win both races? At what odds would it be reasonable to bet on him to win both?

7   Dapper Dan has two chances out of five of winning the Belmont Stakes if he has won the Kentucky Derby and the Preakness. Before any of these races has been run, what is the probability that he will win all three? At what odds would it be reasonable to bet that he will win the Triple Crown? (Take account of information in the previous example.)

8   On earth there are two sexes—male and female—which are equally numerous. On Mars there are three sexes—alpha, beta, and gamma—which are equally numerous. Which is more probable: that an earth couple who are going to have two children will have at least one male child, or that a Martian triple who are going to have three children will have at least one alpha?

C   Discuss the reasoning in each example.

1   We don't know whether there is life on any of the moons of Jupiter. But there are just two possibilities: either there is or there isn't. So, relative

to the information we possess, the probability of life there is ½. It would be reasonable to accept even odds in betting on this.

2 This airline has never had a crash? Well, then, I won't fly with them. They're probably due for a smashup soon.

3 Alec has an even chance to pass mathematics and an even chance to pass physics. So he has one chance in four of passing both courses.

4 I've tossed this coin of yours a dozen times now, and it has always come up heads. So I'm not willing to wager at even odds that it will come up tails on the next toss.

5 We've had mild winters for the last several years. We can't expect this to go on. So probably next winter will be severe.

6 Last term Dave got a "C" in Calculus I. But he has always had a "B" average so far; hence, by the law of averages, he'll probably get "A" in Calculus II this term.

7 Nan, who is twenty-one, has read that twenty-one-year-olds in this country have a long life expectancy. She decides that therefore it's safe for her to take up motorcycling, skydiving, and drug use.

8 When you play slot machines at the casino, don't play just one machine. Move around and try different ones. That way, you'll get diversification, and so you'll have the best prospect of maximizing your winnings.

34 EXPLANATORY HYPOTHESES

So far, we have considered some special types of inductive arguments and the special considerations that bear upon their strength. But there is also a more general way of looking at inductive reasoning, a point of view that is often appropriate when we are evaluating the strength of inductive arguments of various types. We may think of the conclusion of an inductive argument as a hypothesis, a conjecture about the empirical world, and we may think of the premises as data presented in support of that hypothesis. From this point of view, it is possible for us to ask, Is this hypothesis a plausible *explanation* of the data? Asking this question can often help when we are trying to form a clear view of the strength of the inductive argument itself. An inductive argument establishes a high probability for its conclusion, provided that it is possible to regard the conclusion as a hypothesis supplying the best explanation of the data contained in the premises.

To go back to the example used in discussing inductive generalization, let us suppose that we have observed many white swans and have never observed a swan that is not white. How strongly does this evidence support the conclusion that all swans are white? Here it is helpful to adopt this new viewpoint and ask, How well does the hypothesis that all swans are white explain the fact that we have obtained these observations? Our data make the generalization highly probable only if the generalization itself helps to provide the most probable explanation of why these were the data which we obtained. Are there other equally reasonable ways of explaining why it has happened that all the swans we have seen have been white? Is it perhaps that we have looked only at American swans and have missed nonwhite swans in other countries? Is it perhaps that we have looked at swans only in summertime and have missed nonwhite swans in other seasons? In any such case, the inductive argument is weak; if not, it is stronger. Asking ourselves whether the generalization provides the most reasonable explanation of the data is a good way of helping to evaluate the degree of probability that the data confer on the generalization. This general point of view is helpful in connection with any type of inductive inference.

When we adopt this point of view and ask about the reasonableness of some explanatory hypothesis, we should bear in mind that for any set of data there always are many incompatible ways in which the data might conceivably be explained. Sometimes one line of explanation is definitely very much better than all other conflicting lines of explanation. If the silver spoons are missing from their rack on the dining-room wall; if the maid, who had left hastily, is arrested and found to have the spoons concealed in her car; and if she confesses to having stolen them; then, in the light of these data, by far the most reasonable explanation is that the maid stole the spoons, just as she says. We might well say, "That's the only possible explanation," by which we would mean that this is much the best and most probable explanation.

Yet even here it is perfectly conceivable that the true explanation could be something different. Conceivably, there may have been an open window through which a crow, attracted by the glitter of the spoons, carried them off one by one and concealed them in the maid's car; she, having been disappointed in love, was in such a low state of mind when apprehended by the police that she readily confessed to the action of which they accused her. This is a conceivable hypothesis, though a very improbable one. The point is that always, if we use imagination, we can think of alternative explanations. We never are absolutely limited to a single hypothesis since there always are alternative conceivable explanations. We always are faced with choice, and our problem is to choose the most reasonable hypothesis, that is, the one providing the best explanation.

Various factors combine to make one explanatory hypothesis more probable than another. These are not describable in any sharp, precise way, but we can say something about them.

We are likely to think that the extent to which it 'fits the facts' contributes greatly to determining the probability of an explanatory hypothesis. If one hypothesis succeeds in explaining more of the data than another does, this increases the probability of the former. Suppose that only the solid-silver spoons and none of the plated spoons are missing. The hypothesis that the maid stole the spoons explains this, for the maid would know that the plated spoons were of less value, whereas the hypothesis that an unknown crow stole the spoons does not explain this. However, whether a hypothesis fits the facts is not a simple yes-or-no matter. Although the crow hypothesis does not *easily* fit the fact that only the solid-silver spoons are gone, still we could think of some auxiliary hypothesis which, when combined with the crow hypothesis, would provide a conceivable explanation of this troublesome fact. Perhaps there were two crows, both attracted by the shininess of the spoons; the larger crow carried off all the spoons, and then the smaller crow, out of spite, brought back as many spoons as it could but was not strong enough to lift the heavier solid-silver spoons and so returned only the plated ones. This is a far-fetched yet not a totally impossible line of explanation.

There is no limit to the lengths to which we can go in making any hypothesis fit the facts, if we are imaginative enough in thinking of auxiliary hypotheses. In the end, perhaps the best way of looking at the matter is this: We should not think that we have to choose between one single hypothesis and another (e.g., the hypothesis that the maid stole the spoons versus the hypothesis that a crow did). Instead we should think of the choice as lying between whole *sets* of hypotheses (the hypotheses that the maid stole the spoons just as she said and that crows had nothing to do with it, versus the hypotheses that one crow stole the spoons and another brought back some of them, and the maid had a lover who disappointed her, etc.). As we think over the total body of known data, we ask ourselves, Which *set* of hypotheses best explains these data? If one set of hypotheses stands out as giving a much more reasonable line of explanation that does any other set, then all the hypotheses of that set are probably true.

When we compare sets of hypotheses with one another, it is helpful to invoke the notions of *simplicity* and *unifying power*. Other things being equal, the simpler a set of hypotheses and the better it unifies our system of beliefs, the more probable it is as an explanation of the data. Although we cannot define these notions of simplicity and unifying power in any rigorous manner, they can assist us in our reflections. When we supplement the crow hypothesis with auxiliary hypotheses so as to provide a consistent explanation of all the observed data, what makes this line of explanation less reasonable than the line of explanation employing the maid hypothesis? The decisive factor is that the maid hypothesis provides a simpler and more unified line of explanation.

In various ways it is a simpler and more unified explanation. The explanation that makes the maid guilty is simpler because it does not require us to postulate the existence of any entities that have not been observed, whereas the line of explanation making the crow guilty requires us to postulate the existence of two crows and a lover, none of which we have observed. A set of hypotheses is simpler the fewer the entities, and also the fewer the kinds of entities, in which it requires us to believe. Moreover, a set of hypotheses is simpler and more probable if it attributes usual and direct operations to phenomena, rather than elaborate and unusual ones. In this respect too, the crow hypotheses are poor, for they require us to suppose that these crows have carried out a very elaborate operation, which would be very unusual indeed in terms of what we know of crows from our past experience with them and with similar birds.

Occasionally *inconsistency* creeps into an explanation. If there is an inconsistency in the way it treats the facts, an explanation cannot have much probability. To take another example, some people have been puzzled at the paintings of El Greco: the human figures he painted seem strangely distorted, unnaturally tall and thin. Suppose that someone tries to explain this peculiarity of his painting by means of the hypothesis that El Greco suffered from astigmatism, which made him see things in this strangely distorted manner, and as he saw them, so he painted them.

This explanation may sound plausible at first, and yet it is wholly unacceptable as it stands, for it deals inconsistently with the facts. If El Greco had bad eyes that made him see everything in a distorted manner, this defect would have been operative not merely when he looked at his models but also when he looked at his canvases. Thus a distorted figure drawn on his canvas would not have looked the same to him as did his model. This attempted explanation fails to explain; the hypothesis that El Greco had bad eyes could conceivably be true, but it is not supported by the mere fact that he painted in this distorted way. (One could supplement it with the auxiliary hypothesis that he wore corrective glasses when and only when he looked at his canvases; but then we do not have a simple set of explanatory hypotheses.)

A still more extreme inconsistency occurs if the explanatory hypothesis employs a self-contradictory notion. The spoons having disappeared, suppose someone suggests the hypothesis that pixies have carried them off. We point out that no one has seen any pixies, or heard them, or felt or smelled or tasted them. No one has experienced pixies in any way, even though sometimes people have looked for them rather diligently. This person replies, "Well, I think it was invisible pixies that carried away the spoons. The pixies cannot be seen or heard or touched or smelled or tasted; not with the unaided senses, nor with scientific instruments either. But I believe they're there, all the same, even though no one could possibly detect them. Science never will be able to demonstrate their presence, but it cannot prove that they aren't there."

This hypothesis is a queer one. It is advanced as though it were a hypothesis that made sense, that is true rather than false but that never could be verified or refuted. The difficulty here is that we are invited to suppose that there are little manlike creatures which are invisible, intangible, and in every way absolutely undetectable, by anyone, ever. This hypothesis employs a self-contradictory notion. To say that something is really there is to imply that it could conceivably be detected. Being there means being detectable, at least in principle—even though in practice we may not actually be able to detect the thing. The notion of a pixie which is there but absolutely undetectable is inconsistent. The hypothesis that there are absolutely undetectable pixies is necessarily false, as much so as is the hypothesis that there are married bachelors.

We have mentioned some of the factors that determine the degree of probability of an explanatory hypothesis. However, when we ask how *good* an explanation is, this comprehends more than just its probability. Probability is one component that helps to make an explanation good, but it is not the only one. Another component is the power of the explanation to illuminate the phenomena for which it aims to account. We commonly seek an explanation for a phenomenon because the phenomenon is strange, out of the ordinary, different from what was to have been expected or, at any rate, isolated, its connections with other phenomena unknown. We ask "Why are the silver spoons missing?" for this is unexpected when in the past they have always been in their rack. We ask "Why does soda fizz?" because this seems strange when most liquids do not, and soda does so only when the bottle is opened. We ask "Why do the planets move in elliptical orbits?" because this fact seems anomalous and isolated, when we do not grasp its relation to other facts.

In answering this sort of question, the explanation tries to remove the strangeness, the anomaly, the puzzle, by showing how the thing being explained harmonizes with other known and conjectured facts. We explain the action of soda water by pointing out that it contains carbon dioxide under pressure, which must escape when the bottle is opened. (This explanation gives the cause.) Newton explained why the orbits of the planets are elliptical by showing how this is a special case of the inertial and gravitational way in which all bodies everywhere in the universe move. (This is not a causal explanation, but is none the worse for that.[44]) The point here is that a good explanation not only must be probable, in the light of the data, but also must account for the data in an illuminating way that helps us to grasp their connection with other facts. We can see that there is a difference between probability and explanatory force if we remember the old example (from Molière) of someone asking "Why does opium cause sleep?" and receiving the answer "Because of its soporific power." Here the explanation merely redescribes the data in a totally unilluminating manner. It is certain that opium possesses 'soporific power,' but this is just a way of expressing the fact that needs explaining; it is not a good explanation of it.

Perhaps it will be useful to have a checklist of steps to follow when we appraise explanatory hypotheses. Many of us find this sort of guidance valuable.

Our first step should be to pick out clearly what the phenomenon is that needs to be explained. What is the specific fact or event in which we are interested and in what way is it puzzling or strange? Our second step is to marshal a variety of possible explanatory hypotheses that are worth considering. Each should initially seem to have some possible merit as an explanation. We need to be inventive and ingenious here, thinking up as many and varied alternatives as we can. Our next step should be to evaluate the probability of the hypotheses we have invented. For each one that we consider, we should ask whether it clashes with other things that we know; we should ask whether the observations that have been made are enough to constitute a real test of the hypothesis; and we should ask whether adopting the given hypothesis will yield the simplest overall set of beliefs that we can erect on the basis of the observed facts. Next, we should ask how well each of the competing hypotheses would explain the phenomenon which needs explanation. If it were true, would it give us deeper insight into what is occurring, or would it merely be a trivial restatement of the phenomenon itself? Having appraised our hypotheses in these ways, we should go back and see whether we can invent any more worthwhile hypotheses before we stop. If we can think of others, we then repeat this same process to evaluate them. Finally, if all goes well, we shall reach a point where one hypothesis stands out as the most probable. We may then appropriately accept this hypothesis as the best explanation we can find, given our present evidence.

Appraising explanatory hypotheses

1 Specify what phenomenon is to be explained.
   A Just what fact or event needs explaining?
   B In what respect is it puzzling or anomalous?
2 Marshal possible explanations.
   A Think up explanatory hypotheses each of which looks as though it might have merit for explaining the phenomenon.
   B Try to include hypotheses of quite different kinds; don't let them all be too similar.
3 Evaluate the probability of the competing hypotheses; for each one, ask:
   A Does it conflict with established facts or well-confirmed hypotheses?
   B Has it been severely tested by the observations?
   C Would adopting it give us the simplest overall set of beliefs consistent with the observed facts?
      (i) Simplicity of laws and regularities.
      (ii) Simplicity in terms of postulating the fewest entities or processes.
4 Evaluate how well the competing hypotheses would explain; for each, ask:
   A If it were true, how well would this succeed in explaining the puzzling or anomalous aspect of the phenomenon?
   B Would it give us a deeper understanding of the phenomenon, and not merely a truistic restatement of it?
5 Go back to step 2 to see whether you can invent more hypotheses worth considering, and then evaluate them via steps 3 and 4. Repeat this process until you arrive (if possible) at the explanatory hypothesis which is the most probable among those that would provide an illuminating explanation.

Notice that the evaluation we have considered here involves two separate dimensions: probability and explanatory power. The hypothesis that is most probable may be rather trivial and lacking in explanatory power. The hypothesis that has the most explanatory power may be rather improbable. We want to strike a balance between these two dimensions. We look for the hypothesis which has the greatest probability among those which would succeed in providing illuminating explanations.

If someone else has proposed an explanatory hypothesis which we want to appraise, these same steps are to be followed. But now we must think up other different hypotheses to consider in competition with the one that has been proposed. We never can really evaluate a single hypothesis in isolation. We always must think of the process as one which is competitive. A particular hypothesis secures high standing when and only when it is able to stand out above its competitors in terms of the dimensions of probability and explanatory power.

EXERCISE 35

*A What is the phenomenon being explained, and what is there about it that seems to need explaining? Discuss how good the proposed explanations are.

1 The minicar drove up and stopped. One after another, fifty clowns came out of it. The explanation is that they were not all in the car at once. It stopped over a trapdoor through which they entered it.

2 Why did George Washington refuse to let himself be appointed king of the United States? He must not have believed that the proposal was genuine.

3 Why did the crystal goblet shatter when the soprano hit her high note? This was because the air vibrations happened to be at the resonant frequency of the goblet, and so there was maximal transfer of energy.

4 You wonder why eating those mushrooms caused illness? The explanation is that they were poisonous mushrooms.

5 Why did Rob lose his job, and why did his wife divorce him? It's because he broke a mirror, getting 7 years' bad luck.

6 Why does gasoline catch fire so readily? It's because it is inflammable.

7 How could St. Thomas Aquinas have written so many millions of words in his comparatively short lifetime? He must have had other monks who helped him as researchers and scribes.

8 Considerably more people in our city come to eat at the charity soup kitchens than did so a few years ago. It must be that the number of needy people has increased.

9 Why does Bill always wear his ten-gallon hat in the dining hall? It's because he's a slob.

10 Astrology undertakes to explain why human beings have different destinies, and its type of explanation is basically quite plausible. We can see that the movements of the heavenly bodies probably can influence human beings when we reflect that the moon has a large effect on the tides, and so why not on a human being—who is about two-thirds water, after all.

B Discuss each proposed explanation.

1 "How often have I said to you that when you have eliminated the impossible, whatever remains, *however improbable*, must be the truth? He did not come through the door, the window, or the chimney...He could not have been concealed in the room...Whence, then did he come?" "He came through the hole in the roof," I cried.

A. CONAN DOYLE, *The sign of the Four*

2 Boy! Lucius! Fast asleep? it is no matter;
Enjoy the heavy honey-dew of slumber:
Thou has no figures nor no fantasies
Which busy care draws in the brains of men;
Therefore thou sleep'st so sound.

WILLIAM SHAKESPEARE, *Julius Caesar*

3 Among the noteworthy actions of Hannibal is numbered this, that although he had an enormous army, composed of men of all nations and fighting in foreign countries, there never arose any dissension either among them or against the prince...This could not be due to anything but his inhuman cruelty, which together with his infinite other virtues, made him always venerated and terrible in the sight of his soldiers.

NICCOLÓ MACHIAVELLI, *The Prince*

4 Since we learn by experience that abundance of bodies are hard, we therefore justly infer the hardness of individual undivided particles not only of bodies we feel, but of all others. For the hardness of the whole arises from the hardness of the parts.   SIR ISAAC NEWTON, *Principia*

5 The fact that fish are able to remain motionless under water is a conclusive reason for thinking that the material of their bodies has the same specific gravity as that of water; accordingly, if in their makeup there are certain parts which are heavier than water there must be others which are lighter, for otherwise they would not produce equilibrium.

GALILEO, *Two New Sciences*

6 The love of the man sinks perceptibly from the moment it has obtained satisfaction; almost every other woman charms him more than the one he already possesses...The love of the woman, on the other hand, increases just from that moment. This is a consequence of the aim of nature which is directed...to the greatest possible increase, of the species. The man can easily beget over a hundred children a year; the woman..., can yet only bring one child a year into the world...Therefore, the man always looks about after other women; the woman, again, sticks firmly to the man; for nature moves her, instinctively and without reflection, to retain the nourisher and protector of the future offspring.

ARTHUR SCHOPENHAUER, *The World as Will and Idea*

7 When we see that the three classes of modern society, the feudal aristocracy, the bourgeoisie and the proletariat, each have their special morality, we can only draw one conclusion, that men consciously or unconsciously, derive their moral ideas in the last resort from the practical relations on which their class position is based—from the economic relations in which they carry on production and exchange.

FRIEDRICH ENGELS, *Anti-Dühring*

8 It happens that the less a man believes in the soul—that is to say, in his conscious immorality, personal and concrete—the more he will exaggerate the worth of this poor transitory life. This is the source from which springs all that effeminate, sentimental ebullition against war. True, a man ought not to wish to die, but the death to be renounced is the death of the soul.

MIGUEL DE UNAMUNO, *The Tragic Sense of Life*

CHAPTER 8

APPLYING LOGICAL PRINCIPLES

We have now discussed a good many aspects of the logic of deductive and inductive reasoning. There remain some important practical considerations that we should examine. These have to do with how to use our knowledge of logical principles in dealing with actual examples.

36 CHOOSING THE RIGHT DEDUCTIVE FORM

In our study of deductive reasoning we became acquainted with several different styles in which sentences can be symbolized. When we met a deductive argument, we could translate its sentences into traditional categorical form, or into truth-functional form, or into quantificational form. Then, depending on what the form was, we could apply one or another of our logical techniques to test whether the argument was valid.

What we must particularly notice now is that good judgment has to be exercised when we decide what form to put an argument into, and when we choose what logical technique to apply to it. If we symbolize an argument unwisely, or test it by an inappropriate method, we can easily end up with a wrong answer about whether the argument is valid.

Suppose we are interested in the argument "No Frenchmen are Germans; some Germans are Lutherans; so some Lutherans are not Frenchmen." Suppose someone were foolish enough to symbolize the first premise as "P," the second premise as "Q," and the conclusion as "R." This person then symbolizes the whole argument as "P, Q, therefore R." Then, looking at this formula, the person decides that a truth table will provide a good way to test its validity. This is a very foolish approach, and it will of course give the wrong answer—for the original argument was a deductively valid syllogism, but a truth-table test of "*P, Q,* therefore *R*" will yield the answer that it is invalid.

The mistake that has been committed here needs to be described with care. The person who handled the argument in this way has not exactly *mistranslated* the separate sentences of the argument. It is not flatly wrong to symbolize "No Frenchmen are Germans" as "*P,*" or "Some Germans are Lutherans" as "*Q.*" In the context of some other argument, this might be an acceptable way to symbolize these sentences. But the trouble is that symbolizing the various sentences in this way in this argument has the bad effect of obscuring the logical form which is relevant to the validity of the argument. When the argument is symbolized in this way, its syllogistic structure is not exhibited. It is just this syllogistic structure that we need to bring out if we are to see why the argument is valid.

The mistake here is that an unwise choice has been made about how to symbolize the three sentences, as parts of *this* argument. In symbolizing an argument, not only must we avoid misrepresenting any of the sentences in it; also, we must bring out the common structure among the sentences that is relevant to whether the argument is valid.

Our aim should be to give each argument a fair chance. Let each argument be symbolized so as to display whatever logical form gives it its validity, or whatever logical form the arguer may suppose gives it validity. Of course there are no mechanical rules by means of which we can guarantee that this will be accomplished. We have to listen sympathetically to the language of the argument and use our good judgment in interpreting it.

In addition to making the right choice concerning how to symbolize an argument, another kind of choice also is needed. Even after an argument has been symbolized well, we still have to decide what logical method to use in testing whether it is valid. If we make a bad choice of method, things can go wrong. For instance, if we symbolize a syllogism correctly, but then unwisely try to test its validity by means of a truth table, we can get misleading results. What is needed is for us to symbolize each argument judiciously and then select an appropriate method for testing its validity.

Here we should keep in mind that each of the various logical methods we have studied (such as Venn's diagrams, the rules of the syllogism, truth tables, truth-functional deduction, quantificational deduction) is a method which supplies a *sufficient* condition of validity, but not a *necessary* condition. That is, if an argument that has been symbolized well can be shown to be valid according to a truth table, then it is valid. But if it cannot be shown to be valid according to a truth table, this does not guarantee that it is invalid—it might be valid for some other reason (for instance, it might be a syllogism, and a truth table does not test for the validity of this sort of logical structure).

What we can say is that if an argument has no reason for being valid except its syllogistic form, then if it is not valid according to the rules of the syllogism, it is invalid. And if an argument has no reason for being valid except its truth-functional form, then if it is invalid according to a truth table, it is invalid. And so on, for each of our methods.

The method of quantificational deduction studied in Chapters 4 and 5, including as it does the laws of truth-functional deduction, is a method powerful enough to show the validity of all valid deductive arguments of all the main types that we have studied. So using this method will never lead you into the error described above.

However, it is generally wiser on each occasion to employ the most elementary method that will fit the example. By so doing, we usually reduce the work for ourselves and thereby minimize the risk of error. Moreover, unlike the method of quantificational deduction, the more elementary methods of Venn's diagrams, rules of the syllogism, and truth tables, where they are applicable, can provide negative demonstrations of the invalidity of invalid arguments—a significant advantage. Thus, whenever a more elementary method applies, it is usually good strategy to employ it in preference to the method of quantificational deduction.

In the same spirit, when symbolizing an argument, it is wise to employ the fewest letters and the simplest formulas that can suffice to exhibit the relevant logical structure of the reasoning. We do not want to make things more complicated than is strictly necessary, for that again usually increases the amount of work involved and the risk of error.

Thus, when we are confronted with a deductive argument whose validity we want to investigate, we should use our ingenuity to try to find the simplest appropriate way of interpreting that argument. We want to interpret it as being of the simplest kind, and as having the simplest structure within that kind, as will do justice to the meanings of the sentences involved and their intended relationship. We may have to use trial and error to see what interpretation is best. But a growing familiarity with forms of argument gradually develops one's competence at this.

EXERCISE 36

  A Show whether each of the following deductive arguments is valid. Try to use the best method in each case.

    1 If Ted loves Myra, he doesn't love Jean. But he does love Jean. So he doesn't love Myra.

    2 All birds have wings, but no reptiles have wings. So no reptiles are birds.

    3 Either bats are birds or some mammals are birds. But bats aren't birds. So some mammals are birds.

    4 No rationalists are empiricists. Some positivists are empiricists. So some positivists are not rationalists.

    5 If we fly to Australia, our tickets will be costly. If we take a ship to

Australia, our tickets will be costly. We'll either fly or take a ship to Australia. So our tickets are going to be costly.

6 If everything influences everything, then everything influences itself. Everything does influence itself. Therefore, everything influences everything.

7 Illegal actions are dangerous and immoral. Dangerous and immoral actions are not prudent. So prudent actions are not illegal.

8 If some squares are round, then some squares are squares and some squares are not squares. So it's not the case that some squares are round.

9 Everything immortal or perfect is immaterial. Some immortal things are perfect. Hence, some immaterial things are immortal.

10 All bonuses are to be included in taxable income. No gifts are to be included in taxable income. All tips are bonuses. So no tips are gifts.

B Use an appropriate method to test the validity of each of the following deductive arguments.

1 There is someone whom everyone finds attractive. So everyone finds someone or other attractive.

2 Every automobile bought by someone will be admired somewhere. Whatever is going to be admired somewhere will be a source of pride. So every automobile bought by someone will be a source of pride.

3 There is a virus that can destroy any living cell. Phagocytes are living cells. So there is a virus that can destroy any phagocyte.

4 No libertarians favor bigger government. All statists favor bigger government. Some liberals are statists. So some liberals are not libertarians.

5 No oak tree is as old as every redwood. Since there are oak trees, some redwood must be such that no oak is as old as it is.

6 Only those soldiers who have been invited by the mayor will attend the ceremony and march in the parade. So if no soldiers have been invited by the mayor, no soldiers will march in the parade.

7 Whatever farms have been plagued by grasshoppers will need government funds if they are going to get back into production. No government funds are available. So no farms plagued by grasshoppers will get back into production.

8 All pandas are vegetarians, or none of them are. Some pandas eat only bamboo. Whatever eats only bamboo is a vegetarian. So all pandas are vegetarians.

37 THE ENTHYMEME

In ordinary discussion a person often presents an argument without bothering to make explicit what all its premises are. Sometimes the arguer has a premise fairly definitely in mind but regards it as common knowledge and so does not bother to state it. Other times the arguer has not thought of the unstated premise at all, but would embrace it if it were pointed out.

An argument is called an *enthymeme* if at least one of its premises is unstated in this way. Originally the term "enthymeme" was restricted to syllogisms, but nowadays the term is extended to cover all kinds of arguments having unstated premises. And sometimes the term "enthymeme" is extended even further to cover arguments whose conclusions have been left unstated—but such cases are of less interest.

Suppose we meet a deductive argument whose conclusion does not validly follow from the stated premises alone. If we want to determine how sound the argument is, we ought to ask ourselves whether there are any unstated premises that the arguer is taking for granted. If there are, we should try to state these premises explicitly so that we can consider whether they are true and so that we can see in full the logical structure of the argument, to tell whether it is valid.

Suppose that someone argues "Robinson must be a lawyer, for he belongs to the bar association." Is this argument a *non sequitur*, or is it a valid enthymeme? To classify the argument as a *non sequitur* merely because the stated premise does not by itself imply the conclusion would probably be unfair to the speaker's thinking. Instead, we should realize that in all probability the speaker is employing the unstated premise "All persons who belong to the bar association are lawyers." This is a piece of common knowledge, and the speaker probably feels that it does not need to be stated outright. When we notice the unstated premise, we see that the reasoning is valid.

An arguer is perfectly justified in leaving some premises unstated, provided that these are obvious pieces of common knowledge which the audience will recognize that the speaker intends to assume. The arguer is to blame, however, if the unstated premises upon which the argument depends are dubious and questionable, or hard for the audience to fill in for themselves. Still worse, of course, is the mistake of the careless thinker who regards as common knowledge things that are not even true at all. It is the duty of a really conscientious arguer to make explicit all premises that critical listeners might reasonably challenge and all premises that they cannot readily fill in for themselves. An arguer who fails to do this is not presenting the argument as carefully and as candidly as would be desirable.

However, some students of logic get the mistaken idea that all deductive arguments whose conclusions do not validly follow from their stated premises should be regarded as enthymemes. So whenever they meet an argument that is not deductively valid, they immediately start providing premises which would make it valid, and they think that the arguer is committed to accepting these premises. Thus they reconstruct every argument so that it becomes deductively valid. But this is the wrong approach. Fallacies of *non sequitur* do occur in deductive reasoning, and we ought not to adopt a strategy which will make it seem as though there never are any such fallacies.

Suppose, for example, that someone argues "All Marxists are socialists, and so all socialists are Marxists." Should we regard this argument as a valid enthymeme, having, say, the unstated premise "If all Marxists are socialists, then all socialists are Marxists"? No, this would be a poor interpretation. To interpret the argument this way would be to think of it as committing the fallacy of begging the question, since this conditional sentence would not be less doubtful than the conclusion of the argument (for almost all of us, at least). But the original argument surely did not beg the question. It ought to be regarded as a *non sequitur*, instead. The speaker's real mistake most likely lies in thinking that an *A* sentence can be converted. It is a better interpretation to say that the original argument is invalid on account of its form, than to say that it is valid but has an unstated premise which makes it beg the question.

Naturally, it is not always easy to be certain what unstated premises there may be in the back of the mind of the person who states an argument. But we should try to do our best to interpret fairly what it is that the arguer is taking for granted. In making the argument more explicit, our aim should be to do so in a way that the arguer could recognize as expressing what was intended. In light of this, there are two guidelines for us to heed when we are considering whether someone's argument has an unstated premise.

1 If the argument is to express the speaker's own reasoning accurately, then its premises have to be ones which the speaker believes—and this holds for unstated premises too. A sentence can express an unstated premise of someone's argument only if the person quite firmly believes that the sentence is true. If the sentence says something that would be surprising or doubtful to the arguer, then it cannot be a premise of that argument.

2 If one or more sentences express unstated premises of someone's argument, then the argument with these premises added must be the sort of argument that the person would use. If adding the sentences as premises makes the argument into one which the person would not have been likely to use (because it would beg the question, for instance), then it cannot be a fair interpretation to regard these sentences as premises.

Some deductive arguments are enthymemes, and some are not. Those that are can be transformed by making all their premises explicit, so that they cease to be enthymemes.[45] But when it comes to inductive arguments, they must always be and remain enthymemes, if what was said at the end of Section 30 is correct. With an inductive argument, we never can fully succeed in stating all the premises upon which the conclusion depends. We can state more and more of the premises, but we cannot finish the task of making all of them explicit, and so an inductive argument is irremediably an enthymeme. Thus our concern about enthymemes relates more to deductive arguments, whose premises we can succeed in stating fully, than to inductive arguments, where we cannot. Though even with inductive arguments, it can often be very helpful to make explicit especially significant premises that have been left unstated.

EXERCISE 37

*A Which arguments can plausibly be regarded as enthymemes? What are their suppressed premises?

1 She goes to Harding University. So I expect she's very stuck up.
2 He must be rowdy and a troublemaker. After all, he rides a motorcycle.
3 Methodists are all Protestants, but no Swedenborgians are Methodists. So no Swedenborgians are Protestants.
4 That person is wearing a woman's type of hat, and so must be a woman.
5 If the fishing is good, Ted is out in his boat. He is out in his boat. So the fishing is good.
6 All Tunisians are Africans, and all Romans are Italians. Therefore, no Romans are Tunisians.
7 They're going on holiday, but not to any place in the Northern Hemisphere. So they must be going somewhere in the Southern Hemisphere.
8 The person who delivers our mail is not a man. So a woman must be the one who does it.
9 No one came to our party. They must all hate us.
10 Nuclear warfare could destroy the human race. Therefore, we should work for unilateral disarmament.

†B Which examples should be interpreted as enthymemes? What premises are suppressed?

1 Our observations of the stars make it evident...that the earth is a sphere of no great size. For...the stars seen are different, as one moves northward or southward. Indeed...some stars seen in Egypt...are not seen in the northerly regions.   ARISTOTLE, *On the Heavens*

2 Many argue in this way. If all things follow from...the absolutely perfect nature of God, why are there so many imperfections in nature, such, for instance, as things corrupt to the point of putridity, loathsome deformity, confusion, evil, sin, &c.? But these reasoners are...easily confuted, for...things are not more or less perfect, according as they delight or offend human senses, or according as they are serviceable or repugnant to mankind.   BARUCH SPINOZA, *Ethics*

3 The present state is short and transitory; but our state in the other world, is everlasting....Our state in the future world, therefore, being eternal, is of so much greater importance than our state here, that all our concerns in this world should be wholly subordinated to it.   JONATHAN EDWARDS

4 Other men die. I am not another. Therefore, I shall not die.
          VLADIMIR NABOKOV, *Pale Fire*

5 All that is religious is good, for it is only religious as it expresses a common higher life.   FRIEDRICH SCHLEIERMACHER, *On Religion*

6 "For my faith," he continued, "I will not change it. Your own God, as you say, was put to death by the very men whom he created. But mine," he concluded, pointing to his Deity—then alas! sinking in glory behind the mountains—"my God still lives in the heavens and looks down on his children."   WILLIAM H. PRESCOTT, *The Conquest of Peru*

7 The peculiar evil of silencing the expression of an opinion is that it is robbing the human race; posterity as well as the existing generation; those who dissent from the opinion, still more than those who hold it. If the opinion is right, they are deprived of the opportunity of exchanging error for truth: if wrong, they lose, what is almost as great a benefit, the clearer perception and livelier impression of truth, produced by its collision with error.   JOHN STUART MILL, *On Liberty*

8 Death is nothing terrible, else it would have appeared so to Socrates.
      EPICTETUS

9 Accustom thyself to believe that death is nothing to us, for good and evil imply sentience, and death is the privation of all sentience.   EPICURUS

10 We reject all merely probable knowledge and make it a rule to trust only what is completely known and incapable of being doubted....But if we adhere closely to this rule we shall find left but few objects of legitimate study. For there is scarce any question occurring in the sciences about which talented men have not disagreed.
      RENÉ DESCARTES, *Rules for the Direction of the Mind*

38 NONINDUCTIVE REASONING BY ANALOGY

In Section 32 we considered inductive arguments by analogy. One of our examples was the reasoning of a postman who, on the basis of his past experience with boxer dogs that bit, reasons that probably the new boxer looming in his path will bite also, if approached. This is an argument by analogy. Moreover, the reasoning is definitely inductive in nature, for the conclusion (that this dog will bite if approached) embodies conjectures regarding what future sense experience can reveal, conjectures not deductively implied by the present evidence. However, not all reasoning by analogy is inductive in this sense.

Let us consider an example of an argument by analogy which is not inductive. At a certain college the student body has established a rigorous honor code to govern student behavior. The code specifically lists lying and cheating as punishable offenses. The students administer this code and take it seriously. Now suppose it is discovered that a student has written a bad check and used it to purchase merchandise in the town. The question arises whether this student has violated the honor code. Is writing a bad check a violation of the rule against lying and cheating? Let us suppose that those who wrote the code never pronounced on this question and that there are no known precedents about it.

Someone might try to dismiss this question by saying, "Well, it's all a matter of definition. If by 'lying' you mean something that includes writing bad checks, then the rule has been violated. And if you don't mean that by the word 'lying,' then the rule has not been violated. It's just a matter of what you choose to mean by a word. Just decide how you want to define your terms, that's all."

This comment suggests that the question about the interpretation of the honor code is just a trivial verbal question. As we remember from Section 29, a verbal dispute is one that has no true or false solution and that arises solely because people choose to use words differently, not because they differ in their beliefs about what is so. For example, one person may insist that the fox's posterior appendage is the brush and not the tail; someone else may claim that of course it is the tail, for who ever heard of a brush growing on an animal? Here the issue is purely verbal, for the two parties to the dispute do not disagree about what the fox's appendage is like. They disagree only about what it should be called.

But is the question about the honor code a trivial verbal question, in the way the question about the fox's appendage is? Surely not. The question whether a violation of the honor code has been committed is a serious and substantial question. Those who must decide it cannot settle it merely by making an arbitrary decision about how to use a word. That would not be fair to the accused student, and it would not be fair to the rest of the student body, who take their code seriously. The decision that is reached will determine what action is taken with respect to the accused student, and such actions ought not to be arbitrary. Those who must make the decision need to engage in careful thinking if they are to decide fairly. They need to weigh the arguments pro and con.

Deductive arguments are not likely to be of much use in this situation. Suppose someone tries to settle the problem deductively by arguing: "All cases of cheating violate the honor code; all cases of writing bad checks are cases of cheating; therefore, all cases of writing bad checks violate the honor code." Although this argument is valid, it does not succeed in proving its conclusion. If we were dubious about whether the conclusion is true, then we are pretty sure to be at least equally dubious about the minor premise. Here the deduction commits the fallacy of begging the question. No purely deductive line of reasoning is likely to settle this problem.

Nor are inductive arguments likely to help much. Whichever conclusion we want to establish here—that writing a bad check is, or is not, a violation of the honor code—in either case the conclusion does not embody predictive conjectures about future experience that go beyond what is already known. Reaching a conclusion about whether the student is guilty certainly is not the same as predicting how he is going to be treated. Nor is it the same as predicting what observable consequences his behavior is going to have. Such predictions would be inductive, but they are not what we are seeking. No purely inductive line of reasoning is sufficient here, for the conclusion is not of the inductive sort.

What sort of reasoning would be appropriate to this problem? Someone would be making a helpful and relevant contribution to the discussion who reasoned as follows: "Lying and cheating are indisputably offenses against the honor code. Now, writing a bad check is like falsely stating that you have money in the bank. Also, writing a bad check is very like cheating, for you persuade the merchant to accept the check in exchange for merchandise by deceptively suggesting that the check is good. Since writing a bad check is so like lying and cheating in these respects, it therefore resembles them also in being a violation of the honor code." At the heart of this reasoning are the analogies between writing a bad check on the one hand and lying and cheating on the other hand. The whole argument essentially depends upon these analogies—the argument is a good argument if and only if these are good analogies.

Unlike deductive reasoning, this sort of reasoning does not claim to be demonstrative. At best, the truth of the premises gives us only some good reason for accepting the conclusion. Also, as we saw, this sort of reasoning differs from induction—the conclusion being argued for does not embody predictive conjectures going beyond what the premises say.[46]

This sort of noninductive reasoning by analogy is a fundamental way of reasoning. We often resort to it in cases where deductive reasoning and inductive reasoning are not able to give us answers that we need. Although there are no formal rules about when arguments of this sort are good and when they are bad, we can say that the reasoning is good when the analogies are good and that it is bad when the analogies are bad. And it is not just a matter of taste—some analogies really are better than others.

If one thinks that an argument by analogy employs a bad analogy and reaches a wrong conclusion, there are at least two ways to attack it.

One way of attacking it is to point out weaknesses in the analogy. For example, someone might attack the argument about the honor code, claiming that the analogy upon which it rests is not a good analogy. Such a critic might argue that lying and cheating are not that much like writing bad checks. Sometimes a person writes bad checks unintentionally, just because of being mistaken about a bank balance. This is unlike lying, which always is intentional. And even when bad checks are intentionally written, the people who write them often are not intending to defraud their creditors permanently—they just intend to delay the payment for a while.

The original argument drew a parallel between bad-check writing on the one hand and lying and cheating on the other. Now this counterargument claims that the cases are not sufficiently parallel to justify the conclusion that was drawn. This debate may go back and forth for a while, as each side tries to show the other things about the analogy that had not been noticed. Ultimately, if all goes well, the participants to the discussion will end up with a clearer view of the ways in which writing bad checks is like lying and cheating and of the ways in which it is different. This may add up to a definite answer about whether writing bad checks is a violation of the honor code. But even if it does not yield a definite answer to that question, the discussion will have clarified the situation.

Another and more vivid way of attacking an argument that seems to employ a weak analogy and reach a wrong conclusion is to think of a counter-analogy pointing in an opposite direction. Taking a different example, suppose someone says, "Maybe this boy did write bad checks, but emotionally he is just a child, and so we should make allowances for him, as we would for a child." Someone else may reply, "Well, just because he is childlike, he needs to be dealt with severely, for children who are not sharply corrected persist in their delinquent habits." Here the first analogy is met by a counteranalogy. The first argument is shown not to be very strong by showing that reasoning which is about as good can lead to just the opposite conclusion.

The sort of example we have been discussing has an ethical aspect. But the type of noninductive reasoning by analogy that we are considering is in no way limited to ethical cases. With any kind of subject matter this type of reasoning may be helpful.

EXERCISE 38

A In each case, what conclusion is being argued for, and what analogy is employed in the argument? Discuss the soundness of the reasoning.

1 It will be hard to persuade industrial workers to join a union voluntarily and pay its dues if they can enjoy the benefits negotiated by the union without doing so. But all would be better off if all were members. So union membership ought to be compulsory (the closed shop). Imagine depending on voluntary contributions to pay for national defense. It is an analogous situation.

2 Marxism calls itself atheistic, but it's really a religion. It demands a commitment of faith from its followers, it has Marx and Lenin as its prophets, and for its heaven it promises the classless society.

3 When the government expands the supply of money, the effect is exactly the same as when a criminal counterfeits money. In either case, the action reduces the purchasing power of the money that all others hold and so transfers wealth to the creator of the new money. Government expansion of the money supply is really counterfeiting.

4 Moving parts in contact require lubrication to avoid excessive wear. Honorifics and formal politeness provide lubrication when people rub together. Often the young deplore these formalities as 'empty' or 'dishonest,' and scorn to use them. They thereby throw sand into machinery that does not work too well at best.

B Discuss these arguments by analogy.

1 The man who eats in idleness what he has not himself earned, is a thief, and in my eyes, the man who lives on an income paid him by the state for doing nothing, differs little from a highwayman who lives on those who travel his way.　　　　　　　　　　JEAN-JACQUES ROUSSEAU, *Emile*

2 It would not seem open to a man to disown his father (though a father may disown his son); being in debt, he should repay, but there is nothing by doing which a son will have done the equivalent of what he has received, so that he is always in debt. But creditors can remit a debt; and a father can therefore do so too.　　　　　　　　ARISTOTLE, *Nicomachean Ethics*

3 "Then you should say what you mean," the March Hare went on. "I do," Alice hastily replied; "at least—at least I mean what I say—that's the same thing, you know."

"Not the same thing a bit!" said the Hatter. "Why, you might as well say that 'I see what I eat' is the same thing as 'I eat what I see'!"

"You might just as well say," added the March Hare, "that 'I like what I get' is the same thing as 'I get what I like'!"

LEWIS CARROLL, Alice in Wonderland

4 But me—look at the growth of hair in front.
It hangs before me; down my back it tumbles,
Good, rich, coarse hair all up and down my body.
Don't tell me man-grown hair is out of fashion;
A tree's not beautiful when grey and bare,
A horse without his mane's not fit to look at;
Feathers become a bird as wool does sheep,
So a deep-matted run of hair looks handsome
On any man who has the luck to wear it.   OVID, *Metamorphoses*

5 That the agressor, who puts himself into the state of war with another, and unjustly invades another man's right, can, by such an unjust war, never come to have a right over the conquered, will be easily agreed by all men, who will not think that robbers and pirates have a right of empire over whomsoever they have force enough to master.

JOHN LOCKE, Of Civil Government

6 A foolish consistency is the hobgoblin of little minds, adored by little statesmen and philosophers and divines. With consistency a great soul has simply nothing to do. He may as well concern himself with his shadow on the wall.   RALPH WALDO EMERSON, "Self-Reliance"

7 If it be admitted that a man possessing absolute power may misuse that power by wronging his adversaries, why should not a majority be liable to the same reproach?...The power to do everything, which I should refuse to one of my equals, I will never grant to any number of them.

ALEXIS DE TOCQUEVILLE, Democracy in America

8 Our own more 'rational' beliefs are based on evidence exactly similar in nature to that which mystics quote for theirs. Our senses, namely, have assured us of certain states of fact; but mystical experiences are as direct perceptions of fact for those who have them as any sensations ever were for us.   WILLIAM JAMES, *The Varieties of Religious Experience*

39 REASONING IN WRITING

It is one thing to be acquainted with the general principles of logic. It is something else to be able to apply them well. Gaining an acquaintance with logical principles will contribute but little to one's education unless one does become able to apply these principles in one's actual thinking. To do this effectively takes practice, common sense, general knowledge, and mastery of language. It calls for a kind of maturity in thinking which develops only gradually. We can slowly cultivate it in ourselves, but we cannot acquire it overnight.

It is when we are dealing with thoughts presented in writing that we display our logical skills (or lack of them) most clearly. Two rather different sorts of logical skill are involved here. One is a more creative ability: the ability to invent arguments. The other is a critical ability: the ability to evaluate the logical quality of given arguments. When we are doing the writing ourselves and are trying to present arguments in support of some position which we wish to defend, the creative ability to invent arguments is what we need first of all. To invent arguments fluently requires not only understanding of logic, but also firm knowledge of the subject matter under discussion. However, over and above this creative skill, we also of course need the ability to evaluate the validity of the arguments we have invented so that, in our writing, we use only the better ones. Thus, whether we are doing the writing ourselves or merely thinking about the writing of others, in either case this critical skill is called for.

With regard to the more creative skill: of course there are no simple, mechanical rules that can dictate to us how we should go about inventing arguments, or wording and organizing them. What can be said is that a piece of argumentative writing had better make clear just what conclusion is being defended and just what the reasons are which are being put forward in its defense. Practice in writing is what it takes to enable us to improve our skill at creating arguments and presenting them clearly.

Let us consider in a little more detail, however, the second skill, that involved in the criticizing of arguments. It may be helpful to outline a systematic procedure for carrying out this criticism.

When we meet a piece of argumentative discourse that we want to analyze in a systematic fashion, a good first step is to start by unraveling the structure of the reasoning. Is it a single argument, or is it a set of arguments? If it is a single argument, what is its conclusion, and what are the premises? If it is a set of arguments, what are the premises and conclusions of the various ones, and how are these arguments interconnected? (Do some have conclusions which serve as premises of others?) The next main step can be to examine each bit of reasoning. First we should classify it: Is it deductive, inductive, or what? And is it of some special type that has a name? Then we can evaluate the validity of each bit of reasoning by some method appropriate to its type. Also we should consider whether it commits any fallacy. Then the final step is to form an overall evaluation of the reasoning. Are the unproved premises ones which it is reasonable to believe? Does the reasoning succeed in establishing its ultimate conclusion(s)?

A checklist of these suggested steps may be helpful.

To analyze reasoning

1 Unravel the structure of the reasoning.
  A Is it a single argument?
      If so, what is the conclusion? And what are the premises?
  B Is it a set of arguments?
      If so, what are their conclusions and their premises?
      Are they interconnected? If so, how?
2 Examine each argument.
  A What type of argument is it?
      General type: deductive, inductive, noninductive argument by analogy.
      Specific type: syllogism, inductive generalization, etc.
  B Is it valid?
      Test by an appropriate method, where possible.
  C Does it commit any fallacy?
3 Final evaluation.
  A Are the unproved premises reasonable ones to believe?
  B Does the reasoning succeed in establishing its ultimate conclusions?

These guidelines are constructed from the point of view of someone who wants to appraise arguments that others have constructed. But of course the same sequence of steps is appropriate when we are criticizing arguments that we ourselves are constructing. When it is an argument of our own we are dealing with, as soon as we detect a logical error, we can alter the argument so as to avoid that error. The ability to criticize the completed reasoning of others should make us able to criticize our own reasoning, so that we ourselves do not advance defective arguments.

If we remember that we do not just want to criticize the reasoning of others, but also want to criticize our own reasoning, then this will help us to keep in mind that our task is twofold. We want to avoid being deceived by bad reasoning, and we want to recognize good reasoning as good.

People with a glib half-knowledge of logic sometimes understand the former aim without comprehending the latter. Having learned the names of a few fallacies, for instance, they conclude that whenever they meet someone else's reasoning, the proper procedure is to cry out indiscriminately the name of some fallacy; the opponent, who probably has not studied fallacies, will be rocked and intimidated by this. Such people think that logical criticism is all negative criticism, always finding fault, always accusing others of having made mistakes. But this attitude is shallow and harmful. It would be better never to study logic than to develop this attitude. The little that this sort of person has learned is used so crudely that it does more harm than good.

Even more debased than this are the regrettable intellectual habits of those who, perhaps through experience in debating, learn enough about argumentation to realize that a vigorous case can be made on either side of any issue. These people then get the idea that the whole point of logic is always to score debating victories over one's opponent. They are like the ancient Greek Sophists, who developed powerful tactics for intimidating their opponents, but who did not care whether their own conclusions were true or false. These modern sophists focus all their attention on the superficial persuasiveness of arguments, losing sight of validity and soundness. Often they remain perfectly content with whatever thoughtless opinions they themselves happen to have acquired, and they devote all their argumentative talents to the task of persuading others that these opinions are right.

Reasoning at its best is not a competitive but a cooperative enterprise. A balanced attitude must involve a willingness on our part to recognize and to accept good reasoning whenever an opponent is able to present it to us, in addition to a willingness to recognize fallacies whenever they occur and not just when they are committed by others. The ideal is that we should be dispassionate and objective as we distinguish between good and bad arguments, and as we evaluate the degrees and respects in which arguments that are neither wholly good nor wholly bad are good and bad.

If by rhetoric we mean an overall view concerning strategy in argumentation, then it may be helpful here to introduce the phrase "rhetoric of assent." In our reasoning, we should be ready and willing to assent to arguments whenever they are sound. Our attitude should not be the merely sophistical attitude of being ready to find excuses for rejecting other peoples' arguments. A rhetoric which emphasizes negative rejection of arguments may do more harm than would having no overall outlook concerning argumentation at all. The correct attitude is the discriminating one: a willingness to reject and avoid bad arguments, and to accept and employ good ones.

EXERCISE 39

Discuss the quality of the reasoning in each of the following controversies. Then write a short essay formulating and defending your own conclusion concerning the issue.

A Privatizing the postal service
1 **Mr. Pro**: Private enterprise is more efficient than government-run operations. That's why I favor letting private companies carry some or all the mail. This would reduce mailing costs and give better service.
2 **Ms. Con**: But private companies might employ fewer workers at lower wages than the postal service now does. We need more employment and higher wages.

3 **Mr. Con**: Besides, private companies wouldn't deliver cheaply to hard-to-reach places. Delivery there would either become much more expensive, or would have to be subsidized by the taxpayers.

4 **Mr. Pro**: People should pay for the services they get according to what it costs to provide them. Privatizing the mails is the best way to ensure efficiency and fairness.

B Removing immigration barriers

1 **Ms. Pro**: Any person anywhere should be allowed to move to any other country. Down with immigration barriers!

2 **Mr. Con**: We can't afford to have hordes of immigrants from poorer nations flocking to our shores. They would drive down wage levels here, overburden our welfare services, and cause cultural conflict.

3 **Ms. Pro**: But having plenty of immigrants would augment our labor supply, enabling our industries to keep prices down and remain competitive.

4 **Mr. Con**: Our first responsibility is to our own fellow citizens. We can't let foreigners take bread out of their mouths.

5 **Ms. Pro**: Our birthrate is falling below the replacement level. The best way to keep our population increasing is through immigration.

6 **Mr. Con**: We have too many people already. Look how crowded the highways are at rush hour.

7 **Ms. Pro**: The whole question is very simple: are people of all nations members of one great human family, or not? If they are, we cannot in good conscience have immigration barriers.

C Sex distinctions in insurance

1 **Ms. Con**: It's discrimination to treat people according to what race or sex they belong to. This is always wrong.

2 **Mr. Pro**: Well, is it? Must we have unisex restrooms?

3 **Ms. Con**: The point is that the insurance industry continues to practice sexual discrimination by charging different rates to men and women. When a woman of a given age wants to buy an annuity that will pay her a certain amount a year for life, she will be charged more for it than a man the same age would pay. And a man who buys life insurance has to pay more for coverage than a woman the same age pays. This must be stopped.

3 **Mr. Pro**: Annuities cost women more, but they get life insurance more cheaply. For women as a group, it pretty much balances out. So it's not unfair.

4 **Ms. Con**: Obviously we wouldn't let insurance companies use race as a basis for setting rates. So we must outlaw the use of sex, too.

5 **Mr. Pro**: To be actuarialy sound, an insurance scheme has to charge groups differently when they are known to have different degrees of risk. Now, in every age group, women live significantly longer than men. That's why they should pay different rates.

6 **Ms. Con**: Yes, that's the way it has been done. But it's unjust, and must change.

7 **Mr. Pro**: The same kind of reasoning that leads you to think sex shouldn't be considered ought to lead you to think that age shouldn't be considered. But the insurance business couldn't operate without considering age, so your reasoning is absurd.

D Charging for library videotapes

    1 **Ms. Pro**: The public library charges for lending video tapes, but books are lent free. This is the right policy. People who borrow videotapes have video players, so they're well-to-do and can afford the modest charge.

    2 **Mr. Con**: No, it's unfair. A public library should provide the materials the public wants, and shouldn't discriminate.

    4 **Ms. Pro**: Libraries are for books, after all. Videotapes are not their real business.

    5 **Mr. Con**: The electronic revolution is changing all that. Libraries have to move in the direction of new modes of information storage.

E A low speed limit

    1 **Mr. Pro**: The 55 m.p.h. speed limit saves lives and conserves gasoline. It's best.

    2 **Ms. Con**: No, hardly any drivers obey it, so it doesn't have either result. And it undermines respect for law.

    3 **Ms. Pro**: But a higher speed limit encourages drivers to go even faster.

    4 **Ms. Con**: Our better highways were designed for 70 m.p.h.

    5 **Mr. Pro**: But they are safer at 55.

    6 **Ms. Con**: If you seriously wanted highway safety at all costs, you'd slow traffic down to 25 m.p.h., or maybe 15.

CHAPTER 9

THE PHILOSOPHY OF LOGIC

We shall conclude with a brief consideration of some basic philosophical questions concerning the nature and status of logic. The issues selected are ones that emerge readily out of the discussions of logical reasoning in the previous chapters.

40 THE STATUS OF LOGICAL LAWS

Philosophers have long been interested in trying to characterize the nature of the laws of logic. In Chapter 1 some preliminary suggestions were made about this, but now let us try to discuss the matter further, considering alternative views of this controversial question.

When we speak of laws of logic, we are thinking of deductive and inductive principles such as the following.[47]

Every sentence of the form "p and not p" is false.

Every **E** sentence is equivalent to its own converse.

No valid syllogism can have an undistributed middle term.

The probability of a sentence is never less that that of its conjunction with another sentence.

What kind of sentences are these laws, and how do we know them to be true? Let us consider four philosophical views about such laws as these.

Logical Laws as Inductive Generalizations

Some philosophers have held that logical laws are empirical truths about the world, just as the laws of natural science are. They have regarded logical laws as describing especially general facts about the way things always occur in this world we happen to live in. According to this view, we confirm these laws of logic by making observations of phenomena in the world and then generalizing inductively from what we observe.

With an ordinary empirical generalization, such as that all ravens are black, we do reason in just this way. We have observed many black ravens, and we have never observed any ravens that are not black, so we conclude inductively that probably all ravens are black. According to the view that logical laws are inductive generalizations, we arrive at our knowledge of them in just the same manner.

Consider the law that all sentences of the form "p and not p" are false. We have met many sentences having the form mentioned in the law, such as "Today is Tuesday, and it is not," "Snow is white, and it is not," and so on. In each case, we find that the particular sentence is false. We have never come across a sentence of this form which we found to be true. Hence, it seems that we are entitled inductively to conclude that all such sentences are false, and thus the law is established. This would mean that past experience is the real basis of our confidence in logical laws.

Is this a satisfactory view about the nature of the laws of logic? Like many another view in philosophy, this one offers us a comparison of one thing with another, and it is a comparison that is partly misleading and partly illuminating.

To see how it is misleading, let us remember why it is that typical inductive generalizations do need to be supported by observational evidence. Think of the generalization about ravens. When we have observed many ravens, all of which were black, we feel justified in accepting it as an inductive generalization that all ravens are black. We do not expect this generalization to be refuted by further observations, yet we still understand rather clearly what it would be like for the generalization to be refuted by the discovery of a nonblack raven. If we were to hear a report of such a discovery, it would be surprising but not unintelligible. Our past experience with black ravens is needed to support the generalization precisely because the generalization says something that could conceivably be refuted by experience. In contrast, a universal sentence saying something that experience could not conceivably refute (e.g., "All bachelors are unmarried") would not need to be confirmed by observations. Thus it is a characteristic of typical inductive generalizations that we can understand rather clearly what it would be like for observations to refute them.

Do laws of logic share this characteristic with typical inductive generalizations? Can we describe what it would be like, for instance, to make observations refuting the generalization that all sentences of the form "p and not p" are false? Let's think about this. Suppose we meet a creature that claims to be both a man and not a man, or an object which somebody says is both a tree and not a tree. Suppose, moreover, that the creature insists that it is not merely in some ways like a man and in some ways not like a man;

it insists that it both flatly is and flatly is not a man. Similarly, the person insists that the object both flatly is a tree and flatly is not a tree. How should we react?

These claims are quite unlike the matter of a nonblack raven. The possibility of a nonblack raven made sense, but these claims do not. No matter how much we observed of this creature or of this object, nothing about it could prove to us that it flatly has and flatly lacks the very same property. Thus, nothing that we could observe could ever confront us with a situation that we would need to recognize as a counterexample to the proposed logical law.

If there is no way in which observations could refute the proposed logical law, it cannot be correct to suppose that the law needs the support of observations. Thus, our conviction that no sentences of the form "p and not p" are true does not need to be based on our observations. Instead, whatever we could observe has to conform to this logical law. So much for the misleading aspect of the view that laws of logic are inductive generalizations.

However, there is also an illuminating aspect to this comparison of the elementary laws of logic with inductive generalizations. Although these laws do not need evidence from experience to show that they hold true, such evidence serves to show their utility. These laws are of use because the world happens to be the kind of world that it is. This is a generalization based upon experience and could be refuted by experience. Suppose, for instance, that the universe were under the governance of a powerful and malicious demon of superhuman intelligence who disliked anybody who reasoned in accordance with logical laws. The demon might see to it that any such person was supplied with misleading evidence—evidence which, when logically interpreted, led to false conclusions. For instance, if there were both white and black swans in the world, the demon would arrange that logical thinkers observed only the white ones; logical thinkers would then infer the false conclusion that all swans are white. The demon might also arrange that illogical thinkers would be supplied with evidence of kinds such that from it, with habitual illogic, those thinkers would infer true conclusions.

A demon who was clever enough and powerful enough could cause logical people to reach relatively few true conclusions and illogical people to reach relatively many true conclusions. Under these circumstances, logic would lose its utility, and illogical thinking would be more profitable than logical thinking. This is not to say, however, that the principles of logic would be untrue in such a world. Thus, although our knowledge that these elementary laws of logic are true does not rest upon observation, our knowledge of their utility does, for it is through observations and past experience that we know our world not to be like the far-fetched world just described.

Logical Laws as Metaphysical Facts

There are other philosophers, mostly rather traditional ones, who have agreed that laws of logic are necessary truths, but who still have held that these laws are very general facts about the nature of the universe. They have considered them to be facts about the way all beings have to be; that is, metaphysical facts. Yet how can there be necessary metaphysical facts, and how would these be known by us?

According to this view, it is a very fundamental fact about reality that whenever any entity has a property, it cannot also fail to have that property. Thus, if a creature is a man, it cannot fail to be a man. And it is a still more general fact that whenever what a sentence says is true, what its negation says has to be false. Furthermore, it is another very general fact that any conjunction has to be false if at least one of its components is false. Hence, the conjunction of any sentence with its negation always has to be false—and this is a logical law.

The idea is that these are extremely general facts, built into the nature of reality. How are we supposed to know about them? Not by observation or induction, which are methods too feeble for this purpose. Instead, these traditional philosophers postulate that human beings possess a special mental faculty called reason, which enables them to have direct insight into the nature of reality. Reason is regarded as providing us with a vision of the basic structure of reality. Because this special sort of insight is different from sense experience, it is able to apprehend necessary truths in a nonempirical way.

This view also embodies a comparison. Knowledge of logical laws is compared to a sort of vision, a nonsensory vision. This comparison, like the preceding one, has both an illuminating and a misleading aspect. Its illuminating aspect is that it emphasizes the difference between logical laws and empirical generalizations, by insisting that knowledge of logical laws is a priori rather than empirical. By speaking of rational insight, this view rightly suggests that we can grasp the truth of elementary logical laws by 'seeing' that they hold, that is, just by thinking about them.

But there is a definitely misleading aspect to this view also. Speaking of insight into the nature of reality suggests that the process by which we come to know logical laws is a kind of seeing with the eye of reason—seeing into the inner essence of things, seeing general facts essentially embedded in the nature of the world. The view suggests that by a kind of penetrating and occult clairvoyance we succeed in gazing into the abstract innards of the universe. This is misleading, for it makes the whole matter more mysterious, more occult, than necessary.

Even worse, this view that logical laws are metaphysical facts conveys a wrong impression of the reflective thinking that is involved in grasping logical laws. The view seems to suggest that by staring very intently with the mind's eye we come to understand that sentences of the form "p and not p" are false. That is not so, however. We come to understand this through remembering how the words "and" and "not" are used in normal cases, and through fitting together what we remember of this. If you accepted the doctrine of rational insight, you might be inclined to sit blinking your mind's eye and waiting for your rational vision to clear, when what you ought to be doing is marshaling what you know about how certain words are used in our language. The view that logical laws are metaphysical facts misleadingly suggests that someone might fully understand the uses of the words "and" and "not" and yet, lacking unclouded rational insight, might remain ignorant of the law that sentences of the form "p and not p" are false. But this could not happen, for if anyone doubts whether sentences of this form are false, this doubt by itself is sufficient to show that the person does not fully understand the normal uses of these words.

Logical Laws as Psychological Generalizations

Quite a few philosophers have held a third view about the nature of logical laws. They have believed that these laws describe how the human mind works, that they are generalizations about how people think. The real meaning of the logical law that all sentences of the form "p and not p" are false would be that the human mind cannot think a contradiction; the human mind lacks the power to believe a sentence of the form "p and not p," for it is under a compulsion to reject all inconsistency. According to this view, in studying logic we are studying the capacity of the human mind to maintain certain types of beliefs and the compulsions to which the mind is subject that prevent it from maintaining certain other beliefs. Most of those who hold this view would not seek any explanation of why the human mind is subject to such compulsions, except perhaps that God benevolently made it so or that there is evolutionary survival value in having these compulsions.

This view embodies a comparison between logical laws and laws of psychology. Again, there is an illuminating aspect to the comparison, although there is a misleading aspect also. The value of the comparison lies in the fact that logical laws are related to what the mind can believe. For example, it is rather as though the human mind were subject to a compulsion not to believe contradictions, for the more fully a person comprehends that a belief is a contradiction, the harder it is to believe it. People often hold contradictory beliefs, but only when they do not fully recognize what they are doing.

However, this view that logical laws describe how the mind works is misleading insofar as it tends to suggest that logic is a branch of empirical psychology. The principle that people cannot full knowingly believe contradictions really is not an inductive generalization belonging to psychology. Instead, it is a necessary truth reflecting something about what it means to understand a contradiction; part of what it means to say that someone fully understands a contradiction is that the person disbelieves it. Logic, indeed, has very little to do with empirical facts about human minds. (Empirical facts about human psychology enter into logic, if at all, only in connection with the discussion of logical fallacies.) When logic tells us that no sentence of the form "p and not p" is true, this is best regarded as a remark about sentences, not as a remark about minds. Mental phenomena are not the subject matter of logic; its subject matter consists of sentences and arguments, which may be about anything whatever. Logic is not a branch of psychology, for psychology is an empirical, inductive study of how people and animals think and behave, whereas logic is a nonempirical, noninductive study of such matters as the validity of arguments.

Moreover, there is also another respect in which it is misleading to regard logical laws as psychological generalizations. Consider the law of contradiction. Is the essential thing about that law that it tells us human minds are incapable of believing sentences of the form "p and not p"? Surely not. For no reason has been given why what humans cannot believe need be false. Thus the view leaves open the possibility that sentences of the form "p and not p" might be true, despite our inability to believe them. It regards sentences of that form as not necessarily false, then. And this is a misleading and unsatisfactory result, for sentences of that form are among our most clear cases of necessary falsehood.

Logical Laws as Verbal Conventions

Some recent philosophers have advocated still another view about the status of the laws of logic, the view that these are verbal conventions. The logical law that all sentences of the form "p and not p" are false is compared by them to a stipulative definition. According to this view, the meaning of the law is that we have arbitrarily decided always to apply the word "false" to that sort of sentence containing "and" and "not." We maintain this stipulation because it proves to be a convenient way of speaking, but not for any other reason.

From this standpoint, the logical law cannot be regarded as a necessary truth. It really is neither true nor necessary, for all it does is express an arbitrary verbal convention, which we could alter if we decided that it would be convenient to do so. Perhaps it would never prove convenient to alter this particular verbal convention, but some thinkers have actually urged that we alter the corresponding law stating that all sentences of the form "p or not p" are true. They have suggested that it would be more convenient to do without the principle of the excluded middle. As they see it, a logic which regards some sentences as neither true nor false might be more convenient for some purposes than is our standard logic, and would be just as legitimate (for them, there is no question of a logic being true).

This viewpoint rightly calls to our attention that how words are used is a matter of arbitrary convention. It is merely a historical accident that we happen to have come to use the word "and" to express conjunction, and the word "not" for negation. It could be legitimate for us to alter these conventions, if we decided to do so.

Moreover, the view that logical laws are verbal conventions also is right in calling to our attention that the laws of logic are embedded in our language, and that it is the character of language, more than the character of the world, that is revealed by logical laws. To have learned to use the words "and" and "not" in their standard senses is to have learned that sentences of the form "p and not p" are always false. Someone who thinks that a sentence of this form might not be false thereby shows that he does not understand the standard senses of "and" and "not".

However, there is a misleading aspect to this view that logical laws are conventions of our language. This is because it holds that logical laws are arbitrary in nature and that the laws themselves might perfectly well have been otherwise if we had chosen to have them otherwise. But what would it be like for our present logical laws to be untrue? What would it be like for the world to contain, say, things that both were and were not trees—in the standard senses of "and" and "not"? This does not make sense. The law that all sentences of the form "p and not p" are false, when understood in the normal way, is a law that cannot be false. Since it cannot be false, we certainly could not *make* it false by changing our verbal conventions.

Confusion arises here because of an ambiguity. The proponent of this view neglects the difference between a logical law considered merely as dealing with sentences of the form "p and not p" and a logical law considered as dealing with these sentences *understood in the standard manner.* If a logical law dealt merely with marks and sounds, the law could arbitrarily be changed merely by changing the meanings we attach to the marks and to the sounds. For instance, we could decide to let "and" express disjunction; that would certainly change the law. But when the logical law is understood as dealing with sentences understood in a particular way, the law cannot be changed by any human power, or by any power at all, for it is necessarily true.

Conclusion

Looking back over these four views, we can see that each contributes something to our understanding of the matter, and yet none of the four views, by itself, is adequate. It is not good enough to describe the laws of logic as inductive generalizations about how things in the world behave. It is not good enough to call them rational insights into the nature of reality. It is not good enough to call them generalizations about how human minds happen to work. Nor is it good enough to call them verbal conventions. What we should seek is an account of logical laws which combines the merits of these four positions, but without retaining their misleading aspects.

Drawing together some of the points made in this section, we may characterize the laws of logic as follows. Most of them are about sentences and arguments. They hold in virtue of the ways words are used in language. We grasp them through having mastered our language. They are not made true by us, however, and we cannot change them. It is inappropriate to regard them as factual descriptions of the world, of the human mind, of language, or of anything else. Instead, they are necessary truths, knowable a priori.

A main source of philosophical difficulty in thinking about logical laws is that we are too much inclined to suppose that they must either be descriptions of some kind of contingent facts, or be arbitrary verbal conventions. We may feel attracted by the view that logical laws are true, but then we think this has to mean that they are descriptions of facts which have to be known inductively or by rational insight. And we may feel attracted by the view that logical laws are necessary and are knowable a priori; but then we think this has to mean that they express verbal conventions that could arbitrarily be altered. Thus we stay entangled in unsatisfactory views.

What we should try to see is that truths can be necessary, and can be knowable a priori, even when our knowledge of them comes from our mastery of our language, and not from empirical observation or from vision with the eye of reason. There are truths of this type, and logical laws surely are among the most important of them.

EXERCISE 40

Discuss the assertions made in the following conversation. Which points are well taken, and which are confused?

1 **Alpha**: Logic is about thinking, and thinking is a mental process. So the old view that logic deals with the laws of thought is basically right.

2 Logic deals with the way we must think; and it is the structure of our brains that determines how we must think. So, at least indirectly, logic is a study of brain structure.

3 It would obviously be pointless to draw up a system of logic whose rules were ones in accordance with which we could not think.

4 **Beta**: Rubbish. Logic has nothing to do with the brain, or with human psychology. Laboratory research would simply have no relevance to logic.

5 Our laws of logic, both deductive and inductive, are true by definition. They do not describe thinking, or the world, or anything else. All they do is express the prescribed rules of our language. They are linguistic conventions.

6 If we grant this, it obviously leaves open the possibility that we could have employed other, different linguistic conventions instead.

7 For example, our familiar logic allows just two truth values; in it, every sentence must be either true or false. But there could be a different logic in which three values were allowed, so that every sentence had to be, say, true, false, or indeterminate. In a logic of this latter kind, some forms of argument that count as valid in our familiar two-valued logic would not be valid. For instance, *reductio ad absurdum* is not valid within the three-valued logic; showing that a sentence is not true would not suffice in three-valued logic to show that the sentence was false—it might be indeterminate.

8 This illustrates how validity is always *relative* to a specific kind of logic. Since different kinds of logic are possible, there is no such thing as absolute validity. All we are entitled to say is that relative to the usual two-valued system of logic, *reductio ad absurdum* reasoning is valid; but relative to a three-valued system it would not be valid; and so on. Therefore, we cannot just study an argument and determine whether it is valid or invalid; before we do that, we must choose the logical system relative to which validity is to be assessed.

9 How then do we choose among different but equally legitimate systems of logic? The choice must be made on the basis of considerations lying outside the systems of logic among which we are choosing. One of the criteria for the choice of systems seems to be primarily psychological: the logic we usually employ is the one that is generally accepted by common sense, the one that is familiar and natural to us.

10 Another criterion for the selection of systems is utility. For ordinary practical purposes, the common two-valued logic probably is the most useful. But in special situations some other system might be more convenient.

11 Just because there is no ultimate necessity determining the choice of logical systems, it does not mean that logic is irrational, or based on whims. One must, of course, have a set of logical principles that is consistent; no logic could be useful that was inconsistent. And beyond that, our logic should be as psychologically satisfying and as useful as possible.

12 **Alpha**: Well, I'm glad that you came around to my viewpoint, after all. You agree with me, then, that the nature of human psychological processes dictates what logical principles are to be accepted.

13 **Gamma**: I cannot agree with Beta about utility. How can we explain why one kind of logic is more useful than another? Would a logic that was not true be likely to be useful? The simplest explanation of why the normal two-valued logic is the most useful kind of logic for us to use is that its principles are the correct ones.

14 Why do we need to go searching around for some subject matter for logic to be about, such as the psychology of thinking, or the rules of language? Why not just say that logical laws are about negation and conjunction and categorical statements and so on? And that when logical principles are correct, they express the truth about these matters?

15 Also, Beta speaks about the consistency of different systems of logic, and speaks of it as if it were something not relative. Thus he is employing the notion of an absolute consistency. (Systems that were consistent only relative to some other systems would not be preferable to those that weren't, surely.) So if it is all right to speak of absolute consistency, why should it not be all right to speak of absolute logical validity? Thus Beta's whole relativistic outlook collapses.

41 SCEPTICISM ABOUT DEDUCTION AND INDUCTION

If we start thinking sceptically about deductive reasoning as it contrasts with inductive reasoning, a problem seems to arise about each. These two problems have perplexed some philosophers in the past.

Does All Deductive Reasoning Beg the Question?

The distinctive feature of deductive arguments is that they are, or claim to be, demonstrative; that is, a deductive argument makes the claim that since the premises all are true, the conclusion must necessarily be true also. Put another way, the deductive argument claims that there would be an outright contradiction involved if any person were to assert the premises but deny the conclusion. If the conclusion said anything wholly new and independent of the premises, there could not then be any contradiction involved in asserting the premises but denying the conclusion; the argument could not then have the demonstrative character of a valid deductive argument. Thus we see that if an argument is to be both deductive and valid, its conclusion cannot say something new or independent of its premises. In this sense, the conclusion of a valid deductive argument cannot go beyond the content of its premises; it can only bring out what is already contained in the premises. But this fact gives rise to a philosophical puzzle.

This puzzle has troubled philosophers since the time of Plato, but the classic statement of the puzzle was offered by John Stuart Mill.[48] Mill was particularly concerned with the categorical syllogism, because in traditional logic the syllogism was regarded as the fundamental kind of deductive argument. Mill considered the syllogism, noted that its conclusion must always be contained in the premises if the argument is to be valid, and concluded that this makes the syllogism a worthless style of reasoning.

Consider the syllogism "All teetotalers are avaricious; Mr. White is a teetotaler; therefore Mr. White must be avaricious." Mill charged that an argument like this is worthless because it must beg the question. How could you really know that all teetotalers are avaricious, unless you had already observed each teetotaler and found every last one to be avaricious? But in doing this, you would have had to observe Mr. White himself and note that he is avaricious. Thus you would have had to learn that the conclusion is true *before* you could have learned that the major premise is true. This makes the syllogism worthless as a means of proving the conclusion. The syllogism is a *petitio principii,* for anyone who was in doubt about the conclusion should be at least equally in doubt about the premises.

Not all syllogisms are quite like this example. We might have a syllogism that involved no circularity of reasoning with respect to its major premise, for instance, "All bachelors are unmarried; Aristotle was a bachelor, and so he must have been unmarried." This syllogism has a necessary major premise, and we do not have to observe all bachelors including Aristotle before we can know that all of them are unmarried; we know this in virtue of the meanings of the words involved. Even in this example, however, there still remains a circularity in the reasoning. For how could we know that Aristotle was a bachelor unless we first had found out that he was unmarried? If we did not know that he was unmarried, we could not possibly know that he was a bachelor. Thus again we have to know the conclusion *before* we can know a premise. Here the circularity arises with respect to the minor premise rather than the major, but the reasoning again is a begging of the question.

Mill considered that all deductive reasoning suffered from this sort of circularity. No deductive argument could ever be used really to prove anything, for always one would have to know the truth of the conclusion before one could know the truth of all the premises; always the premises would be at least as dubious as the conclusion itself. Because all deductive reasoning seemed to him to be useless, Mill came to the conclusion that all genuine reasoning that proves anything is what we would call inductive in nature.

Suppose I am trying to prove that Mr. White is avaricious. The evidence from which I really reason is that Mr. Brown, whom I've met, is an avaricious teetotaler; that Mr. Gray, whom I've met, is an avaricious teetotaler; and so on. The actual evidence that I have is about other particular individuals. This is the evidence upon which I must rely if I am to make a useful inference about whether Mr. White is avaricious. An argument of this type, in which one reasons from evidence about some individual cases to a conclusion about another individual case, is what we have called an inductive argument by analogy. Mill in effect contended that this was the fundamental type of argument that we use in our thinking whenever we are employing reasoning that can really prove anything.

Is Mill right about this? Can it be true that deductive reasoning, which we have spent so much time studying, always is basically worthless and never can prove anything? The idea that deductive reasoning always commits the fallacy of begging the question sounds very paradoxical and puzzling; yet can we maintain that deduction is of any use when we admit that the conclusion of a valid deductive argument has to be contained in its premises?

Mill surely was right in insisting that inductive reasoning is extremely important in our thinking and that our empirical beliefs about the phenomena of nature, about past history, and about future predictions ultimately involve inductive reasoning and not deduction alone. How do we know that the sun will rise tomorrow? Our knowledge of this is based upon our observations of the regular behavior of the sun and other heavenly bodies in the past. How do we know that the the classroom building will be here tomorrow and will not vanish into thin air overnight? It is because of our past observations of the durability of buildings. As we go speeding down the highway, what right do we have to assume that the pavement continues out of sight around the bend rather than plunging into a fiery pit? It is because of our past experience with the reliability of highways.

No doubt we can justify some of the facts that we know about the world by deducing them from other more general facts that we know about the world. But, in the end, those more general facts must themselves be established inductively if we are to know them. Mill is surely right that induction (as we call it; he used the word somewhat differently) is very important and that merely deductive proofs of empirical conclusions would never be complete. He rightly emphasizes the importance of induction and the limitations of deduction in our reasoning about empirical matters.

However, Mill surely puts his point too strongly. It is a misleading exaggeration to say that whenever we have an argument whose conclusion is deductively contained in its premises, there we always have a fallacy of begging the question. Sometimes we can have arguments which are deductively valid, whose conclusions are indeed contained in their premises, yet which are of real value as proofs.

Suppose that a man lives in the suburbs but works in the city; he com-
mutes every day. He knows perfectly well that it takes him ten minutes to
get from his house to the station, thirty-five minutes by train into the city,
ten minutes by subway, and then five minutes to walk to his office, and the
same on the way back. And he knows perfectly well that 10 plus 35 plus 10
plus 5 equals 60, and that there are sixty minutes in an hour. He knows
these separate facts very well indeed. But it may come as a surprise to him,
and perhaps a shock, if someone now points out that he is spending two full
hours every working day of his life just traveling back and forth. This conclusion follows deductively from the premises; the man knew perfectly well
that the premises of the argument are true, but he had not noticed the conclusion contained in the premises.

An argument begs the question if its conclusion is contained in its premises in such a way that a person would not know the premises to be true
without having noticed that the conclusion is true too. The example just
given is a simple deduction that does not beg the question. Its conclusion is
indeed contained in its premises, but it takes some thinking to detect that
the conclusion is there, and so the argument can succeed in showing the
man something important that he had not noticed before. This is the kind of
case in which deduction has its value. The point of deductive reasoning is
that it helps us to grasp consequences that we had not noticed but that are
contained in what we already believe. And naturally in more complicated
cases the conclusion might be far more deeply hidden. This happens often
in mathematical reasoning, where very elaborate deductive arguments
sometimes are employed in order to bring out the consequences of sets of
premises.

Is All Inductive Reasoning Invalid?

Mill believed that he had discovered a fatal weakness in deductive reasoning, and so he put his faith in inductive reasoning instead. But is inductive
reasoning really legitimate? Here too a philosophical puzzle arises.

The Scottish philosopher David Hume in the eighteenth century had already raised a serious question about induction.[49] He asked: What right do
we have to trust inductive reasoning? In any inductive argument the conclusion goes beyond what the premises say and makes some kind of prediction or conjecture which further observations may or may not support.
There never is any logical contradiction involved in asserting the premises
of an inductive argument but denying the conclusion. This means that there
never is any logical certainty that the conclusion must be true just because
the premises are. If this is so, how can an inductive argument have any logical force at all? If the truth of the premises does not guarantee the truth of
the conclusion, why should we trust or rely upon inductive reasoning?

Consider examples. In our past experience we have always found that
bread is nourishing to eat and arsenic is poisonous. We have observed many

occasions when people have eaten bread and stayed healthy, and we have observed some occasions when people ate arsenic and died. But have we any logical right to believe that this must continue to be so in the future? It is logically possible that from tomorrow onward people who eat arsenic will be nourished by it whereas those who eat bread will be poisoned by it. If this is so, how can we claim that what we have observed in the past gives us any real reason for making inferences about what must happen in the future? How can we claim really to know anything about what will poison us and what will not?

Hume came to the conclusion that we do not have any reason for trusting inductive arguments. Inductive reasoning is invalid and never really enables us to know anything, he held. Thus Hume was led to a sceptical point of view, doubting that we ever can know anything about as yet unobserved phenomena. Hume recognized that people constantly indulge in inductive thinking, and he developed a theory to explain why people do this. He theorized that human minds are constructed in such a way that they have a built-in tendency to expect for the future the same sort of thing they have experienced in the past. Anyone who has observed something happening often in the past expects to find the same thing happening in the future; the more frequent the past experience has been, the stronger is the expectation for the future. But this is a nonrational tendency in human nature, Hume thought. Our minds work this way, but there is no logical justification for it.

Some philosophers, seeking to escape Hume's sceptical conclusion, have thought that we may justify inductive reasoning by noticing how successful it has been in the past. Looking at our past experience, we see that inductive thinking has frequently led us to true conclusions. Is this not a good reason for trusting induction for the future too? This sort of argument is unsatisfactory as a reply to Hume's scepticism; it offers an inductive argument in favor of the reliability of induction, and that begs the question so far as the sceptic is concerned. The sceptic who is dubious of the legitimacy of induction will be at least equally dubious regarding this particular piece of inductive reasoning. Here is a subtler kind of *petitio principii,* in which it is the form of reasoning itself that is begging the question.

Other philosophers have thought that we may justify inductive reasoning by introducing the assumption that nature is uniform and regular and that the kinds of things that have happened in the past will continue to happen in the future. If we take it as an additional premise in our reasoning that things in nature happen uniformly, this supposedly gives us reason for believing, say, that arsenic which has always poisoned in the past will continue to do so in the future. The idea is that if we assume the 'uniformity of nature,' we can infer that what has happened in the past will continue to happen in the future. However, there are two difficulties about this approach.

First, it is very hard to see how we could formulate a sentence that would adequately perform the role required of this proposed additional premise.

(What kind of uniformity would it be, and how much?) Second, even if we were able to word such a sentence satisfactorily, we would have no way of knowing it to be true, except by induction. There is nothing else we know from which we could deduce such a sentence. Our thinking would be circular if we used inductive reasoning to justify the sentence that itself is introduced for the purpose of justifying inductive reasoning. Thus it seems that we have no way of justifying induction.

The conclusion that we have no real reason for believing that bread is not going to poison us or that arsenic is going to do so is paradoxical and puzzling. We use inductive thinking all the time; can it really be an illogical process without any justification?

Hume's criticism of induction was a valuable contribution to philosophy, for Hume made it because he had recognized that inductive arguments are not demonstrative; one always can consistently deny the conclusion without contradicting the premises. Earlier philosophers had not clearly understood this and had not fully grasped the differences between induction and deduction.

Hume was surely not correct, however, in believing that this means that inductive thinking is not good reasoning at all, that it has no logical force whatever. The trouble arose because Hume thought deductive reasoning is the only legitimate type of reasoning; when he found that inductive arguments are not deductive in nature, he rejected them as illegitimate. But deduction and induction are two different yet equally important types of reasoning, neither of which need be reduced to the other, or justified in terms of the other. It is a misunderstanding to criticize induction just because it is not deductive. We have no more right to do that than we would have to criticize deduction for not being inductive.

The misleading aspect of Hume's sceptical viewpoint becomes still clearer if we notice what it implies. Hume says that we have no real reason for accepting inductive conclusions; this would imply that someone who chooses to eat arsenic in preference to bread is not less reasonable than someone who elects the opposite menu. Hume thinks we have no rational basis for predicting the future; this implies that one kind of thinking is no more logical than any other kind of thinking for making predictions about the future. It implies that the careful scientist who makes predictions is thinking in no more rational a way than the careless person who relies on 'intuitions' or superstitions. They are all in the same category, all completely nonrational in their reasoning, if induction really is without logical justification.

This viewpoint, however, embodies a misuse of the words "rational" and "logical" (and the whole family of words associated with them). For if we use these words in their normal sense, we have to say that the scientist is more rational and logical in his thinking than is a superstitious person. That is part of what it means to be rational and logical: that one uses carefully scientific inductive methods of thinking rather than carelessly superstitious ones. There is no confusion or mistake involved in this normal use of the terms. The mistake arises only in the minds of people who misunderstand their normal use.

EXERCISE 41

A Discuss the following questions.

1 Do all deductively valid syllogisms beg the question? Do they all have an equal tendency to do so?

2 Do all deductively valid truth-functional arguments beg the question? Do they all have an equal tendency to do so?

3 Do all deductively valid quantificational arguments beg the question? Do they all tend to do so equally?

4 Do some invalid deductive arguments beg the question?

5 Can an inductive argument beg the question?

6 Can the same argument beg the question to different degrees, depending on the context of the discussion within which it is used?

7 Can an inductive argument be a good argument if its conclusion does not follow deductively from the premises?

8 Can we give a good deductive proof that induction is reliable?

9 Can we give a good inductive proof that deduction is reliable?

10 Is it necessary to reduce deduction to induction, or induction to deduction?

†B Discuss the following quotation, and consider its bearing on the problem of induction.

In all inference, form alone is essential: the particular subject-matter is irrelevant except as securing the truth of the premises. This is one reason for the great importance of logical form. When I say, "Socrates was a man, all men are mortal, therefore Socrates was mortal," the connection of premises and conclusion does not in any way depend upon its being Socrates and man and mortality that I am mentioning. The general form of the inference may be expressed in some such words as, "If a thing has a certain property, and whatever has this property has a certain other property, then the thing in question also has that other property." Here no particular things or properties are mentioned: the proposition is absolutely general. All inferences, when stated fully, are instances of propositions having this kind of generality. If they seem to depend on the subject-matter otherwise than as regards the truth of the premisses, that is because the premisses have not been all explicitly stated.
BERTRAND RUSSELL, *Our Knowledge of the External World*

42 THE ETHICS OF BELIEF

People form their beliefs in many different ways. Here are a few examples.

1 Jim has invested all his savings in his business of selling an electronic mousetrap. He very much wants his business to succeed for the long run. Some doubters have questioned whether his mousetraps are effective. Jim has conducted no experiments to investigate this, but he is well aware that his prospects for long-run success in this business depend to a considerable extent upon the effectiveness of his mousetraps. Jim tells all prospective customers that his mousetraps are the most effective ones on the market, and he himself firmly believes that this is so. Here Jim is believing something because he *wants* it to be true.

2 Marie has read in the newspaper about people being killed in their homes by robbers who broke in. She is terrified of this. At night she awakens and hears a strange little sound. Without going to investigate it, she becomes convinced that the sound is of robbers breaking in. Here Marie is believing something because she *fears* it is true.

3 Ron has found that people are more respectful toward him when he voices confident opinions. He knows next to nothing about meteorology, but he has heard somewhere that volcanic eruptions may affect the weather. He tells his acquaintances firmly that this year's unusual weather has been caused by volcanic eruptions; and he believes this. Here Ron is believing something *in order to have an opinion.*

4 Chris wondered what type of fertilizing would be of most benefit to the variety of tomato plants she likes to grow. So she tried out the five methods that had been most recommended. Each summer she grew twenty-five plants, dividing them randomly into five groups, treating the groups by her five methods. She recorded the weight of good tomatoes produced by each plant. Upon studying her data, she found that the plants fertilized by one of her methods had quite steadily produced a 15 percent heavier crop than had the plants fertilized by any of the other methods. She decided that this method was the best of the five. Here Chris has sought evidence and has come to believe something on the basis of a *logical appraisal of the evidence.*

People do form beliefs in many different ways. But some of these ways seem to be objectionable and blameworthy. How ought people to form their beliefs?

Many philosophers have maintained that only one method of forming beliefs is legitimate and respectable, the method of logically appraising evidence. They hold that one should collect the relevant evidence that is available and then one should believe all and only those conclusions which follow from the evidence. One ought to believe whatever the evidence logically indicates is so, and one ought to believe nothing else.

We shall not pause to discuss problems that could be raised concerning the notion of evidence. Instead, let us suppose that we are pretty much in agreement about what evidence is and about how it should be obtained. Let us concentrate on the question whether everyone ought always to form beliefs solely on the basis of evidence. In other words, should we always have logical proofs for what we believe (at least, for whatever we believe that is not itself evidence)?

W. K. Clifford, an English thinker, was an especially strong advocate of this position. In an essay entitled "The Ethics of Belief"[50] Clifford declares that the practice of always being guided solely by the evidence is a practice of great value to society. The more widely accepted this practice becomes, the truer will be people's beliefs on the average, and the more will foolish and superstitious beliefs tend to be eliminated. Clifford thought that the advancement of the human race requires people to train themselves always to believe solely in accordance with the evidence. He declared that anyone who believes anything contrary to the evidence is setting a bad example and thereby is "sinning against all mankind."

In holding that we ought to believe all and only those things which the evidence supports, Clifford presumably was not intending to hold that one ought to be *aware* of a proof for each thing one believes. Each of us believes many things without being aware of proofs for them (one believes that Columbus came to America in 1492 and that π is 3.1416, but it may well be that one cannot at the moment think of any proofs of these things). It surely is not blameworthy to believe in this way. Presumably Clifford did not intend to say that we ought to give up these beliefs just because we are not at the moment aware of proofs for them. Probably he would permit us to retain these beliefs as long as there *are* proofs which *could* be given—even though we are not aware of the proofs.

More recent writers have given the name "evidentialism" to Clifford's position. It is an attractive and appealing position. Obviously, people cause much harm for themselves and others by believing without evidence, or contrary to the evidence. Surely we shall be better off, on the average and in the long run, if we believe mostly in accordance with the evidence—rather than believing what we wish were true, or what we fear is true, or believing merely for the sake of having an opinion.

However, evidentialism is a faulty doctrine: it is not true that we ought to believe all and only those things which the evidence indicates are true. William James disagreed with Clifford and rejected evidentialism. In an essay entitled "The Will to Believe"[51] he argued that situations arise in which one ought to believe things that are not supported by the evidence. In these situations there are reasons for believing, but these are not reasons showing that what is believed is true. Let us think about the following case (an elaboration of an example that James gives).

Suppose a man is on a mountain alone and has climbed into a position from which he cannot retreat. His only hope of escape is to go forward by leaping across a chasm. The distance across is a distance which, in his previous jumping, he has seldom succeeded in covering; let us suppose that he has made it only one time in a hundred. What shall he now believe about whether he is going to succeed in leaping across this chasm? If he lets his belief be determined solely by a disinterested, scientific review of the evidence, he will come to the conclusion that he is not going to make it. However, he also knows that confidence enhances jumping ability, and that his slim chance of getting across this chasm will be significantly improved (say, ten-fold) if he can bring himself to believe firmly that he is going to succeed. Under these circumstances, it will be in his own best interest for him to make himself believe that he is going to succeed. Moreover, in the case as we are imagining it, the possible benefit to himself far outweighs any harm likely to be done to others. Therefore, it surely is ethically permissible for him to try to induce himself to believe contrary to the evidence. And if he has a family who are dependent on his support, it will be ethically obligatory for him to do this in order to improve his chance of survival.

This case tells decisively against the doctrine of evidentialism. It is not always obligatory to believe strictly in accordance with the evidence.

Of course it will be irrational, in one sense of that word, for the mountain climber to induce in himself a belief contrary to what disinterested, scientific weighing of the evidence would have led him to believe. However, in a deeper and more important sense, it is not irrational for him to induce belief in himself—for he is prudently setting aside that narrower kind of rationality in order to do what he can see is in his own best interest. In a deeper sense, rationality means choosing the most suitable means for achieving one's ultimate objectives—he is being rational in this deeper sense.

Someone may object that people cannot just induce themselves to believe things. Someone who has been trained in scientific thinking will find it just impossible to believe contrary to the evidence. But this is not as much the case as the objector imagines. Most people do have all too much ability to make themselves believe what they strongly want to believe. Moreover, those who do not have very much of this ability could easily develop more of it in themselves if they wanted to. It is not that we should encourage others to develop this ability. The point is merely that our counterexample to evidentialism cannot be undermined by the idea that people are incapable of believing contrary to the evidence.

The ethics of belief would have been a simpler and more clear-cut topic if evidentialism had been true. But evidentialism is false. Where does this leave us?

For the broad range of situations that we encounter in most of daily life, the best policy surely is to form our beliefs according to what the evidence indicates is true. We can see from experience that any wide departures from this policy tend to cause harm in these ordinary situations. But we cannot rule out the possibility of special situations, like that of the mountain climber, in which it is a better policy not to believe just what the evidence indicates to be true.

Advocates of logic sometimes preach a sort of extended evidentialism. They declare that people ought to believe all and only those things that can be proved logically, whether the proofs are inductively based on evidence or are deductive in character. They scorn both the person who believes something without being able to state good reasons why it is true and the person who refuses to believe something after good reasons have been offered in favor of its truth. They are logical imperialists: they want to plant the flag of logic everywhere and make everyone salute it, all the time.

For the most part, these preachments probably tend to do more good than harm. Most of us are indeed too much inclined to adopt beliefs without good reason, and are too much inclined to fail to adopt beliefs after good reason has been found.

However, as we have seen, it is not true that people always are blameworthy when they form some of their beliefs contrary to evidence and logic. The legitimate scope of logic is not so total. Logical proofs are very important in life, but they ought not to be wholly determinative of belief in all possible situations. Not everything we believe need be proved, and not everything proved need be believed. It is difficult to offer any general rule for distinguishing between cases in which belief ought to be in accordance with the evidence and cases in which it is permissible, or even desirable, to believe without adequate evidence. However, as we develop in maturity and wisdom, we may hope to become increasingly able to make this distinction.

EXERCISE 42

In each example, how inadequate are the grounds for the belief? Discuss the pros and cons of believing in that manner.

1 There are two outs in the bottom of the ninth inning, as the home team trails by three runs. Smigly strides up to the plate. "Come on, Smigly," the rooters cry. "You can do it! A nice base hit!" But the fans know that Smigly has not had a hit in his last ten times at bat, and almost never has hit against a left-handed pitcher.

2 Clara admits that there's not much evidence in favor of astrology. But she believes in it. She says that believing in astrology gives you the feeling that you don't have to take responsibility for what happens to you, since it's all in the stars. She finds this a very comforting thought.

3 Jon has lived all his life in Plainville. He believes it is the best little town in the whole world. He cannot imagine wanting to live anywhere else. However, he has traveled little, and his knowledge of the wider world is slight.

4 Marc has tried to give up smoking but has not succeeded. He knows that lots of scientists say it is dangerous to health, but he prefers not to believe that. Why believe things that are just going to make you feel guilty and miserable?

5 Dr. Blue specializes in the treatment of a dangerous disease. She finds that patients who have this disease usually do not recover. However, when such patients remain cheerful and optimistic rather than becoming despondent their chance of recovery, while still small, is considerably better. Her policy is to explain the prognosis very candidly to each patient, giving the statistics about recovery rates.

6 Maud is extremely fond of her dog. She dresses it up in little costumes and lets it eat from her own plate. She has decided that her dog is so charming that it is worth a million dollars.

7 Ted wants to complete college and then go to medical school. "I know I can do it," he says; "I believe that I can be whatever I want to be." But Ted's grades and test scores are far below average, and he has a great deal of trouble with mathematics and science.

8 The Kookodours are a religious sect with special beliefs. They hold that on the first day of the year 2001 all members of the sect who are then in good standing will be taken straight to Heaven, while all nonmembers will be consigned to Hell. Meanwhile, they live lives of honesty, kindness, and purity. They suffer little physical illness and almost no mental illness, and they rejoice constantly in their fellowship with one another and in their assurance of salvation.

GLOSSARY OF TERMS

abusive *ad hominem* argument   Any *ad hominem* argument that tries to refute a view by attacking the character, qualifications, or motives of the person who advocates the view, rather than by offering direct reasons why the view is false.

***ad baculum* argument (appeal to force)**   Strictly speaking, an *ad baculum* argument is any argument that fallaciously employs a threat as though it were a logical reason for believing a conclusion. In a looser sense, when someone stops offering arguments and resorts to force, he may be said to be resorting to the *ad baculum* 'argument.'

addition   A form of deductive argument in which from a premise a conclusion is derived that is a disjunction having one component that is just the same as the premise. This is schematically represented as "$p, \therefore p \lor q$."

***ad hominem* argument**   Any argument whose premises, rather than containing evidence having a direct bearing on the conclusion, talk instead about the opponent who refuses to agree to the conclusion. Such arguments are often, though not always, fallacious.

adjunction   A form of deductive argument where from two premises a conclusion that is their conjunction is derived. This is schematically represented as "$p, q, \therefore p \mathbin{\&} q$."

***ad misericordiam* argument (appeal to pity)**   Any argument whose premises, rather than containing evidence having a direct bearing on the conclusion, instead give reasons why acceptance of the conclusion would reduce someone's misery.

***ad verecundiam* argument (appeal to authority)**   Any argument whose premises, rather than containing evidence having a direct bearing on the conclusion, instead give evidence that some supposed authority advocates the conclusion. Such arguments are often, but not always, fallacious.

affirmative sentence   Any categorical sentence is affirmative if it is in **A** or **I** form.

affirming the consequent   A form of reasoning in which one premise is a conditional and the other premise is the same as the consequent of that conditional. This is schematically represented as "$p \supset q, q, \therefore p$." This form of reasoning is not deductively valid.

alternation   Disjunction.

ambiguity   To say that an expression is ambiguous is to say that it is unclear which of two or more quite different meanings the expression has.

ambiguity, fallacy of   Any *non sequitur* in which some ambiguity in the argument leads people to misunderstand the logical form of the argument, thus making them regard the argument as valid when it is not.

analogy   A similarity between different things. Sometimes analogies are used for purposes of description, sometimes for purposes of reasoning.

analytical definition   Any definition that aims to describe the accepted meaning of a word or symbol.

antecedent   In a conditional sentence, the component governed by the word "if."

a posteriori sentence   Empirical sentence.

appeal to authority   *Ad verecundiam* argument.

appeal to force   *Ad baculum* argument.

appeal to pity   *Ad misericordiam* argument.

a priori knowledge   Knowledge that we can possess without possessing supporting evidence drawn from sense experience.

a priori sentence   Any sentence that can be known to be true or known to be false a priori.

argument   A formulation in words of one or more premises and of a conclusion that the speaker infers from them or wants his hearers to infer from them.

association   Principles to the effect that in a conjunction of more than two components, or in a disjunction of more than two components, grouping does not matter. Schematically represented, "$(p \& q) \& r$" is equivalent to "$p \& (q \& r)$," and "$(p \lor q) \lor r$" is equivalent to "$p \lor (q \lor r)$."

atomic sentence   Any sentence not containing any other shorter sentence as a component of itself.

begging the question   *Petitio principii.*

biconditional sentence   Any sentence of the form "p if and only if q."

black-and-white thinking   Thinking in extremes; because a sentence is false, it is inferred that some very contrary sentence must be true.

bound variable   To say that a variable in a quantificational formula is bound is to say that the variable there is governed by a quantifier.

broad   To say that an analytical definition is too broad is to say that the definiens applies to some things to which the definiendum does not apply.

categorical sentence   Any sentence in **A, E, I,** or **O** form.

chain argument (hypothetical syllogism)   An argument consisting of three or more conditionals. This is represented schematically by "$p \supset q, q \supset r, \therefore p \supset r$."

circumstantial *ad hominem* argument   Any *ad hominem* argument that offers reasons why the opponent would want to accept the conclusion, rather than reasons why the conclusion is true.

collectively   To speak of the members of a group collectively is to speak about the whole group considered as one unit. What is said may not be true of the members of the group considered individually.

commutation   Principles to the effect that in a conjunction and in a disjunction the order of the components does not matter. Represented schematically "*p* & *q*" is equivalent to "*q* & *p*," and "*p* ∨ *q*" is equivalent to "*q* ∨ *p*."

complex question   Any question worded so as to contain a concealed questionable assumption.

complex question, fallacy of   Any fallacy caused by the presence of an unjustified assumption concealed in a question.

component   The simpler sentences that together make up a compound sentence are called its components.

composition, fallacy of   The fallacy of inferring a conclusion that speaks of a group collectively from a premise that speaks of the group distributively, when such a conclusion does not follow.

compound sentence   Any sentence containing one or more shorter sentences as part of itself.

conclusion   In an inference, that which is inferred from the premises.

conditional sentence   Any "if-then" sentence.

conjunction   Any "and" sentence.

conjunction, law of   Law for calculating the probability of a conjunction. The probability of one event *and* another equals the probability of the first, times the probability that the second would have, assuming that the first is true.

conjunctive argument   Any of various forms of argument that depend upon conjunction; as represented schematically, especially "–(*p* & *q*), *p*, ∴ –*q*."

consequent   In a conditional sentence, the component not governed by "if."

consistency   A group of sentences is consistent if and only if it is not necessarily impossible that all the sentences may be true.

contingent sentence   A sentence whose meaning is such as to leave open both the possibility that the sentence may be true and the possibility that it may be false. Empirical sentences are contingent.

contradiction   To say that a sentence is a contradiction is to say that is necessarily false.

contradictory sentences   Two sentences are contradictories of each other if and only if they are necessarily opposite as regards truth and falsity.

contradictory terms   Two terms are contradictories of each other if and only if it is impossible that there could be anything to which both terms apply, yet one or the other must apply to each thing.

contraposition   The contrapositive of a categorical sentence is got by making subject and predicate trade places and negating each. The contrapositive of a conditional is obtained by making the antecedent and consequent trade places and negating each.

contrary sentences   Two sentences are contraries of each other if and only if they cannot both be true but might both be false.

contrary terms   Two terms are contraries of each other if and only if it is impossible that there could be anything to which both apply but possible that there may be things to which neither applies.

conversion, by limitation   The converse by limitation of a universal categorical sentence is got by making subject and predicate trade places and changing the quantity to particular.

conversion, simple   The simple converse of a categorical sentence is got by making subject and predicate trade places. The converse of a conditional is got by making antecedent and consequent trade places.

copula In categorical sentences, the words "are" and "are not," serving to link subject with predicate.

counteranalogy An argument by analogy constructed for the purpose of countering or opposing some other argument by analogy.

deduction Inference in which the conclusion follows necessarily from the premises, or at any rate in which the speaker claims that it does so. Also, an argument is called a deduction in a narrower and more special sense if it is formally arranged in a series of lines so that each line either is a premise or is inferred from earlier lines by means of some standard principle of inference.

definiendum In a definition, the word or symbol being defined.

definiens That part of a definition which gives the meaning of the word or symbol being defined.

definition A verbal formation of the meaning of a word or symbol; a rule or recipe for translating sentences in which a word or symbol occurs into equivalent sentences that do not contain it. But, in a different and looser sense, any description of the essential nature of a thing is called a definition.

definition in context A definition that shows how to translate sentences containing the definiendum into sentences that do not contain it. This definition does not provide any one fixed combination of words or symbols that can always be substituted for the definiendum.

demonstrative argument Any argument whose conclusion strictly follows from its premises, so that if the premises are true, the conclusion must necessarily be true also.

DeMorgan's laws Laws that the negation of a conjunction is equivalent to a disjunction of negations and that the negation of a disjunction is equivalent to a conjunction of negations. Schematically represented, "$-(p \ \& \ q)$" is equivalent to "$-p \lor -q$," and "$-(p \lor q)$" is equivalent to "$-p \ \& \ -q$."

denying the antecedent Form of argument in which one premise is a conditional and the other is the same as the negation of its antecedent. This is represented schematically by "$p \supset q, \ -p, \ \therefore -q$." This is not deductively valid.

dilemma Form of argument having three premises, two of which are conditionals and the other a disjunction. A simple dilemma contains three distinct basic components; a complex dilemma contains four. In a constructive dilemma the components of the disjunctive premise are the same as the antecedents of the conditional premises; in a destructive dilemma the components of the disjunctive premise are negations of the consequents of the conditionals.

disjunction (alternation) Any "or" sentence.

disjunction, law of Law for calculating the probability of a disjunction. The probability of one event or another equals the probability of the first plus the probability of the second minus the probability that both will occur.

disjunctive argument Any of various arguments that depend on disjunction; represented schematically, especially "$p \lor q, \ -p, \ \therefore q$."

distribution, law of Principle that a conjunction one of whose components is a disjunction is equivalent to a disjunction both of whose components are conjunctions, and that a disjunction one of whose components is a conjunction is equivalent to a conjunction both of whose components are disjunctions. Thus, represented schematically, "$p \ \& \ (q \lor r)$" is equivalent to "$(p \ \& \ q) \lor (p \ \& \ r)$," and "$p \lor (q \ \& \ r)$" is equivalent to "$(p \lor q) \ \& \ (p \lor r)$."

distribution of terms The subject, "S," of a categorical sentence is distributed in that sentence if and only if the sentence says something about every kind of S; the predicate, P, of a categorical sentence is distributed in that sentence if and only if the sentence says something about every kind of P.

distributively To speak of the members of a group distributively is to say something that applies to each member of the group considered singly. What it said need not be true of the group considered as one unit.

division, fallacy of Fallacy of inferring a conclusion that speaks of a group distributively from a premise that speaks of the group collectively, when such a conclusion does not follow.

double negation Principle that the negation of the negation of a sentence is equivalent to the sentence itself; represented schematically, "–(–p)" is equivalent to "p." Also, the principle that the negation of the negation of a term means the same as the term itself; e.g., "non-nonS" means "S."

empirical knowledge Knowledge that a person having only ordinary faculties cannot possess without having evidence drawn from sense experience to support it.

empirical sentence Any sentence that people who possess only ordinary faculties can know to be true or know to be false only on the basis of evidence drawn from sense experience.

enthymeme Any argument one or more of whose premises is unstated.

equivalence Two sentences are equivalent if and only if they must necessarily be alike as regards truth or falsity. When two sentences are equivalent because of their truth-functional form, they are said to be truth-functionally equivalent; when two sentences are equivalent because of their quantificational form, they are said to be quantificationally equivalent.

equivocation, fallacy of Any fallacy of ambiguity in which the ambiguity of some particular word or phrase causes the fallacy.

exclusive disjunction Any "or" sentence whose meaning is such that the sentence is false if both components are true.

existential instantiation (E.I.) Rule of inference according to which we may infer from an existential quantification any instance of it, with the restriction that the name in the instance must be new to the deduction.

existential quantification Any symbolized sentence that starts with an existential quantifier whose scope is all the rest of the sentence.

existential quantifier The expression "($\exists$)," where any variable may be put in the gap. "($\exists$x)" means "At least one thing x is such that."

existential viewpoint In discussing the interrelations of categorical sentences, any viewpoint from which one takes for granted the existence of things of some or all of the kinds under discussion.

explanation Any way of fitting some strange or puzzling phenomenon into the fabric of one's knowledge by pointing out its cause or by showing that it is a special case of some more general phenomenon. Explanation differs from proof at least in this respect, that one asks for an explanation of a phenomenon only when one is ready to grant that it does occur; one asks for a proof of a phenomenon only when one is not ready to take for granted that it occurs.

explicit definition Any definition giving as the definiens a single word or phrase that can be substituted for the definiendum.

exportation A principle of equivalence involving conditionals. Represented schematically, "p $\supset$ (q $\supset$ r)" is equivalent to "(p & q) $\supset$ r."

expression Any word or symbol, or combination of words or symbols.

extension of a general term All those things to which the term applies.

fair bet A bet is fair when every party to the bet has the same mathematical expectation of gain and the same mathematical expectation of loss.

fallacy Any logically defective argument that is capable of misleading people into thinking that it is logically correct.

figure In a categorical syllogism, the pattern of arrangement of the terms.

forgetful induction Invalid inductive reasoning in which the mistake is that some of the relevant available data have not been taken into account.

formal fallacy Any fallacy in deductive reasoning in which the mistake arises because of pure misunderstanding of logical principles.

formula Any sentence written with logical symbols; also any expression containing logical symbols which, though not itself a sentence, displays some logical structure that a sentence could have.

free variable In a symbolized quantificational formula, a variable not governed by any quantifier.

general term Any word or phrase that would make sense if used as subject or predicate in categorical sentences.

hasty induction In inductive reasoning, the fallacy of overconfidently inferring a sweeping conclusion from weak evidence.

hypothetical sentence Any conditional sentence.

hypothetical syllogism Chain argument.

hypothetical viewpoint In discussing the interrelations of categorical sentences, the viewpoint from which one leaves it an open question whether there exist things of the kinds under discussion.

identity To say that x and y are identical is to say that they are one and the same thing. The verb "is," in one of its senses, expresses identity.

ignoratio elenchi Fallacy of irrelevance.

illicit obversion Fallacious obversion, in which the mistake arises because the term that ought to be replaced by its contradictory is replaced instead by a contrary term.

illicit process In categorical syllogisms, the fallacy of allowing a term to be distributed in the conclusion when it is not distributed in a premise.

immediate inference Deductive inference in which a categorical conclusion is inferred from a single categorical premise.

implication To say that one sentence, or group of sentences, implies another sentence is to say that if the former is true, then the latter must necessarily be true too. Where the implication results from the truth-functional forms of the sentences, it is called truth-functional implication; where it results from their quantificational forms, it is called quantificational implication.

inconsistency, fallacy of The fallacy of reasoning from premises that are inconsistent with one another.

inconsistent sentences A group of sentences are inconsistent with one another if and only if it is necessarily impossible for them all to be true. An inconsistent group of sentences either contains sentences of the form "p" and "$-p$" or implies them.

induction Nondeductive inference in which the conclusion expresses an empirical conjecture that goes beyond what the premises say; that is, the conclusion implies something, not implied by the premises, that can be confirmed or refuted only on the basis of evidence drawn from sense experience.

inductive analogy Inductive reasoning that reaches a conclusion about a single case on the basis of a similarity between that case and other previously observed cases.

inductive generalization Inductive reasoning that passes from evidence about some observed members of a class to a conclusion about the whole class.

inference The deriving of a conclusion from premises.

instance In the logic of quantification, an instance of a quantification is a sentence exactly like the quantification except that the quantifier has been removed and a name has been substituted for the variable of quantification. In inductive reasoning, individual cases to which a generalization applies or which bear out an analogy are called instances of that generalization or instances of that analogy.

intension of a general term All those characteristics that a thing must necessarily possess in order that the term correctly apply to it.

invalidity To say that an argument is invalid is to say that the conclusion does not follow from the premises, or, at any rate, that it does not follow with the degree of probability that the speaker claims for it.

irrelevance, fallacy of Any *non sequitur* that is neither a pure fallacy nor a fallacy of ambiguity. A fallacy of this sort is misleading when something about the premises distracts attention from the fact that they have no logical bearing upon the conclusion.

large numbers, law of Statistical principle to the effect that if, for example, a coin is to be tossed (in this case the probability of heads in a single toss is ½), then the greater the number of tosses, the higher the probability that the fraction of them yielding heads will closely approximate the probability of the single case (i.e., ½).

logical analogy Reasoning by analogy which aims to show that an argument is invalid (or that it is valid) by pointing out that other similar arguments are invalid (or valid).

logical form In a sentence or an argument, the logical structure obtained if all nonlogical words are removed, leaving only such logical words as "all," "some," "not," "and," "or," etc.

logical laws Principles about what kinds of sentences are true because of their logical form; principles about what sentences may be inferred from others; and so on. Also, in another sense, a sentence that is necessarily true because of its logical form may be called a law of logic.

major premise In a categorical syllogism, the premise containing the major term.

major term In a categorical syllogism, the term that is the predicate of the conclusion.

mathematical expectation In a gambling situation, the amount the gambler stands to gain (or lose) multiplied by the probability of winning (or by the probability of losing).

method of agreement A method of reasoning about causes, using the principle that the cause of a phenomenon must be a factor that is present in every case in which the phenomenon occurs.

method of concomitant variations A method of reasoning about causes, using the principle that the cause of a phenomenon must be present to the same degree as is the phenomenon.

method of difference A method of reasoning about causes, using the principle that any factor present when the phenomenon does not occur cannot be the cause of it.

middle term In a categorical syllogism, the term that occurs in both premises but not in the conclusion.

Mill's methods Ways of finding the causes of phenomena, based on the general principle that the cause of a phenomenon must be present when and only when the phenomenon occurs.

minor premise In a categorical syllogism, the premise containing the minor term.

minor term In a categorical syllogism, the term that occurs as subject of the conclusion.

modus ponens A form of conditional argument. It is represented schematically by "$p \supset q, p, \therefore q$."

modus tollens A form of conditional argument. It is represented schematically by "$p \supset q, -q, \therefore -p$."

monadic quantification Quantificational symbolism is monadic when each capital letter that is followed by any variables is followed by only one variable at a time.

Monte Carlo fallacy In inductive reasoning, the fallacy of inferring that because an event has occurred less often in the recent past than was to have been expected, there is therefore an increased probability of its occurring in the near future.

mood In a categorical syllogism, the forms of the sentences in the syllogism; thus, a syllogism is in the mood **EAE**, for instance, if its major premise is an **E** sentence, its minor an **A**, and its conclusion an **E**.

narrow An analytical definition is too narrow if the definiendum applies to some things to which the definiens does not apply.

necessary condition If all cases of *A* are cases of *B*, then *B* is said to be a necessary condition of *A*. For example, having a middle term that is distributed is a necessary condition of being a valid syllogism. A sentence stating that *A* is a necessary condition of *B* may itself be a necessary sentence, or it may be an empirical sentence.

necessary sentence Any sentence which, if true, is necessarily true and could not have been false, or which, if false, is necessarily false and could not have been true. The truth or falsity of a necessary sentence can be known a priori.

negation Any "not" sentence.

negation, law of Law for calculating the probability of a negation; the probability that something is *not* so equals 1 minus the probability that it is so.

negation of a sentence The result of writing the sentence with a negation sign (which means "It's not the case that") prefixed to it as a whole. This result is contradictory to the original sentence.

negation of a term The result of writing the term with "non" prefixed to it as a whole. This resulting term is contradictory to the original term.

negative analogy In inductive reasoning by generalization or analogy, the extent of the observed differences among the previously observed cases.

negative sentences Categorical sentences are said to be negative if and only if they are in **E** or **O** form.

nonexclusive disjunction Any "or" sentence that counts as true if both components are true.

noninductive reasoning by analogy Reasoning by analogy in which the conclusion does not express any empirical conjecture going beyond the statements of the premises.

non sequitur Any invalid argument, where the conclusion does not follow from the premises.

obversion A categorical sentence is obverted by changing its quality and negating its predicate.

parentheses We use parentheses in logical formulas when and only when they are needed to make clear what grouping is intended. A negation sign or a quantifier is always understood so as to govern as little of what follows as will make sense.

particular sentence Any categorical sentence that is in **I** or **O** form.

petitio principii **(begging the question)** Fallacy of using a premise (or a form of inference) whose acceptability is bound to be at least as doubtful as is that of the conclusion supposedly being proved.

positive analogy In inductive reasoning by generalization or analogy, the extent of the observed similarities among the already observed instances.

post hoc, ergo propter hoc In inductive reasoning about causes, the fallacy of inferring that just because one thing happened after another, the later was caused by the earlier.

predicate In a categorical sentence, the term after the copula.

premise In an inference, an assumption upon which the conclusion depends.

probability In inductive reasoning, the degree of confidence that it is reasonable to accord to the conclusion, relative to the available evidence.

proof Any argument that succeeds in establishing its conclusion.

pure fallacy Any *non sequitur* that arises purely from misunderstanding of logical principles and not from ambiguities of language or irrelevant distractions.

quality To specify the quality of a categorical sentence is to state whether the sentence is affirmative or negative.

quantifier A word or symbol that indicates how many things a sentence is talking about; the words "all," "no," and "some" and the symbols "(x)" and "($\exists$x)" are quantifiers.

quantity To specify the quantity of a categorical sentence is to state whether the sentence is universal or particular.

real definition Many traditional philosophers believed that there is one and only one correct way of describing the nature of each natural being; such description they called a real definition.

reasoning Thinking that includes the making of inferences.

reductio ad absurdum Deductive reasoning in which a conclusion is established by showing that its negation leads to something necessarily false. Schematically, one form is "$p \supset (q \ \& \ {-}q), \therefore {-}p$."

relevance In inductive reasoning by generalization or analogy, the extent to which one's background knowledge makes it reasonable to expect that one thing will be associated with another.

revelatory definition Any description that, by means of a metaphor or in some other way, attempts to point out something fundamental about the nature of the thing being described.

scope of a quantifier In a symbolized sentence containing a quantifier, that portion of the sentence governed by the quantifier.

self-contained argument Any argument whose premises can be stated completely so that, in determining whether the conclusion validly follows from them, one need take no account of the truth or falsity of any other sentences (except for sentences expressing logical laws).

sentence Any combination of words that can serve as a complete utterance, according to the rules of language. In logic the concern is with sentences used to make true or false statements.

simplification Conjunctive argument whose single premise is a conjunction and whose conclusion is the same as one component of that conjunction. This is represented schematically by "p & q, $\therefore$ p."

singular sentence   A sentence containing at least one singular term. An example is "Socrates is mortal"; this example can be symbolized "All S are M" (if "S" is taken to mean "persons identical with Socrates"), or it can be symbolized as "Ma" (if "a" stands for Socrates).

singular term   A word or phrase whose meaning makes it purport to apply to exactly one thing. Proper names are one kind of singular term.

slothful induction   In inductive reasoning, the mistake of underrating the degree of probability with which a conclusion follows from evidence.

sorites   An argument whose conclusion is derivable from premises through use of a series of two or more categorical syllogisms.

square of opposition   A traditional diagram for illustrating the logical interrelations of the different forms of categorical sentence, when all have the same subject and all have the same predicate.

statement   An assertion. To make a statement is to utter (or write) a sentence in such a way as to say something true or false. Strictly speaking, the same sentence might be used on different occasions to make different statements. (By uttering the sentence "You're clever" while addressing Smith one may make a true statement; yet by uttering that same sentence while addressing Jones one perhaps makes a false statement.) In logic a sentence is called true when the statement that the sentence would normally be used to make is a true statement.

stipulative definition   A definition that arbitrarily assigns a new meaning to the word or symbol being defined.

subcontraries   To call two sentences subcontraries is to say that they cannot both be false but may both be true.

subject   In a categorical sentence, the term between the quantifier and the copula.

sufficient condition   To say that A is a sufficient condition of B is to say that all cases of A are cases of B. Having an undistributed middle term is a sufficient condition for being an invalid categorical syllogism.

syllogism   A categorical syllogism is any deductive argument consisting of three categorical sentences that contain three different terms, each term occurring twice, in two different sentences.

symmetry of a relation   To say that a relation is symmetrical is to say that whenever it holds between a first thing and a second, then it holds also between the second and the first. This is represented schematically by "$(x)(y)(Rxy \supset Ryx)$."

tautology   Any sentence that is necessarily true in virtue of its truth-functional form.

term   In categorical sentences, the words or phrases occurring as subjects and predicates are called "terms." More generally, any word or phrase that it could make sense to apply to a thing is called a term. (But not all words are terms; the word "not" is not a term, for it makes no sense to say "This thing is a not.")

transitivity of a relation   To say that a relation is transitive is to say that whenever it holds between a first thing and a second and between the second and a third, then it holds also between the first and the third. This is represented schematically by "$(x)(y)(z)[(Rxy$ & $Ryz) \supset Rxz]$."

truth function   To say that a compound sentence is a truth function of its component sentences is to say that the truth or falsity of the compound is settled once the truth or falsity of each component has been settled.

truth table   Table that shows whether a compound sentence is true or whether it is false, for each possible combination of truth and falsity of its components.

undistributed middle, fallacy of   For a categorical syllogism to commit this fallacy is for its middle term to be distributed neither in the major nor in the minor premise.

universal instantiation   In deductive reasoning, the principle that allows one to infer from a universal quantification any instance of it.

universal quantification   A symbolized sentence that starts with a universal quantifier whose scope is all the rest of the sentence.

universal quantifier   The expression "( )," where any variable may be put in the gap. "(x)" means "Each thing x is such that."

universal sentence   To call a categorical sentence universal is to say that it is in **A** or **E** form.

vagueness   To say that a word is vague is to say that there is no way of telling where the correct application of it is supposed to stop, as things vary in degree.

validity   To say that an argument is valid is to say that its conclusion logically follows from its premise, as the argument claims. A deductive argument is valid if and only if the relation between premises and conclusion is such that the truth of the premises would strictly guarantee the truth of the conclusion. A deductive argument valid on account of its truth-functional form is called truth-functionally valid; if valid on account of its quantificational form, it is called quantificationally valid. An inductive argument is valid if and only if the degree of support which it claims that its premises provide for the conclusion is indeed the degree of support that the premises do provide for the conclusion.

variable   Any of the letters "x," "y," "z," etc., as used in quantificational symbolism.

variable of quantification   In a universal quantification or an existential quantification, the variable whose occurrences are governed by the quantifier that comes at the beginning.

verbal dispute   A disagreement caused not by any difference of opinion concerning anything true or false but merely by a difference in verbal usage; one speaker prefers to use a word in one way, while his opponent prefers to use the word in another way.

GLOSSARY OF SYMBOLS

Letters

A,E,I,O: These four boldface capital letters refer to the four forms of categorical sentence.

A, B, C, etc.: Italic capital letters are used in several ways. In Chapter 2 they are used as abbreviations for terms; thus "All S are P" can symbolize "All Slavs are prudes." In Chapter 3 they are used as abbreviations for whole sentences; thus "S ⊃ P" can symbolize "If Socrates was wise, then Plato was wise." In chapters 4 and 5 they are used in quantified sentences to express properties and relations; thus "Sx" can symbolize "x is a Slav" and "Pxy" can symbolize "x precedes y."

a, b, c, etc.: Small italic letters from the beginning of the alphabet are used in Chapters 4 and 5 as names of particular objects; they function as proper names do.

p, q, r, etc.: Small italic letters starting with "p" are used in Chapter 3 to display the logical skeletons of compound sentences; they function as ellipses do: "p v q" is like "... or /// ."

x, y, z, etc.: Small italic letters from the end of the alphabet are used in Chapters 4 and 5 as variables; they function as pronouns do.

Truth-Functional Symbols

− : The dash expresses negation. "−p" is read "not p," or "it is not the case that p."

& : The ampersand expresses conjunction. "p & q" is read "p and q."

v : The wedge expresses disjunction, in the nonexclusive sense. "p v q" is read "p or q."

⊃: The horseshoe expresses the conditional, in its truth-functional sense. "p ⊃ q" is read "if p then q," or "p only if q."

≡ : The three lines express the biconditional. "p ≡ q" is read "p if and only if q."

Quantificational Symbols

(x) : Any variable enclosed within parentheses is a universal quantifier. "(x)" may be read "each thing x is such that."

(∃x) : Any variable preceded by a backward "E" and enclosed within parentheses is an existential quantifier. "(∃x)" may be read "at least one thing x is such that."

Identity Symbol

= : We write this sign between names or variables to express the relation of strict identity.

Probability Symbol

// : The double stroke is used to express probability. These two strokes appear between one sentence and another to form an overall expression that refers to the probability of the first sentence relative to the second. "p // q" may be read "the probability of p, given q."

NOTES

1 When we get to studying the principles of logic, we shall want to have examples of arguments to illustrate them. Then it will not matter much whether our sample arguments are actual ones that someone has put forward or merely possible ones that someone might conceivably put forward. However, this distinction between actual and potential arguments is important when we are trying to criticize thinking that has occurred. Suppose someone's remarks seem to contain an argument, and we notice that what seem to be its premises are not all true. Only if the argument is an actual argument are we entitled to criticize the thinker for having made the mistake of using a false premise. If the thinker is merely considering a potential argument, there is nothing wrong with letting the so-called premises be false.

Our discussion here has not taken account of the method of conditional proof, a more sophisticated form of reasoning in which a premise can be tentatively put forward, only to be later canceled out so as to yield an "if-then" conclusion. For example, Will might reason as follows: "Suppose, for the sake of argument, that my income for next year increases by 7 percent and the inflation rate is 5 percent. Now, I know that under these circumstances taxes would take an added 3 percent of my income. So I would be worse off financially. And therefore, if my income increases by 7 percent and inflation is 5 percent, I shall be worse off financially." Here Will's initial supposition is never asserted as true, and it does not need to be true in order for him to draw his "if-then" conclusion. The method of conditional proof is often used in more advanced logic, but will not be dealt with in this book.

2 This is not a complete definition of the words "argument," "reasoning," "inference," and "proof." Although they are closely related in meaning, these terms are not exact synonyms. More complete definitions must distinguish their meanings from one another.

Inference, in the basic sense of the word, is the mental act of reaching a conclusion from one's premises, the achievement of coming to believe the conclusion because one comes to see (or thinks one sees) that it follows from the premises which one already accepts as true. *Reasoning* is the broader mental activity of marshaling one's premises, detecting logical connections, and making inferences. An *argument* (that is, an actual argument) is a formulation in words or other symbols of premises and of a conclusion that the speaker is inferring from them, or is urging the audience to infer. A *proof,* in the basic logical sense of this term, is an argument which succeeds in showing that its conclusion is true.

However, some mathematicians and logicians use the word "proof" also in a weaker sense. They call it a proof when one shows that some specific conclusion would strictly follow from specific premises, even when one does not accept the premises and thus has no reason to accept the conclusion. Even further removed from the basic sense of the term is the way of using the word "proof" that has been introduced by modern mathematical logicians—they define proofs as sequences of marks that fulfill certain formalistic requirements. These uses of the word "proof" are perfectly legitimate, but they have only a distant kinship with the basic, central meaning of the term.

3 In other words, the conclusion is 'empirical,' in the sense to be discussed in the next section. There is no unanimity among logicians about how to define induction. The definition adopted here is not the simplest in current use, but it is perhaps the least likely to be misleading overall.

An old-fashioned idea was that by definition deductive arguments always move from the general to the less general, and that inductive arguments always move from the less general to the more general. However, if we accepted that usage, we would have a distinction of much less value for the analysis of reasoning.

4 To say that the premises and conclusions of arguments are *sentences* is a serviceable but crude way of speaking. It is serviceable in enabling us to talk about parts of arguments without having to speak in tedious circumlocutions. It is crude, however, because it glosses over the distinction between a declarative sentence and the statement, or assertion, that a speaker makes by uttering the sentence on a particular occasion. Saying that the premises and conclusion of an argument are sentences may misleadingly seem to suggest that sentences as such are true or false, and that we can analyze the logic of an argument merely by studying the sentences (series of words) that occur in it. But we cannot do that. Suppose a man argued: "If Jones is mad, he needs psychiatric treatment; and he is mad; so he needs psychiatric treatment." Whether this argument is valid depends, for one thing, upon whether the word "mad" is used in the same sense in both premises. If in uttering the first sentence the speaker is asserting that if Jones is insane then he needs treatment, while in uttering the second sentence the speaker was asserting that Jones is angry, then the argument is not good logic. Merely by inspecting the words themselves, one cannot determine how the speaker is using them, and one cannot determine whether the argument is good or bad logic. To determine those things, one must consider the *context* in which these sentences are uttered. Perhaps one must take account of what the speaker said before or afterward, what he saw and knew, and his gestures and tone of voice.

A less crude way of speaking would be to say that the premises and conclusions of arguments are not the sentences that speakers utter but rather are the things they are saying by uttering these sentences. The difficulty is that this way of speaking would be very cumbersome later on when we come to discuss the logical forms of arguments. In the rest of this book, whenever a remark is made about some logical aspect of a sentence, the meticulous reader should understand this is short for a more cumbrous remark about some aspect of what it is that a speaker would normally be saying by uttering that sentence.

Writers on logic have used various terms for referring to the items that serve as premises and conclusions of arguments. Some have spoken of *propositions*, some of *judgments*, some of *statements*.

In our discussion of reasoning, we are speaking of the premises and conclusions as *true or false*. This is a fundamental and important way of considering reasoning. However, we should note in passing that some logicians have maintained that not all premises and conclusions need to be true or false. They have talked about a logic of commands, where a conclusion that is a command can be inferred from premises which include commands; and of a logic of questions, where a question can be inferred as a conclusion from other questions. And there are other variant types of reasoning where the premises and conclusions include sentences of kinds not capable of being true or false. These are of philosophical interest, but we shall not be giving them further consideration.

5 Some writers on logic restrict the term "valid" to good deductive arguments. They do not choose to call an inductive argument valid, no matter how good it is. We shall not follow that usage, however. Notice that we are using the word "valid" in a special logical sense and are applying it only to arguments. In ordinary language the word is used more broadly, as a synonym for "true"—as when people speak of valid opinions, etc.

6 This is the only notion of implication that we shall employ. However, many modern logic writers follow the somewhat confusing precedent set by Russell, who used the word "implication" as a name for the truth-functional conditional (which we shall discuss in Chapter 3). We shall regard implication as a relation between sentences, never as a type of sentence.

7 Let us leave it an open question whether there are other sentences which are knowable a priori but which are not necessary in this sense. If there are any contingent but a priori sentences (Descartes' "I am thinking" and "I exist" might be examples), they are rather special cases.

Also we shall not be concerned with weaker senses of necessity, such as the 'physical necessity' supposedly expressed by sentences such as "Taking arsenic *must be* fatal."

8 The term "categorical" traditionally has been used because of its connection with the term "category," which comes from the Greek word for predicate. Thus, categorical sentences are sentences in which a predicate is connected with a subject. In Aristotle's philosophy, predicates were classified into some ten basic types such as substance (e.g., "man"), quantity (e.g., "2 feet long"), quality (e.g., "white"), and others. These types of predicates, also regarded as corresponding to types of real entity in the universe, came to be called the *categories*. It was thought that in every categorical sentence the predicate had to belong to one of these categories.

9 The distinction between general and singular terms is of some importance for logic. A *general term* is a word or phrase whose grammar allows it to apply to any number of individual things—to none, to one, or to many. Thus, the general term "dog" happens to apply to millions of individual dogs, the general term "natural satellite of the earth" happens to apply just to the moon, and the general term "unicorn" happens to apply to nothing. A speaker can use a general term (e.g., "dodoes") in saying many things that he knows to be true (e.g., in saying "No dogs are dodoes," "Some birds are not dodoes," etc.) regardless of whether there is anything to which the term applies.

In contrast, a *singular term* is a word or phrase whose grammar makes it purport to refer to just one thing, on any particular occasion. A speaker can use a singular term (e.g., the proper name "Fido") in saying a variety of things that he knows to be true (e.g., in saying "Fido is an intelligent dog," "Fido is not a cat," etc.) only if the term as he is using it does refer to just one individual thing. If he had made a mistake and there were no such dog as the one he thought he was referring to, then he would not have said anything true or false by uttering those sentences.

Another distinction which is going to be important to us is that between compound sentences and atomic sentences. Sentences are said to be *compound* if they contain other simpler sentences as logical components. Sentences are said to be *atomic* if they do not contain other simpler sentences. Thus the sentences "Birds have wings, and birds can fly," "If birds have wings, then birds can fly," and "Birds can fly because birds have wings" are examples of compound sentences. This is because each contains the shorter sentences "Birds have wings" and "Birds can fly."

Categorical sentences are not compound, as such. That is, a categorical sentences does not need to contain other simpler sentences as components of itself, and most categorical sentences do not. However, it would be incorrect to say that all categorical sentences are atomic, for some categorical sentences do contain other simpler sentences. For example, the categorical sentence "All persons who believe that birds can fly are persons who believe that birds have wings" is compound, since it contains the simpler sentences "Birds can fly" and "Birds have wings." Some categorical sentences are compound, and some are atomic.

10 A more rigorous formulation of the definition of distribution is as follows: Suppose that T is a term which occurs as subject or predicate in a categorical sentence s. Where T' is any other term, let s' be the sentence that is exactly like s except for containing the compound term T' & T wherever s contains T. Now, T is said to be distributed in s if and only if, for every term T', s logically implies s'.

To see the meaning of this definition, consider an example. Suppose that T is the term "prohibitionists" and s is the sentence "Some seamen are not prohibitionists." Then if T' is the term "rich," s' will be the sentence "Some seamen are not rich prohibitionists." To say that T is distributed in s is to say that every sentence of the form "Some seamen are not...prohibitionists" is logically implied by s.

Old-fashioned logic books do not explain the notion of distribution in this way. They usually say that a term in a categorical sentence is distributed if and only if the sentence 'refers to' all members of the class of things to which the term applies. But this explanation is obscure and misleading in at least two ways.

One way is this. The sentence "All equilateral triangles are equiangular triangles" seems to refer to all equilateral triangles, and since these necessarily are equilateral triangles, it would appear that the sentence refers to all equilateral triangles also. In that case, the predicate should be considered to be distributed. However, contrary to this the traditional view was that the predicate of an **A** sentence always has to be distributed.

Another unsatisfactory aspect of the old-fashioned account has to do with its treatment of the **O** form. To claim that the sentence "Some seamen are not prohibitionists" refers to all prohibitionists is to make an unsatisfactory claim, because it is so obscure. The notion of 'reference' employed in this old-fashioned account is too ill-defined to enable us to understand why the predicate of an **O** sentence is supposed to be undistributed.

11 Some of the words used to describe the relationships of this traditional square of opposition for the existential viewpoint are used *loosely*. This is a point which old-fashioned logic books often did not make clear.

In the strict sense, to say that one sentence *implies* another is to say that if the first is true, this alone is sufficient to guarantee that the second must be true also. **A** does not imply **I**, nor does **E** imply **O**, in this strict sense. These pairs of sentences involve implication only in the looser sense that if the existential presupposition is true, then if **A** is true **I** must be true; and if the existential presupposition is true, then if **E** is true **O** must be true.

Similarly, to say that two sentences are *contraries* in the strict sense is to say that it is logically impossible for them both to be true. **A** and **E** are not contraries in this strict sense. They are contraries only in the looser sense that if the existential presupposition is true, then **A** and **E** cannot both be true. Also, **I** and **O** are subcontraries only in a correspondingly loose sense. Furthermore, it is only for nonnecessary sentences that we can count on **A** and **E** to be contraries and **I** and **O** to be subcontraries, even in these weaker senses. With necessary sentences these relationships can fail to hold: e.g., "All men are humans" and "No men are humans" fail to be contraries, as they cannot both be false.

To say that two sentences are contradictories in the strict sense is to say that one asserts just what the other denies, no more and no less. As we are understanding them, **A** and **O** are contradictories in this strict sense, as are **E** and **I**.

If we had regarded the existential presupposition that at least one S exists as part of the meaning of each universal sentence, the situation would have been different. Then **A** would be understood as meaning "If anything is an S, it is a P, and there is at least one S," and **E** would be understood as meaning "Nothing is both an S and a P, and there is at least one S." Under these circumstances, with the assumption that there is at least one S built into the meanings of the universal sentences, rather than being treated as a presupposition underlying our whole discussion of the interrelationships, **A** would not be the contradictory of **O**, nor would **E** be the contradictory of **I**. Also, **I** and **O** would not be subcontraries. Because these consequences are inconvenient, we do not adopt this approach.

12 In medieval times each valid form of syllogism was given a name, the vowels in the name indicating its mood. Thus **AAA** in the first figure was called "*Barbara*," and **EAE** in the first figure was called "*Celarent*." In traditional discussion of the syllogism, an existential viewpoint always was adopted. Some lines of Latin verse were used to help students remember the names of the valid forms:

Barbara, Celarent, Darii, Ferioque prioris;
Cesare, Camestres, Festino, Baroco secundae;
Tertia *Darapti, Disamis, Datisi, Felapton,*
Bocardo, Ferison habet; quarta insuper addit
Bramantip, Camenes, Dimaris, Fesapo, Fresison.

These lines omit **AAI** and **EAO** in the first figure, **AEO** and **EAO** in the second, and **AEO** in the fourth. Those five forms, though recognized as valid, were looked down upon by medieval logicians. They called them 'weakened' forms, because in each of them a particular conclusion is drawn from premises from which a universal conclusion can validly be derived. Medieval logicians thought it pointless to get a particular conclusion when one could get the universal conclusion instead.

13 Some philosophers, such as Bertrand Russell, have believed that every assertion has just one essential logical form. They have held, for instance, that a sentence such as "Brutus betrayed Caesar" cannot legitimately be regarded as having the logical form of an **A** sentence; they maintain that it is an essentially relational sentence, and the only proper way to analyze it is according to the relational style (which we shall discuss in Chapter 5).

This attitude is misguided, however. It is only in the context of some specific argument that a sentence needs to be analyzed as, say, relational rather than categorical. In some other argument the same sentence might properly be analyzed in the opposite fashion.

For example, consider the argument "Brutus betrayed Caesar, and Caesar was the conqueror of Gaul; so Brutus betrayed the conqueror of Gaul." Here "betrayed" should be interpreted as a relation and symbolized as a two-placed predicate (see Chapter 5). But contrast this with the argument "Brutus betrayed Caesar, and Brutus was the noblest of Romans; so the noblest of Romans betrayed Caesar." Here it is permissible to interpret "betrayed Caesar" as expressing a property of Brutus, and to analyze the argument as a categorical syllogism.

14 This is usually but not invariably so. Here is an example where we would be led astray by this procedure. The argument "The vase will not be dropped; therefore, if the vase is dropped, it will break" is a silly and invalid argument; but if we blindly symbolized it in the form "–*D*, therefore *D* ⊃ *B*" and then tested its validity by the truth-table method presented later in this chapter, we would get the incorrect answer that the argument is valid. When we replace non-truth-functional sentences by the corresponding truth-functional sentences that they imply, we should keep in mind the following principles: If an argument is valid, any argument exactly like it except for having one or more stronger premises must be valid too; and if an argument is invalid, then any argument exactly like it except for having a stronger conclusion must be invalid too. Replacing non-truth-functional sentences by the corresponding truth-functional sentences that they imply can be counted on to yield correct answers only when the procedure can be justified by appeal to these principles.

15 An optional stronger version of this rule is as follows. We may write down *any* tautology as a new line in a formal deduction, whether the sentence has one of the forms on our list or not. If the tautology does not have one of the familiar forms on the list, then a truth table should be constructed to establish that it is indeed a tautology. The stronger version of the rule permits some formal deductions to have slightly fewer lines.

Teachers who wish to do so should give their students permission to use the stronger version of the rule. Other teachers, who do not care to mix the truth-table method with formal deductions, should limit use of the rule to the short list of tautologous forms given in Section 15.

16 One simple way to build such a unit would be by using a single-pole double-throw switch controlled by an electromagnet (Figure A). The output is connected to the pole of the switch. The input is connected to the electromagnet. When the input is zero, the electromagnet is not energized, and a spring holds the switch in the lower position, connecting the positive voltage of the power supply to the output. When the input is positive, this energizes the electromagnet, which overpowers the spring and throws the switch in the opposite direction, grounding the output (that is, connecting it to the nonpositive side of the power supply).

Figure A

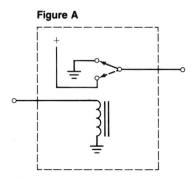

17 A simple way to build this type of unit would be by using two single-pole double-throw switches, each controlled by an electromagnet (Figure B). The two switches are connected in series between the positive voltage of the power supply and the output ("in series" means that both switches must be thrown in the upward direction for positive voltage to reach the output). With this arrange-

Figure B

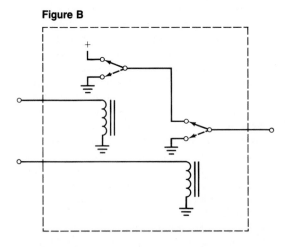

ment, the output is positive when and only when both electromagnets are energized, that is, when and only when both inputs are positive.

18 This unit can be built from a pair of the same kind of switches controlled by electromagnets (Figure C). Now we must wire the two switches in parallel, so that the output will be positive when and only when at least one switch connects it to the positive voltage; this will occur when and only when at least one input is positive.

Figure C

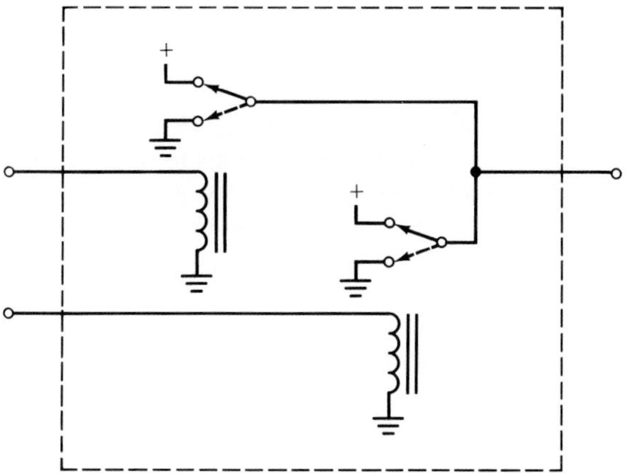

19 Here we want the word "thing" to be understood in a broad sense so as not to exclude persons; persons are to be included among things. However, if that seems too awkward a way of speaking, we may understand the existential quantifier "($\exists$x)" as meaning "there is at least one *being* such that", and the universal quantifier "(x)" as meaning "Each *being* is such that".

20 Whenever there would be ambiguity without them, we use parentheses or brackets to enclose all that falls within the scope of a quantifier. But instead of writing "(x) [–(x is solid)]" we write simply "(x)–(x is solid)," as there is no danger of misunderstanding here. In the absence of parentheses or brackets, we always interpret the scope of the quantifier as being as short as would make sense.

21 In more advanced discussions of quantification, the variables of quantification are said to 'range over' or to 'take as their values' all the things in the universe of discourse. To understand this way of speaking, let us introduce a new way of regarding free variables. Consider the free variable "x" in the expression "x is physical." Let us think of this "x" as a name for some particular thing selected from the universe of discourse. Suppose that on any particular occasion we allow this "x" to name only one thing, but on different occasions we allow this "x" to name different things, and any thing in the universe of discourse may at some time be selected for this "x" to name. In this sense, we are making the variable 'range over' all the things in the universe of discourse; we are allowing this "x" to 'take as its value' any one of these things. Now, the meaning of the universal quantification "(x)(x is physical)" can be explained thus: It means that "x is

physical" becomes a true statement whatever thing from the universe of discourse "x" is regarded as naming (or 'taking as its value'). And the existential quantification "(∃x)(x is mental)" can be explained as meaning that "x is mental" becomes a true statement for at least one choice of thing from the universe of discourse for "x" to name (that is, for at least one 'value' of "x").

22 A third way of handling this argument would be to leave the universe of discourse unlimited, but to alter the meanings of the capital letters, so that the simpler set of formulas can express the argument. To do this, we would have to build the notion of being a person into the meanings of the other letters. Suppose we reinterpret "S" so that now it will be short for "is a person over 7 feet tall," and we reinterpret "E" to mean "is an Eskimo person." With the capital letters understood in this way, the second set of formulas serves as a satisfactory translation of the original argument.

23 Here we take it for granted that no free variables are involved, as we are not permitting free variables. It might still seem that there are exceptions to this principle. Consider "(x)Fx ∨ (x)Gx"; can this be rewritten as "(x)[Fx ∨ (x)Gx]"? This is not an exception to the principle, however, as the rewriting is correct. The new universal quantification looks odd, but it is equivalent to the original one. In the new quantification, the inner quantifier governs the second occurrence of "x," while the outer quantifier governs only the first occurrence of "x." The formula goes into words as "Each thing is such that either it's an F or everything is G."

This principle of equivalence can itself be justified in terms of the principles we already have. To show that "(x)(Mx ∨ B)" is equivalent to "(x)Mx ∨ B," we show that each implies the other. This requires two deductions.

1 [(x)Mx ∨ B] & −(x)(Mx ∨ B)	Premise
2 −(x)(Mx ∨ B)	1, c.s.
3 (∃x)−(Mx ∨ B)	2, Q.E.
4 −(Ma ∨ B)	3, E.I.
5 −Ma & −B	4, De Morgan
6 −B	5, c.s.
7 (x)Mx ∨ B	1, c.s.
8 (x)Mx	7, 6, disj. arg.
9 Ma	8, U.I.
10 −Ma	5, c.s.
11 Ma & −Ma	9, 10, c.a.

1 (x)(Mx ∨ B) & −[(x)Mx ∨ B]	Premise
2 −[(x)Mx ∨ B]	1, c.s.
3 −(x)Mx & −B	2, De Morgan
4 −(x)Mx	3, c.s.
5 (∃x)−Mx	4, Q.E.
6 −Ma	5, E.I.
7 (x)(Mx ∨ B)	1, c.s.
8 Ma ∨ B	7, U.I.
9 B	6, 8, disj.
10 −B	3, c.s.
11 B & −B	9, 10, c.a.

Since each can be shown to follow from the other, the sentences are equivalent. Thus our new principle of equivalence has been justified in terms of principles that we already had. We need this new principle, to complete our method, but the idea it involves depends on our earlier principles.

24 This principle can also be justified by appeal to our earlier principles, using a pair of deductions similar to those in note 23. Here too we take for granted that no free variables are present.

25 By adding these principles of equivalence we make the method complete. That is, every valid argument of this part of logic can be shown to be valid by the method.

As has been noted, in discussing these two principles of equivalence we have taken it for granted that the sentences with which we are concerned do not contain any free variables. These principles would have to be restated in narrower form if they were to hold good for expressions containing free variables.

Teachers who wish to do so may instruct their students to use an optional short-cut which will streamline truth-functional steps in quantificational deductions. This is the principle of truth-functional inference (T. F. I.): We may add as a new line in a deduction *any* sentence that is truth-functionally implied by one or more preceding lines. If we use this rule, we may combine several truth-functional steps into one. However, if anyone challenges a move we have made by T. F. I., we must be ready to justify what we have done by breaking it down into smaller steps, each one of which is specifically justified by one of our earlier rules.

26 Notice that we have not dealt with and have not yet ruled out the possibility that it might be a contradiction for some other reason—although in this example there is no other reason that merits consideration. Being a contradiction on account of its logical form is a sufficient though not a necessary condition for a sentence to be a contradiction. A sentence like "Some wealthy persons are not rich" is a contradiction even though its quantificational form—presumably, "($\exists$x) (Wx & −Rx)"—is not what makes it so. What does make it a contradiction is that the terms "wealthy" and "rich", when understood in their normal senses, are contrary terms.

27 The form of argument "Fa, $a = b$, ∴ Fb" is correlated with the necessary truths of this family. This form of argument is valid for a wide range of ordinary cases. However, there are three types of cases in which it fails to be valid (and in which the correlated conditional sentences fail to be necessarily true).

1 One type of exception arises when the name in the second premise is mentioned rather than used. For example, it would be invalid to argue.

Boise is Idaho's capital.
"Boise" is a five-letter word.
Therefore Idaho's capital is a five-letter word.

2 Further exceptions arise when the name occurs in the second premise within a sentence saying that something is necessary, not necessary, possible, not possible, or the like. Thus it would be invalid to argue:

Nine is the number of planets.
Nine is necessarily greater than seven.
Therefore, the number of planets is necessarily greater than seven.

Also belonging to this group of exceptions are kindred cases where the second premise declares that something is provable or unprovable in a certain way, knowable or unknowable by certain means, and the like.

3 Still further exceptions can arise when the name occurs in the second premise within the scope of a verb that expresses some psychological attitude such as believing, desiring, fearing, or the like. Suppose someone argues:

Matilda is Hugo's future wife.
Hugo fears that Matilda will reject his proposal of marriage.
Therefore Hugo fears that his future wife will reject his proposal of marriage.

If the conclusion is understood as telling what it is that Hugo is fearful of (and this is the most straightforward way of understanding it), then the argument is definitely fallacious. But aside from these three types of exceptions, this form of identity reasoning is reliable.

28 This account is informal. To state the matter with exactitude would require more advanced terminology for discussing formulas and their interpretation.

29 For *practically* everyone this argument would be question-begging. However, it is just conceivable that there might be some person who already knew for sure that Jones is demented but did not know for sure whether Jones is insane (this person might be more familiar with the word "demented" than with the word "insane"). For such a person, the argument might not be question-begging; it might be able to show the person logically that the conclusion is to be believed.

This illustrates how whether an argument begs the question will depend upon the state of knowledge of the audience at whom it is directed. In this regard, begging the question is quite different from any formal fallacy.

30 Use of this example does not express any criticism of religion. It does illustrate how matters of religious faith often are believed by people who do not know how to give good arguments in support of what they believe. Theologians (especially those of Islam) often emphasized that proofs of matters of faith cannot be given. Ought we sometimes to believe things for which we cannot give good arguments? This point will be discussed further in Section 42.

An argument that begs the question usually does so on account of its premises. But is that the only way to commit this fallacy? Suppose someone argues: "All syllogisms conforming to the five rules of the syllogism are valid; some syllogisms conforming to the five rules are in the mood **AII**, third figure; therefore, some syllogisms in the mood **AII**, third figure, are valid." Here nothing is especially objectionable about the premises. But the peculiarity is that the argument itself is in the mood **AII**, third figure. Consequently, anyone who has any doubt about the truth of the conclusion ought to be at least equally doubtful about the validity of the argument. Hence the argument cannot succeed in establishing its conclusion. It should be classified as a *petitio principii*. What makes it question-begging is the unseemly relationship between its logical form (that is, the 'rule of inference' by which it proceeds) and its conclusion.

31 Someone might object that this way of distinguishing among the three main categories of fallacies permits them to overlap. What shall we say about a person who includes contrary sentences among his premises because he believes it is a correct principle of logic that contraries can both be true? Such a person has committed a formal fallacy and a fallacy of inconsistency too. And what shall we say about a person who uses the conclusion as a premise, believing it to be a correct principle of logic that a sentence can validly follow only from itself? Such a person has committed a *petitio principii* and a formal fallacy as well.

However, in both these cases the formal fallacy is the more basic error. Anyway, these are very degenerate cases. A more ordinary error in reasoning, when fully understood, will almost always be seen to fit into just one of our three categories.

32 To be sure, the fallacy of composition is not always a fallacy of equivocation. It will be a formal fallacy in the rather unlikely event that the speaker is clear about how to symbolize the argument correctly but thinks it a valid logical principle that whatever holds true of each member of a group must hold true also of the group considered as a whole. Here the mistake would be caused by pure misunderstanding of logical principles, rather than by equivocation.

33 The fallacy of division also could be a formal fallacy. This will happen in the rather unlikely event that the speaker is clear about what the premises say but thinks it is a valid logical principle that whatever holds true of a group considered as a whole must hold true also of each member of that group.

34 Not all definitions are explicit ones. In a dictionary many words have to be defined not by giving one exact equivalent but by giving several partial synonyms. Thus "honesty" may be defined as "refraining from lying, cheating, or stealing; being truthful, trustworthy, upright, sincere, fair, straightforward or chaste." Here the meaning of the definiendum is adequately if not rigorously explained, but this is not an explicit definition, for we are not given some one other word or phrase that always means just the same as the definiendum.

In logic and mathematics, rigorous definitions that are not explicit definitions sometimes are used. For example, if we wish to define the biconditional symbol, we can say "$p \equiv q$" is defined as "$(q \supset p) \& (p \supset q)$." This is called a *definition in context*; it supplies a rule enabling us to rewrite any expression containing the biconditional sign so that it will contain the horseshoe and ampersand instead. If we already understand the horseshoe and ampersand, this definition shows us exactly what the biconditional sign means. But this is not an explicit definition, for the whole expression containing the biconditional sign must be rearranged completely; we do not just remove the biconditional sign and put some other sign combination in its place.

35 The situation is different with regard to general terms. It is all right to define the general term "unicorn" as "horse with a horn in its forehead." There are no unicorns, but the definition tells us that if there were any horse with a horn in its forehead, it would be called a unicorn. We can use the general term "unicorn" even though there are no unicorns, but we must beware of using the letter "n" as a singular term unless we know that there is such a number.

36 Traditional philosophers, in line with Aristotle and scholasticism, emphasized what were called *real* definitions. Like the definitions which we are calling revelatory, real definitions were not supposed to state the meanings of words but rather were supposed to describe things in a fundamental way. It was believed, however, that there must be only one proper real definition of each species of natural being. For instance, it was held that the real definition of the human species is that it is the species of rational animals. According to this traditional point of view, it would have been thought incorrect to define humans as the tool-using animals or the animals with language, let alone as the neurotic animals. The weakness of this traditional view is that it fails to recognize how the same thing may be defined in different yet perhaps equally legitimate ways which reveal different aspects of its nature.

37 We shall speak of inductive conclusions as being probable, no matter how well established they are. This is a departure from ordinary usage, for in ordinary discourse a well-established inductive conclusion, e.g., that the sun will rise tomorrow, is called certain rather than highly probable. But for purposes of logic it is convenient to conceive of probability in a broader sense, ascribing it to the conclusions of all arguments that are not deductive. By using the term in this way, we emphasize the difference between deductive and nondeductive reasoning.

38 Some philosophers have held that an argument like this, which reaches a singular conclusion, ought to be interpreted as involving two steps: first, the inferring of an inductive generalization ("Since a, b, c each has been observed to be S and P, therefore probably all S are P"); and second, a deductive syllogism ("All S are P; d is an S; therefore d is P"). However, there is no reason why we must interpret the reasoning in this way. Moreover, this interpretation misleadingly suggests that the singular conclusion is no more probable than the inductive generalization, whereas actually the singular conclusion usually would be more probable than the corresponding generalization.

39 There are necessary sentences about causal relations, e.g., "Fatal wounds cause death." But these are comparatively trivial and uninteresting.

40 Some people might object to what has been said, on the ground that it is vague to speak of "cases of some certain kind" or of cases that are "appropriately similar." To this we must reply that of course it is vague, but that is not a ground for objecting. The general notion of causation is a rather vague notion, though not on that account a useless notion.

Another aspect of the notion of cause is that we commonly speak about *the* cause of an event. For instance, a coroner is asked to determine *the* cause of a victim's death. There are innumerable events, each of which in a sense could be said to have caused the death: the victim died because his brain ceased to receive oxygen, because his blood stopped circulating, because his heart stopped beating, because a bullet traveled toward his body, because his enemy pulled the trigger, and so on. Each of these events is such that death in closely similar cases occurs if and only if the given event occurs. But the coroner will report as the cause of death that a bullet passed through the heart. When he calls this *the* cause of death, the coroner is not denying that many other events belonged to the chain of causes and effects that eventuated in death; the coroner is doing his duty by focusing attention upon one especially significant event in the chain. This event, which he calls *the* cause, is especially significant because it is the event upon which we can best focus our attention if we want to assign responsibility for such a death and upon which we can best focus our efforts if we want to prevent or control deaths of this type.

41 In his *System of Logic*, Mill discusses two additional methods, the joint method of agreement and difference and the method of residues. But these are just slightly more complicated ways of using the method of agreement and the method of difference; they do not introduce any new principle.

42 Gain and loss should perhaps be measured in terms of utility (amount of benefit or harm), not just in terms of money. If winning \$9 would merely make one a little less poor, while losing \$7 would drive one into bankruptcy, then the expectation of loss on the bet is really greater than the expectation of gain, though not in dollar terms.

43 The mathematical notion of limit is needed for a more exact formulation of this principle. Let x be the probability of a certain outcome (such as getting a total of 7 in rolling two dice). Let y be the number of trials (the number of times the dice are rolled). Let z be the fraction of these trials in which that certain outcome occurs. And let w be an arbitrarily chosen percentage (such as 1 percent, 0.01 percent, etc.). Then the principle is that, for each choice of w, the probability that the absolute value of the difference between z and x will be less than w increases toward 1 as its limit, as y increases without bound.

44 With regard to Newton and gravitation, sometimes we speak of gravitation as *causing* objects to fall, and so on. Certainly gravitation may be called the cause; but gravitation is not the cause of falling in the sense in which, say, germs are the cause of malaria. The germs are entities distinct from the pathological results they produce; it would not be senseless to speak of germs without malaria or of malaria without germs. But gravitation is not some additional entity, over and above moving bodies; to talk about gravitation is to talk about how bodies move.

Thinking of work like Newton's on gravitation, people sometimes say, "Science doesn't tell us why things happen, only how they happen; it doesn't really explain; it only describes." They say this because they imagine that the only way to explain is to point out the hidden inner entity which is the cause, and they see that science does not do that for gravitation and other fundamental forces. However, this remark reflects a misunderstanding of the nature of explanation, for not all good explanations point out hidden causes.

45 Another issue that comes up in connection with enthymemes is, How far should we go in supplying *necessary* truths as supposedly suppressed premises? Suppose that someone has argued "No Lutherans are Buddhists, and so no Buddhists are Lutherans," and someone else wants to regard this as an enthymeme. The second person thinks the argument has as a suppressed premise the necessary truth "If no so-and-so's are such-and-such's, then no such-and-such's are so-and-so's." Is that a good interpretation of the argument? No, it is not. It is inappropriate here to regard this necessary truth as a premise; instead, it should be regarded as expressing the *principle* according to which the inference proceeds. More explicitly stated, the principle is that from "No so-and-so's are such-and-such's" we may infer "no such-and-such's are so-and-so's."

Clearly, any argument of the sorts we have been dealing with must have at least one premise and must proceed according to some principle of inference. But how should we tell the difference between a premise of the argument and the principle according to which the argument proceeds? What is our justification for regarding the necessary truth in the preceding paragraph as the principle, rather than as a premise? The best answer for our purposes is in terms of their different *levels of certainty*.

A premise is something which the person arguing is committed to accepting, but which is not beyond question within the context of that particular discussion. It needs to be stated as a premise just in order that listeners who may want to challenge it will have it explicitly before them. In contrast, the principle according to which an argument proceeds (its rule of inference) should have an altogether higher level of certainty than the premises do. In the example we were considering, the necessary truth is so certain that it is utterly uncontroversial, whereas the statement that no Lutherans are Buddhists is more questionable. Thus the latter should be considered a premise (it could not do the job of serving as a rule of inference here, anyway), while the former should be considered the rule of inference of this argument (especially so, since no equally plausible alternative is available in this case).

As another example, consider the argument "This is red; therefore this is colored." Is this an enthymeme, with the suppressed premise "Everything red is colored," or is the argument complete as it stands, with its principle of inference being that from "x is red" we may infer "x is colored"? Here the latter answer is the better one. The principle that being red entails being colored is so obvious and uncontroversial (in most contexts of discussion) that it is better to regard this as the principle according to which the argument proceeds, rather than as a premise.

We should not conclude from this that necessary truths never can serve as premises of arguments. When they are at least a bit questionable and controversial, then it is better to treat them as premises. But when they are highly obvious to all concerned, it is better not to think of them as premises; sometimes then they should be regarded as rules of inference, and in other cases they need not be taken note of at all, so far as our analysis of arguments is concerned.

46 Someone may object that this sort of argument ought to be interpreted as an enthymeme having an unstated premise. The idea would be that if an appropriate additional premise were supplied, the argument would become definitely deductive. But there are two difficulties with this idea. First, in this sort of case it is hard to state another premise which is both known to us and sufficient to render the argument deductively valid. Second, even if we could state such a premise, adding it to the argument would surely make the argument into a *petitio principii*. For instance, the auxiliary premise "Whatever is like lying and cheating ought to count as an honor offense," even if we did not know it to be false, would be more dubious than the conclusion that we are trying to establish. It would seem that someone who insists upon regarding this argument as a deductive enthymeme must say either that the argument is a *non sequitur* or that it depends upon false premises or that it begs the question; in any of these three cases, he will have to say that the argument is of no value for proving its conclusion. But this argument and others like it are not worthless for proving conclusions. They sometimes are very good arguments, whose premises provide real reason for believing their conclusions.

47 Some writers use the phrase "laws of logic" to refer only to sentences that are logically true on account of their form, such as "Snow is white, or it is not," rather than to sentences that mention other sentences, as our examples do. According to that more pedantic usage, our examples would have to be referred to as "laws of metalogic."

48 Mill treats this matter in his *System of Logic*, book II, chapter III.

49 Hume considers this in his *Enquiry Concerning Human Understanding*, section IV.

50 This essay is found in Clifford's book *Dissertations and Discussions*.

51 In this essay James was especially concerned with religious belief. He considered that our observational evidence is wholly indecisive with respect to religious doctrines (especially the doctrine that God exists). That is, according to him, nothing we can observe suffices to make these religious beliefs probable, and nothing we can observe suffices to make them improbable. Evidence and logical proofs cannot settle such questions, he held. James maintained, however, that there are benefits (even in the present life) which believers have a chance of attaining, while unbelievers have no chance of getting these benefits. Under these circumstances, we ought to embrace religious belief, James says—we should choose to believe, exerting the "will to believe." Doing so is the best policy.

James says that he recommends the will to believe only for situations where evidence and proofs cannot settle the matter; he does not recommend willing to believe *contrary* to the evidence. But his own example about the mountain climber shows that this restriction is inappropriate; the mountain climber is in a situation where he has evidence, and yet he ought to believe contrary to the evidence.

James's position involves issues about religious belief which go far beyond the scope of our discussion here. Is there no evidence or proof which makes these religious beliefs either probable or improbable? Do we have good reason to suppose that believers have a chance of gaining benefits that are foreclosed to nonbelievers? Regardless of whether James's position on these points is correct, his essay provides a valuable antidote to evidentialism.

INDEX

Principles for Use in Quantificational Deductions

I. Truth-functional inference
We may use any of the principles of truth-functional deduction that were listed in Chapter 3.

II. Quantificational rules of inference
Universal instantiation (U.I.): From any universal quantification we may validly infer any instance of it.

Existential instantiation (E.I.): From an existential quantification we may validly infer any instance of it, provided that the name being introduced into the instance is new to the deduction.

III. Quantificational equivalences (Q.E.)
From a sentence we may validly infer any sentence that is equivalent to it according to these rules:

1 Two sentences are equivalent if they are exactly alike except that where one contains a negation sign immediately followed by a universal quantifier, the other contains an existential quantifier immediately followed by a negation sign; e.g., "$-(x)$ Fx" is equivalent to "$(\exists x) - Fx$."

2 Two sentences always are equivalent if they are exactly alike except that where one contains a negation sign immediately followed by an existential quantifier, the other contains a universal quantifier immediately followed by a negation sign; e.g., "$-(\exists x)$ Fx" is equivalent to "$(x) - Fx$."

3 Any disjunction, one component of which is a universal quantification, may be rewritten in the equivalent form of a universal quantification of a disjunction; for example, "(x) Mx ∨ B" is equivalent to "(x) $(Mx$ ∨ $B)$."

4 Any disjunction, one component of which is an existential quantification, may be rewritten in the equivalent form of an existential quantification of a disjunction; for example, "$(\exists x)$ Mx ∨ Z" is equivalent to "$(\exists x)(Mx$ ∨ $Z)$."